CHRIST'S HEALING TOUCH

VOLUME I

UNDERSTANDING HOW TO TAKE
GOD'S HEALING POWER
TO THE WORLD

Todd Bentley

Christ's Healing Touch

Volume I

Understanding How to Take God's Healing Power *to The World*

Foreword: Mahesh Chavda

Managing Editor: Kevin Paterson

Assistant Editors:
Michael Kerry Jackie Macgirvin Janelle Mierau

Christ's Healing Touch: *Understanding How to Take God's Healing Power to the World*

ISBN 0-9736387-0-2

The New King James Version of the Bible has been used for all Scripture references unless otherwise indicated.

Individual testimonies and revival reports may have been edited for the sake of space or language. However, the content or message has not been changed.

Printed by Hemlock Printers Ltd.
Suite 320 – 1070 Douglas St.
Victoria, BC, Canada
V8W 2C4

Printed in Canada

Cover artwork and graphic design by Steve Stanczyk
Page layout by Steve Stanczyk and Dan Brennan

Fresh Fire Ministries contact information for orders:

Fresh Fire Ministries
P.O. Box 2525
Abbotsford, BC
Canada, V2T 6R3

Toll free phone line: 1-866-853-9041
On line ordering: www.freshfire.ca

We want to hear from you. Please send your comments about this book to Fresh Fire Ministries' mailing address above.

DEDICATION

I dedicate this book to Jehovah-Rapha, the great physician, and to the truth about divine healing, a lost message in the church.

ACKNOWLEDGMENTS

I want to thank the following people for sowing into this book and into my healing ministry:

- My Abba Father—for all His perfect gifts to me—gifts of salvation, friendship with Jesus, intimacy with the Holy Spirit and healing anointing, as well as for all the people He's given to love and support me.

- The Holy Spirit for sweet fellowship, for mentoring me in the healing ministry and for teaching me all the truths that I've been able to share in this book.

- My beautiful wife, Shonnah, and my three wonderful children—Lauralee, Esther and Elijah—for sharing me with the world.

- Patricia King for being a cheerleader and always telling me to go for it! She believed in the bigness of the call of God on my life.

- The generals of the faith and those who have pioneered in the healing ministry in the last century—people like John G. Lake, T. L. Osborn, Smith Wigglesworth, F.F. Bosworth, Aimee Semple MacPherson, A.A. Allen, Jack Coe, Maria Woodworth-Etter and many others. We need to honor our fathers and mothers in the faith who have made it possible to come this far in the healing ministry.

- Kevin Paterson for managing this huge project and for the many months of writing, rewriting and editing. Wow, we did it! Together we are discipling the nations in healing ministry!

- Steve Stanczyk for the inspired artwork on the cover of the book and for the weeks of layout and design work.

- Mike Kerry and Jackie Macgirvin for all the editing and proofing work; for helping dot the "i"s and cross the "t"s.

- Janelle Mierau for transcribing tape after tape and for the leg work in putting together the testimony chapter.

- Dan Brennan who oversaw the layout and looked after all the publishing details.

- All my staff who serve so hard in crusades and conferences where God demonstrates His healing power.

- All my fellow comrades who continue to pioneer with me in restoring the healing ministry to the world today.

- You, the hungry believer, who places a demand on the healing ministry and who also desires to take God's power to a lost and dying world.

Endorsements

"Todd Bentley has done it again—he has provided us with an invaluable tool helping us bring an authentic gospel to the streets of this nation and beyond. Instead of reinforcing the misconception of 'miracles are for superstars,' he equips us with the insights necessary to pursue healing as a Biblical mandate. It's his personal story that completes the picture by creating in us a hunger to passionately pursue Jesus, the true Healer."

~Bill Johnson, Pastor, Bethel Church, Author, *When Heaven Invades Earth, The Supernatural Power of the Transformed Mind*
Redding, CA, USA

"Christ's Healing Touch is a book loaded with 'fresh oil' that will become 'fresh fire' in you as you read its pages. Todd's faith for healing is sure to 'get all over you' as you allow the revelations found in this book to touch your life. The doctrine is sound, the testimonies are astounding, and the flavor—'real.' Hmm, all of these things describe Todd Bentley. Imbibe deeply—you will truly be ruined for the ordinary!"

~Patricia King, President of Extreme Prophetic
Kelowna, B.C., Canada

"Todd's book, Christ's Healing Touch, is dynamic, informative and powerful. I highly recommend it."

~Dr. Che Ahn, Senior Pastor, Harvest Rock Church
Pasadena, CA, USA

"Todd's faith in the miraculous power of God is infectious. Like the good and faithful steward in the parable of the talents, he has a passion to see everything in the kingdom multiplied. As you read this book, Christ's Healing Touch, get ready to receive an impartation of faith for healing so you yourself can pray for miracles and experience the supernatural power of God in your own life and ministry."

~Wesley & Stacey Campbell, Founders of New Life Church,
Praying the Bible International and Revival Now Ministries,
Kelowna, B.C.,Canada

"A few years ago I began to hear and read about a new "nobody" that God had raised up—Todd Bentley. This was in connection with God using Todd for a great outpouring of healing in Albany, Oregon. I remembered the prophecies that I had heard in the desert years of the church in the late 1980's and early 1990's, prophecies about God sending a future revival through a nameless faceless revival.

When I first read about Todd, I knew here was another of the nameless that God was raising up; here was someone, that no one had ever heard about, about to be catapulted into international ministry. The fact that Todd has had little education and no formal theological education prior to his calling from God reminds us that Jesus still calls people from the mills and other market places to come follow Him and to join Him in what He is doing.

I have since met Todd and ministered with him on several occasions. I find him full of the Holy Spirit, full of the divine energy of God, full of faith and confidence in God, full of compassion for the poor and the sick, full of Jesus. It is also encouraging to read that Todd's teams are often used for the miraculous and that the ministry isn't dependent upon him. His new book on healing is a wonderful wake up call to the church to enter into the new healing revival that is going on around the world.

In this day in which so many put such an emphasis upon the style of ministry, let me say, that though our styles of ministry are quite different, I am grateful to God for raising up such a young man. He's a man from outside the camp, who God is using to actually embarrass many who have been in the ministry for a long time (and many who have much training) for their latent unbelief and lack of power. May Todd's life, ministry, and books provoke us to a holy jealousy and stir in us a desire to see and experience more of the biblical promises in our lives. I recommend this book as one which will increase your faith and understanding regarding the ministry of healing and the miraculous. I am going to add it to the reading list for my interns."

~Randy Clark, Founder and President of Global Awakening,
Mechanicsburg, PA, USA

Contents

FOREWORD

The heart of God can be summarized in Christ's words as He emerges from the wilderness, ministers healing and deliverance and declares, "The Spirit of the Lord is upon Me, because He has anointed Me to preach the gospel to the poor; He has sent Me to heal the brokenhearted, to proclaim liberty to the captives and recovery of sight to the blind, to set at liberty those who are oppressed; to proclaim the acceptable year of the Lord," (Luke 4:18-19). God's heart of compassion has never changed. He still desires to heal and set free the poor, the captive, the brokenhearted and oppressed. And so Christ, through the centuries, has commissioned His disciples "to go into all the world, preach good news" with signs following.

In the last century, gifted men and women have brought this message with amazing confirming signs. Among them were Aimee Semple MacPherson, A.A. Allen, T.L. Osborn, William Branham, Oral Roberts, Kathryn Kuhlman, John G. Lake and many others.

About five years ago, I heard of another special gift that God was raising up in Canada who was touching nations with a powerful healing gift. He was a young man in his mid-twenties, recently delivered of drugs, who had been called and anointed of God with a special healing gift. His name was Todd Bentley. He invited me to come up to Canada and minister with him.

I spent quality time not just with him, but also his wife, his pastor, his father and his team. In their midst I smelled the life-giving fragrance of the Holy Spirit, mingled with zeal, holiness and humility. I invited Todd to come to our healing center in Charlotte to minister. I saw the healing gift truly touching lives. Since that time we have had more quality time to compare notes.

In this book you will hear the voice of a genuine healing gift raised up for our generation. Todd has a burden to disciple and release others in this anointing.

The roll call of nations and cities that have already been impacted by his ministry is astounding. When one is around Todd Bentley, one gets the burden of his heart to touch every nation and every soul with the healing gospel of Christ as soon as possible.

In this, the first decade of a new millennium, I believe we are looking to move into the greatest expansion of the glorious gospel of the kingdom of God. Todd Bentley's book, undergirded by a genuine and powerful gift of healing, is an anointed tool to disciple you to do the works of Christ and impact your generation with the power of Christ.

Dr. Mahesh Chavda
Senior Pastor, All Nations Church
Ft. Mill, SC, USA
August 2004

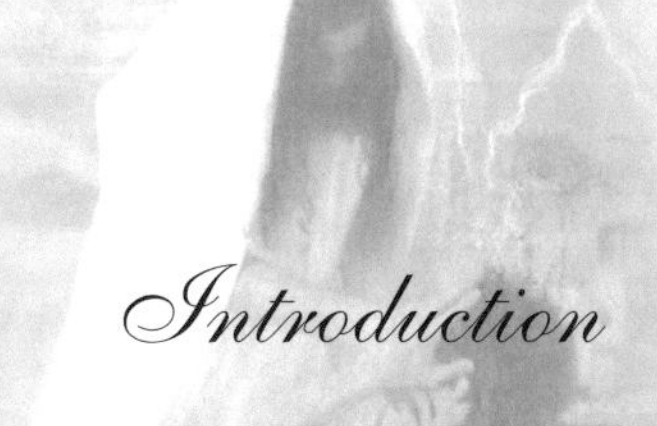

Introduction

YOUR CALL INTO HEALING MINISTRY

Christ's Healing Touch is written as a complete war manual on the healing ministry, so you, like Jesus, can heal all who are "oppressed by the devil" (Acts 10:38), and with God's power, "destroy the works" of the enemy" (1 Jn. 3:8). Together Volume I & II will help give you a complete theological understanding of healing and will impart a new passion and anointing for doing the supernatural works of Jesus. (Volume I focuses mostly on the powerful theology of healing, while Volume II deals mainly with spiritual warfare and overcoming the enemies to healing.)

The healing truths in this book have been growing in me since shortly after my dramatic conversion to Christ in my early teens. Since that day, I've had a great desire to see the God of the Bible made real in my life and the lives of other believers.

God is raising up a healing army that can demonstrate a gospel of power to the world. This book is written for those who really desire to fully share the gospel with others, not in word only, but in the demonstration of the Spirit and in power (1 Cor. 2:4).

Through this book, I believe, the healing anointing will be imparted and activated in your life. As you read these pages, you will grow in faith for a healing or miracle in your own life and receive a greater revelation of the

Father's passion for His people to walk in divine health. My passion is that through the teaching in this book you would learn how miracles function and then receive a whole new revelation, God is releasing today, as to how you can walk in the faith and healing anointing for miracles.

Jesus made a sure promise in John 14:12 saying: ***"Most assuredly, I say to you, he who believes in Me, the works that I do he will do also; and greater works than these he will do, because I go to My Father."*** This is not only a promise, but also a wonderful birthright for every believer who would dare walk into this realm of the supernatural that Jesus modeled for us on the earth.

My prayer is that, as you read this book, you will receive supernatural healing revelation and impartation and that, ultimately, you will receive God's call to take His healing power to the world!

Todd Bentley
Healing Evangelist & Revivalist
Fresh Fire Ministries

MY PERSONAL JOURNEY INTO THE HEALING MINISTRY

Through the years of my ministry and Christian life, I have come to see that most believers are desperate to see God made real to them in their every day life. They want their faith to be more than just some fancy theological words, nice doctrine or a three-point sermon. They want a Christian life that reflects the Christianity of the Bible, a Christianity in which healings, miracles, signs and wonders are regular and normal experiences. Most believers yearn, deep inside, to find a Christianity powerful enough to meet their needs in body, soul and spirit. They want a faith that's real, that's exciting, that makes unbelievers sit up and take notice. This book is designed to take you into that world of the supernatural, of the power of God, and of faith adventures with God that rock your world and the world around you.

Before we dive into the teaching chapters on healing, I want to give you some personal insights about my journey into the healing ministry. I have told my entire life story and testimony in my first book, "Journey into the Miraculous." In this chapter you can "listen in" on an interview and conversation between me and the book's editor, and personal friend, Kevin Paterson. (Kevin was a youth pastor that helped start and lead Fresh Fire years ago, when it was still a youth ministry and before it became my international evangelistic ministry.) My prayer is that through my responses below, you will begin to catch some of my passion and heart for Jesus and His healing ministry. I am praying that the Lord will begin to impart to you some of the radical faith that the Lord has gifted me with so I can help pioneer and restore the healing ministry to the church today. The church is preparing for a massive healing revival and we need as many gifted and trained healing warriors as we can get. Get ready to receive impartation and to be equipped for healing ministry as you read!

The Interview

Kevin: *Todd, how did your healing ministry start?*

Todd: Desire. I was hungry for the kind of power of God that I read about in the Gospels and in the book of Acts. When I looked at the church and the manifestation of the Spirit in the church, I didn't see the kind of miracles we read about in the Gospels and in the book of Acts. So I began to ask myself, if the kingdom of God was power and not in word only then where was the power? "If Paul's preaching didn't come with the persuasive words of human wisdom but in a demonstration of the Spirit of God and power," I wondered, "what does that look like in the church today?" I began to examine the Scripture, verse by verse, chapter by chapter—not just the Gospels, but what the entire Bible had to say about healing and the healing ministry.

I began to ask what the healing ministry of Jesus and the disciples looked like. I became convinced that from the beginning of the Bible to the end, divine healing was a vital part of God's plan of redemption and restoration on earth. I became certain that God is a good God who wants His people to prosper and be in good health (3 John 1:2). I saw that message throughout the entire Bible and so I became hungry to see God's healing power. The Bible says to earnestly desire spiritual gifts such as gifts of faith, healings and miracles. So I said, "I am going to desire!" Then I would take a day, two days, sometimes three days, praying and fasting for the manifestation and the experience of what I was reading in the Scriptures. The whole time I would read nothing else in the Bible except stories and verses about healing. I would go through the Gospels—Mathew, Mark, Luke and John—three or four times in a day, focusing on the accounts of healing and praying for the manifestation of those things in my life.

I also fed my spirit with the teachings of F.F. Bosworth, T. L. Osbourne (*Healing the Sick*) and John G. Lake. I was being provoked by the lives of men and women that God had used in the past in healing ministry. Today, I meet a lot of people hungry for revival and hungry for the power of God. All of them have read the classics like Smith Wigglesworth, John G. Lake or Maria Woodworth-Etter (*The Diary of Signs and Wonders*). They have been through the life and the testimony of Kathryn Kuhlman and they are excited about what God is doing in some of the contemporary healing guys today like Reinhard Bonnke and Benny Hinn. They have read all the books. Any one who has been to any kind of Bible School has looked at the lives of those that God has used in revival. They've all done that. I've done that too. But I had a deep hunger in my heart for the gift and ministry of healing to operate in my life. After studying the scriptures, I said, "There is nowhere in the Scriptures that says it's not for me. Healing is for today; I see it in the Bible. Jesus is the same today, yesterday, and forever, so healing must continue today."

Still, I had some questions to resolve: "Am I called to the healing ministry? Is this for me or is it only for the ones that God has used in healing. Am I called?" I knew healing is biblical and is for today. But I needed to find out whether this healing gift was for me or just for Benny Hinn and Reinhard Bonnke. I wondered, "Do I have to be called, or can God use me?"

Then I saw in Scripture that "the prayer of faith will save the sick." (James 5:15) I said, "It's the prayer of faith, not the prayer of Todd Bentley and not the anointing of Todd Bentley." I realized that healing is in the prayer, not in the person praying the prayer." Then I saw Mark 16:17 which says, "These signs will follow them who believe." I said, "I am a believer!" As I

A recent crusade in Arusha, Tanzania. Thousands of people are saved, healed and delivered

continued to read those verses, I said to myself: "This is for me!" The Bible says to earnestly desire spiritual gifts, and spiritual gifts are faith, healing and miracles. So I asked myself, "Why would God want me to desire something He didn't want me to have?"

During those days, the Lord answered three main questions for me. First, I wanted to know whether it is God's heart to heal—I became convinced in my heart that it *is* His heart. My second question was: "How many will God heal?" The Holy Spirit showed me in Scripture that healing is for all, all the time. The third question God answered is this: "Is healing for me?" I began to realize that it is God's will to use me just as much as He has used anyone else in healing throughout history. That's when miracles started for me.

After my questions were answered, then it was on to step #2—I realized that if I believed it, I needed to preach it and that the Holy Ghost would confirm the Word with signs and wonders. I knew He would work with me. You know—Mark 16—the Lord working to confirm the Word. The Lord had shown me that, "if I want healing, I need to preach healing. If I want prosperity, I need to preach prosperity. If I want deliverance I need to preach deliverance. If I want fruit in the family, I need to preach family." So I began to preach healing wherever I could. I preached everything that the classic healing evangelists did; I preached everything on healing and then I prayed for the sick in faith. I believed that God would confirm the Word if I laid my hands on the sick believing that God would do what He said He would do. Very simply—I followed the faith model. I talk more about this in the chapter on the Four Levels of Healing, but that is basically how it all started for me.

Kevin: *What stirred the passion in you for healing and miracles?*

Todd: What really stirred that passion was the fact that I wanted the deaf to hear because my mother was deaf. God actually used that situation in my life to fuel the fire in me. When I learnt that healing was a part of the Christian faith I asked, "God, are you going to heal my Mom?" After I got saved I prayed over and over that God would heal my Mom. This was even before I started pursuing healing in my own life and ministry. When my Mom wasn't healed, a holy zeal and determination rose up within me: "The deaf are going to hear!" It became a rage within me, fuel for the fire for healing to work through me. My number one passion in the healing ministry was that the deaf would hear. So in my healing meetings I would always go for healing of the deaf—that would sometimes be one of the first altar calls that I would give. In those days, I remember inviting all the deaf up for prayer and none would hear, or perhaps one would partially hear. But that was how I began to increase in my healing gift. I teach more on this in the chapter about the deaf and dumb spirit.

Kevin: *Describe how you got into the healing ministry and how you developed your gifts and your anointing.*

Todd: All the different healing ministers kind of helped mentor me in my early days of healing ministry. I would look at the strengths of healing ministers like T. L. Osbourne and notice that their strong points were in the Word, faith and authority. Then I would look at ministers like Kathryn Kuhlman and Benny Hinn and the healings that came through the worship, the atmosphere, the anointing and the Presence. Then you have guys like Kenneth Hagin and Oral Roberts—although anointed healing ministers, their strength and ministry of healing came through the presentation of faith and the belief that "faith comes by hearing." I would ask, "God, how can I take the best of every stream?" Then I would look at prophets like William Branham and I would wonder: "How can I combine the prophetic gift with healing ministry, so it's not just about anointing and faith?" I wanted to be able to combine the office of the prophet with that of the evangelist in healing ministry.

I know that today God has placed on our ministry an apostolic anointing in which my two strongest suits are the call of prophet and the call of evangelist. I've had to learn how to operate in the office of the prophet and the office of the evangelist and then learn how to mix those two gifts together in the healing ministry. The Lord taught me how to move in Elijah/Elisha-type miracles by preaching the Word of God, speaking the word of knowledge and by decreeing what the Lord is doing; He also taught me how to operate in healing ministry by the faith model. So I would combine all those elements: prophesying healing; inviting the healing presence of the Lord as well as releasing healing by the Word and faith. Examining the strengths and weaknesses of different healing ministries allowed me to learn from each one.

William Branham would hardly even preach, at times, in the beginning of his ministry. He would just do the word of knowledge and healing stuff. On the other hand, F.F. Bosworth and others had tremendous teaching ministries for healing—but when they saw the prophetic gift on people like William Branham, they made room for the guys with the powerful revelatory gift for healing. Today, through Fresh Fire, we seek to combine the revelatory gift for healing, while strongly emphasizing the presence, anointing and the atmosphere of the Holy Ghost and the scriptural teaching of healing to stir faith. Past healing ministries would seldom walk in more than one of these many aspects of healing ministry. We are operating in what I call faith, anointing and prophetic—each facet comes from the Holy Spirit, but they all operate in different ways.

Kevin: *Describe how you developed your gifts.*

Todd: I grew in the healing ministry by believing that God gave gifts of healing and gifts of miracles—more than one healing gift, more than one miracle gift. I came to see that there could be one hundred people in a room with gifts of healing but that the gift would function and flow through their lives in different ways and strengths. Each one may see all kinds of healings but will probably have what I call a healing strength—yours could be backs; Mike's may be blind eyes while Joe's specialty is cripples. My healing strength is deaf ears. I've been especially blessed with a strong gift of healing for the

Man's ears completely healed in Germany—he shows Todd his hearing aid

deaf. Yet we have still seen healings from just about every kind of sickness and disease. I can't think of a healing that we haven't seen, other than the dead being raised…and that would be a creative miracle. Still, we are contending and praying for the dead to be raised all the time.

But here is the thing. I didn't always have a healing gift for the deaf. It's developed gradually as I've exercised it. I've always had a healing anointing for all sickness because healing is for all. But how did I develop a healing strength so that today, in some meetings, all the deaf hear, whether it is 20 or 30? I've been in meetings where 80 percent of the people would hear or all but two would hear. So what happened? I developed strength in healing. I believe, even though you have a healing gift, a healing anointing and a healing call, you can cultivate special healing strengths in several areas. I've learned how to develop the healing anointing into a healing gift specifically for the deaf. I began to pray for the deaf and when the deaf didn't hear, I'd pray for the deaf. And when the deaf didn't hear I'd pray for the deaf and when the deaf didn't hear I'd keep on praying for the deaf!

Wherever I was not seeing a great level of success, I would focus my prayer and faith. If I was seeing many arthritics healed, lots of deaf people healed and many people with pains in the stomach healed, yet there were no blind seeing in my meetings, I would begin to contend for breakthrough. I'd say, "OK, tonight we are going for the blind. Before I do anything else, I'm going to pray for the blind." And I'd do that in every meeting until the blind began to see and I developed authority in that area. As I contended for victory in an area of sickness, I would increase in authority until I was seeing miracles and until I got several healed of that affliction. Suddenly those types of healings became easy. Then I would go, "Now where am I a little weak? Is it cripples?" So I would begin to open up meetings by saying, "Let's pray for all the cripples first." Instead of seeing one out of every 100 cripples healed, soon it would be one in every 20 cripples, all because I took time to specifically sow into that area until it became a strength, an area of new authority in my ministry.

Kevin: *Describe the greatest influences that propelled or helped you walk into the healing ministry.*

Todd: When I look at men of God today who stir me to go deeper and higher, I think of guys like Reinhard Bonnke who is reaching millions in a crusade when we are reaching 10's of thousands in our crusades. So I am saying, "Holy Spirit, that's where I want to be." And I think of guys like Benny Hinn and the healing ministry that God has placed on his life today. I'm not even so much moved by the kind of healings that happen, but by the Presence of God involved. I was deeply touched by Benny's ministry, years ago, when I was only saved a few months. At that time, in my first six months as a Christian, I would consume anything that I could get my hands on that Benny had taught, both books and tapes. So, as for contemporary guys—as I've grown in the Lord I've continued to love and be blessed by the anointing and presence of God upon Benny's ministry, while being challenged by the miracles and crowds in the ministry of Reinhard Bonnke. But as for guys from the past, the greatest influences for me would be John G. Lake and William Branham. Benny was the first to expose me to anything to do with the anointing, the presence of God and miracles—that's how I came to learn about Kathryn Kuhlman. I had only been saved two months and so I knew nothing about anything. I didn't know that there was anybody who, years ago, had been used in healing or had a healing ministry. All I ever knew was the reality of the Holy Spirit and Benny Hinn. I was living in a small community of about 3,000 people, just coming off the street as a drug addict. I hadn't even seen Benny Hinn on TV at this time. I just had his book "Good Morning Holy Spirit."

It was at that time, in those first few months, as I began to listen to tapes and videos of Benny Hinn, that I said, "Holy Spirit I'll pay the price." Just like Benny Hinn said, "I'll pay the price" for the anointing he saw on Kathryn Kuhlman, I said, "I'll pay the price" for the anointing that was on both Kuhlman and Benny Hinn. That decision became rooted deep within me. That was before I even knew there were guys named Kenneth Hagen, T.L. Osborn or Reinhard Bonnke. That was before I knew anything about church history and revival. I just got saved and was filled with the Holy Ghost at the Full Gospel Business Men's meetings. I was reading the Bible everyday and praying and hungering for God when somebody gave me Benny Hinn's book on the Holy Spirit and that was it. I said, "God that's what I want! That's what I want on my life. I want to do that. I want to do healing. And that was how it all started.

I learned to move in my healing anointing by developing my personal intimate fellowship with the Holy Spirit. It became as natural as breathing for me. People ask "Todd, how did you learn to give out words of knowledge?" or, "Todd, how did you learn to prophesy?" or, "Todd, how did you learn how to move in the power of God?" It's become second nature to me. It's become like breathing. People ask, "How did it become so normal and easy for you to flow in miracles, to flow in words of knowledge and to flow in prophecy?" I'd say that it came out of those 4-12 hours a day those early months as a new Christian coming into those personal intimate encounters with the person of the Holy Spirit. I kept saying, "Holy Spirit I want to know you." As I developed in my intimate relationship with the Holy Spirit, asking Him questions and coming to know Him as a person, all that other stuff just began to happen—like a river, it began to flow. It was without effort. I didn't have to struggle to get into the word of knowledge. It became second nature because of the Holy Spirit. Some of those other things teachings from men of God helped me learn to flow and direct my river. So, intimacy with the Holy Spirit was the foundation for all the other stuff.

Kevin: *Tell me, what was the role of the early Fresh Fire youth ministry in helping launch you into your present ministry?*

Todd: Kevin, most people don't know that Fresh Fire began as youth meetings with you and several youth pastors in the basement of an Anglican church on Friday nights. As youth pastors, you guys had been praying for youth and revival in Abbotsford for almost two years, before you felt led to start weekly interchurch youth revival meetings—you called it Fresh Fire. In 1997, you guys began meeting with a small group of spiritually hungry youth and months later you invited me to speak once. I really connected with your vision to worship, pray, hear God, prophesy, preach and ignite revival fire through youth of the city. It was awesome to see all these spiritually hungry youth from Baptist, Mennonite, Pentecostal, Anglican, independent charismatic, and various other evangelical churches. About this time I started having encounters with the Holy Spirit during my 3-month soaking season and began to be invited to preach more at the youth meetings.

I'd say that those early Fresh Fire youth meetings became a real opportunity for me to practice. My heart was full—I was full of knowledge and there was a fire on my life. I just didn't have an opportunity or a platform to heal the sick and preach all the revelation that I was receiving in my times of visitation. I wasn't being invited into the nations, I didn't have the opportunity to preach in church and so I was working in the mill. I was asked to come every Friday and speak—those meetings became an opportunity for me to develop and to use the gifts that the Holy Spirit had given me. It became my platform. So I was able to go in and practice healing and I was able to practice prophecy because now I had a group of 50, 60 to 100 youth every Friday night that were hungry for the things of God. I could go in and share the things that I was getting in my visitation experiences and I could go in and prophesy over the kids. I could pray for them and they would get healed and filled with the Holy Ghost. It became an opportunity for me to develop my gifts.

If it wasn't for that season in my life in those early Fresh Fire meetings, I would never have been able to develop my gift in preaching or my confidence in preaching to crowds. I would never have had the opportunity to meet with a group of leaders where we could go over what just happened in each meeting and talk about my strengths and weaknesses. There was an opportunity for mentoring in my gifts as I was able to meet the other key men and talk about the various things that happened at each meeting. So, the youth ministry became a real training and mentoring opportunity for me; it became a bouncing board where I would ask, "How did that go? How could we have done this more?" It also became an opportunity for me to grow without having to worry about a reputation—I was working in the saw mill. I was in the midst of a three-month visitation of the Holy Ghost and I was full. I wanted to share and spread my wings.

I remember seeing my first healing in those meetings in the basement of St. Matthew's Anglican. One young woman's back was crooked and she couldn't stand up straight. It was in those meetings that she was healed. I remember another one of the young men had scoliosis and had curvature of the spine for years. I can still remember the tears flowing down his face as he said, "My back was healed. I felt heat flow through my back; I felt it crack and I could stand up straight for the first time." I remember some of those key healing testimonies from those youth meetings.

Kevin: *What are some of the specific memories from the early youth ministry that really touched your life, things that impacted you in that season?*

Todd: When I think back to those early Fresh Fire days, I remember my first meeting in the inner city in Vancouver, when we took a team of youth to minister at the Street Church. I was able to share my testimony with a crowd of people who were mostly unsaved—alcoholics, drug addicts and prostitutes. This was my first real evangelistic opportunity where I was able to give my testimony, give an altar call, then pray for the sick and for those who wanted to be set free from drugs and alcohol. In my eyes, it was a mini crusade. Even as I shared my testimony there was such a move of God's Spirit that some people came up to the altar to give their lives to Jesus or to rededicate their life to Him even before I was done speaking or got to the altar call. "Why are these people coming up to the front while I'm still speaking?" I remember asking. After someone from the ministry team investigated, he said, "Todd, they are coming up to get saved." Also, in that meeting, I remember praying for a woman who was a prostitute and a cocaine addict with AIDS. I still remember her today! She began manifesting devils and so we cast them out. I remember hearing a report, weeks later, of a drug-addicted woman in Vancouver who had gotten saved and later testified of a powerful healing. I was actually in one of Patricia King's meetings in Mission, B.C. when a woman came up to me and said, "I was just in Vancouver at this inner city church and a woman who had received prayer just weeks earlier was delivered from an addiction to cocaine. She also testified that she had just been to the doctor's and got her HIV test back showing that she was totally healed

Salvations and healings on the streets of England

of AIDS." That's when the Holy Spirit said to me, "That's the one you prayed for." The person she described was in the same service I was in. The Lord allowed me to hear the testimony through the grape vine.

I remember that incident to this day. I recall walking out of that inner city meeting which, to me, was like my first evangelistic crusade. I remember saying, "This is what I want to do the rest of my life." It was that night that I became desperate and hungry for God to release me into healing ministry. I said, "God I want to do this the rest of my life." It was that night and into the next day that my three month soaking visitation season began.

Kevin: *I remember that. You were so pumped about that day and about these people running to the altar. That experience gave you the hunger to spend all that time soaking.*

Todd: I wanted to get anointed. I wanted to receive everything. So I remember specifically the healing of that young man and the curvature of his spine and how he was weeping and his back cracked and how he stood straight for the first time. I remember some of the outreaches where we would take handfuls of Fresh Fire young people after the services were over and we would go out to Subway or Tim Hortons (a Canadian coffee/donut shop). I recall lining up people in the restaurants or in the streets and prophesying over them. I also remember preaching on repentance and giving an altar call and all the youth would be on their faces, laying their sin at the altar. I really began to stretch my John-the-Baptist wings, calling for repentance like Charles Finney used to do. I even remember some of the first messages that I preached on loving your neighbor as yourself. "If you love yourself enough that you don't want to go to hell and make sure that your soul is right with God, then love your neighbor enough to make sure that his soul is right with God," I would say, challenging the young people into evangelism.

Kevin: *Describe a few of your greatest revelations in the area of healing, when it was just like a light went on?*

Todd: Healing went to a whole other level for me when I understood how to make myself available to receive the word of knowledge and I began to operate in the prophetic in healing. That was the greatest revelation for me. Then I was able to come to God before the service and say, "Father, even before I go into the service, I ask you to show me now who is going to be healed and what is going to happen." The greatest revelation for increasing healing in my life and ministry was when I asked the Holy Spirit to show me things to come. God could now take me in a vision into the meeting, hours and days before the meeting took place. I only wanted to do those things that I saw the Father doing, so I began to take time at the beginning of each day or before each service to say, "Father, show me what you want me to act out tonight." Then I began to understand, not only God's word of knowledge and healing, but that I could position myself to wait on Him, receive a vision from heaven and then bring it to pass. In listening prayer, I would wait before the Lord saying, "Here I am God, what do you want to do tonight." I would write down those things that I saw, felt or heard. I would do that everyday. I wanted to walk like Jesus, who said, ***"the Son can do nothing of Himself, but what He sees the Father do; for whatever He does, the Son also does in like manner" (John 5:19).***

I remember doing that in the extended meetings in Albany Oregon. It went on for weeks and months. I remember taking 1-3 hours a day, not to pray, but to listen and say, "Father, show me who is going to be healed tonight. What kind of miracles do you want to do? What is going to happen and when is it going to happen? What's the first thing that you want me to do?" I'd ask for ten words of knowledge, then 15. I'd even begin to push for detail; I'd get a word of knowledge and then I'd begin to ask for specifics about that word of knowledge. "Lord, tell me the name of that person. Tell me where that person lives. Tell me what year the accident happened. Tell me the age and gender of the person." I'd ask for some keys that would go with the word of knowledge. If there was a back that God was going to heal, I'd ask for a sense of where the person was sitting, what side of the room and other details about the person. When I eventually began to minister at the meeting, I'd be able to say, "Here are ten miracles that I saw even before I got into the service." And I knew that was possible because I believed in the gifts of the Spirit. I just needed to increase my level of faith by waiting on the Father every day. That's how Jesus did only what He saw the Father doing. Realizing that I could walk in that realm of the prophetic was the greatest revelation for me.

Kevin: *Looking back on your years in healing ministry, what would be some of the highlights for you?*

Todd: India. The cities of Bombay and Goa in India. In six nights we saw 139 deaf mutes healed. That's a highlight for me. There was something about all those healings. Another highlight for me would be the first time I witnessed the Holy Spirit healing a Polio victim in India. This 16-year-old girl's legs were not even half the size of a teenage girl's legs. Both her legs were twisted where the knee was and curved out toward the hip. She had two big metal braces and crutches and she walked like a penguin. She had to sway like a penguin and her body had to twist to the right and left. I remember praying for her for two nights and nothing happened. She was in tears wanting to be healed—they would push her to the front of the healing line every night when I prayed for the cripples. One night I remember passing her by and thinking "oh, I've prayed for her 5 or 6 times and all my team has prayed for her. I prayed again, but just a kind of nonchalant courtesy prayer. "I'll just get her under the spirit and the anointing—she'll fall down and I'll go on praying for the rest of the cripples." I thought this way because I had given up. So I just kind of reached over and said, "Bless her Lord." I knew she was sensitive to the presence of the Lord and that if I touched her she would fall under the power. Then it would look like something was happening, so I could move on without feeling guilty because I had already prayed for her five times.

After I prayed for her and moved on, I heard a scream behind me and turned to see her running. I'll never forget her face; I'll never forget her smile; I'll never forget the tears flowing down her face. And she wasn't just trying to walk for the first time, she was running. She had one usher on each arm. And as she ran you could see her glee and hear her breathing like someone who had run up 100 flights of stairs, even though she had only run a few feet. Her respiratory system was weak because she had never been able to run or even walk fast. I remember her face when she would fall down and people would go to help her. She would push them away when they tried to slow her down and tell her to take slow steps. She didn't want to take little; she wanted to run right away. She would run up to me, all out of breath, and give me a hug. I'll never forget that girl with polio from birth, completely healed.

Another highlight for me was a woman without a breast in Ginga, Uganda. She had cancer and her breast was surgically removed. She began screaming because her breast had grown back. She had a brand new breast. That one miracle made such an impact on the crowd that it led to 34,000 salvations. That one miracle also led to several thousand people being set free from the power of witchcraft. That one miracle brought the witch doctors, the soothsayers and sorcerers. They came wondering, "What kind of power does the white man possess that he can even make body parts grow back?" The crowds swelled from 8 to10,000 up to 60,000 on the last night. During the altar calls, instead of 200 being saved, after that creative miracle, thousands were coming to Jesus. It was a powerful experience for me to see how one miracle can shake a city for God.

There were testimonies in Kansas City. I remember I was at a meeting in the inner city in Kansas City. Yes, miracles happen in the United States too. One night three blind people, each totally blind in one eye, all received their sight. I remember these three blind people all getting healed and within two minutes of one another they all received their sight. Then something incredible happened—an angel appeared in the balcony at that service. It was the healing angel that I talk about. Not only did I see him, but my Dad saw him. I hadn't said anything to anyone about angels. I was aware that the healing angel was making his presence known in the top left hand part of the balcony in Kansas. Then my Dad looked over at me and asked, "Did you know that your healing angel is sitting in the balcony in the top left." I knew something was going to happen that night, and sure enough, it did. Three blind eyes were opened—that was a real highlight for me of God's power at work in the United States.

Also, in North America, there have been numerous meetings where unusual miracles took place, whether it was gold in people's mouths (dental miracles) or God manifesting His presence with gold and glory dust on people's faces. These meetings would often go on until 4 a.m., with a strong presence of God and with prophecy.

Kevin: *So, whether in Africa or North America, you have seen every kind of miracle, pretty much?*

Todd: Yes. Incredible testimonies of healing. I remember one summer we had an incredible six-week run in California. I've lost track of how many deaf, but more than 18 people that were deaf received their healing. Also, we saw that six or seven cases of MS, some who had been crippled for years and hadn't walked, were healed of MS. I remember hearing testimonies when I was in Vista, California of people with cancer, Lupis and tumors who were healed—those were highlights for me. A small Four Square Church that really wanted to pursue evangelism and the power of God with no holds barred and 3,000 people showed up in the parking lot for food on an outreach before our crusade. I remember being in those meetings and baptizing people right at the crusade. There were testimonies of healing every night of people who were blind or crippled.

I also remember the story of the boy that came out of the coma in Grant's Pass. In a trance the Lord told me about a boy in a coma in the hospital. I saw that I would make a prophetic announcement about a man in my meeting who would come on behalf of a woman that was in the hospital at the bedside of her boy in a coma. The woman, which I had believed to be the mother of that boy had come to me in that vision and spoke to me about her boy in the coma and how she had a friend, a man that she had sent to that tent meeting to stand in the gap for that boy in the coma. I saw myself pray for the man who came forward, then announce prophetically that the newspaper headlines would read, "Boy Comes out of Coma." There were about 1,000 people that night in the tent in Grant's Pass Oregon in December of 2000—I gave the word of knowledge and, months later, sure enough, I heard from elders in that church that headlines on the front of the local papers read, "Boy comes out of the coma." That was a real highlight for me.

Those meetings in Grant's Pass were a real launching time for me in ministry. I had been invited to be the healing evangelist to minister alongside key prophets of today like Paul Keith Davis, Bob Jones, Bobby Conners and John Paul Jackson. The organizers wanted someone with a healing anointing to partner with the prophetic guys and to help re-dig the ancient healing well. Because a move of healing was already beginning to take place in those early months of August and November 2000, they said, "We know this man Todd Bentley. He's an evangelist. He's been doing meetings for us up the road from us for three hours. Let's have him come in."

Cripple boy healed at crusade in India

In the same place (Grant's Pass, Oregon) in 1950, God used William Branham and Paul Cain to start a healing revival in the Northwest. It was when "The Voice of Healing" magazine was born. Paul Cain, a seasoned prophet today, was at that time a young man working with William Branham in Grant's Pass. In 1950 they were dedicating a tabernacle of healing.

It was in our healing meetings 50 years later where we joined together in a jubilee time to contend for the same healing anointing that broke out in the Northwest in the days of the Voice of Healing. It was at that time that people began to accept the validity of my ministry and my prophetic word because I was ministering alongside Bob Jones, John Paul Jackson and Bobby Conners. They began to think, "Well, Todd must have a word from the Lord." So I was received more on an international level because I had ministered alongside more recognized, seasoned prophets who were known internationally. No more were we just going into a city and doing meetings with a hundred people because nobody knew who Todd Bentley or Fresh Fire was. It was in Grant's Pass, during that weekend of December 5, 2000 where I had a profound visitation from an angel by the name of Healing Revival. The first time I had a visitation of an angel was in my home before my traveling ministry started. I said, "There is an angel towering in the apartment above me." People can read that part of my testimony in my book *Journey into the Miraculous*.

Anyway, three weeks after the Grant's Pass meetings, God used this same healing angel to help ignite a healing revival in Albany, Oregon at the Vineyard church. I had already preached in Albany twice, in August and November 2000, and there were already signs that God wanted to move for an extended time. When I came to Albany in January 2001, the healing revival meetings went on for months and people came from all over the United Sates and from other nations to receive a healing touch from God. These meetings continued with several speakers coming in and feeding the fire each week right up until May 2001.

Once I saw a woman who was pushing her bicycle through the parking lot of the church. I ran outside and asked, "Do you know what's happening in here? It's a healing revival." I found out she was a Swedish woman who had been deaf in one ear almost all her life. I prayed for her and she was totally healed in the parking lot. People were lining up for hours early to get into the healing service that night. The strength of that healing revival went for 8-9 months. It was considered a legitimate revival in North America. This move of God propelled our ministry—it is what really launched us.

Every ministry has milestones or markers, times when people can say this meeting or this conference or this revival is where God really launched the ministry to a whole new level. For us, although I had been traveling for two years already, it was in those Grant's pass meetings and those early weeks of the revival of healing in Albany, Oregon that God really began to put an international favor on our ministry. I would say it was one of God's promotion times. There have been other such times, but during this season it was as if God gave us a big stamp of validation followed by far greater opportunity for our ministry on a more international level.

Why? It wasn't so much about the crowds, the numbers, the healings or anything like that in those meetings in Albany, but it was the friendship I developed with Steve Shultz from the Elijah List (a prophetic internet/e-mail resource). Steve is part of the local church in Albany, Oregon and his Elijah list was reaching 50- to 60-thousand people at that time over the internet. So it was a real tool to get the word out about what God was doing and saying. Steve and I had lunch together and developed a friendship. He was in some of those meetings in Oregon where he witnessed how the prophetic and the word of knowledge were key demonstrations of God's power in healing. He saw and heard the testimonies of healing himself. Things really took off when Steve began to send out reports on the Elijah list weekly, sometimes nightly, about what was happening in his local church in Albany, Oregon with a young man by the name of Todd Bentley.

Very quickly news spread that there were extended healing meetings where real significant miracles—healings of the deaf, blind, crippled and Hepatitis C sufferers. Meetings took place every night for months. Pastors who wanted a healing impartation for their church flew in. The same healing anointing had been upon my life before but we hadn't had the exposure. So God used Albany, Oregon and the friendship Steve Shultz and I began to promote what God was doing in both Oregon and Albany through Fresh Fire and Denny Kline's Vineyard Church. The Elijah list became exposure for the anointing that was already on my life and I would say that the meetings in Albany were the manifestation and the result of the visitation in Grant's Pass of the angel named Healing Revival.

Kevin: *Tell us more about the healing angel and how the visitations have impacted your life and ministry.*

Todd: During the time I call my "soaking season" (which readers can learn more about in my testimony book *Journey into the Miraculous)* the Lord began to launch me into ministry. It was in that season (early 1998) that I had a visitation of an angel in my home. You were there Kevin and so was my wife. I was on the floor and I yelled out, "There's an angel standing in the middle of the apartment and he is towering into the apartment above me." Remember, you asked me, "Why is he here? Who is he?" I said, "I don't know. It's just an angel and I just saw him." At the time, I had no idea what this visitation was all about. It was within weeks of that visitation, on Mother's day in May, that I was called out publicly and commissioned into full-time ministry at a Patricia King conference after the Holy Spirit showed up in power during a time I was to share a testimony.

I didn't realize at the time how significant the angel's first appearance was in connection to my release into ministry. It was not until the angel appeared to me later in Albany, Oregon (February 2001) that I understood that this was the same angel that visited me in my apartment and in Grant's Pass. Here in Albany, I heard the audible voice of the Lord tell me that this angel's name was Healing Revival and that it was like the angel in John 5 that stirred the waters at the Pool of Bethesda and brought healing. The Lord told me that this angel had been a key part of three other healing movements in church history. He also said that this same kind of angel was visiting us and that there was a real call on my life, not just to move in healing, but to be a part of sparking healing revival. In that meeting of four or five hundred people in Albany, many actually saw the angel while others sensed the presence of the angel in this, one of the most unusual meetings that I have ever done.

The Lord also gave us many signs that the angel really was visiting us. Children were having visitations of angels while several other people screamed out, "I'm healed" and announced that they were touched by an angelic presence before they were healed. One woman, crippled from birth, yelled out that she was healed. One woman with a broken neck yelled out that she was healed. Anybody who stepped up within six feet of the spot where the angel had appeared would fall under the power without hands being laid on them and many of them would get up healed. That meeting went on until 11 p.m. with no preaching. Whether people could see the angel or not, it was clear that something was going on.

Later, the Lord began to show me the purposes behind these visitations at different times in my life. When the angel visited me on December 5 in Grant's Pass, I was knocked out of my body and had an out-of-body experience (like the apostle Paul did). It was at that time that the word of knowledge increased in my life. There has been an increase in my accuracy and frequency of delivering the word of knowledge since that visitation. All of a sudden I began to experience more open visions, more trances and more seer/prophet stuff in which my eyes would be open to the invisible realm and what was going on in the realm of angels and demons. Through different prophetic ministry friends I have since come to understand that I received a real deposit of that same kind of revelatory gift that God placed upon William Branham years ago. It was only after that visitation that I was able to touch people with my left hand and accurately diagnose their sicknesses. This is same kind of gift that William Branham during the Voice of Healing revival exactly 50 years before.

When the angel visited again weeks later in Albany, I understood that this was the same angel I had seen in Grant's Pass. "Where have you seen this angel before Grant's Pass?" the Lord asked me. "What do you mean 'before'?" I asked in surprise. "Remember back in your home during that season of soaking? That was the first time that I assigned the angel to you." Then the Lord reminded me that my commissioning into full-time ministry took place just weeks after He sent the angel to my apartment. "That was the day that you were commissioned—it wasn't when Pat (Patricia King) called you out at her conference," the Lord explained.

During the third visitation the Holy Spirit said, "I've commissioned you to take healing revival—like that which has begun in Oregon—to other places. This is more than Todd moving in healing; it's a resident healing anointing. I've commissioned you to be one of many, but a key part of sparking the next healing revival." The Spirit told me that my ministry would leave a resident healing anointing. "When you come in, there will be healings. But, ultimately, I'm going to assign this kind of angel to whole cities and regions and do what I did in the days of John Lake in Spokane (Washington) where again there will be whole cities overcome with my healing anointing."

The angel showed up a fourth time in Kansas City—that is the night those three blind people saw. Since then I've seen him in Kansas City and Mexico. The angel was also seen as I was praying for the sick in Tanzania and many other cities. Today, many times when I pray for the sick, people tell me that they see an angel standing behind me on the left side. And I know this because now I don't even see the angel as much but I can feel his presence standing behind me on my left and he whispers in my ear words of knowledge. It's like I'll feel the presence of the angel and I know He's there to help me. Scripture describes this angelic role in ministry: ***"Are they not all ministering spirits, sent out to render service for the sake of those who will inherit salvation?" (Heb. 1:14).*** Scripture tells us that Jesus has given us authority on earth to speak and bind and loose (allow and disallow)—the Father wants to answer our prayers and back up our words. We also know that angels do God's bidding:

> ***"I Bless the LORD, O my soul; and all that is within me, bless His holy name! Bless the LORD, O my soul, and forget not all His benefits: Who forgives all your iniquities, Who heals all your diseases... Bless the LORD, you His angels, who excel in strength, who do His word, heeding the voice of His word" (Ps. 103:1–3,20).***

It is clear that God will send angels to back us up and to assist in bringing salvation, wholeness and healing to people. Jesus is the healer but angels are a part of all that we do in healing, like they were in John 5. Jesus is the healing Word, but angels also carry out His word. So, when this angel visits me on my left side, there is this knowing that comes into my mind when I feel his presence. I get this knowing of who is in the room, accurate details about their life, their history, their sickness, how long they've had it, their names, where they are sitting and so on.

Kevin: *So what do you see as this angel's role in your ministry?*

Todd: When the angel's presence is manifest and we become aware that the angel is here (it's happened in more than 30 meetings), it's as if the presence of this angel clears the air and pushes back the darkness in such a way that there is a freedom to move in the gifts of the Spirit without all the warfare that usually comes with it. There seems to be an increase in accuracy in the kinds of words of knowledge that I get and my ability to discern conditions and sickness. When I am accurate in the word of knowledge, the faith level in the room increases so there is just a whole new thickness of the healing anointing. It seems (if you want to gage the meeting) that when the angel's presence becomes known or visits me before a meeting, the power of the meeting will be an 8 or a 9 verses a 5 or 6 normally. There is just a definite increased awareness of atmosphere, faith, the accuracy of the prophetic, as well as the kinds and frequency of miracles that take place. I feel that he comes as a messenger with revelatory communications from the Father, like Gabriel was a messenger to Daniel. As I receive the message, I can speak what I hear and the accuracy of the words is so bang on that the faith of the people increases. If I can tell you your name and your condition, your faith for healing will dramatically increase.

Kevin: *So you think that this angel isn't in every meeting, just some meetings?*

Todd: I think everywhere, all the time, all believers have angels with them, but this particular angel definitely does not manifest in every meeting. I believe I have angels with me as every believer does, but I don't believe that they always visit on the same level. Usually when I become aware of the visitation of the healing angel, I'm to prophecy in the church or that city or that region that a healing revival is coming and that God is going to release part of the anointing similar to that in Spokane with John G. Lake and the healing rooms. The Lord has shown me that He is going to create healing pools like the pool of Bethesda in John 5. When the angel's presence becomes known, I know that city or region is one of the end-times places where God is really going to open up a healing pool. When the angel visits, I receive an authority to prophecy that this area or place is going to become a healing pool or a healing center in the end-time move of God. I can prophesy a healing anointing and usually I will leave and the healing anointing will continue on—that doesn't happen everywhere I go. But usually in those places where the angel shows up, the healing wave continues.

Kevin: *Why does the angel appear on your left side, Todd?*

Todd: I have no idea why the angel appears on my left side and not on my right. I always feel the gift in my left hand. The electricity goes through my arm. Sometimes I'll lay my right hand on the sick, but sometimes I will grab people with my left hand. I'll feel electricity in my left arm and I'll become aware of a presence beside me. Sometimes it will be as if that presence is whispering in my ear all these little things and sometimes I'll even feel like wind is blowing in my ear. Other times I'll hear an inner audible voice, or I'll just get a knowing. Maybe I'm praying for you and then it's like "boom," a shot of lightning and I have instant, accurate knowledge about you that I didn't have five seconds before. Then all of a sudden your faith level increases as the Lord prepares you for the healing prayer that I am about to give you. The angel may suddenly show up when I am on the platform or ministering or even preaching and I'll stop the meeting and go, "Let's see what he wants to do." Then he'll tell me, "There is a woman called Donna over here on the right that has a kidney disease." Then Donna will stand up and scream and all of a sudden we will move into healing ministry.

Woman healed of back problems in Africa

Kevin: *Does that gift happen all the time?*

Todd: This gift of healing that manifests in my left hand happens in meetings, not just when the angel comes, but most often when the angel's presence is near. It's not all the time for everybody. Sometimes the angel comes several times a week, sometimes once a month and sometimes once every two months. Sometimes he'll come every day for a few days and sometimes he'll show up in every meeting in a city.

Kevin: *So you may get the gift of healing, in the same meeting, for one person and not for another.*

Todd: Let's call it the discerning gift of healing which allows me to bring an accurate word of knowledge. Healing will operate in many other ways for other people and this discerning gift in my hand is just one unusual way the gift operates. If you look at healing ministries that God has used throughout history, every one of them had a characteristic that was maybe a little bit different or unusual. John G. Lake and William Branham had gifts like that. Smith Wigglesworth had a unique gift of radical faith that led him to pray for people in very unusual ways. Kathryn Kuhlman would say, "He's here," whenever she sensed the Holy Spirit present to heal. Everybody had a signature, something they did that made them unique—for me it's just one way that the healing gift operates but it's one of the more unusual manifestations at times in my meetings. This gift brings accuracy in the word of knowledge and gives me sharp discernment which increases faith in the room so healing can flow more freely. The angel's presence opens things up. It's also a sign to me that I am to prophesy that this church, city or region is one of the healing pools God is preparing.

Kevin: *You believe is it the same angel in your ministry as in the healing ministries of John Knox, William Branham and John G. Lake?*

Todd: I don't believe that it is the exact same angel. However, I do believe it as an angel with the same nature as the angel that would operate in John Knox's life and that worked alongside the revival or reformation parts of His ministry. Like Knox, we at FFM are called to more than just healing meetings; we are called to see cities and nations transformed by God's power. We need to see a reformation of healing power in the church today. Although we don't endorse every part of John Knox's ministry, he definitely had a revivalist-type mantle for reformation that God has called us to walk in as well. In William Branham's life there was also a prophetic element of healing. I really feel like God has called me as both a prophet, like Branham, as well as an evangelist. My favorite gift is that of evangelist even though my prophet gift has become as strong. Today, I'm able to walk in both mantles. John G Lake's ministry was something more than just a four-day healing conference; he delivered the resident tangible anointing that would remain in a church or city in an ongoing way. John Lake was about training the body of Christ to do healing ministry; it wasn't just about John Lake being anointed. He raised up others. His anointing became resident in other places. He believed in contending in faith for healing. Lake believed that if people are not healed, then we are to pray again and keep on praying and soaking them until they are healed. So, I believe it was a healing angel in John G Lake meetings at times and in William Branham and John Knox meetings at times.

John G. Lake

Those different ministry anointings are what our ministry is about: revival, word of knowledge, the prophetic and then contending faith for an abiding healing anointing. We want to see the anointing released when we come into a city and we want people to catch it after we are gone. So usually on the last night of my meetings I will pray for everyone for an impartation of healing. I want the healing anointing to be sparked in others. That is one of the characteristics of "The Voice of Healing Revival." There were over 100 or more prominent healing evangelists at one time. You think of Gordon Lindsay, Jack Coe, A.A. Allen, William Branham and Oral Roberts. Even T.L. Osborn's ministry was sparked in a William Branham meeting. Those are just a few key household names.

Yet, several other guys, that you don't even know of, were also launched into healing ministry out of that healing movement in the 40's and 50's. My heart is that, in this next healing wave, not just Todd Bentley will move in gifts of healing as an evangelist, but that through tangible impartation God will raise up a healing army. This mighty army will carry elements found in the ministries of John Knox (that of revival reformation), William Branham (the prophetic and revelatory transferable anointing) and John G Lake who modeled the training aspect of healing and how to maintain and sustain that anointing in your city through the healing rooms.

I mean, who knows how much the angelic realm is really involved in our meetings. In order for us to increase in a healing anointing today, we need to become more aware of how the angelic realm or the realm of heaven is involved in what we want to get done on earth. Only when we begin to give credit to that realm and begin to talk about it without being afraid are we going to see an increase of "as it is in heaven" on the earth. But as long as we are afraid of all this stuff we won't see the power of God come in a real way so that heaven begins to touch earth.

Kevin: *Describe a few of the greatest discouragements and struggles in the ministry.*

Todd: In the beginning, the greatest struggle was over "How many will God heal?" I had to wrestle with the theology of healing, studying Scripture after Scripture until I believed healing was for all, all the time. I had to overcome the discouragement of praying for 100 and only seeing one healed. At other times I would be in meetings when there was no real visible sign of any healings other than a little pain in somebody's knee or back. I remember during the low times asking God: "Why was this person with a broken bone healed but these two blind people weren't?" I've come home from meetings again and again, as each of us do, wanting to say thank you for what God did but we can't help think about all the things that didn't seem to happen. I would have to wrestle through in my own heart why these five were healed and those five weren't or why these kinds of sicknesses were healed and those kinds of sicknesses weren't healed. I would go through the disappointment of believing I was as strong in faith for the blind as I was for arthritis. I would see people healed of arthritis but when I prayed for the blind, little or no manifestation would take place. I would cry out saying, "But Holy Spirit it's the same anointing for healing arthritis as it is healing for the blind. It doesn't take any more faith and power. Why are the blind not being healed?"

Teaching and preaching God's desire to heal all and then not seeing the immediate manifestation of healing has been discouraging for me, at times. In the early days, I would pray for the deaf and they just wouldn't hear. I believed that the deaf would hear but they weren't hearing. I had to continue contending for the manifestation even when I was tempted to be discouraged. At times, when I compared myself to other healing ministers, I'd ask, "Why did they see these kinds of miracles and I'm not. Why are they at a higher level? If I'm seeing one wheel chair, how come they are getting thirty in a meeting? How come Jack Coe had over 100 wheel chairs in one meeting and I am struggling to get one in four days. And yet I've seen numerous deaf and numerous people crippled with arthritis healed. I've even seen tumors disappear and yet these three people over here on cots aren't getting up.

I've learned that every healing ministry goes through these struggles. I've had to wrestle this through in my own heart with the understanding that there is a difference between healing and miracles. Miracles are instant, healings tend to be "they will recover"—they are progressive. There needs to be room in healing today, like the story of the 10 lepers, where they were cleansed as they went. I've heard hundreds of times, now, of people who were healed two or three days after being in a meeting.

Today our ministry sees so many powerful healings, however, people still ask how I deal with the disappointment of all the ones that we pray for who don't see any immediate change. I've had to train my ministry teams by sharing the revelation that has helped me overcome my own disappointment and discouragement—I have come to understand that I can't really say that people weren't healed or that they are not going to be healed. It isn't my job to try figure out if and when they are going to be healed. I just need to believe in faith that regardless of what I've seen, God is faithful to His Word and my job is to lay hands on the sick and God does the rest. Healings can be progressive and they can occur even as people travel home. So we don't know that the ones we prayed for tonight aren't going to travel home and wake up healed two days from now. I am not going to beat myself up about what I don't know, so I just live and pray as if I'm trusting that all of them are going to be healed as they go. I'm not saying they are, but in my own heart, so I can have peace and victory, I just leave it to God to sort out. I can't think all night about the blind boy that I prayed for that didn't get healed on the platform because I might be beating myself up for nothing. He might just get healed in three days.

In many crusades I've had to struggle with the thoughts: "I've put all this time and money into this crusade; it was going to be our biggest and now it is raining and the crowds aren't showing up." I've had to deal with, again and again, how come these kinds of sicknesses are being healed and these others aren't. I had to realize in my heart that it is OK not to be instantly healed and come to understand that a miracle and a healing are different. I just had to purpose in my heart that three things remain: faith, hope and love.

People still say, "Todd, it's easy for you to preach and teach that message. But have you had somebody close to you die after you prayed in faith for them to be healed?" My answer is, "Yes." In the midst of a healing revival when thousands of people were coming from all over America, from almost every state, with people being healed every night—my mother died. In this healing revival in Albany, Oregon, people were even being healed of strokes, yet my mother died of a stroke. I had already prayed for her in person to be healed of that stroke more than 10 times. I saw her recover and then regress. After I prayed for her, she recovered miraculously from her first stroke; she began talking and walking again. Then, as a result of continuous seizures, she regressed and then she ended up getting pneumonia and dying.

Just the day before, I was just in a meeting when two or three people, crippled and paralyzed from stroke, were instantly healed and all their symptoms disappeared. I could think about all the others that had been healed of pneumonia, stroke, seizures and epilepsy throughout the years—I had already been in healing ministry and here I was faced with the news of my mother's death. Yet, I had to hang on to my message: "These things remain: faith, hope and love." I just needed to believe that, as the Scripture says, many died not yet receiving the promise, but their death becomes a martyr's seed for the healing ministry. Sometimes it is in death that 100-fold return comes. I could respond to this death in discouragement, disappointment or anger towards God, saying, "Why, God, would you let my mother die in the midst of healing revival, even in the midst of hearing testimonies of people healed of stroke. I'm faithfully serving you in the nations, praying for all these other people; couldn't you at least heal this one for me?"

Again and again I would hear powerful healing testimonies. Yet my wife and my children are sick while I'm in the most glorious healing revival. Then I was ministering in India and had to battle through why the Lord wasn't covering my family: "Lord, I've been praying and asking in faith for healing for my family. Yet, people with conditions ten times worse than my family were healed just today." I've been challenged over and over with the message that I preach and believe. How do I go on in healing ministry when somebody close to me has died (like my mother), or somebody close to me is battling sickness (like my mother-in-law's father struggling with cancer, or my children and wife suffering from the common 'flu)? How do I battle through all that?

I've realized that it's not as much about how you believe today; it's about where your faith ends up. It's how you go out that counts. It's not about how you believe today. Some people can have strength to believe for healing for six months while they start to get better. Months later the diagnosis gets worse. Then two years pass, they have been to one hundred healing meetings and they are not yet healed. Their faith isn't as strong as it was in those first 6 months. So I've decided that if I'm going to be as strong in faith for ten years as I was in the first 6 months, then I have to commit to God that these three things remain: "Faith, hope and love" and that, "Many died not yet receiving the promise." I've decided its OK to have questions and that it is OK not to have answers. I just don't change God's Word or my message based on what does or does not happen.

Kevin: *I think part of it is realizing that there are many reasons why healing may or may not happen. We don't know which reason it is why the healing didn't happen.*

Todd: In this book we've listed thirty reasons why miracles happen and thirty reasons why miracles don't happen. And there are many more—I have to recognize that I don't always know from the Lord which one of those reasons it may have been. I can't go around trying to figure that out. So, I don't try to pin a reason on everybody for not being healed and play the blame game. Forget it! I just leave it alone and continue to love people, preach healing and pray for the sick—God does the rest.

My wife needs a brand new back even though I can think of so many people I have prayed for who God has given a brand new back. I've had to deal with the car accident my wife had three or four years ago when somebody rear ended her, fracturing her spine. I've had to believe God for healing so she can overcome the pain.

Kevin: *Todd, is the healing ministry for everyone?*

Todd: I believe that healing ministry is for everyone. The Scripture is clear about our healing commission: ***"Most assuredly, I say to you, he who believes in Me, the works that I do he will do also; and greater works than these he***

will do, because I go to My Father" (John 14:12). Jesus also commissioned His disciples saying:

> ***"...Go into all the world and preach the gospel to every creature. He who believes and is baptized will be saved; but he who does not believe will be condemned. And these signs will follow those who believe: In My name they will cast out demons; they will speak with new tongues; they will take up serpents; and if they drink anything deadly, it will by no means hurt them; they will lay hands on the sick, and they will recover" (Mark 16:15).***

Then James 5:15 tells us that ***"the prayer of faith will save the sick, and the Lord will raise him up."*** It's the prayer of faith that saves the sick, not the prayer of Reinhard Bonnke. It's not the prayer of William Branham or the prayer of John G Lake; it's not the prayer of Todd Bentley—it's the prayer of faith. If a three-year-old can pray in faith that God would do what He said he would do, it will save the sick. It doesn't matter if it's an elder, a housewife, or a businessman, healing is for everyone because of Romans 8:11—this Scripture shows us that the same Spirit that raised Jesus Christ from the dead lives in us. The same Spirit lives in every born again believer. According to Acts 10:38, the Holy Spirit anointed Jesus to do good and heal everyone oppressed of the devil. **Jesus did not do one miracle as God**. Every miracle that Jesus did, He did as one anointed with the Holy Ghost and power. And we have that same Spirit that raised Jesus Christ from the dead in us. It's the Holy Spirit who is the key to miracles in Jesus' ministry and in our lives. We don't all have the desire; we don't all have the faith level but we all have the same potential to walk in healing power because it's a believer's ministry.

Kevin: *Are there different levels of healing, depending on a person's office?*

Todd: Yes. There is a level of healing that comes with the office gift of an evangelist or a prophet. There is different authority, influence and platform. Not everyone is going to fill stadiums. Not everyone is going to do mass crusades. But everybody has the right to operate in healing in their home, in their business and at the hospital. Everyone can pray for healing of others in their church, but not everyone is going to have the same influence, platform and opportunity as Reinhard Bonnke, Benny Hinn or T.L. Osborn but they can have a gift of healing.

Believers can also develop an area of strength in healing ministry because there are "gifts of healing." I also believe that there are special strengths that come with office calls—the fivefold ministry call of Ephesians 4:11 (Apostle, Prophet, Pastor, Teacher and Evangelist.) So if you are called as an apostle or a prophet or an evangelist, there is an authority, an anointing and a strength to produce, not just signs and wonders, but signs and wonders of the frequency that comes with being an apostle, prophet or evangelist. So there is definitely a difference. Average believers might see the healing of one deaf ear in five years but they are not going to have the opportunity to pray for one thousand deaf in a big crusade because they don't have that call as an evangelist. If I have ten blind people in my meeting, I have a better chance of getting the blind healed than a businessman or saw mill worker who doesn't meet blind people every week. They are not up on a platform in a meeting with 10,000 people. There is greater frequency of healing that comes with the office gift.

So what's the main difference between the work of the saints and the office gift? It's not that all believers can't prophesy, but they will probably not have the influence in the lives of kings or presidents. You might not have international recognition and opportunity to speak in conferences with 5, 000 people. It's all about platform, influence and authority.

Kevin: *How do ordinary people acquire and maintain the gift of healing?*

Todd: Use it or lose it. People can increase their anointing by getting around others that have more than what they have, if they are humble enough to say, "Pray for me to get more of what you have." If you want more anointing, get as many people as you can that move in more healing than you do to lay hands on you. Get as much impartation as you can. Remember Matthew 10:8—***"Freely you have received, freely give."*** So you need to be receiving and giving. If you are receiving impartation by a mighty ministry that is laying hands on you and you are not giving it away, you are going to lose what you got. So my thing is, get prayer and use it; get prayer and use it as quickly as you get it.

Kevin: *So Todd, people who don't have a healing ministry and don't have the platform that you or others have, how do they use their healing gifts?*

Todd: There are several opportunities in the church today. Maybe it's a healing ministry, healing rooms in your city or hospital visitation. Rather than going out in the streets and doing evangelism, maybe you can start going door to door and ask, "Is there anyone sick in your home that I can pray for?" Talk to your pastor or your ministry team leader at your church and ask if there is opportunity for people to pray for healing on Sundays. Ask if you can be part of the team or whether you can start a healing team. There are numerous opportunities to pray for the sick in everyday life. We need to create opportunity. If there isn't an opportunity for you to hook into what God is already doing, then maybe you can create the opportunity in your church or community to pray for the sick. Pray for your neighbors, start a healing room or do whatever you can to create an opportunity wherever you can for God's healing river to flow.

Woman receives ministry at the Abbotsford, BC Tent Revival Meetings

SOZO—FULL SALVATION FOR SPIRIT, SOUL AND BODY

In this chapter I want to examine the scriptural foundation of salvation, rooted in the Greek word *sozo*, which speaks of salvation and wholeness for the spirit, soul and body. We need to recognize the full extent of the gospel and of our commission. If we are going to walk in divine health and be released into the ministry of praying for the sick, we must have a revelation of the heart of God for both spiritual and physical wholeness. We need to know that God's desire is to heal every sick person. The Bible tells us that Jesus was moved with compassion and healed all the sick. He healed every sickness and every disease that people were afflicted with (Matt. 4:23,24).

In these first few chapters I would like to share with you some of the biblical truths of divine healing found in the redemptive names of God as well as the covenant of healing and deliverance. We will examine what these truths mean to us as believers, how they can work in our lives and how we can appropriate God's healing, redemptive plan and covenant for our lives. I also want to give a full biblical understanding of what it really means to be saved. This message of *sozo* (complete salvation) is probably one of the most important for you to understand if you want to lay a foundation of faith in your life so you can believe God for healing—not just for some, but for all people.

Jesus Healed Everyone

God wants to impart to every Christian the same power He gave to the disciples in Matthew 10:1: ***"He gave them power over unclean spirits to cast them out and to heal all kinds of sickness and all kinds of disease."*** That is what we are after as we journey through this book—the power to heal all kinds of sickness and to heal all kinds of disease. When I travel to Africa and around the world to preach in mass crusades, I usually preach this message of *sozo*. Quite often, at the moment of salvation, many people who were Muslim, Hindu or Buddhist, with no previous exposure to Christianity, are delivered of every devil and healed of every sickness and disease. These people don't have to wait 10 years to discover the truth about divine healing. They are a testimony of the power of the message of *sozo*.

You will find more power in your life and your ministry, as one who ministers healing, when you believe and preach this message. Receiving the revelation of *sozo* will not just impart to us faith to receive healing, but will allow us to accept and participate in the complete Great Commission to preach the full gospel to all nations. This message of *sozo* is the foundation for our faith in divine healing.

Sozo: Complete Salvation

Scripture tells us, ***"that if you confess with your mouth the Lord Jesus and believe in your heart that God has raised Him from the dead, you will be saved" (Rom. 10:9).*** However, what does that word "saved" really mean? As Christians we talk about being "saved" or "born again" all the time. During altar calls preachers usually say things like, "If you want to give your life to Jesus tonight, then come to the altar and be saved." We often throw around other Christian clichés like: "Pray the sinners' prayer", "Your name will be written in the Lamb's book of life", or "We welcome you to the kingdom of God". Yet, do we really understand the language we use; do we understand the most basic concept of being "saved"? Just say it, "I'm saved." What do you feel when you say, "I'm saved"? What do you think about when you hear the word "saved"?

Sozo **defined.** Let's first define this Greek word. Here's the definition of *Sozo* from *Strong's Exhaustive Concordance of the Bible:*

> *4982* ***sozo****, sode-zo; from a prim. Sos (contr. For obsol. Saos, "safe"); to save, i.e. deliver or protect (lit. or fig.):--heal, preserve, save (self), do well, be (make) whole.*

Sozo is described as salvation for the body, soul and spirit at the moment of salvation. Here's another definition of the word *sozo*, taken from *Vines Expository Dictionary of New Testament Words*:

> ***Save, Saving*** *<A-1,Verb,4982,sozo> "to save," is used (as with the noun soteria, "salvation") (a) of material and temporal deliverance from danger, suffering, etc., e.g., Matt. 8:25; Mark 13:20; Luke 23:35; John 12:27; 1 Tim. 2:15; 2 Tim. 4:18 (AV, "preserve"); Jude 1:5; from sickness, Matt. 9:22, "made ... whole" (RV, marg., "saved"); so Mark 5:34; Luke 8:48; Jas. 5:15; (b) of the spiritual and eternal salvation granted immediately by God to those who believe on the Lord Jesus Christ, e.g., Acts 2:47, RV "(those that) were being saved;" 16:31; Rom. 8:24, RV, "were we saved;" Eph. 2:5,8: 1 Tim. 2:4; 2 Tim. 1:9; Titus 3:5; of human agency in this, Rom. 11:14; 1 Cor. 7:16; 9:22; (c) of the present experiences of God's power to deliver from the bondage of sin, e.g., Matt. 1:21; Rom. 5:10; 1 Cor. 15:2; Heb. 7:25; Jas. 1:21; 1 Pet. 3:21; of human agency in this, 1 Tim. 4:16; (d) of the future deliverance of believers at the second coming of Christ for His saints, being deliverance from the wrath of God to be executed upon the ungodly at the close of this age and from eternal doom, e.g., Rom. 5:9; (e) of the deliverance of the nation of Israel at the second advent of Christ, e.g., Rom. 11: 26; (f) inclusively for all the blessings bestowed by God on men in Christ, e.g., Luke 19:10; John 10:9; 1 Cor. 10:33; 1 Tim. 1:15; (g) of those who endure to the end of the time of the Great Tribulation, Matt. 10:22; Mark 13:13; (h) of the individual believer, who, though losing his reward at the Judgment-Seat of Christ hereafter, will not lose his salvation, 1 Cor. 3:15; 5:5; (i) of the deliverance of the nations at the Millennium, Rev. 21:24 (in some mss.).*

Now let's just break it down a little bit. The word means to be saved from spiritual death through forgiveness of sin; to be saved from physical death by healing; it means "heal." The word also means "to preserve, make whole, keep you safe and sound, rescue from danger or destruction." This word covers everything that hinders you from receiving the manifestation of everything that is good, heavenly and holy, including blessing, healing and deliverance. It means to be delivered from every evil that obstructs and hinders.

Sozo Prophesied

This kind of complete salvation was prophesied years before the ministry of Jesus and the blessings of the cross were won. Let me show you the kind of salvation God promised in the book of Joel. What I'm about to share with you is the "full gospel" that we seldom hear preached as part of the salvation message. Consequently, ***"God's people are destroyed for lack of knowledge" (Hosea 4:6).*** The Devil's greatest weapon today is to steal and hide truth or just to twist it and bring error. For instance, think about a salvation altar call. What do you see? Probably you see people giving their lives to Jesus, being saved from hell and going to heaven forgiven of their sin. Yes, that's true and wonderful. But salvation is so much more than that! In Joel 2:32 the promise of *sozo* salvation is prophesied: ***"And it shall come to pass that whoever calls upon the name of the Lord shall be saved. For in Mount Zion in Jerusalem there shall be deliverance."*** Now do you believe that? Do you believe, "whoever shall call upon the name of the Lord shall be saved?" Now let's put in the full meaning of that word saved. Let me just change it: "Whoever shall call upon the name of the Lord shall be delivered," or "Whoever shall call upon the name of the Lord shall be healed, for in Mount Zion in Jerusalem there shall be salvation." Obviously spiritual, born again salvation is included in the verse too. So, we can now see that in Mount Zion and Jerusalem there shall be salvation, deliverance and healing.

An altar call in Ethiopia

How can I use those words interchangeably? Because this Scripture is prophetic of the salvation which was to come through Jesus Christ, a *sozo* salvation spoken of in Acts 2:21 when Peter quotes the Joel 2:32 passage we've been examining. Here at the outpouring of the Spirit, Peter claims the fulfillment of this salvation Scripture. When he again proclaims, "Whoever shall call upon the name of the Lord shall be saved," he uses the Greek word *sozo*. The word means salvation, healing and deliverance. So when the Bible says, "Whoever shall call upon the name of the Lord shall be saved," it is also saying, "Whoever shall call upon the name of the Lord shall be healed (or delivered)." Different pictures flash through our minds when we hear the words salvation, deliverance and healing. When we picture salvation, we see someone praying the sinner's prayer to receive Jesus; when we picture healing, we picture someone laying hands on a sick person; when we picture deliverance, we see a person writhing on the floor, getting set free from a demon. We even separate people's ministries into salvation, healing and deliverance ministries. For instance: "That guy is a salvation guy; he has a healing ministry and those people over there do deliverance and cast out demons." However, the Bible sees all three areas as the same thing. *sozo* encompasses all three areas—it is salvation for the complete human being—body, soul and spirit. *sozo* gathers all three into one and calls it "to make whole." Now let's just look at more New Testament scriptures which use the Greek word *sozo* for all three areas.

Sozo: Salvation, Deliverance and Healing

Mathew 1:21 uses *sozo* for the word "save" when it says, ***"And she will bring forth a Son, and you shall call His name Jesus, for He shall <u>save</u> His people from His sins.***

The word is used again for "saved" in Acts 2:47. It says, ***"(The people were) praising God and having favor with all the people. And the Lord added to the church daily those who were being <u>saved</u>."***

Now lets look at Luke 8:36 where the same word *sozo* is used for the area of deliverance: ***"They also had seen it had told them by what means he who had been demon possessed was <u>healed</u>."*** Here *sozo* is no longer referring to wholeness for the spirit, but wholeness for the soul in the form of deliverance from demons.

Then Scripture uses the word *sozo*, in the story of the woman with the issue of blood, to speak about healing or wholeness for the body. "And He said to her, ***"Daughter, your faith has made you <u>well</u>. Go in peace, and be healed of your affliction" (Mark 5:34).*** In the book of James, the word *sozo* is again used in reference to healing for the body: ***"And the prayer of faith will <u>save</u> the sick, and the Lord will raise him up. And if he has committed sins, he will be forgiven" (James 5:15).***

James says the prayer of faith will save (or *sozo*) the sick... and the Lord will raise him up. In these previous passages, we see the word *sozo* in reference to deliverance—the healing of the demon possessed—we see it in reference to salvation for the spirit—speaking of Jesus saving His people from their sins—and now we see the word speaking of physical healing. It's the same word! The word *sozo* is used again in Romans 10:9: ***"...if you confess with your mouth the Lord Jesus and believe in your heart that God has raised Him from the dead, you will be saved (sozo)."*** If you confess with your mouth and believe in your heart, you will be what? You will be saved! It's clearly salvation for the spirit.

In Christian circles we tend to only think of salvation as for the spirit. We don't realize that in the Bible God also uses the same word for salvation and wholeness of the soul and body as well. Mark 6:56 again confirms this idea of salvation for the body: ***"...(they) begged Him that they might just touch the hem of His garment. And as many as touched Him were made well."*** Again, in this Scripture, "made well" is the Greek word *sozo* meaning "made whole" in the context of Jesus healing everybody.

Do you know what "made whole" means? It means that if you're missing an arm, you grow a brand new arm back; if you're missing an eye-ball, a brand new eye ball appears in the socket. It's clear in Scripture that God sees spiritual redemption, deliverance and physical healing as requiring the same remedy—salvation. However, because many people in the church today just think of salvation in a spiritual context, they are destroyed for a lack of knowledge. So we have all these people in North America saved and forgiven of their sin, yet still sick in their body and possessed or tormented by devils.

When I present this powerful message of salvation for body, soul and spirit in crusades in Africa, India or South America, at the moment of salvation people are instantly healed from their physical infirmities and are set free from fear, depression, addictions and other demonic oppression. In fact, we get them filled with the Holy Ghost, cast out all the devils and get them healed all at once—at the altar call for salvation. During my last crusade in Malawi, we saw about 10, 000 people come to Jesus for salvation. It was awesome! (In 2003 we saw over 140,000 people give their lives to Christ. Spiritual salvation is the greatest miracle.) During the altar call in Malawi, after about 3,800 people had responded, the Holy Spirit said to me, "They're saved, but let's pray for the fire to fall and get them filled with the Holy Ghost and speaking in tongues." So we prayed en mass for the Holy Spirit. His fire started falling and people began weeping, shaking, and crying as they were healed and set free.

During the actual prayer for the baptism of the Holy Spirit, my team and I all saw the Lord Himself appear in the crowd as a man, without His glory. I wondered, "Is that the Lord?" Then the Spirit whispered to me: "Yes, it's the man of suffering. It's not the glorified risen Christ; it's the man that died on the cross for the sin of the world." His only glorious aspect was His robe. He wore a scarlet robe that went down just below His ankles and almost dragged on the ground. The robe was blood red and shimmered with glory; the robe itself was like crystal, emanating beams of glory. But Jesus himself appeared as a plain man, not even a good-looking guy. I'm sorry if that offends you, but my description does fits in with the Bible which describes Christ as just a guy with long hair, a beard and a scarred up face. He actually looked kind of old, older than 33. He looked to be in His 40s.

The Lord walked from one end of the altar to the other—everyone fell under the power like dominos as the Lord walked down the aisle! He left a line of fallen bodies wherever He walked, like long grass cut down by a lawn mower. As I watched with awe, I screamed, "Jesus is walking through the crowd!" It happened so quickly but we were still able to get it on video. After this powerful altar call, people got up completely healed of physical conditions. Many AIDS victims went back to their doctors and got blood tests which confirmed that they had been totally healed of AIDS! Then, two hours later, the local witchdoctor, who was out in the crowd, came up on the platform trembling under the power, having realized that the power of Jesus is greater than the power of darkness. Every devil had left him the moment Jesus went by.

The full power of *sozo*—wholeness for spirit, soul and body—had been released at the moment of salvation. That day Jesus released tremendous *sozo* miracles!

Out of Egypt

Even in the Old Testament, God revealed His heart for complete wholeness for the entire person—spirit, soul and body. The Bible tells us that during the exodus from Egypt, God ***"brought them up out of Egypt with silver and gold and there was not one feeble among their tribes" (Ps. 105:37).*** When God's people came out of Egypt there was not one weak! Think about it—three million or more people and not one feeble, sick person among all the tribes of Israel. After the Israelites had experienced the Passover in which the lambs had been slain and the blood was applied, then came the powerful manifestation of healing. This Passover lamb was a type of Christ, the Lamb of God; it prophesied the coming salvation and healing through Jesus.

Later in prophetic history, Jesus appeared in Israel. John the Baptist said of Him: "Behold the Lamb of God that was slain." Jesus came to earth as a prophetic picture of *sozo* (salvation, healing and deliverance), as the complete atonement for our wholeness. Then, in one of John's epistles, we read again of God's desire for our complete wholeness: ***"I wish above all things that you would prosper and be in health even as your soul prospers" (3 John :2).*** Remember, even in the Old Testament, when the people came up out of Egypt, they came out with silver and gold. God continued prospering them in the wilderness—even after forty years of wandering, their shoes and their clothing had not worn out. I've said to God, "I need that anointing on my kids' clothes and on my wife's clothes. The Israelites' shoes and clothes stayed as new as when they left Egypt. That's pretty good—they probably weren't all that new when they left 40 years before. The kids grew up with the same shoes on. Their feet grew—their shoes grew!"

The Jewish people were not only completely healthy, but their clothing and shoes did not wear out for 40 years! Divine prosperity and health! Those are the blessings our God has for us! Hallelujah!

A Type of Calvary

God's people had come out of Egypt, which was a type of the world, or sin, bondage and oppression. As they came out, they all entered into God's blessings. In the same way, when we come out of sin and bondage through Christ, we enter into all the blessings paid for us at Calvary. The book of Exodus also gives us another prophetic picture of Jesus' atoning sacrifice at Calvary:

> ***"So he cried out to the Lord, and the Lord showed him a tree. When he cast it into the waters, the waters were made sweet. There He made a statute and an ordinance for them, and there He tested them, and said, 'If you diligently heed the voice of the Lord your God and do what is right in His sight, give ear to His commandments and keep all His statutes, I will put none of the diseases on you which I have brought on the Egyptians. For I am the Lord who heals you' " (Ex. 15:25,26).***

In this passage, the Lord showed him a tree, a type of the cross. Then the Lord told them that if they would obey His commands, they wouldn't get any of the diseases the Egyptians did. Let me share with you one of the literal translations of this verse from the original language: "I will not permit to come on you any of the diseases I permitted to come on the Egyptians." Now that's a different angle on this verse! God was saying, "I will not permit… I will not give permission for sickness to come on you my people. You are in covenant with me, under the umbrella of my protection. I will not permit the diseases I permitted to come on Egypt."

See it's a whole lot different than God Himself coming down and saying, "Here is sickness. Here is cancer. Here are boils." I don't picture God that way. However, He does grant permission to the Devil to afflict. In fact, we could say that we give permission to the enemy to afflict us through disobedience, sin or unbelief. But it is the Devil afflicting, not God. God is not the author of

Seeking a touch from the Lord

disease! (We'll talk more about that topic later.) God doesn't have it in heaven to give it to you. It's not even up there. He created it. He uses it. He gives permission. But He doesn't do it Himself. He will not afflict you with sickness. God will not do it. It doesn't mean that we don't step out from under the umbrella of covenant and from God's plan by disobeying His commandments or by not listening to Him. In these cases, we open ourselves to attacks of sickness. However, although God may give permission, it's always the Devil who afflicts with disease.

In the passage in Exodus, God promises His people that He will not give permission for diseases to come upon them. Then whom did the diseases come on? The Egyptians. Why? Because Egypt is the world; Egypt is sin and bondage. Diseases still comes on Egypt today. If you are living in Egypt, you are going to get every sickness and disease that's in Egypt until you repent. I mean, sickness is just there. God has ordained it. So when you step into Egypt, you step back out into the world, into bondage and into everything that Egypt represents. Remember, when the people came out of Egypt, they always wanted to go back. To the Israelites, Egypt looked better. They would look back saying: "I remember our days in Egypt. The food was better. The pleasures in Egypt were amazing. I want to go back." Today, God's people still fight that same lure of the world. We are tempted to always look back.

Healing of a Nation

When God says, "I am the Lord who heals you," there could have been as many as three million people sick at the time. They had lived in the sinful environment of Egypt and they had been oppressed for over 400 years. Slaves! Likely, their food had little nutritional value. They weren't getting their multi-vitamins. So they were broken down, sick, exhausted people under cruel slave-masters. They weren't all healthy and they weren't all strong. Does the Scripture we are making reference to—***"they were all strong and none were sick and feeble,"*** imply that they were all healthy? No! Most of them were probably sick and there were 600,000 men plus woman and children—as many as three million. Talk about a healing service!

The Lord told them if they would do what it right, stay in relationship with Him and come under the umbrella of His protection, then He would be their healer, not the Lord who curses them or who brings diseases. Then every one of them was divinely healed at that moment. Boom! However, what very significant event had just preceded this massive wave of healing? Just before they left Egypt they had practiced the first Passover. On that night, every Israeli home had sacrificed a lamb that was without spot or blemish. They took the blood of the lamb and applied it to the door posts of their house so destruction and death would pass them by in the night. This event was a prophetic picture of Jesus Chris, the Lamb of God, without spot or blemish, who was killed as a sacrifice for sin. Jesus was the Lamb of God who took away the sin of the world. Today, when we apply the blood of the Lamb to our lives, death and destruction, which are the wages of sin, will pass us by.

And then what was the next thing that they were to do? They were to eat the flesh of the lamb, which is a prophetic picture for us of receiving Jesus into our life, of partaking of Jesus, the Bread of Life. Shortly after that Passover event, at the beginning of the exodus, God took His people through the Red Sea, rescued them from the Egyptians and healed every one of them. This series of events was a prophetic picture of *sozo*. It gives us a type or picture of Calvary, of salvation. The lamb was slain, the blood was applied, they were freed from sin, death and destruction and they all received the Lamb (representing Jesus) into their life. Right after that God said***, "I am the Lord who heals you" (Ex. 15:26).*** Imagine them all standing there receiving their healing saying, "John, your tumor is gone. Mary—your blind eye is healed. Look at my son Tommy—he is walking!" Visibly every one of them was healed—the Bible tells us that not one was sick or weak! It was not until after the healing was demonstrated that the Lord said, ***"I am the Lord who heals you and if you want to keep your healing, do what is right in my sight."*** According to Psalm 105:37, every one of them became healthy!

The God Who Heals

From the beginning of the Bible right through to the New Testament, the Lord always healed all. He didn't heal some of the sick when they came out of Egypt. He healed all, as a type of Calvary. When the Israelites were bitten by snakes in the desert, God again showed His heart to heal all. The people became very discouraged on the way and spoke against God and Moses, ***"Why have you brought us up out of Egypt to die in the wilderness? ...So the Lord***

sent fiery serpents among the people, and they bit the people; and many of the people of Israel died" (Num. 21:5,6). The interesting thing here is that it is the fiery serpents that brought the sickness here, not the Lord. The Lord permitted the serpents (which are symbolic in Scripture of demonic power). Later in Scripture, Jesus told the disciples He was giving them power to tread on serpents and every work of the enemy (Luke 10:19).

After the fiery serpents bit the people, many got sick and died. After they cried out and repented of their sin, ***"... the Lord said to Moses, 'Make a fiery serpent and set it on a pole and it shall be that everyone who is bitten*** (all the sick)***, when he looks at it, shall live" (Num. 21:8).*** So Moses made a bronze serpent and put it on a pole. Everyone bitten by a serpent would be healed if they looked at the bronze serpent. Everyone had to look for themselves. Again, this story is a picture of Calvary; it's a picture of the cross. Notice, they were not healed when they looked at Moses or when they looked at the man with the healing gift. It's not when they looked at the man with a healing ministry, when they went to the healing crusade or when they looked to the doctor. They were healed when they looked to the Lord.

Victory Over Sin First

Just as the Israelites were delivered from the curse of the serpents, we, as New Testament believers, have been delivered from the curse of the law. The apostle Paul says this: ***"For the law of the Spirit of life in Christ Jesus has made me free from the law of sin and death" (Rom. 8:2).*** Under the law, sin, sickness, disease, death and poverty work together. Sickness is the manifestation of physical death and sin is the manifestation of spiritual death. Those who live in sin under this severe law, will live in the realm of sickness, disease, death, poverty, oppression and bondage. However, there is a new law in Christ Jesus called the law of the spirit of life. It's a divine law and all heaven is going to back it up. It doesn't mean that the Devil won't trespass once in a while. You can put up all the "No Trespassing"

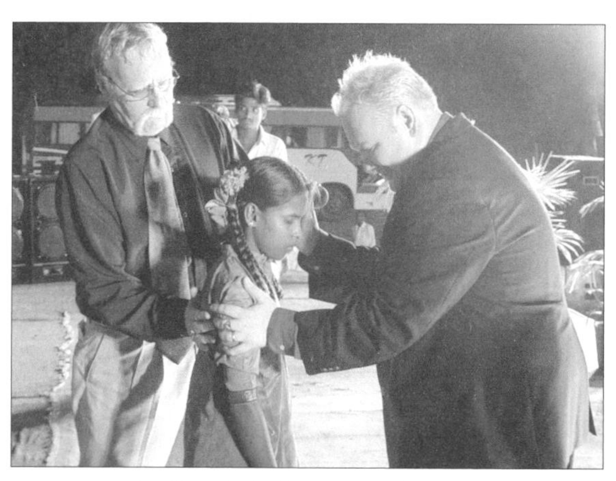

Girl healed of deafness in India

signs that you want to. The Devil is still going to test you to see if you are an enforcer of your covenant rights. If you will enforce the law of life in faith through prayer and declaration, all the angels of heaven are ready to back you up. I mean, if something is law, that's it! Evildoers on earth must bow to the law when it is enforced. Even more, the Enemy must bow to this law of life if we stand on God's Word. God doesn't just talk about freedom from sickness, disease, death and poverty—He calls it the law.

Stripes For Our Healing

Now I'm going to show you some things, in Isaiah 53, that perhaps you have never seen before. This passage again confirms that healing is for all: ***"But He was wounded for our transgressions, He was bruised for our iniquities; the chastisement for our peace was upon Him, and by His stripes we are healed."*** Now look at verse 4. ***"Surely he has borne our griefs and carried our sorrows."*** God says "surely"—this healing work of the cross is a done deal. The word "borne" in this context means "suffered for". In other words: surely He has suffered for our griefs and for our sorrows. Obviously, the griefs and sorrows also come in the form of pain, sicknesses and diseases. But He has suffered for our sicknesses, disease and pains.

In the New Testament, the apostle Peter confirms the healing power of Jesus' suffering. Again, using the word "bore," he says***: "… who Himself bore our sins in His own body on the tree, that we, having died to sins, might live for righteousness—by whose stripes you were healed" (1 Pet. 2:24)***. This passage takes Christ's healing work one step further. He says that we <u>were</u> healed— past tense. In Isaiah 53, it's ***"we are healed"*** but in 1 Peter 2:24 it's ***"we were healed."*** In both references it tells us how Jesus paid for sin and healing all at once through the atonement. In the same way Jesus suffered for, and bore, our sins in his body, he also "surely" bore our sicknesses. This New Testament Scripture is obviously a prophetic fulfillment of Isaiah 53.

The passage in Isaiah refers to Christ's suffering for our sins three times ("transgression" and "iniquities" twice), however, it highlights the healing aspect of Christ's sacrifice even more than that. This prophetic passage uses phrases like, "He has borne our griefs", "carried our sorrows," and "the chastisement for our peace was upon Him." The word chastisement here speaks of the suffering for our peace—the word peace is *shalom* which means peace, prosperity and wholeness. Think back to the blessings of coming out of Egypt: wholeness and healing for everyone of God's people as well as gold and great prosperity. Jesus suffered for us to have peace, prosperity and wholeness - that's the cross. Again, verse 5 confirms our healing inheritance saying, ***"by His stripes we are healed."***

So what's the bottom line according to Isaiah? As you have seen, he is very clear that Christ suffered for our sickness in the same way He "surely" suffered for our sins. Yet, in the church today, we still struggle to believe this truth. Our failure to receive divine healing in the church is directly related to how we view God. Verse 4 says this: ***"Yet we esteemed Him stricken, smitten by God, and afflicted."*** Do you know what Isaiah is saying? Jesus endured beating, wounds, suffering, rejection, pain, torment and the loss of His precious blood to carry our disease. However, we "esteemed" or saw Him as afflicted but failed to see the victorious purpose of the suffering. Still today we see Him as the suffering wounded Messiah. We need to see the realities of the suffering of the cross of Jesus as the price to carry away our sickness and disease. He was wounded for our transgression and our sin.

Jesus Conquered Sickness

Although we see and acknowledge Christ's suffering for our cleansing and healing, we must also see Him as the overcoming one. He didn't merely suffer; He actually conquered sin, disease, death and the grave! We must see Him as the victorious Christ who rose up on the third day with resurrection power over sickness, disease and death! He took the curse of the law and redeemed us so we could once again come into the blessing of Abraham and be whole in body, soul and spirit. Christians today often fail to see Him as the resurrected, victorious, Christ—they still relate to Him as the suffering, afflicted, wounded Jesus on the cross. That's the way much of the church presents Jesus today. Isaiah is saying that SURELY, in the SAME way that He has suffered for our iniquities, He was beaten for our sicknesses so we can walk in victorious power over sin and disease. YET we still see or esteem Him as the suffering one. We missed the powerful message of the cross—He didn't just suffer, He was victorious! It is vital that the church begins to emphasize the overcoming power of Christ! He is the victorious, conquering One who has overcome sin, sickness, disease, death and poverty. If we will put our faith in the victorious Christ, we can receive the blessing of *sozo*, the forgiveness, liberty and healing He has provided for all through His atoning sacrifice—a sacrifice freely given so we can live a victorious Christian life.

Chapter Three

THE SEVEN REDEMPTIVE NAMES OF GOD

The Old Testament refers to seven different variations of 'Jehovah' often called *The Seven Redemptive Names of God.* 'Redemption' can be defined as "the deliverance of a prisoner or hostage upon payment of a ransom." Christ redeemed us through His death; He paid the ultimate price. The seven redemptive names demonstrate God's great love for us, a love that motivated Him to offer the ultimate sacrifice of His son's life. This sacrifice was made to restore us to relationship with Him, Jehovah God, and to bring us out of bondage to sin and its consequences.

'Jehovah' actually refers to God's relationship to man—He is our Lord. The name Jehovah is the name of deity. Literally, Jehovah means the self-existent one who reveals Himself and keeps on revealing Himself. Jesus said if you love me and obey my commands, I will manifest Myself to you. Truly our God is the One who reveals Himself. In the area of healing we can either say, "Wow, the blind see!" or we can say "the self-existent One reveals Himself". We need to think about how much of God has come close to us for a healing to take place. We can think of healing as the blessing and provision of God or we can look to the nature and heart of God released through healing.

It is important to realize that God is revealing Himself in every miracle and in every healing in the Bible—every time we see Christ's healing touch we can receive new revelation about the One who heals. Yet many people see only the mighty acts and not the wonderful God who performs the acts. That's why Jesus rebuked Capernaum in Matthew 11:21, saying that if the same mighty works had been done in Sodom or Gomorrah, those cities would have repented. He rebuked them because even when mighty works were done, their hearts didn't change; they didn't come into *relationship* with the healer—they only knew about the *works* of the healer. So, when we talk about the seven redemptive names, we're actually talking about intimacy with God which leads us to the privileges and blessings of Calvary. Now let's draw near to our God through seven of His wonderful names.

Jehovah Shammah

Jehovah Shammah means "the Lord is there." The greatest blessing to God's people on earth is His presence. Our greatest passion needs to be that He would be with us. Like Moses, we need to say, "God, unless You go with us (You are there), we don't want to go to the Promised Land." We desperately need the presence of the God who is there.

Fortunately, He has made a way for us to come into the holy of holies, before the throne of grace. The only reason we can experience God's presence is because His death on the cross brought us near by His blood.

The fire that continually burned on the temple altar was a symbol of God's presence with His people:

> ***"And the fire on the altar shall be kept burning on it; it shall not be put out. And the priest shall burn wood on it every morning, and lay the burnt offering in order on it; and he shall burn on it the fat of the peace offerings" (Lev. 26:12).***

In the New Testament Jesus promised He would be present with them, not just in the Holy of Holies, but whenever His people gathered: ***"For where two or three are gathered together in My name, I am there in the midst of them" (Matt. 18:20).***

In the Old Testament Ezekiel prophesies to the nation of Israel—its temple had been destroyed and they were in captivity. The prophet looked past the trials, bitter tears, satanic oppression and persecution to the victorious closing days of church history. Speaking to a people enslaved in a strange land, Ezekiel, after giving a vision of the future and describing the new temple, says this: ***"The city shall be 18,000 cubits, round about; and the name of the city from that day shall be, 'The LORD is there'" (Ez. 48:35).*** Yes, the

Lord is there in the sanctuary of His people! His presence rested in the temple in Jerusalem just like His presence dwells in the lives (the temples) of His children today.

God also wants His people to know that even in the midst of their troubles, even during the darkest of times Jehovah is there walking with them (Isa. 63:9), to comfort, teach, deliver and preserve those He loves.

Speaking of this ever-present God, the psalmist asks,

> ***"Where can I go from Your Spirit? Or where can I flee from Your presence? If I ascend into heaven, You are there; if I make my bed in hell, behold, You are there. If I take the wings of the morning, and dwell in the uttermost parts of the sea, Even there Your hand shall lead me, and Your right hand shall hold me. If I say, 'Surely the darkness shall fall on me,' even the night shall be light about me; Indeed, the darkness shall not hide from You, but the night shines as the day; the darkness and the light are both alike to You" (Ps. 139:7-12).***

As David so poetically declared, there is no place to hide from God's presence. One day His tabernacle will rest among men and God will live with us. Every tear shall be wiped away and there will be no more death.

The omnipresent God Who will make all things new is Jehovah Shammah, the Lord who is there. Yes, it is true that God is omnipresent, but this special name speaks of God dwelling with us in a visible, tangible way. The prophet Zephaniah spoke of this special presence of the Lord saying, ***"The LORD your God in your midst, the Mighty One, will save; He will rejoice over you with gladness, He will quiet you with His love, He will rejoice over you with singing" (Zeph. 3:17).*** The Lord Himself even made us this promise: ***"I will be unto her a wall of fire round about, and will be the glory in the midst of her" (Zech. 2:5).*** All of these things God has promised to His church and that which is true of the whole body is true of every member of the body.

In the Beginning. One of the most powerful manifestations of Jehovah Shammah was revealed at creation… for the Lord was there! Our awesome Creator spoke the universe into existence and then He formed man and woman in His image. He designed everything, including man, with great beauty, splendor and majesty—then He called it "GOOD." But what was the purpose of this created paradise? It was the place, the setting, in which God wanted fellowship with Adam and Eve. In this beautiful place God walked with man—The Lord was there!

Even though Adam and Eve fell from fellowship, the Lord continued to pursue that intimate relationship. God continued to make Himself known. Though He would destroy the world with a flood, He prepared a way of salvation for mankind and the Lord was there with Noah in the ark. When Jacob fled from Esau, God gave him a dream of a ladder reaching from earth to heaven. Jacob called the place Bethel, the house of God, because the Lord was there.

Throughout those ancient days, whenever people worshipped or believed God, the Lord was there. In the tabernacle in the wilderness, in the land of Canaan, during the times of the Judges, the Kings, and the Prophets in Israel, the Lord was there. God revealed His presence both at the dedication of Solomon's magnificent temple and then, many years later, in a filthy cow stable, at the birth of Jesus, the son of God—for the Lord was there.

Christ Himself. The name Jehovah Shammah is embodied in the man Christ Jesus. At His birth in Bethlehem, the Scripture speaks of Jesus as "Wonderful, Counselor, the Mighty God, the Everlasting Father and the Prince of Peace" (Is. 9:6). His name is Immanuel (Is 7:14) which means "God with us!" Jesus Christ is God in bodily form; He is Jehovah-Shammah, for wherever Jesus Christ is, "The Lord is There." The apostle Paul states that all the fullness of the Godhead lives in the body of the man Jesus Christ (Col. 2:9).

Throughout Jesus' earthly life, God was in Christ reconciling the world to Himself. Wherever Jesus walked during His life, He was Jehovah Shammah, "The Lord is There." When Jesus was crucified, suffered and hung dying in agony, He revealed Himself as Jehovah Shammah, "the Lord is There" (II Cor. 5:21; Isa. 5:9-12).

Every believer. The same spirit that raised Jesus from the dead lives in every born-again believer (Rom. 8:11). Whenever we see or interact with another Christian, we can truly say Jehovah Shammah or, "The Lord is There."

Scripture tells us that the Lord is there by His Spirit, wooing and convicting sinners. The Lord is there in saving power at conversion to waken dead spirits, impart faith and to turn hearts to Christ.

I remember one of the first times that I truly had the revelation that the Lord was with me. I had been in an encounter with the Holy Spirit and God's presence became so real to me that, at times, when I stepped out onto the street to go for a walk I would feel a presence moving with me on my right side. It was as if something was hovering over my shoulder. I was aware that this was the Holy Spirit's presence.

Once I jumped into my vehicle and as soon as I shut the door I felt the sensation of someone jumping into the seat next to me, but there was nobody there. I remember hearing the Lord say, "I am with you." Tears ran down my face; I was aware of a person's presence. I don't know if the Holy Spirit has a form but I definitely felt His presence in the actual form of a person. It's the same sensation you would get if someone stood behind you reading the newspaper over your shoulder. You just sense it. I vividly remember times in my life when the presence of the Holy Spirit would come daily in such a manifest way that I felt that an invisible person was with me wherever I went.

I experienced one of the most profound revelations of Jehovah Shammah's presence with me in my home. I was in my living room in prayer when a young woman by the name of Joelle attempted to walk straight out of the kitchen into the living room. She hit an electrical force field and was thrown back several feet. She asked, "What's that? I feel an electrical current." That day I was very aware that the Holy Spirit was strongly with me.

Not only can we know His presence today, but we can also be assured that He will be with us in the future. When the appointed time comes for God's people to go to heaven, "the Lord is there" (Jn. 14:1-3).

The church. Today, wherever you find the church of God on earth, Jehovah Shammah, "the Lord is there." (Matt. 18:20; 28:20). Wherever you find local gatherings of God's people, "The Lord is There!" God's ever-present nature is the source of the believer's security and strength in the midst of trials; it is the source of supernatural power for God's people; it is the fountain-head of love, joy, peace and unity for every believer. It is all because "The Lord is there!"

His eternal presence. A day is coming when the city of God will be completed and the church will be raptured into God's presence to be eternally joined to Jesus at the marriage supper of the Lamb. God's house will be full and the end-time glory of the bride, the Groom and their final home will be revealed. And the great glory of that City will be Jehovah Shammah, "The Lord is there."

Healing crusade in Peru

Jehovah Shalom

This literally means "the Lord our peace." Jesus is the Prince of Peace. God wants us to allow His peace to rule our hearts and minds. The peace of God is a spiritual impartation; it's something absolutely unexplainable. God's shalom allows us to have peace in the midst of any kind of trial and tribulation.

God's people in the Old Testament knew this peace. Gideon, facing destruction at the hands of the powerful forces of Midian, along with Israel, knew God's peace. For seven years, a prodigal Israel had known nothing but war. In total desperation, Israel cried out for peace and returned to the true and living God. How would peace come? The Lord graciously sent an angel to Gideon while he was threshing wheat in the wine press. The angel told Gideon of God's call for him to deliver Israel. This commission came despite Gideon's lack of power, influence or affluence. The Lord gave Gideon a confirming sign and then sent fire from heaven to consume a sacrifice. In awe at God's power and His confirming signs, ***"… Gideon built an altar there to the LORD, and called it The-LORD-Is-Peace (Jehovah Shalom)" (Jud. 6:24).***

David also had a revelation of Jehovah Shalom. He said, ***"Great peace have those who love Your law, and nothing causes them to stumble" (Ps. 119:165).*** David understood that obedience to God's law releases peace into our lives.

Long after David's time, and following centuries of God's people walking away from His Shalom, God made a new covenant of peace with His people. He sent Jesus, as the mediator, so we could receive that gift freely, by faith. Hundreds of years before Jesus came to earth, Isaiah said, ***"For unto us a Child is born, unto us a Son is given; and the government will be upon His shoulder. And His name will be called Wonderful, Counselor, Mighty God, Everlasting Father, <u>Prince of Peace</u>" (Isa. 9:6).***

The Bible declares that the chastisement of our peace was upon Him. Christ's suffering paid for our peace and allowed Him to say, ***"Peace I leave with you, My peace I give to you; not as the world gives do I give to you. Let not your heart be troubled, neither let it be afraid" (Jn. 14:27).***

As a result of Jesus' visit to earth as Prince of Peace, the apostle Paul recognized that we need not be afraid or anxious for anything because ***"…the peace of God, which surpasses all understanding, will guard your hearts and minds through Christ Jesus (Phil. 4:7).***

On several occasions I've known God by His supernatural peace when I've been in third world countries. In some African hot spots it's dangerous to present the gospel. The police chief in Uganda once informed us that they feared there was a bomb under our platform. In another situation, after a meeting I was told that a militant, sword-wielding Muslim had come toward the platform to assault me. Numerous times we've faced threats of terrorist attacks from militant Muslims and impending riots by crowds of people pressing in, desperate for healing. Yet, in the midst of these dangerous circumstances nothing seemed to faze me.

We don't shy away from people with AIDS or other diseases. We get close to, and lay hands on lepers, or we go into hospitals where there are people with terminal, contagious diseases. Yet, there is a peace that covers us. I would describe it as a force field in which natural dangers, that would normally cause you to fear or worry, don't affect you. That has happened to me several times in crusades--everyone around me was fearful but it's as if I was wrapped in an invisible cocoon so that no matter what was going on around me, I was safe in the shelter of Jehovah Shalom.

Jehovah Rohi

Scripture also tells us that Jesus is Jehovah Rohi, which means, "the Lord is my Shepherd." The term shepherd appears about 80 times in Scripture, speaking of the Lord as our feeder, herdsman, companion, keeper, pastor and friend.

You have a right to receive abundant life, healing and provision; you have full access to His guidance and to the wisdom and revelation of heaven (Jn. 10:26) because the Shepherd has given His life for the sheep.

According to God's Word, you have a right to receive guidance from the Shepherd of your soul:

> ***"The LORD is my shepherd; I shall not want. He makes me to lie down in green pastures; He leads me beside the still waters. He restores my soul; He leads me in the paths of righteousness for His name's sake" (Ps. 23:1-3).***

Jesus truly is the good shepherd—it was the provision that came through His death that gave us access to all the abundant blessings of heaven:

> ***"...I have come that they may have life, and that they may have it more abundantly. I am the good shepherd. The good shepherd gives His life for the sheep" (Jn. 10:10-11).***

The Hebrew name for God, Jehovah Rohi, literally means Jehovah the shepherd, or Jehovah the herdsman, or Jehovah the companion. Yes, our great God is not a fearsome overseer, but a gentle, kind and compassionate shepherd of His flock. He is a loving guide and companion who cares for each of His sheep. God has promised a day when He, as the great shepherd, would gather His scattered people.

> ***"I will establish one shepherd over them, and he shall feed them--My servant David. He shall feed them and be their shepherd. 24 And I, the LORD, will be their God, and My servant David a prince among them; I, the LORD, have spoken. 31 'You are My flock, the flock of My pasture; you are men, and I am your God,' says the Lord GOD" (Ez. 34:23).***

A few chapters later the prophet tells us that God's people ***"shall all have one shepherd" (Ez. 37:24).*** Another prophet, Zechariah, then foretells the good shepherd's death:

> ***"Awake, O sword, against My Shepherd, against the Man who is My Companion," Says the LORD of hosts. "Strike the Shepherd, and the sheep will be scattered; then I will turn My hand against the little ones" (Zech. 13:7).***

The apostle Paul describes Christ as ***"that great Shepherd of the sheep"*** who has given us ***"the blood of the everlasting covenant" (Heb. 13: 20).*** The apostle Peter says this: ***"For you were like sheep going astray, but have now returned to the Shepherd and Overseer of your souls" (I Pet. 2: 25).*** Then he assures us that ***"...when the Chief Shepherd appears, you will receive the crown of glory that does not fade away" (I Pet. 5:4)***. Those who have received Him can take comfort in His words: ***"I am the good shepherd; and I know My sheep, and am known by My own" (Jn. 10:14).***

Christ's blood has paid the price, for our salvation, intimate relationship, healing, freedom, and provision. Notice what David says in his 23rd Psalm—because the Lord is Jehovah our shepherd, we "shall not want"! Yes, as we follow this wonderful shepherd, we will not have any needs or wants; He will provide for them all. Oh, what an awesome Shepherd we have!

There are times in my life when I am dependent on Him as a friend to share His inner secrets. Most often He reveals Himself to me in times of waiting in His presence and asking Him "when, what, where" and "how?" He guides my preaching and meetings and teaches me how to move in the anointing. He gives me words of knowledge. Before every meeting my heart's cry is, "I'm totally dependent on You. I need You to guide me. God I don't just want another service. I want to see Your power and glory come—I want to go from glory to glory. I thank You for what You've done in the past, but I'm dependent on You again to guide me." I'll often wait in His presence for an answer to a question. I depend on Him as my shepherd. He is the One who leads me by green pastures.

Jehovah Jireh

Our God is also known as Jehovah Jireh, "the Lord will provide." God has always provided for the needs of His people who put their trust in Him. As New Testament believers, we have the right to have all our needs filled according to His riches in glory (Phil. 4:19).

I remember the first time that God supernaturally provided for me—it was out of friendship. In those days God would sometimes visit me so powerfully that I felt like Moses speaking to God face to face as a friend speaks to a friend.

During one encounter the glory showed up on my face. When I came out of my room, my wife instantly fell under the power in the kitchen and her friend (who didn't really believe in the supernatural charismatic side of Christianity) screamed that my face was glowing! As I was walking through the kitchen I thought, "I'd like to have a peanut butter sandwich." My wife and I had been married just a few weeks and I wasn't working so our food supplies were low. I checked the cupboard and there was no peanut butter. I didn't mention it or pray about it. I just went back into the room and started seeking Him.

My wife woke up the next morning and opened the door and there was a jar of peanut butter on the step. Because I delighted myself in Him the desire of my heart became real to Him. That was the first time I realized that God really knows the things I need and that He can provide even the simplest of things.

After extended encounters with the Holy Spirit and within a few days of being called publicly in to the ministry, Patricia King said, "Come along Todd, be on my team and trust God to provide for you." My rent was due in a few days. I told God if it was really Him who had called me into the ministry then I needed Him to provide supernaturally for us. "Though my wife and I are telling no one, Lord, I believe You are going to provide my rent," I said. I clearly remember that first time He provided. Shonnah and I were worshiping God in a meeting and the rent was due the next day. A woman came up to us and said, "I don't know anything about you but while we were worshipping the Lord spoke to me and said I was supposed to go empty my bank account and give you all the money that I have." She gave us $500, my month's rent. God has been providing ever since.

It's one thing to ask God to give me $500 and it's another thing to cry out to Jehovah Jireh asking, "Where is Your provision?" It's one thing to say, "God I'm hungry" and it's another thing to say, "God where do I go to get food?"

During a famine in Israel, God led His servant Elijah to the provision. It takes the leading of God to get the provision of God. God sent Elijah to the brook where the ravens brought him meat. Then God sent him to a widow. God said, "I have commanded the widow to provide for you." So the question is, "Where is my widow and where is my brook?"

Todd ministering to aids orphans in Ethiopia

Our Jehovah Jireh has made His provision readily accessible to us by faith, through grace, because Christ sacrificed His life at Calvary. The offering of the cross of Calvary made Him our personal Jehovah Jireh.

We see, in Abraham's story, the first mention of Jehovah Jireh in Scripture. Genesis 22 speaks directly of God as Jehovah Jireh at the climax of Abraham's most severe trial. God called upon Abraham to endure a heart-rending trial in order to test and prove his faith. However, at the eleventh hour, just before Abraham plunged a knife into his son's chest in obedience to divine instruction, God provided a ram to die in Isaac's place. Abraham built a memorial to God and ***"...called the name of the place, The-LORD-Will-Provide (Jehovah Jireh); as it is said to this day, 'In the Mount of the LORD it shall be provided' " (Gen. 22:14).***

Abraham's test was not merely to try his faith, but to fulfill prophecy; his experience gives us a picture of Christ's death. Father Abraham offers his son as a sacrifice on Mt. Moriah and 2000 years later our Heavenly Father offered His Son as an atoning sacrifice for our sin. The moral of the story is found in John 12:24: ***"Most assuredly, I say to you, unless a grain of wheat falls into the ground and dies, it remains alone; but if it dies, it produces***

much grain." Isaac had to die (or be willing to die) in order to fulfill the promise that Abraham would be the father of a nation. In the same way, Jesus had to die in order to reproduce a nation of spiritual children for Father God.

King David, in Psalm 23, suggests this divine name of provider saying, ***"The Lord is my shepherd; I shall not want…"*** Scripture repeatedly promises provision to God's children with words like these:

> ***"The Lord will guide you continually, and satisfy your soul in drought, and strengthen your bones; you shall be like a watered garden" (Isa. 58:11).***

> ***"Now if God so clothes the grass of the field, which today is, and tomorrow is thrown into the oven, will He not much more clothe you, O you of little faith?" (Matt. 6:30).***

Our heavenly Father is also described elsewhere as the One who sees and provides. As already mentioned, the apostle Paul describes this provider God in one of his letters: ***"And my God shall supply all your need according to His riches in glory by Christ Jesus" (Phi. 4:19).*** Jesus, in the gospel of Matthew, also speaks of His Father as the one who cares for the material needs of His people:

> ***"Therefore do not worry, saying, 'What shall we eat?' or What 'shall we drink?' or 'What shall we wear?' For after all these things the Gentiles seek. For your heavenly Father knows that you need all these things. But seek first the kingdom of God and His righteousness, and all these things shall be added to you" (Matt. 6: 31-33).***

Yes, Scripture is clear, material provision is part of our inheritance as God's children. The apostle John confirms God's desire to bless us materially as he prays under the inspiration of the Holy Spirit: ***"Beloved, I pray that you may prosper in all things and be in health, just as your soul prospers" (3 Jn. 1:2).***

The first time we had to trust Jehovah Jireh for $500 to pay our rent. Since then I've learned that whether it is $50, $500 or $5,000, faith in God as our Provider still works the same today. Today we trust for million of dollars to fund crusades and provide for the poor in third world countries. Yes, like Abraham and Paul, we can say, "Our God provides!" We serve, not only the Great Shepherd, but the Great Provider!

Jehovah Nissi

Jehovah Nissi means "the Lord is my banner, captain and victor." He has triumphed over every power and principality. At Calvary He shed His blood, paid the penalty of sin and removed the sting of death. As a born-again believer, you have power over the works of the devil—you have the authority to tread on serpents and scorpions and every power of the enemy. When He triumphed over the enemy at the cross of Calvary, Jesus became our banner and victor, just as it was prophesied:

> ***"And in that day there shall be a Root of Jesse, Who shall stand as a banner to the people; for the Gentiles shall seek Him, and His resting place shall be glorious" (Isa. 11:10).***

The Bible repeatedly speaks of God raising up a banner, a battle ensign, as a sign or token which will strike fear in the enemy's camps:

> ***"So shall they fear the name of the LORD from the west, and His glory from the rising of the sun; when the enemy comes in like a flood, the Spirit of the LORD will lift up a standard (a banner) against him." (Isa. 59:19).***

> ***"Thus says the Lord GOD: 'Behold, I will lift My hand in an oath to the nations, and set up My standard (banner) for the peoples; they shall bring your sons in their arms, and your daughters shall be carried on their shoulders'" (Isa. 49:22).***

> ***"Thou art beautiful, O my love, as Tirzah, comely as Jerusalem, terrible as an army with banners" (S.S. 6:4).***

In the book of Exodus, we read the story of Moses leading the people to victory against their enemies. With the rod of God in his hand, he sat on top of a hill overlooking the valley of Rephidim where the Israeli army battled the hosts of Amelek. Aaron and Hur stood beside Moses supporting his arms in an act of intercession. When Moses raised his arms, Israel prevailed; when he lowered his arms, Amalek began to win. When the army of Israel could not see the rod, their faith in the Lord their banner wavered and the Amalekites began to defeat them. So Aaron and Hur found a stone and put it under Moses to support him. Then they held up his hands until the sun went down. Eventually

Joshua and the army defeated the Amalekites. No wonder, after this great victory, ***"... Moses built an altar and called its name, The-LORD-Is-My-Banner (Jehovah Nissi)" (Ex. 17:15).***

We need to hear the words of Jesus our captain, ***"Be of good cheer; I have overcome the world" (Jn. 16:33).*** We are a lot like the Israelite army. At times it looks like our spiritual battle will surely end in defeat. Like Moses, we get tired and our arms grow weak. However, just when we have run out of strength, Christ our High Priest, represented by Aaron, and the Spirit of God, represented by Hur, come to our rescue. Jesus and the Holy Spirit help us lift our hands in prayer as we rest on Christ, our solid foundation stone. When we fix our eyes on Jesus, our banner of victory, and as we rest in Him, we prevail over our enemies. As we fight our spiritual battles and as we win, like Moses, we too can build an altar by worshipping Jehovah Nissi, our banner and sure victory.

King David also speaks of Jehovah Nissi, the Lord Our Banner, in Psalm 23 as the one who prepares a table for us in the midst our enemies! We feast while God deals with them. Even with enemies on every side, we can rest. No one can prevail against us as we put our trust in God, for He is our banner.

The Apostles Paul and John also understood the nature of God as our captain and victor. Their letters are peppered with words of victory like these:

> ***"What then shall we say to these things? If God is for us, who can be against us? (Rom. 8:31).***
>
> ***"Yet in all these things we are more than conquerors through Him who loved us" (Rom. 8:37).***
>
> ***"...who delivered us from so great a death, and does deliver us; in whom we trust that He will still deliver us" (2 Corinthians 1:10).***
>
> ***"You are of God, little children, and have overcome them, because He who is in you is greater than he who is in the world" (1 Jn. 4:4).***
>
> ***"For whatever is born of God overcomes the world. And this is the victory that has overcome the world--our faith" (1 Jn. 5:4).***

Yes, from start to finish, Scripture truly reveals Jesus, the captain of the host, as our victorious banner, always fighting with us and putting our enemy to flight. With Him at our side, we overcome in every circumstance of life.

In my life I've discovered that, as Isaiah says, when the enemy comes in like a flood the Holy Spirit will lift up a standard. I believe the correct reading of this verse, from the original language, is that when the enemy comes in (no comma here) then like a flood the Holy Spirit will lift up a standard. We usually read the verse as if it's the enemy that comes in like a flood. But really, we need to realize that the Holy Ghost is the flood that keeps away the enemy's attacks.

I've experienced this protective power of God several times. Because I came out of a rough background and a drug-lifestyle I was bound by fear. I had struggled with the spirit of fear since I was 12 years old and that fear continued to attack me, even as a Christian. I burned a lot of bridges and I had reason to fear harm from the whole underworld of drugs and gangs. I had death threats on my life.

As a believer, one of the first things I needed to learn was a trust in God to protect, to comfort and to keep back the enemy. I had read the promise of protection from God our banner and captain, but I didn't know how God was going to keep His Word in my life. I can remember one of my earliest encounters with God as my banner. I was walking down the road talking to a friend about how God was going to protect me, even if someone was to jump out of a bush or out of a car to hurt me. Just then somebody jumped out of the bushes and lunged at me. When he came within a few feet, it was as if he bounced off an invisible, electrical force field—he was stunned and ran down the street. I saw him turning and looking back over and over again; he looked like a whimpering dog. I realized that an angel, or even the Lord Himself, had appeared in front of me. I could sense the presence of a being, 12 to 14 feet tall, keeping my attacker away. That was when I knew that the Lord is my banner and that He drives out my enemies. From that day forward I trusted God to fight my battles and to protect me.

People have asked me how I can deal with the witchcraft in Africa. "Todd, what's the key to your boldness in confronting not just one or two people but hundreds of individuals bound by witchcraft?"

In the early days, one of the most powerful witchdoctors in Uganda came to the crusade to challenge and publicly curse me. The pastors were fearful because this witchdoctor's curses had caused sickness and accidents. They credited numerous traumatic events to this old man's demonic craft which he had been practicing for many years. I was new in the ministry and preaching at one of my first crusades. I was 22 or 23 years old and he had come to publicly challenge me. At first, it appeared that his power was greater—as he released his demonic chants, storm clouds appeared and rain fell. I had a sense that the Lord was with me and that I had authority to confront, bind and take authority over this man's power. Not only did the Lord lead me to bind the occult powers, but He also prompted me to prophesy publicly that the man would have an encounter with Jesus and that he would no longer operate in witchcraft. I didn't know how that was going to take place but I knew that God was my banner.

I had a sense that an angelic host was around me. Jesus is the Commander of the Army of the Lord and my commands were coming from Him. Every time that we've confronted witchcraft I've had to wait until I get the command from the army in heaven. In these situations, there is a strategic day—sometimes it is the first day and sometimes it's the third day. But there will come a command in prayer and God will say, "Today I will give you the authority over witchcraft." I can't confront that level of witchcraft at will. I have to wait until I hear, in prayer, the word from the Commander of the Army of the Lord. In Uganda, the Lord gave me the confidence to confront witchcraft for the first time in a large gathering.

That night the Lord translated me in the spirit into the man's room as he was in a demonic trance. I shared the gospel with him and he gave his life to Jesus. He was at the crusade the next night, no longer operating in witchcraft. He was born-again and on the platform on his hands and knees asking for forgiveness and sharing the account of how I had appeared in his home in a trance. Even though I didn't fully realize it, I was actually translated in the spirit. (These two sentences seem to contradict each other. Was he translated, or was it his angel?) The Lord must have sent my angel—probably like the story of Peter showing up at the door of the praying disciples when they thought it was his angel. Although it was Peter, their words indicate that they were aware of encounters in which people's angels showed up looking like those people.

Today, every time I need to deal with witchcraft I have to wait until I hear, in prayer, from my Commander when He will release an Elijah spirit to confront the power of witchcraft *en masse*. I am not talking about casting out demons in individual people. I am talking about taking authority over witchcraft in the air. I have to wait until my Commander, Jehovah Nissi, gives the order.

Jehovah Tsidkenu

The sixth name of God, Jehovah Tsidkenu, means "all righteousness." We understand, of course, that our God is holy, pure and righteous; no sin can enter His presence. A righteous King first appeared to Abram in Genesis. ***"Then Melchizedek king of Salem brought out bread and wine; he was the priest***

of God most High" (Gen. 14:18). Melchizedek means king of righteousness. Many theologians believe that Melchizedek was actually Jesus, the son of God, before He was born on earth.

Scripture also prophesies, in the book of Jeremiah, about this King from the lineage of David, who is referred to as a Branch of Righteousness and who ***"...shall reign and prosper, and execute judgment and righteousness in the earth. 6 In His days Judah will be saved, and Israel will dwell safely; now this is His name by which He will be called: THE LORD OUR RIGHTEOUSNESS (Jehovah Tsidkenu in Hebrew)" (Jer. 23:5-6).***

The kingdom of "The Lord our Righteousness" as prophesied, was fulfilled, in part, when Jesus Christ began His ministry on earth to establish the kingdom of God. John the Baptist preached, ***"The time is fulfilled, and the kingdom of God is at hand. Repent, and believe in the gospel" (Mark 1:15).*** Repentance and new birth is the key to His kingdom (Matt.3:1-8; Jn. 3:3) and ***"...the kingdom of God is not eating and drinking, but righteousness and peace and joy in the Holy Spirit" (Rom. 14:17).***

Jesus has established His kingdom in righteousness (uprightness before God). Speaking to His disciples He said, ***"... unless your righteousness exceeds the righteousness of the scribes and Pharisees, you will by no means enter the kingdom of heaven" (Matt.5:20).***

Although Jesus brought the good news of the kingdom of righteousness to Israel, most of His people did not receive the message. He was righteous, holy and without deceit. Yet, He was led, as a spotless lamb, to the slaughter; He didn't open His mouth but laid His life down freely.

Establishing this kingdom cost Jesus His life. He said, ***"13 Greater love has no one than this, than to lay down one's life for his friends" (Jn. 15:13).*** He also said, ***"...I lay down My life... No one takes it from Me" (10:17-18).*** Although He didn't deserve death, Jesus, the only righteous, holy and perfect man who ever lived, willingly laid down His life for His sheep. He offered himself as a righteous offering for sin, shedding His blood to give us the gift of righteousness. He brought us into right standing with God and gave us access to the holy of holies, the place of God's very presence. This gift of righteousness can now be received by anyone, not through good works, but by faith, through grace alone.

The Lord wants us, as His people, ***"those who receive an abundance of grace and of the gift of righteousness... (to) reign in life through the One, Jesus Christ" (Rom. 5:17b).*** As we reign as kings in life, we are to execute judgment and righteousness through prayer and acts of faith. Today, the Church, Christ's body on earth, represents the kingdom of righteousness. We are keepers of this kingdom. The question is this: "Are we reigning, prospering and establishing victory and the rule of Jesus' righteousness on earth?" The

Lord wants us to rule in compassionate righteousness, not like the servant in Jesus' parables who was left in charge of his master's kingdom, yet beat the messengers sent by His master and eventually killed His master's son. (Mark 12:1-9). He also wants to find us faithfully serving when He comes, not asleep on the job. (Mark 13: 34-36).

Jesus preached the way of righteousness but the religious leaders didn't believe. However, the publicans, harlots, tax collectors and other "less desirable people" believed Him and repented . Similarly, these days, there are many people belonging to other religions that believe Jesus Christ, forsake sin and enter the kingdom of God. On the other hand, we see many Christians, claiming to be born-again or Spirit-filled people, who still live in sin. They are like the Pharisees and the chief priests, who professed to be religious but were full of hypocrisy and pride. They followed religious rules and rituals yet do not righteously follow God from their hearts. They find fault with the weak sheep but do not help them. Preachers today often merely preach candy-coated messages which allow believers to walk into divorce and abortion with no fear of God. God will hold such preachers responsible for diluting His Word.

Receiving prayer for healing in Denmark

However, God wants us to both preach and practice righteousness so people know we belong to Him (I Jn. 2:29; 3:7). Also, as soldiers of the King of righteousness, through spiritual warfare, we are called to fight for justice and righteousness. Today, the same kingdom of righteousness we are advancing on earth will be extended after Christ returns during His 1000-year reign. Because of His very nature, Jehovah Tsidkenu will never tolerate deliberate sin among His chosen people. He will judge them because judgment begins in the House of God.

Although God wants us to have His zeal for righteousness, we can't possibly fulfill the righteous requirements of the law in our own strength. God's laws are too high, too holy, too pure and too perfect. Though we have passed from death to life, the old sin nature of Adam still struggles for dominion within us. In our own strength, the good we want to do, we often won't do; the evil we hate, we will perform. There is nothing good or righteous in any man of himself (Rom. 7:14-24).

I remember one of the first revelations of my righteousness in Christ came through the teaching of Kenneth Copeland. I was given a tape series on the gift of righteousness In my early days as a believer I struggled a lot in this area. To this day, I remember listening to the tapes three or four times, over and over, on how I was righteous in Christ by faith.

I learned how righteousness was a gift I received because of Christ's sacrifice. I discovered that I had already been presented before the Father totally blameless and above reproach (because of the sacrifice of Jesus, not because of what I have or haven't done.)

Up until that time, I had struggled with a guilty conscience, condemnation and shame. I was so aware that I'd come short of God's standards and that I hadn't lived up to my standard of desperation in prayer or in soaking. When you come from the kind of background I do, there is a tendency to shrink back and feel unworthy.

But the teaching of righteousness from Romans 5 and the revelation of who I was and what I had because of Christ and His sacrifice brought incredible freedom. I realized that by remaining in Him (not through anything that I had done) I was freed from condemnation. So, even to this day, I use the weapons of Romans 5, 6, 7 and 8. Because faith comes by hearing, I often re-read these powerful scriptures about my righteousness. If I am struggling in that area I refresh myself in those chapters and I return to walking in my freedom.

Without the revelation of the Lord as my righteousness I would have disqualified myself—even if I continued to run the race, I wouldn't have run with the authority and power we have seen demonstrated in our meetings. I would have become so aware of my shortcomings and felt so unworthy that it would have come through in my teaching and in my prayer. Even if I went through the motions of ministry but was without that sense of my righteous in Christ (not righteousness because of what I have or haven't done) I just know that I wouldn't have been able to grow in faith. I would not have been able to believe God for the miraculous and powerful things He is doing today.

Without the revelation of righteousness, I would have focused on my unworthiness. So the revelation of Jehovah as my righteousness has made a huge impact because it's given me a sense of "it's Him and not me." You see, my struggle has been with wondering, "Why me? Why the favor? Why the anointing and ministry?" However, if you live in "Why me?" you will never come to the place of "Why not me?" Recognizing that, in Christ, God has made me worthy, has given me power, confidence and boldness.

Even today, if I'm not walking in that revelation of righteousness, or not reading the Bible or praying like I should, I start to fear God won't release His power in a meeting, or that He won't provide what I need in some area of my life. For all of us, there is this tendency to feel confident when we're reading the Word and praying every day and haven't been in any gross sin—we start to have a sense of earned righteousness. When we feel like we have been falling short, there is more of a tendency to shrink back and not to ask boldly. This type of thinking can bring us into bondage unless we begin to walk in the light of Christ's righteousness.

Praise be to God for His grace and empowerment that enables us to walk as ambassadors of righteousness. We need to constantly walk in the revelation of Jehovah Tsidkenu, our righteousness, and then lean on His strength to live it out and extend His kingdom to the ends of the earth. As king David says, He leads us in ***"paths of righteousness for His name sake" (Ps. 23:3).*** If we want to be righteous, we must have the righteousness of another. Thank God that when we exchange our life for His, Jesus gives us His righteousness—for His name is Jehovah Tsidkenu. Yes, Jesus is The Lord our Righteousness!

Jehovah Rapha

The seventh redemptive name of God is Jehovah Rapha– "I am the Lord who heals you."

> ***"...If you diligently heed the voice of the Lord your God and do what is right in His sight, give ear to His commandments and keep all His statutes, I will put none of the diseases on you which I have brought on the Egyptians. For I am the Lord who heals you. (Jehovah Rapha)" (Ex. 15:26).***

Yes, the Lord is our physician. The only reason we can believe God heals every sickness and disease, and the only reason we can believe and accurately declare God's will is to heal everyone, is because He bore our sickness in His body. At Calvary, Jesus bore upon His body our griefs, our sorrows and our pain—He carried them away. As Scripture clearly states: ***"... by His stripes we are healed."***

> ***"But He was wounded for our transgressions, He was bruised for our iniquities; the chastisement for our peace was upon Him, and by His stripes we are healed" (Isa. 53:5).***

His shed blood has made this healing covenant come alive. He can never forsake the office of "I am the Lord that heals you" because that's who He is. And that's why miracles and healings have not passed away. That's why miracles cannot pass away. For Scripture tells us that ***"Jesus Christ is the same yesterday, today, and forever" (Heb. 13:8).***

God made a promise of healing to His people after they murmured about the bitter water in the desert at Marah. The Lord made the waters sweet for them and then gave them a promise of healing if they would listen to Him and obey. The scriptures above and below clearly show that God is truly the One who heals and that healing is definitely part of the atonement through Jesus:

> ***"So Moses made a bronze serpent, and put it on a pole; and so it was, if a serpent had bitten anyone, when he looked at the bronze serpent, he lived" (Num. 21:9).***

> ***"He also brought them out with silver and gold, and there was none feeble among the tribes" (Ps. 105:37).***

> ***"Who Himself bore our sins in His own body on the tree, that we, having died to sins, might live for righteousness—by whose stripes you were healed" (1 Pet. 2:24).***

The Lord revealed himself to His people as savior *and healer* by bringing them out of Egypt (which represents sin and the world). Through the exodus He was saying, "I am the Savior and also, the healer of your body." Think about it—not one of them was sick or weak. Probably millions of Israelites left Egypt, yet every single one came out with divine health. This supernatural act was a shadow of things to come through Calvary.

Most Christians do not understand their healing inheritance so the devil afflicts their bodies—they are destroyed for lack of knowledge. The devil has robbed God's people of the full blessing of salvation, which includes healing, because they have believed it's God's will that some are sick. People place more credibility on their negative experiences than on the Word of God.

Children wanting more of Jesus

They begin to think that if God isn't healing everyone then healing can't be His will. But that is just wrong thinking.

Can we say the same for salvation? "Not every one is getting saved, therefore God doesn't want everyone to get saved. He must want some to go to hell." That sounds harsh, but that is the same logic many people use in the area of healing. We need to recognize that many factors can hinder healing, but it is never that God has changed His mind about healing.

I believe the body of Christ has been destroyed for lack of knowledge—we cannot have faith to receive what God has for us if we don't know what God says about the healing blessings He has for us. We need to be absolutely convinced God's will is to heal us of every sickness and disease before we can have the faith to receive healing.

If we really believed that God is Jehovah Rapha, we would see tremendous healings. All we have to do is believe God is who He says He is and be willing to put His Word to the test. We need to meditate on His Word and His name until the revelation grows inside of us and until we are absolutely convinced God wants to heal us. Then we need to receive the revelation that He wants us to take His healing power to others—physical healing is a vital doctrine of the church. God didn't just ask us to heal others, He commanded us to do so:

> ***"Go into all the world and preach the gospel… and these signs will follow those who believe: In My name they will cast out demons; they will speak with new tongues… they will lay hands on the sick, and they will recover" (Mark 16:15-18).***

Healing is not a good idea, friends, it's a command! Now let's look at what Jesus went through for us and why it is an injustice to God not to receive His healing blessings.

Scripture tells us that by His stripes and by His beating that we are healed. Look at how Jesus was treated, even before He went to the cross:

> ***"Then the high priest tore his clothes, saying, 'He has spoken blasphemy! What further need do we have of witnesses? Look, now you have heard His blasphemy!' 'What do you think?' they answered and said, 'He is deserving of death.' He was innocent but they said, 'he is deserving of death.' Then they spat in His face and beat Him; and others struck Him with the palms of their hands, saying, 'Prophesy to us, Christ! Who is the one who struck You?' " (Mat. 26:65-68)***

We know from this Scripture and others, that Jesus' body was terribly beaten. ***"Just as many were astonished at you, my people, so His appearance was marred more than any man and His form more than the sons of men" (Isa. 52:14).*** Jesus was beaten so badly that He was unrecognizable. He was literally beaten to a pulp; His image was marred more than any other man. The Bible even says that they literally ripped the beard out of His face. Imagine His beard pulled out with chunks of flesh.

You need to realize that by the time Jesus got to the cross, He was almost dead. Before He got to the cross His body was covered in blood from the top of His head down to His feet. He bore all this anguish for our healing, wholeness and salvation.

Jesus didn't shed His blood so you could be healed when you get to heaven. There is no sorrow, no pain, no tears and no sickness in heaven. You won't need to be healed then. Healing is now. Scripture <u>does not</u> tell us that "by His stripes you <u>will be</u> healed" (future tense); it says, in Isaiah 53:5, ***"by His stripes we <u>ARE</u> healed"*** (present tense).

Jesus came to bring the kingdom of God to earth, to deposit the kingdom of God inside us by His Spirit. He tells us in the gospels that the kingdom of God is within us and that He wants us to experience the reality of that kingdom inheritance on earth now. Jesus wants us to enjoy today all He paid for at Calvary. Wherever Jesus brought the kingdom of God on earth, people were healed and set free.

Today, Jesus is saying, "I want the reality of the kingdom of God to be yours now. I want you to experience who I am and what I have achieved for you. I want you to experience the inheritance of the kingdom of heaven on the earth now. I don't want you to wait for it."

We need to determine in our hearts to have everything Jesus intended for us to have. We can see everything He wanted us to have when we see the full provision of the cross—let us settle for nothing else. The good news is that the provision of salvation, healing and deliverance is a gift—we don't have to do anything to earn it. For us not to believe and receive these blessings is an injustice to God. We need to see the price of a miracle. We need to see every blood drop that came out of Jesus' body for our healing. We need to say, "That's why we must be healed—that's why we must preach the gospel, heal the sick, cleanse the lepers and raise the dead."

The good news is that Jesus not only died, but rose from the dead. Now the same Spirit that raised Christ from the dead lives in us (Rom. 8:11). Because He has risen, He has made us more than conquerors (Rom. 8:37). Because He has risen you can do all things through Christ who strengthens you (Phil. 4:13). Because He has risen, He has made us to sit in heavenly places where He sits at the right hand of God far above all powers, far above all dominion, far above all might and far above every name that can be named (Eph. 2:6). He has made us victorious over the power of sin, sickness, disease and death. The spirit of life in Christ Jesus has set us free from the law of sin and death (Rom. 8:2). Where the law says you must be conquered by the curse and by sickness, the law of the Spirit of life in Christ Jesus says you must be free from the law of sin and death; you must be free from your sin; you must be healed of your sickness.

Yes, the spirit of life has freed us from the laws of this world, from the natural laws. You no longer have to believe what medical science tells you. You no longer have to live by the rule of poverty and lack or under the curse of the land. The apostle Paul describes the abundance that comes in Christ: ***"Blessed be the God and Father of our Lord Jesus Christ, who has blessed us with every spiritual blessing in the heavenly places in Christ…" (Eph. 1:3).*** Also, according to Ephesians 2:6, He has made us to sit with Him, high above all these things. Jesus has given us access to God's throne. And because He is the Alpha and the Omega, the beginning and the end, He knows no limits! What is impossible with man is not impossible with God.

I remember one of the first times that I truly had the revelation that not only was He a God that heals but He was also a God that heals when Todd prays for the sick. It's one thing to know that He can; it's another thing to know that He will; and it's even another thing to know that He will heal when *you* pray.

I really wanted that anointing. Before I had been called publicly to the healing ministry; before I had an encounter with the healing angel; before I had any kind of supernatural manifestation of healing gifts and words of knowledge operating in my life and before I had any supernatural encounters with God, I had desire. I was hungry for gifts of faith, healing and miracles. And I believed in God's healing power that I read about in the gospels and the book of Acts.

So I began to ask, "Where is the God of Elijah and the God that demonstrated His power in the Bible?" I'd hear about how God was demonstrating that kind of power through some contemporary healing evangelists like Benny Hinn, T.L. Osborn, Reinhard Bonnke and others. These people were living out the gospels and the book of Acts.

According to Jesus in John 14:12, ***"He who believes in me will do the works that I do and greater."*** I began to wonder: "God, I am a believer, but is healing ministry really for me? Maybe it was only for Kathryn Kuhlman and Aimee Semple MacPherson."

I decided I was going to step out in faith and apply the healing principles of the Word and of various healing evangelists. Years ago I resolved to do this whether there was any angelic visitation, whether someone prophesied over me about healing or whether there was any kind of supernatural manifestation, I was just going to preach healing.

At first, all I had was theory. I began to pray for healing when Fresh Fire was just a local youth ministry lead by a group of youth pastors. I remember praying for what seemed like hundreds before anyone got healed. I purposed in my heart that regardless of what I felt or saw, if nobody was healed, I'd continue to pray for thousands. I was not going to give up.

I realized that not every one is called to pack out stadiums and go to the nations. But the Lord began to give me the revelation that He does heal, that He is the same yesterday, today and forever and that He will heal through me. So I hungered and I desired because I knew this same power was available today.

One night God performed an incredible miracle. A teenage girl named Julie asked me to pray for her unsaved grandfather who was in a hospital in Pittsburgh. He had suffered a stroke and was paralyzed on his left side. "Pray that he would be healed and know that Jesus was the one who did the miracle," she said. As I prayed, the Lord translated me in a vision into the man's hospital room. I saw him hooked up to IV's and a heart monitor. I laid my hands on him and rebuked the effects of the stroke. Immediately, I saw him rise up out of his bed and run down the hallway with the IV still in his arm. Within hours the telephone rang in Canada. Julie answered it and heard these words, "Praise Jesus, praise Jesus, I've been healed." Her grandfather shared how the power of God came into his body and supernaturally healed him.

On another occasion, just after I was released into full-time ministry, I was in a healing meeting in Prince George when the Lord whispered to me: "This deaf child has a deaf and dumb spirit." I saw in Scripture that when Jesus cast the deaf and dumb spirit out of the boy, he both heard and spoke. So I commanded that spirit to come out and she heard. From that day forward I had success when I prayed for the deaf. It was then that I experienced a tremendous breakthrough in healing. Through those early healing breakthroughs, the Lord strengthened in my heart the powerful revelation of my Jehovah Rapha, the healer.

Today I believe that He wants to be the healer for every one of us. We need to make up our minds to have every blessing Jesus intended for us to have. Let's not settle for anything else but all He paid for us to have. Healing (and every other blessing) is a gift and we don't have to do anything for it. We need to see the price of a miracle; we need to see every drop of blood that came out of Jesus' body. Then we will know why we must be healed and why we must preach the gospel, heal the sick, cleanse the lepers and raise the dead (Matt. 10:7).

He has given you access to the throne of God because He is who He is. He will be who He is forever, the beginning and the end, the Alpha and the Omega. He wants you to know something: "I know no limits!" What is impossible with man is not impossible with God. And, as the apostle John prays, the Lord wants you to ***"prosper in all things and be in health, just as your soul prospers" (3 Jn. 2)*** for He is Jehovah Rapha, the Lord who heals.

The Power of Jehovah's Names

After examining the awesome names of our Jehovah God, you can see that He is really the only one whose very nature can fulfill your every desire. Yes, all you need is found in Jesus. As you continue to meditate on His names, you will be inspired to praise your great God for who He is. As you grow closer to Him, the provision of His nature becomes yours.

When you are lonely or need the safety and comfort of a friend or a father, call and the Lord will meet you. No matter where you have been, where you are, or where you may find yourself—if you are God's child, the Lord is there; He is Jehovah Shammah. When a spiritual battle is raging and the enemy is seeking to bring destruction to your life, His name is Jehovah-Nissi—The Lord Our Banner. No one can raise a standard against you, for Christ is your standard. Are you in desperate need of natural provision? Does it seem like there is no help and no way out? Remember, His name is Jehovah-Jireh—The Lord Will Provide. Wherever you are and whatever your need, our Great God will supply! Do you need spiritual or physical health? Are you struggling with an affliction? Rejoice in the fact that His name is Jehovah-Rapha—The Lord That Heals You. When struggling to overcome sin, a revelation of the nature of God will help us overcome. As forgiven children, we have a right to appropriate His purity, for He is Jehovah-Tsidkenu—The Lord Our Righteousness. When you need peace in your soul or in your circumstances, remember, our God still calms storms. His name is Jehovah-Shalom—The Lord Our Peace. Throughout life's journey, even when the road is winding and dark and you can't seem to find your way, the Lord will be your guide. Yes, Jesus came as Jehovah-Rohi—"The Lord My Shepherd."

As we embrace the names of our Lord, we receive abundant life and the blessings of the Lord will begin to overtake us. As king David said,

> ***"1 Praise the LORD! Praise, O servants of the LORD, praise the name of the LORD! 2 Blessed be the name of the LORD From this time forth and forevermore! 3 From the rising of the sun to its going down the LORD's name is to be praised" (Ps. 113:1-3).***

Some of the writing above was gleaned from information at the following websites:

www1.itech.net/~ydl/The_Seven_Redemptive_Names.htm

www.freegrace.net/dfbooks/dfnamesGodbk/NAMES8.htm

www.geocities.com/Heartland/9170/THOUGHT7.HTM

www1.itech.net/~ydl/The_Seven_Redemptive_Names.htm

www.gracegems.org/MacDuffs/pp06.htm

www.geocities.com/Heartland/9170/THOUGHT7.HTM

www.geocities.com/Heartland/9170/THOUGHT7.HTM

www1.itech.net/~ydl/The_Seven_Redemptive_Names.htm

www.gracegems.org/MacDuffs/pp06.htm and

www.geocities.com/Heartland/9170/THOUGHT7.HTM

www.gloryofhiscross.org/promises.htm

www.geocities.com/Heartland/9170/THOUGHT7.HTM

www1.itech.net/~ydl/The_Seven_Redemptive_Names.htm

www.holybible.com/resources/names_of_lord.htm

FREEDOM FROM SICKNESS AND DISEASE

When God began to use me in the healing ministry, I began to hunger for more of the power of God for healing. So I started to meditate on Jesus' healing ministry in the gospels—Mathew, Mark, Luke and John. For days, and even weeks, I would read the gospel accounts of healing and nothing else. That's all I would read. Each day I would go through the four gospels in about two or three hours, sometimes with fasting—I was just desperate to grow in faith and anointing in the area of healing.

It definitely is good to go through all the scriptures about healing, in both Old and New Testaments. However, there is something special about studying the *Sozo* (salvation for spirit, soul and body) power of the cross and there is something powerful about meditating on the healing ministry of Jesus. I've always said that, even if you could find something anywhere else in the Bible that seems to dispute healing, there is nothing that can take away from the atonement and healing provision of the cross because it is the greatest event that has ever happened in history. And if, in His ministry, Jesus healed everyone who came to Him, it doesn't matter if I don't understand why Paul left somebody sick because His ministry doesn't carry as much weight as Jesus' ministry and atoning sacrifice. As I meditated on the accounts of healing in the gospels, the Lord began to stir greater faith in my heart for healing. The Holy Spirit would teach me about the healing ministry as I dissected each account of healing to see what made it work and how it happened.

So far we've talked about our inheritance in Jesus and the high price he paid at Calvary for our wholeness. We honor Him by receiving healing and His other gifts to us through active faith. In this chapter we will be looking at our responsibility as Christians to walk in healings, miracles, signs and wonders. We will also develop a scriptural understanding and learn some of the basic principles we need to release these gifts in our lives. In addition, I want to deal with some unscriptural beliefs about healing that many Christians hold today.

Made in God's Image

We need to look at the beginning, at the creation of man, to gain a full understanding of God's views on healing. It's important to recognize, in the first chapters of Genesis, that every time God creates something, it is good. He would create the day, the stars, the land, the sea and the animals—then He would call them "good". But notice that after God creates man He calls this creation "VERY good." Before making man, God said, ***"Let Us make man in Our image, according to Our likeness; let them have dominion over the fish of the sea, over the birds of the air, over the cattle, over all the earth and over every creeping thing that creeps on the earth" (Gen. 1:26).*** After this final creation God describes it as "very good."

If God has created us in His image, where did sickness and disease come from? If God is good and created us in His image, sickness can't be from His presence. So where did it come from?

Sickness obviously wasn't from God—Jesus devoted much of His ministry to destroying it. He says, in the gospel of Luke, that the Spirit of the Lord had anointed Him to preach to the poor and to ***"heal the brokenhearted, to proclaim liberty to the captives and recovery of sight to the blind" (Luke 4: 18).*** Jesus also gave the great commission to all believers, commanding them to carry on His healing ministry. After all—we are made in God's image. Here are Jesus' words: ***"Go into all the world and preach the gospel… these signs will follow those who believe: in My name they will cast out demons; they will speak with new tongues… they will lay hands on the sick, and they will recover" (Mark 16:15, 17).*** Jesus promised that we would do the same healing works as Him***: "… he who believes in Me, the works that I do he will do also; and greater works than these he will do…" (John 14:12).*** The apostle Paul also tells us that Jesus came to give us the Spirit of Life and to destroy the power of sin and death over our lives so that the Holy Spirit could give life to our ***"mortal bodies" (Rom. 8:2,11).***

Suffering versus Sickness

To really understand the source of sickness, we must closely examine some scriptures. People often misuse scriptures to argue that God heals some, but not all of the sick, and to suggest that some sickness and disease is actually from God. Let's be clear—I believe Scripture shows, especially in the original language, that God permits sickness, but doesn't give it to people. We've already looked at this idea in Exodus 15:26 where God says (in the original Hebrew) that He will not permit sickness to come on His people like He permitted it to come on the Egyptians.

Let's look at Psalm 34:19, another commonly misinterpreted Scripture which people use all the time when they want to argue against divine healing. They say, "Todd, 'many are the afflictions of the righteous, but the Lord delivers him out of them all.'" Let's first investigate the word for "affliction" in this verse. The definition of the word affliction means "hardship, trials, trouble and persecution." I don't see any sickness in there. You might call sickness a trial—I don't. We will talk more about these words later because this is a big one for many Christians and may go against everything you have ever believed. So "God, I ask that you'd give me the hammer! …the hammer of truth."

Deaf man healed—shows Todd his hearing aid

Let me show you the difference between suffering and sickness. Let's look at James 5:13-15:

> ***"Is anyone among you suffering? Let him pray. Is anyone cheerful? Let him sing psalms. Is anyone among you sick? Let him call for the elders of the church, and let them pray over him, anointing him with oil in the name of the Lord. And the prayer of faith will save the sick, and the Lord will raise him up."***

Let's look at that verse again—you have probably never seen these verses in this way before. Watch this! ***"Is anyone among you suffering, let him pray."*** You don't pray away trials, hardship and suffering. You don't rebuke your trials or your persecution. The Bible says if you are suffering, you should pray—don't even go to some spiritual leader for prayer—pray yourself. But then this passage says this: ***"Is anyone among you sick? Let him call for the elders of the church, and let them pray over him, anointing him with oil in the name of the Lord. And the prayer of faith will save the sick."*** Notice that James differentiates between suffering and sickness—they are different.

If sickness and suffering were one and the same, then why would you be trying to get rid of something that God gave you to develop your character? See, if you are suffering, you are to pray. You don't come to the church elders to pray away your trial, hardships and suffering. However, this Scripture does tell you if you're sick to go to the elders for prayer so you can be healed! It is obvious here that sickness and suffering are two different things; suffering we are to endure, while sickness we are to get rid of! If you're sick, get prayer and be healed. Obviously God doesn't want you to endure sickness as if it is a suffering or a trial. Is any one among you suffering? Pray. Is anyone among you sick? Come and get rid of it. That is what it says! You don't have to take your sickness and say, "God doesn't want to heal me because He is using sickness to teach me." God has many other good ways to teach and train you.

Now let's examine another Scripture which people also use as an objection to the ministry of healing:

> ***"And you have forgotten the exhortation which speaks to you as to sons: 'My son, do not despise the chastening of the Lord, nor be discouraged when you are rebuked by Him; for whom the Lord loves He chastens, and scourges every son whom He receives.' If you endure chastening, God deals with you as with sons; for what son is there whom a Father does not chasten?" (Hebrews 12:5).***

Here the writer says that God disciplines His children. However, nowhere does He say that He would do it with sickness. He speaks of "chastening," "scourging" and "rebuke", but not once does he mention sickness. You need to understand that I am only speaking of immunity to sickness within the bounds of covenant relationship with Jesus. Such protection does not apply if you are under the law of sin and death, letting sin reign in your life and stepping out from underneath the umbrella of God's protection. When people walk in sin and disobedience, God's hands are tied—He is not going to invade free will. I am talking about protection from disease and sickness if you're in a loving relationship with God, doing what is right in His sight, praying and keeping your life clean as the Lord convicts you.

This passage speaks of God bringing discipline, not just permitting it. The Greek word for chastening means to discipline, correct and nurture. It's a picture of God lovingly training and teaching as a teacher trains his pupil. Now what would you do if your son went to school today and his teacher said, "I am going to give your son a cancer to teach him a lesson"? What kind of teacher trains his pupil by giving him diabetes? What kind of teacher trains his pupil by giving him some kind of gross liver disease or making him go blind. Imagine a teacher like that: "That's it! I'll teach you a lesson; you will never talk in class again! Get over here right now. I am going to pop your ear drum with this pencil." If this scenario is so shocking to us, why would we think God is like this? What is wrong with us?!

The original language of this passage also refers to training and molding a child's character. Now I have three children—Elijah, Lauralee and Esther. I want to be sure to mold the character of my son. So when my son doesn't listen, am I going to press his hand on the stove and burn it purposely? I want to train up my children; I want to rebuke, correct and chastise them so they learn. So, I am going to teach my daughter Lauralee a lesson. Am I going to give her the worst kind of Crohn's disease and irritable bowel disease until she learns how to eat all her dinner? Such acts would be considered child abuse in our society. I mean, it just doesn't make sense that anyone would consider doing such things to their child.

It's pretty simple—God is good! The religious crowd has a hard time believing this truth. When someone says, "God is good" I shout "Amen!" He's so good that sometimes I can hardly stand it. Jesus says this: ***"If you then, being evil, know how to give good gifts to your children, how much more will your Father who is in heaven give good things to those who ask Him!" (Matt. 7:11).*** Now how many of you are giving good gifts to your children like cancer, tumors, blood disorders, blind eyes, deaf ears and paralysis? How many people would even do that before they were saved? No one! Would that be good parenting? Would that be giving good gifts to your children? Can you even imagine a parent today introducing some sort of viral bacteria, disease or terminal illness to their children's environment, hoping for them to catch it? Can you even imagine waking up in the morning and saying, "I think I would like to rebuke, correct and teach my son today to mold his character. I really would like to see him have epilepsy?"

Yet somehow we can actually think of God this way. But the Bible says that if even sinful parents know how to give good gifts to their children, surely God knows even more how to give good gifts to His kids. You wouldn't even think about disciplining your children with sickness; it wouldn't even enter your mind. Most parents would rather be sick in place of their child—they'd rather take the hurt and pain than see their child suffer. No matter how bad they were, no child is deserving of sickness or disease. But God can inflict these things on His kids?! We must remember, God is a good Father and knows how to give good gifts to His children.

Job's Suffering

Let's look at another Bible story which seems to challenge the view that God always wants to heal everyone. When they hear about the ministry of healing, people often ask, "What about Job?" So, let's talk about old Job! Some say Job's whole ordeal lasted 18 months. I don't know if that's true, but I will show you one thing in Job 2:7: ***"So Satan went up to the presence of the Lord and struck Job with painful boils."*** So who struck Job? Yes God permitted it to happen, but who actually afflicted Job? Who is the author of sickness and disease? Satan went up to the presence of the Lord and struck Job. "Well, how could that happen?" people ask. "Job was holy; he was blameless." What about Job 3:25? In this verse Job says, "…the thing I greatly feared has come upon me." Whether it was the area of fear or something else, God wouldn't have permitted his affliction if there wasn't an open door, an area that needed to be dealt with in Job's life. And even though God gave permission, it was still the Devil that gave the sickness. Could fear have provided the open door for the enemy to walk through?

People often ask, "What about Job?" I just reply, "What about Job? The Devil did it!" Perhaps God gave permission because Job had issues of fear and self-righteousness (think of his defensive protests to his friends) and God

Young boy who was brought over 300 miles to our meeting in Latvia has his vision completely restored

allowed sickness for his instruction… so it was the love of God which allowed Job's afflictions. However, in the end God healed him—that's the bottom line. Satan afflicted him with the boils and God healed him—so what about Job? God allowed him to endure sickness for a season, but God wasn't the source. I actually think that we often bring sickness on ourselves even though God doesn't want us to have it. But if we choose to do our own thing or not listen to God, we can bring it upon ourselves.

Also, realize that not every sickness or disease is a result of sin! Do you understand that? Because the Devil is a liar, you can put up all the "No Trespassing" signs you want but he is still going to trespass. He is the thief that comes to kill, steal and destroy. There are innocent victims of the Devil's destructive attacks throughout the world today. God's people need to have a good understanding of their healing rights so they can enforce them when the Devil comes trespassing. We also need to realize that Job was not under the New Covenant which has provided for healing in Christ's atonement. Many theologians believe that Job actually lived in a time period before the Old Covenant and the law. So Job did not have the blessings of any covenant with God. Whether Job lived under the Old Covenant or not, today, as the Scripture tells us, we live under a far better covenant. This New Covenant has provided *Sozo* to all God's children.

Even though Scripture constantly speaks of God's goodness, many Christians still hold on to the idea that their sickness is of God. I know a great many men and woman who say, "You know what, Todd? If it wasn't for that tumor; if it wasn't for that cancer, my whole family wouldn't be saved. If it wasn't for that sickness, I wouldn't be where I am today in the kingdom." We have all these testimonies of good that has come out of sickness and disease. Here is what I say about that: God didn't cause it, but God will use it. God will use anything! He causes all things to work together for good. You may say, "I'm glad that it happened to me; I'm glad that I was laid up in the hospital for months." In the end Job also said, "Hallelujah! Praise God! Now I can really see you!" Yes, even though sickness is not God's will for his children, when we sin or unwittingly open the door to illness, or when the Devil trespasses in our lives, God still causes all things to work together for good. However, God wasn't the source of the sickness. He just used it. He will use anything. Good can come out of sickness, but let's just understand where it came from. God always wants to teach us and to shower good things on our lives and He has better ways of doing in than through sickness. Even though the enemy is the source of sickness, God will even turn this demonic strategy to good for His children.

Paul's Thorn

Besides the account of Job's suffering, the passage describing Paul's thorn has become the other great proof text to support a theological stance with the idea that sickness is God's will. In 2 Corinthians 11 Paul lists the many ordeals he's been through—what he calls suffering, hardships and trials—yet he never once mentions sickness. You may still be thinking that sickness can be a hardship and a trial. Well, let's see what Paul says about the subject—here's the list of the many hardships he suffered for Christ:

> ***"...in labors, more abundant, in stripes above measure, in prisons more frequently, in deaths often. From the Jews five times I received forty stripes minus one. Three times I was beaten with rods; once I was stoned; three times I was ship-wrecked; a night and a day I have been in the deep; in journeys often, in perils of waters, in perils of robbers, in perils of my own countrymen, in perils of the Gentiles, in perils of the city, in perils in the wilderness, in perils in the sea, in perils among false brethren; in weariness and toil, in sleeplessness often, in hunger and thirst, in fastings often, in cold and nakedness—besides the other things, what comes upon me daily: my deep concern for all the churches" (2 Cor. 11:23-28).***

Now did you notice Paul talking about his cancer, his diabetes, his blood condition and his migraine headaches in this passage? Do you see it in there? Nowhere does he list sickness and disease as a suffering, hardship or trial. Now let me just say this. God always causes external pressures not internal pressures. When God wants to teach you and bring you closer to Him, He'll never afflict you internally. Often the outside pressures come at us from every direction. It's like being in a pressure cooker, but it's all outside stuff. Notice that having many beatings is not sickness or disease. Yes, it's still pain; it's still suffering for Christ. However, a beating or stoning is not an internal terminal disease, diabetes, liver disease, blindness or deafness—it is an external pressure, not an internal pressure. God always uses external pressure. He is not going to afflict your body inside with some kind of sickness or disease. It doesn't mean that He won't allow the enemy or others to bring external sufferings, pressures, beatings and martyrdom our way. But those things are not sickness or disease.

Now let's look at the verse that speaks specifically about Paul's thorn in the flesh. It is pretty simple to me:

"And lest I should be exalted above measure by the abundance of the revelations, a thorn in the flesh was given to me, a messenger of Satan to buffet me, lest I be exalted above measure. Concerning this thing I pleaded with the Lord three times that it might depart from me. And He said to me, 'My grace is sufficient for you, for my strength is made perfect in weakness.' Therefore most gladly I will rather boast in my infirmities, that the power of Christ may rest upon me. Therefore I take pleasure in infirmities, in reproaches, in needs, in persecutions, in distresses, for Christ's sake. For when I am weak, then I am strong" (2 Cor. 12:7-10).

Paul was saying that he was going to boast in his infirmities so that the power of Christ would rest upon him. Now let's look closely at his words in verse 10: ***"Therefore I take pleasure in infirmities, in reproaches, in needs, in persecutions, in distresses, for Christ's sake. For when I am weak, then I am strong."*** Did you see sickness and disease mentioned there? I take pleasure in what? Reproaches. Distresses. Persecutions. Needs. Infirmities. "For when I am weak, then I am strong." Paul was saying that, "these things force my total dependency on Christ because I can't do it in my own strength. It's either God provides or I am toast." That is the idea of weakness here. In the midst of all Paul's struggles and weaknesses, God still delivered him and worked in powerful ways through him. So Paul would boast in these things because it showed who his dependence was on and highlighted the fact that it was God, not Paul, who was the power source.

A Messenger of Satan

Now let's look at this passage more closely. Paul said, ***"A thorn in the flesh was given to me."*** What is a thorn in the flesh? Let's keep reading—here it is: ***"a messenger of Satan to buffet me…" (v. 7)*** Clearly Paul's thorn is not a sickness—it is a messenger of Satan. Messenger in this Scripture is "anglos" or "angel"—so this was a demonic angel or messenger sent to buffet him. The word "buffet" in this verse means to beat repeatedly, or a more literal meaning would be, "blow after blow." Now think of Paul's description of his buffeting: persecutions, sleeplessness, fastings, beatings, scourgings, in prison often and in need. His ordeals definitely sound like "blow after blow," don't they? It's as if everywhere he went a hornet's nest was stirred up around him. A riot erupts in Ephesus; he is thrown out of cities; he is stoned and left for dead and he is repeatedly rejected. One demonic blow after another! Not internal attacks of sickness, but external buffeting from persecution and extremely difficult circumstances. The purpose of this buffeting, according to Paul, was to keep him from being "exalted." These constant attacks would keep him humble because he was kept in a continual state of weakness and was forced to place his total dependency on Christ.

Now let's continue to examine the phrase "thorn in the flesh." When we do word studies like this, it's important to look at other scriptural references to the word. Look at this Old Testament passage:

> ***"But if you do not drive out the inhabitants of the land from before you, then it shall be that those whom you let remain shall be irritants (or pricks) in your eyes and thorns in your sides, and they shall harass you in the land where you dwell" (Num. 33:55).***

So clearly, when God is talking about the thorns, He is talking about enemies that harass you. Again, these thorns are outward, external and constant irritations—they are constantly there irritating you and may not necessarily be causing great pain or huge damage to your life. Have you ever got a little thorn right in your finger, under the skin? I tried to pull one out of my daughter the other day. "NO! Daddy! Please No!" I said "Honey, it's only a little thorn." She said, "Daddy, it hurts!" It took me ten minutes to convince her to let me pull it out. Thorns in our flesh are just enough to cause us great irritation, but they don't cause life-threatening damage. You are always aware that the thorn is there; it constantly harasses you.

Infirmity Versus Sickness

Ok, now you may be wondering what to make of verse eight: "***Concerning this thing I pleaded with the Lord three times that it might depart from me. And He said to me, "My grace is sufficient for you, for my strength is made perfect in weakness."*** Then Paul's response to the Lord is: ***"Therefore most gladly I will rather boast in my infirmities, that the power of Christ may rest upon me."*** We need to understand what the word "infirmities" means here. Notice first that in context Paul is talking about weakness, not sickness. This same Greek word is also used in Romans 8:26 (which again uses the English word infirmity in the King James Version): ***"Likewise the Spirit also helpeth our infirmities: for we know not what we should pray for as we ought: but the Spirit itself maketh intercession for us with groanings which cannot*** *be uttered."* The word infirmity in this context doesn't sound like sickness to me. Rather, the verse suggests that when you do not know how to pray, the spirit helps in our weaknesses and makes intercession for us. Even though the original word "astheneia" could be translated as feebleness of body or mind, moral frailty, sickness or weakness, in context, the only reading that could be correct is "weakness." In the American Standard Version of the Bible, this Greek word "astheneia," in Romans 8:26, is also translated as "weakness" rather than "infirmity".

Woman receives ministry from Shonnah Bentley

The original Greek word for weakness here is the same word used in the verse ***"When I am weak then I am strong"(2 Cor. 12:10).*** Paul had a revelation of the power in weakness when he said, ***"I can do all things through Christ who strengthens me" (Phil. 4:13).*** You see, when we are weak and the situation is impossible and out of our hands, then I am forced to depend on God and His Word. It is in this place that God can move in power because we can't get it done in our own strength. That is why it is so dangerous to trust in military might, riches or our own skills and abilities. The danger of trusting in these false securities is that we begin to move out of total dependency on God because we are no longer weak. We no longer need to be dependent on Him if we have all the money in the world. We don't need to be dependent on Him if we aren't in need and without distresses, reproaches and persecutions. These external pressures are the infirmities and lead to the weaknesses that Paul refers to in this passage about his thorn.

Let's look at one more Scripture that people use to argue that Paul's thorn in the flesh was a sickness. I love this one—it's so amusing because people have actually tried to figure out what sickness Paul had. Here is what some have said: "Paul had an oriental eye disease." Have you heard that one? Come on now?! How do people come up with this stuff? Let's just examine Galatians 6:11 and diffuse that argument. Here Paul says, ***"See with what large letters I have written to you with my own hand."*** People have actually read into that verse that Paul had an eye problem because he had to write with such large letters (large writing) so he could see his own writing.

Firstly, there is no reference to sickness, eye disease or physical problems in this passage. The only reason people would interpret this verse as Paul having a sickness is if they had already decided that his thorn or infirmity was a sickness. However, we've already examined the true meanings of those words. This verse about large letters, rather than referring to the quality of Paul's writing, seems more likely to refer to the size of his epistles. It's not how big his 'a' is or how big his 'p's or 'c's are. He is speaking of the volume of his writing, of how big this letter is they are about to receive in the mail. Perhaps it's four pages this time instead of one page. Here's what he is saying: "This letter is bigger than the letters I usually write. It's not because I have an eye disease or an eye problem." In fact the King James Version of the Bible translates the verse this same way: ***"Ye see how large a letter I have written unto you with mine own hand."*** Amen—So be it!

The Author of Sickness and Disease

Even though we can show in Scripture that God does not afflict His children with "thorns" of sickness and that He does desire our wholeness, you may be wondering how sickness arrived on planet earth in the first place. In those first chapters of Genesis, everything God made was good, except the creation of man and woman, which was *very* good. After those seven days of creation, no sickness, disease, death or poverty existed in the Garden of Eden. So where did those things come from in the first place?

It's not until after man disobeys God and falls into sin in Genesis 3 that

African boys radically touched by the fire of God

sin comes into the world. Later, in Deuteronomy 28, the Bible lists the results of the curse of the law. Do you know that just about every major category of sickness and disease in the world today—such as blindness, tumors, skin conditions, irritations and barrenness—can be found in Deuteronomy 28? You see, sin was the door for sickness, disease, death and poverty. Those human afflictions did not exist until sin opened the door. And so, as we discovered in our lesson on *Sozo*, when we receive forgiveness of sin, we can also receive healing—to forgive sin is to heal and to heal is to forgive sin—we've seen this truth in the book of James 5:15. This Scripture tells us that ***"...the prayer of faith will save the sick, and the Lord will raise him up. And if he has committed sins, he will be forgiven."*** James is telling us that when we receive healing prayer, we receive forgiveness of sins too. According to this verse, you don't even need to be asking for forgiveness when you're receiving healing prayer, because healing and forgiveness are the same. Remember, back in the garden, sin was the open door for sickness to walk into the human race.

The apostle Paul also refers to this link between sin and sickness or death:

> ***"Therefore, just as through one man sin entered the world, and death through sin, and thus death spread to all men... Therefore, as through one man's offense judgment came to all men, resulting in condemnation, even so through one's man righteous act the free gift came to all men, resulting in justification of life. For as by one man's disobedience many were made sinners, so also by one Man's obedience many will be made righteous" (Rom. 5:12,18).***

According to this passage, when sin came into the world, death spread to all men—I believe that was death in both the spiritual and the natural realms. The result of spiritual death is separation from intimate relationship with God, while the early symptoms of physical death manifest in the form of sickness and disease. As a result of one man's sin in the beginning death spread to all of us. However, in the same way, through one man's (Jesus') righteousness, how much more will the power or righteous spread to the world. Now I also believe that if death can spread to the human race because of one man's sin, then healing can spread to all people because of Jesus' righteous act.

I believe Romans 5 clearly shows that healing is for everyone all the time. Think about it—sin brought death in spirit (separation from God) and also death and sickness for the body. Also, sin was the door for sickness, disease, death and poverty because they did not exist until sin entered the world after the fall of man. So, if it is true that one man's disobedient act brought the curse of death and sickness to humanity, then it must also be true that Jesus Christ's atoning work brought life and restored relationship to God as well as healing from sickness. If Jesus bore the curse of the law at Calvary, and the curse includes every known sickness as listed in Deuteronomy 28, then Jesus must have born every sickness that affects humans today! Isn't that incredible!

So every Christian is delivered from the curse of the law of sin and death and set free from the barrier separating them from God as well as the attack of physical sickness. So that is where sickness and disease came from. Consequently, although God created sickness, sin opened the door for it to afflict mankind and the Devil uses it to attack and destroy people made in God's image. Yet, the Devil can't use sickness without God's permission. Scripture calls Satan the god of this world we live in; so bad things can obviously happen to innocent people because we live in the Devil's playground.

Sickness and Sin

Although sickness has invaded our world through the door of generational sin from Adam, I don't believe that sickness in a person's life is always because they are in personal sin. Sin gave the Devil permission to attack people with sickness, starting in Genesis, but that doesn't mean the enemy is always able to afflict them or that God permits him to afflict them. However, at times, God may permit sickness in cases of persistent individual sin. Always remember though, God may permit sickness, but it is always Satan who gives sickness—his goal is to steal, kill, and destroy. Sorrow, pain, sickness and death do not exist in heaven! It's not there. You're not going to accidentally find a room in heaven where they keep all these viruses and bacteria. It is just not there. You won't find pain or sorrow there, only life, health, goodness and joy.

At times, here on earth, God permits sickness in order to show us our faults so that we will repent and get back under His umbrella of protection and be healed. If we remain under God's covenant of protection through obedience and faith, we can continually receive His healing grace. God can permit sickness to purify us from sin, however, that route is one of His last choices—He would rather teach us through His Word, His voice or through relationships and circumstances. At times, I believe, when people continue to resist God's other methods of teaching, He will allow sickness as a visible sign of God's judgement on a nation or an individual.

Remember, though, sin is only one reason for sickness—other reasons could include the existence of a generational curse in someone's life or just natural things such as poor diet and lifestyle. Also, if I cut my finger off on a table saw by accident, neither God or the Devil is necessarily to blame. Sickness could also be the result of Christians' ignorance of their *Sozo* covenant and they need to meditate on Scripture to grow in faith for healing. Even though God may allow sickness at times, we see in Hosea 6 that God will always be there when we are broken and bruised and wounded to draw us back to Himself so we can be healed. That is His heart. But it is always the Devil that is the instrument of sickness and disease, not God.

Healing those Oppressed by Satan

Now let's establish, once and for all, the author of sickness and disease. Is it God or is it the Devil? Here's one more powerful Scripture that should remove any remaining doubt: ***"How God anointed Jesus of Nazareth with the Holy Spirit and with power, who went about doing good and healing all who were oppressed by the Devil, for God was with Him" (Acts 10:38).*** Notice that Jesus went about doing good and healing. Healing who? All those who were what? All those who were oppressed of the Devil. So by healing people, Jesus was actually destroying works of the Devil! This mandate is in perfect harmony with Jesus mission statement in 1 John 3:8: ***"For this purpose the Son of God was manifested, that He might destroy the works of the Devil."*** Jesus came to destroy the works of the Devil. And how did He do that? He healed people! Now let me ask you what kind of people did Jesus heal? All people oppressed of the Devil.

So if He healed every sickness and every disease among the people (Matt. 9:35), does that make every sickness and every disease an oppression of the Devil in God's eyes? Think about it—if Jesus healed Peter's mother-in-law's fever, God saw it as an oppression of the Devil. He wouldn't go around healing fever if, in his eyes, fever wasn't considered an oppression and work of the Devil. The same goes for every healing of blindness, deafness, epilepsy and every other sickness and disease Jesus healed. Now, just because you're sick, doesn't mean you have a devil or that you're demon possessed. However, we live in a fallen world system in which sickness, death and oppression has spread to everyone. The Devil has come to kill, steal and destroy in order to oppress mankind. Jesus went around healing people to free them from the Devil's oppression.

So when He healed blind eyes, He was destroying an oppression of the Devil. When He healed fever, paralysis, arthritis or deafness, He was destroying oppression of the Devil.

Now let's take a quick overview of the Bible's treatment of healing. It is interesting that in the first chapters of Genesis, mankind starts with perfect health. God didn't create Adam and say, "Aw man, I am sorry Adam, dude, I only gave you one eyeball." God didn't create Eve and then discover she had cataracts. They didn't have diabetes. They didn't have all these different physical conditions. God created them perfectly. He didn't forget things. Can you imagine God saying, "Oh yeah, I'm sorry, I forgot to give you the other lung. I created you with a faulty kidney." They were perfect. They were strong and whole until Genesis 3 when sin entered the world and spread death to all men.

Then in Deuteronomy 28 we see that the curse of the law actually led to every sickness and disease that we have in the world today. Later, in the New Testament, Jesus showed his heart for people's wholeness by healing every sickness and disease of everyone who came to Him. Then Paul, in Romans 8, talks about the law of sin and death. As we've already discussed, the fruit of the law of sin is sickness, disease, death and poverty. I mean it's law! Those things go together. And then when we get to the last chapter in the Bible, Revelation 22, we discover that Scripture also ends with healing. In Revelations 22 you have the river and the trees and the leaves of the trees which are for the healing of the nations. Scripture starts with perfect healing and ends with perfect healing. In the beginning, at the end, and throughout the whole New Testament, it was healing ALL, ALL the time! Praise the Lord!

Demons that Cause Sickness

As we are talking about the author of sickness and disease, it's important that we talk about some of the specific demons that cause sickness. For instance, in Luke 13, we see a woman who was bound for 18 years by a spirit of infirmity. Do you remember where the spirit of infirmity was? It was in her spine. She was bent over and could not stand up straight on her feet. It was a spirit of infirmity that caused a back condition. In one of my meetings I actually had a vision of a spirit of infirmity as a large snake on a man squeezing his back and lungs. Again, this spirit was causing physical sickness.

Another example of a demon causing sickness is mentioned in Mathew 17:14-15—it's the story of an epileptic boy. In other passages in the gospels, "epileptic" is also translated as "lunatic," meaning madness or mental illness. This epileptic boy suffered severely and would often fall into fire or into water—but the word for epileptic is also lunatic. So Scripture actually shows us a demonic cause for mental disorders, which could include bi-polar syndrome, schizophrenia and other types of mental illness. Another Scripture which speaks of a demonic source for illness, is found in ***Isaiah 61:3: "Put on the garment of praise for the spirit of heaviness."*** This verse suggests that there is a demonic spirit that causes heaviness and depression.

The Bible, in Mark 9:25, also refers to a demon called the deaf and dumb spirit. When a father brought his deaf and dumb son to Jesus, the Lord said, "Deaf and dumb spirit, I command you, come out of him and enter him no more." Another Scripture, Matthew 9:32-33 refers to a demon afflicting a man with muteness. I have had considerable experience with this affliction. When I minister in Africa, I would say that about one out of every 10 children is either deaf or mute. We have had considerable success in healing the deaf by casting out the spirit causing the deafness or muteness. In this example in the gospel of Matthew, when Jesus cast out the demon, the mute man spoke. A few chapters later, we read about a demonized man who was both mute and blind (Matt. 12:22). Yes, there is a demon that makes people blind as well. When Jesus healed him, the man spoke and saw. Scripture gives so much evidence which points to the demonic origin of sickness. As we've already seen, Acts 10:38 speaks of all sickness as the Devil's work because Jesus ***"went about doing good and healing all who were oppressed by the Devil."*** So Jesus, our Lord and teacher, clearly saw all sickness as the Devil's work.

In my healing ministry, I can think of numerous instances when people were healed when I cast out devils. On one occasion, in Portland, a sweet woman came for prayer saying she had a disorder in her stomach. When I went to lay hands on her to pray for her stomache, the room filled up with a foul-smelling odor like raw sewage. Then I heard the Lord say that this stomach infirmity was caused by an unclean devil and from involvement in lust and perversion. I knew that she was either involved in sexual sin or that she had been raped and until this demonic oppression was dealt with we wouldn't be able to deal with the stomach disorder. When we cast out the demons, she was healed from her stomach disorder.

Most often when I deal with scoliosis or a crooked spine or any kind of degenerate arthritis of the spine, bones or joints, I need to deal with the spirit of infirmity. Just about every time I cast this demon out, even if the person is suffering from rheumatoid arthritis, it comes out through the person's back. Scoliosis, especially, is usually caused by a demon, as supported by the story in Luke 18. In this story, the spirit of infirmity had bound a woman for years so that she was bent over and couldn't stand up straight—the demon actually affected her spine. In my experience, whether it's a spinal condition or just a chronic illness or chronic pain like fibromyalgia, this spirit of infirmity often manifests in the persons back and comes out through the spine. If I lay my hands on the people's backs when I am casting out the spirit of infirmity, quite often they will see healing of chronic pain and illnesses, arthritis, fibromialgia or chronic pain. Its not that they necessarily had a problem with their back, but that's where the demon will manifest and leave.

Satan Gives Sickness, Jesus Gives Life

It seems clear from these experiences, and after our examination of Scripture, that the devil is the source of sickness, either in a general or in a specific sense. I'll tell you this, the reason Christians actually believe that somehow God is the source of sickness or that He gives us "thorns of sickness" is not rooted in Scripture. These beliefs are usually based on our experiences with people we know—we keep trying to figure, with our own understanding, why this good man or woman is sick. Then we look for thoughts or explanations (scriptural or not) which seem to bring comfort to them in their sickness. We've spoken our ideas with the right heart—wanting to give comfort and love to our brother or sister. However, the theological understanding was faulty and did not help them get well.

So let's not say that everybody who is sick is in sin. Let's understand that our enemy, the Devil, is the source of all sickness and disease. People are not the source of sickness, although they can contribute to it. Knowing the enemy of our health will stir us so much more to want to war and contend for people's healing until we see the answer manifest. And just because they die of their sickness (many died in the Bible not yet receiving the promise) should not stop us from contending for healing and miracles in people's bodies. It's OK not to have the answers for everything. However, I believe that our discussion in this chapter will help you understand the goodness of God and pour more fuel on your fire for the healing ministry—you will be inspired to war for your healing inheritance in Christ. So God uses sickness but does not want us to have it—He permits it, but the Devil is always the one that makes it happen. If we will read everything the Word says about healing, begin to rid ourselves of the spirit of unbelief and ask God to help our unbelief, then we will begin to see the greater works we are called to do.

Jesus comes that we might have abundant life while the Devil comes to kill, steal and destroy. We have been redeemed from the curse of the law, but can choose to live in willful sin and rebellion and, by that, remove ourselves from under His umbrella of healing grace. Christ has made provision for our healing—the glorious truth is that the Father has made a way, through Jesus, for us to overcome the works of the enemy and to walk free of sickness. All we have to do is take hold of this inheritance by faith, in the same way we receive salvation by faith. Together, let's start living in this wonderful healing inheritance that God is offering us today.

Chapter Five

TOUCHING GOD ON COVENANT

In this chapter we will continue to strengthen our biblical foundation of faith for healing. We will examine the difference between believing and faith; we will also define biblical covenant and its power for every believer. This covenant provides for health, healing and miracles. His great promises to us can anchor our faith for His supernatural healing provision. The Father has a passionate desire for our healing and for confirming the powerful covenant He has cut with us. This covenant provides for health, healing and miracles.

Our covenant blessings all started with God's promise to Abraham in ***Genesis 17:6: "I will make you exceedingly fruitful; and I will make nations of you…."*** Remember, this is God speaking to you, not just Abraham. As the Apostle Paul says, ***"Christ has redeemed us from the curse of the law, having become a curse for us (for it is written, 'Cursed is everyone who hangs on a tree'), that the blessing of Abraham might come upon the Gentiles in Christ Jesus" (Gal. 3:13-14).*** Often we remove ourselves from the promises of God in Scripture because it may have been originally spoken to David, Moses or Abraham. We need to realize that God is a God of generational covenants—covenants which extend to His people's descendents forever. So when I read this Genesis 17 promise, I know God is talking to me and not just Abraham!

When you read about God's promises to Abraham, you need to say, "God is talking to me." Just remove Abraham from the picture and say, "I am one of the descendents. I am part of the sand of the sea shore—it passed on to Isaac, Jacob and Joseph and now it's ME. Thank you God! You are going to make ME exceedingly fruitful! Hallelujah! Here God is talking to me—'I will make nations of you!' Yah! That's my promise too. It was Abraham's and I'm his seed and in his seed all the families of the earth are blessed. This is my promise now. God says, 'Kings shall come from you'—I declare this over my children. "Kingship!" See, you need to do that every once in a while. Are you getting it? That was just a Holy Ghost download!

Now let's look at God's covenant with Abraham which is ours in Jesus:

> ***"And I will establish my covenant between me and you and your descendants after you in their generations, for an everlasting covenant, to be God to you and your descendants after you. Also I give to you and to your descendants after you the land in which you are a stranger, all the land of Canaan, as an everlasting possession; and I will be their God" (Gen. 17:7-8).***

God establishes a covenant here between Himself and Abraham. By definition, a covenant is a contract or a pledge, an agreement between two individuals—a King and his people, God and his people, a husband and a wife or even two parties in a business deal. The business world refers to such an agreement as a contract. Each party agrees to their rights, responsibilities and financial commitment. They then draw up a contract which both parties sign as a pledge of commitment to the terms of the deal. Legally, if one of those parties does not keep up their end of the bargain, the contract is annulled.

A marriage covenant is made in a similar way. In this agreement, a husband and wife covenant together (with a public vow and signature) before God and the government to fulfill certain responsibilities as faithful, loving spouses. Motivated by love, a couple signs a binding contract and they are married. However, if one marriage partner is unfaithful to his or her spouse, the other partner is released from the covenant. In covenant or contract law, when one person doesn't fulfill his end of the bargain, the covenant is dissolved.

So when God made a covenant with Abraham, each party became responsible for fulfilling certain terms. The promises of God to us in Scripture operate in a similar way. Have you ever noticed that for every promise in Scripture there is an "if" or an implied condition? You will often see phrases like, "If you do what is right in His eyes" or "If you obey my Word." Those little "ifs" seem to sneak in there all the time. Yes, often what we do or don't do can make or break the promise. I don't speak of prophetic words as guarantees anymore—I call them "potential." Just as the promises to Abraham depended on his faith and obedience, so do our prophetic promises and even scriptural promises.

Think about all the wonderful, divine scriptural promises. God repeatedly says things like: "I want to bless My people; I want to heal My people; I want them to prosper; I want them to live in health, peace, joy, and righteousness; I want them to be overcomers; I want to give them land and vineyards; I want My blessings to overtake them; I want them to be the head and not the tail, above and not beneath; I want to enable them to do all things through Christ who strengthens them; I want them to be very rich; I want them to have more than enough provision— exceedingly, abundantly above all that they could dream of." Yes, the American dream and more—God wants you to have it. He wants to bless you, heal you and set you free from the curse of the law. He wants to free you from demonic torment—He doesn't want you to suffer.

So, in order to pour out these many blessings on His people, God decided to make a covenant with man. Think about God's wonderful love—He created the entire universe and then He said, "I want a loving relationship with the man and woman, so I'm going to give them the choice to love Me. I'll give them dominion over everything on the earth." Think of how small we are, as human beings, in the scheme of the entire universe, and yet God loves us and wants to bless us.

The covenant blessings started in Genesis 15 when God made a pledge to Abraham to be His God and His descendants' God forever. God's covenant with Abraham is the eternal foundation stone of Israel's relationship with God, and all other Bible promises are based on this one. By sealing this covenant with blood, God secured His covenant blessings with His people, including all the benefits of salvation. When He cut a covenant with Abraham He passed between the parts of the sacrifice and initiated, in love, the first blood sacrifice. However, this was a unique covenant—look at this powerful account:

> ***"And it came to pass, when the sun went down and it was dark, that behold, there appeared a smoking oven and a burning torch that passed between those pieces. On the same day the Lord made a covenant with Abram, saying: 'To your descendants I have given this land…'" (Gen. 15:17-18).***

God knew that man was incapable of keeping a covenant and He did not want anything to hinder the blessing so He would eventually fulfill both sides of this agreement. He said, "Listen, I know what is in man, for all have sinned and fallen short of My glory. No one is righteous, not one. Yet, I love them and I want them to have all the benefits of My goodness." Those benefits included salvation, healing, deliverance, victory, peace, every spiritual blessing, all the provision of God's seven redemptive names, all the blessing of *Sozo* as well as all the provision of prosperity and healing. However, to ensure this covenant would not fail, God decided to fulfill both sides of the covenant because He knew man could not live up to his end of the deal. So the Father sent His own Son as a man to keep the requirements of the covenant by living a sinless life and then to die on the cross to pay our price for the blessings of heaven. He knew that we would mess it up. God so loved the world that HE GAVE.

When God cut the covenant with Abraham He also gave a special guarantee that it would come to pass: ***"For when God made a promise to Abraham, because He could swear by no one greater, He swore by Himself" (Heb. 6:13).*** God swore by Himself to secure the covenant and then ultimately fulfilled the agreement for both parties in Christ. Now that's love!

We need to realize that a covenant with God is extremely powerful and totally sure because God is a God of His Word. The Bible tells us that He holds His Word above His name (Ps. 138:2). He is saying that His promises are even surer than His name, than His very nature as God. God has bound Himself to His Word. The Word tells us that God does what He says He'll do: ***"...in hope of eternal life which God, who cannot lie, promised before time began" (Titus 1:2).*** God couldn't even lie if He wanted to—it's not in His nature. If He promises something, He does it—it's as simple as that! So when we read God's healing promises, such as 1 Pet. 2:24 which says, ***"...by whose stripes you were healed"*** then we can bank on that word. Miracles and healings happen because God has made a sure, loving covenant with His people.

Healing—Getting Started!

"Do You Want to be Made Well?"

That's the question in John 5:6 that Jesus asked of the man with the infirmity for 38 years. In this story people, perhaps from all around the world, have come to the pool of Bethesda—the lame, sick and paralyzed. A healing angel would stir up the waters of the pool and whoever stepped in first was healed of whatever disease or sickness he had. It was "whoever" was healed of "whatever" sickness and disease he had because of the healing anointing that

Woman's ears open in Edmonton, Canada

came with the angel. Jesus knew that this man had been in need for 38 years.

You see, Jesus knows whether you have been waiting for your healing a few months or a few decades. So imagine that suddenly the Lord shows up. It's the day that the Lord is going to heal you! This sick man at the pool has been pressing in, warring and contending. Who knows how many times he has asked for healing and gotten prayer? After 38 years the Lord shows up and says, "Do you want to be made whole?" I know people that think they want to be made whole, but they really don't.

People Who Want to Stay Sick

Let me share an example with you. I was in this meeting in White Horse, Yukon and we met a blind lady who came to the altar every day for prayer saying, "I want to see! I want to see!" She had me pray for her every night—she was so desperate that when she didn't get healed one night, she came back to me and said, "I want you to pray for me again. I want my eyesight. I want to be healed" Every night it was the same. I really didn't have any faith because I had prayed for her so many times and had seen nothing. So I was thinking, "If God wants to He can. I'm just the instrument." I did a courtesy prayer and said, "God come open these blind eyes."

Later, in the middle of that meeting she screamed, "I can see! I can see!" Then, seconds later, as God began to progressively heal her eyesight, she screamed out, "I don't want to see! I am scared! I'm scared! I don't want to see! Take it away!" After being blind from birth, it was so overwhelming that she decided that she didn't want to see after all and tragically, she lost her healing. At first her response to Jesus' question, "Do you want to be made whole?" was "Yes, Yes!" But really she was saying, "I *think* I want to be made whole." With every healing and miracle, comes a responsibility—we need to walk that healing out into an unknown realm that can provoke fear. Before and after every healing, God is calling us out of fear and into faith.

I was in another meeting where we met a lady who was completely deaf without the use of hearing aids. She had scraped together a deposit so that she could buy them and was making monthly payments. She came into one of our healing services as a skeptic when one of her friends said, "It's obvious that there are healings taking place. Go get prayer." The woman really didn't think that anything was going to happen. I laid my hands on her and, no sooner did I say "Jesus," than she screamed and grabbed her ears. "I can hear!" She took her hearing aids off. She was ecstatic; overwhelmed with joy that God was so good to her. "He touched me! It's real! It's happening!" She went home that day healed, carrying her hearing aids.

Later she was watching T.V. when she began to think, "Wait a minute, I just paid a thousand dollars (or whatever it was) for these hearing aids—for the next two years I have to make monthly payments for hearing aids I don't even need because I can hear! Why would God heal me?"

Well, the enemy tormented her with those thoughts for a while—she eventually gave in and lost her hearing. What was this woman's true answer to Jesus' question, "Do you want to be made whole?" Her answer was "No"—she didn't really want to be made whole. She ended up coming back to one of our services and repenting. When she got her heart right with God, He instantly healed her again, while she sat in her seat.

I know people in the church today that really don't want to be made whole because of the responsibility and the price that comes with every healing and miracle. Their lives would have to change. They may have to go back to work. They would have to make many adjustments after adapting to their illness for so many years. Some people begin to enjoy the attention their sickness brings them. No longer can they lean on their illness for their identity, depend on government disability support or find comfort in the sympathy of others. They get so used to the toys and the comforts that come with a life of infirmity that they really don't want to be healed. Whatever the reason, some people just want to stay sick.

The Assurance of Covenant Healing.

In His sovereignty and His love God will heal people whether they are Christians or not, but He doesn't have to. However, God will heal all those who touch Him on covenant. In the ministry of healing, God heals all those who initiate or claim His covenant provision. Others, God only heals on the principle of sovereignty—but sovereignty isn't a guarantee. Sovereignty means God does whatever He pleases; if He decides to heal you in the midst of 1,000 other people, He does it. He reaches down and touches this one, then that one. Those healed out in the crowd give praise for God's blessing, but may still wonder, "Why didn't God touch Chuck or Mary?" Another believer may think: "I've been believing, fasting and praying for healing and then God heals an unbeliever, a skeptic who doesn't even meet the requirements?" Some people think, "If God wants to touch me He can touch me in my seat. I don't have to go up to the front. That's the way it happened for Jack." Why does this happen? The answer is sovereignty.

But God heals all who initiate and lay hold of His covenant provision. Not once when man took the initiative in Scripture and touched Him on the principles of covenant did God say no. Based on the principle of God's covenant, which calls for man to initiate and approach God, God heals all, all the time. There is not one occasion in Jesus' ministry where He ever turned away one person who approached Him for healing. Not one time. But, in His sovereignty, He passed by the sick every day. If we need healing, we can wait, hoping for His sovereign touch to come to us… or we can approach God today. So, do you want to be made whole?

Standing in the Gap

Let's examine this scriptural example of standing before God in someone else's place. ***Mathew 8:13: "Then Jesus said to the centurion, 'Go your way; and as you have believed, so let it be done for you.' And his servant was healed that same hour."*** He loves us so much that He will allow us to stand in the gap for another person and receive prayer for a loved one in another location. Look back at verses 5 and 6 in the same chapter: ***"Now when Jesus had entered Capernaum, a centurion came to Him, pleading with Him, saying, 'Lord, my servant is lying at home paralyzed, dreadfully tormented.'"*** Notice, the sick man was not present; he was in another location. And secondly, we don't know whether he was even a believer. He was the servant of the centurion who was a gentile, an unbeliever, according to the Jews. Did he have faith in healing?

Yet in spite of the fact that the man wasn't at the healing service and was probably an unbeliever, Jesus was immediately willing to go and heal him. He wasn't even asked to come yet, but Jesus was so eager to go. The centurion was still describing the problem and the Lord responds, "Let's take care of it; let's go. I'm on my way. I'll go heal him." And the centurion says, "No, no, wait a minute. I don't want You to come to my house." Then he says to Jesus, ***"But only speak a word, and my servant will be healed" (v. 8).*** Look at Jesus' response in verse 10: ***"Assuredly, I say to you, I have not found such great faith, not even in Israel!"***

So my question is this? What was the great faith and who had the faith

African man who was crippled testifies that Jesus healed him

for the man to be healed? I believe that God can touch and heal an unbeliever in another country even if they don't have faith. Someone else, on the basis of their faith, can carry the sick person through to healing.

The centurion demonstrated his faith in Jesus' authority over sickness by believing that Jesus could just speak the word and it would happen. You see, the centurion was a man who had others under his authority and he believed that Jesus was also a man of authority. Perhaps the centurion had such great faith that he believed that Jesus commanded unseen angels to do His bidding. As a gentile outside of God's covenant, he was able to lay hold of healing for his servant who was in another place through his great faith.

I already told the story about praying for Julie's grandfather who was in a hospital in Pittsburgh with a stroke. What I didn't tell you earlier is that I was struggling to believe for a miracle for a man in another country. I saw the desperation in Julie's eyes and I didn't want to say no so I did a courtesy prayer. I prayed a prayer that sounded like I had faith—it included lots of scriptures, confessions, rebukes, decrees and anything else I could think of.

During the prayer the Lord asked me: "What are you doing?" It can be quite a shock when you're praying and the Lord shows up and asks what you're doing. "I'm praying to You. I'm telling You about the problem, God." Then the Lord said, "What are you going to do about it?" In Scripture, Jesus also said something similar to the disciples. I wonder how they felt when Jesus asked them how much bread they had and then told them to give thousands of people something to eat?

Well, in my situation—before I even had time to answer—I was instantly in the spirit in the hospital room. In my imagination I saw myself lay hands on him and watched as the power of God hit him. He came to believe in Christ because of the faith of a 14-year-old girl in another country who stood in the gap for him. God loved her so much He touched her unbelieving grandfather in another nation.

As you can see, God responds to faith, whether it's the faith of the prayer minister, the sick person or even a loved one who is standing in the gap.

In this last case, it wasn't about the faith of the guy in Pittsburgh, nor was it about my faith. God honored the faith of this one 14-year-old girl laying hold of her covenant rights—that's what got the miracle.

Faith: More than Believing

Mathew 9:28 records the story of two blind men that came to Jesus for a touch. They were just like many people today who come to healing schools, healing conferences and healing meetings. When they came for healing, Jesus asked some questions: ***"Do you want to be made whole?"*** and, ***"Do you believe that I am able to do this?"*** When the two blind men said, ***"Yes, Lord,"*** Jesus replied, ***"According to your faith let it be to you."*** Then they were healed.

Faith Means Action

We need to realize, however, that faith is more than believing. People say, "I believe, I believe, I believe." Yes, they may believe, but they don't do anything with what they believe. Their belief is really just knowledge. Faith requires action. It involves moving. Faith without works is dead.

Scripture shows us that faith is more than believing—it's belief in motion. Look at this example:

> ***"And in Lystra a certain man without strength in his feet was sitting, a cripple from his mother's womb, who had never walked. This man heard Paul speaking. Paul, observing him intently and seeing that he had faith to be healed, said with a loud voice, 'Stand up straight on your feet!' And he leaped and walked" (Acts 14:8-10).***

How do you think Paul knew the crippled man had faith? Do you think he was holding up a big sign that said, "I believe that if the Apostle Paul prays for me right now I will be healed"? Was he flailing his arms and shouting, "Hey Paul, over here I believe God"? Or was it something that Paul saw in the spirit? Scripture tells us that ***"faith is the substance of things hoped for, the evidence of things not seen" (Heb. 12:1).*** So Paul must have seen the substance of the man's faith.

The Lord sometimes allows me to *see* who has faith. I can't detect faith by the color of people's hair, clothing or skin—faith actually has a look, an appearance, which I can see over people. I may say, "That person has faith" and everyone else may look at him and say, "He looks like anyone else. What do you mean he's got faith?" I've been in meetings where I can pick out entire rows of people who have faith to be healed—I'll just know that if I pray for them right then, they will be healed. Now, if I was to ask most people if they had faith, or whether they believed that God would heal them, they would say yes. Very few people are going to say no. However, deep down inside they might be saying, "I hope so," or "I think so" or "Maybe some day."

Paul saw visible faith—probably through the 'discerning of spirits' gift—then he said with a loud voice, ***"Stand up straight on your feet!"*** The man was still crippled when Paul spoke. Many people think that crippled or paralyzed people first receive healing and then decide to walk. That's not how it works. The healing usually occurs as they attempt to get up. It's simultaneous; it's as they go. Faith without works is dead. As people take action and move, or attempt to do something they couldn't do before, the healing happens. In this situation if the man was thinking logically, he could have said, "How can I stand? I haven't used my feet in 25 years." Had he hesitated and thought about what Paul said, he would have remained crippled. The power of God didn't heal his legs before Paul told him to stand. It was simultaneous. As the man tried to move his legs (which could not move), in an instant, in that one impulse, it happened.

The same thing happened to the man with the withered hand. The guy has basically got no arm and Jesus said, "Stretch forth your hand." Imagine what he must have been thinking: "Stretch forth my hand? What hand?" The Lord didn't first recreate his hand and then tell him to stretch it out. He gave the authoritative healing command.

So many people hinder their healing because they don't take action after they've received prayer. Often at healing meetings, after I pray for a large group of people and then tell them to move their body and do something they couldn't do before, perhaps only five people out of a group of 500 actually begin to move. When we ask people later why they didn't move they say, "Because I knew I was still sick—the pain was still there. I didn't feel anything. So why even bother trying to move?"

Many times I have prayed a healing prayer, taking ten minutes to rebuke every demon, sickness and disease? Then a healing anointing comes and I ask people to move their body. More often than not, people just stand there looking back at me. Later they come to me saying, "Todd pray for me. I've got a problem in my back." Then I'll tell them, "You are one of the people I saw out there who wouldn't act in faith to the word the Lord gave me and now you want me to pray for you?" God wants us to act in faith even before we feel anything—sometimes we will not see our healing manifest until we do so.

So much of the church is programmed to think unbelieving thoughts:

"He prayed but I didn't feel anything—nothing changed." So even though the preacher may yell out, "Stand up on your feet," they look at their feet and decide, based on feelings, that they are still crippled. Often they won't even try to stand up. But you see—the miracle is prompted by, or simultaneous with, the action! When Jesus told the crippled man to take up his bed and walk, the healing happened *as* he attempted to move. He heard the word, made the decision to act and then moved to grab his bed. Then the healing manifested.

So many people in the church today just don't understand that faith is more than believing. . Faith involves moving; it's an action—"Stretch out your hand! Get up on your feet! Move your legs! Do something you couldn't do before!" Until you act on the word you won't initiate the release of the healing flow. That is why Paul, in the middle of his sermon, before the guy could even think about it, said, "Stand up on your feet!" Before he could reason it through, he was healed.

Now, not all healing comes that way. But if I can get the cripples moving, the cripples get healed. Action begins to break the unbelieving mindset of always looking at the natural, of focusing on the condition of their body instead of God's power to heal.

People receive healing because they jump up on their feet before their mind says, "I can't walk" However, often, after they start walking, they start thinking about it and then lose their healing. They end up back in their wheelchair because they were thinking about how impossible it is to do what they just did. When they allow their natural mind to kick back in, they come out of faith and they lose the healing. People need to get rid of that natural thinking that leads to unbelief.

Faith Means Expectation

Faith is more than believing; faith is also expectation. The story of the crippled man in Mark 2 is a good example of expectation. This man's friends actually laid him on a mat, climbed up on the house where Jesus was, ripped off the roof and lowered him on the mat. These guys had expectation. Jesus saw their faith so he gave them His attention (Mark 2:5).

In Acts 5, Peter and John came across a man at the Gate Beautiful who had been crippled from birth. The man gave them his attention, expecting to receive something from them. Unlike this man, most of us aren't expecting, we are hoping. Faith is more than hoping —we need to have an expectation working in us to activate healing. What you say you believe is not faith. What you hope for is not faith. Faith arises from what you DO. Faith moves. We have to get that kind of faith.

The story of Lazarus in John 11 also illustrates the difference between hope and faith. The Lord knew Lazarus was going to die but He stayed where He was two more days. Thanks a lot God! An already dark situation gets darker.

Finally, Jesus announces, ***"Lazarus is dead" (Jn. 11:14).*** Then He says, ***"And I am glad for your sakes that I was not there, that you may believe."*** Think about that—Lazarus is dead and Jesus is saying, "Hey, guys, I'm glad for your sakes that I wasn't there, hallelujah—so you will be able to believe." Why? Because faith is not what you believe, it's what you do. Jesus knows what He is doing and what He is about to do. Jesus says Martha, ***"Your brother will rise again."*** Martha responds, ***"I know he will rise again in the resurrection on the last day" (Jn. 11:24).*** She thought she was speaking words of faith when, really, she was speaking out of hope.

So what does Jesus say to Martha's hope statement? He makes a powerful promise to shake her out of the future and bring her into faith for the present. Jesus says, ***"I am the resurrection and the life. He who believes in Me, though he may die, he shall live. And whoever lives and believes in Me shall never die. Do you believe this?" (Jn. 11:25).*** Jesus was talking about "now" but she was thinking "future."

Today, for this same reason, many Christians fail to receive God's healing promises. Christians today make similar statements when we proclaim all the scriptural truth about divine healing. Then they say, "I know that He will heal me one day. I know I will be healed when I get to heaven." They place healing in the future. One day. Out there. When they put the answer way out in the future, really they don't have faith, they have hope.

After Jesus announces that He is the resurrection and the life Martha says, ***"Yes, Lord, I believe that You are the Christ, the Son of God, who is to come into the world" (Jn. 11:27).*** Later, in verse 40, He says to her: ***"Did I not say to you that if you would believe you would see the glory of God?"***

Throughout the passage Jesus is trying to teach her what true faith is. Martha was confusing belief, hope and faith. She believed that Jesus could resurrect her brother. She also believed that Jesus would raise Him in the future, in the last day (this was hope). She didn't interpret that as a "now" word. Martha did not believe that Jesus would raise her brother "now." But faith is action! Faith is now!

Yes, she believed that Jesus was the life, that He would raise the dead and that He was Lord. She had great doctrine and theology; she had a great confession of belief. But she still didn't have faith. Jesus wanted to illumine the true condition of their faith (both for Martha and the disciples). Then He demonstrated His Lordship in the present to draw them into true faith. Jesus raised Lazarus from the dead.

Faith is more than mental assent; it's more than acknowledging that certain statements are true. Faith is acting; it's putting your life or reputation on the line for what you believe. Jesus wanted them to have true faith, which is based on expectation and worked out through action.

Martha and the others were brought to the place where they needed to have faith for the impossible. This situation was so impossible that it would take an absolute miracle. When Jesus demonstrates that He is the God of the impossible, it boosted their faith so that they could believe for a miracle next time they faced an impossible situation. They would know that what is impossible with man is not impossible with God. The next time they faced the same kind of situation, they would have the kind of faith that God was looking for!

Authoritative Commands of Faith

When I first discovered this principle of active faith for healing, I was in a meeting in Rocky Mountain House, Alberta, Canada; I think it was my first year of ministry. I met a girl, about 17 or 18—she was partly crippled with rheumatoid arthritis. The disease was attacking her bones and joints, giving her a lot of chronic, constant pain. "OK, so you need Jesus to touch your body and heal you?" I asked her. "Yes, I need a miracle," she said. "All right then," I said as I prepared to pray for her. Before I could start praying, the Lord spoke to me. "No, don't pray. Tell her what to do." You see—one of our problems in the church today is that we pray for the sick. Praying for the sick is all right, but the Lord really didn't call us to pray for the sick. He commanded us to, ***"heal the sick" (Matt. 10:8; Lk. 9:2).***

Well, in this situation, I heard the Lord say, "Tell her to go up on the platform (which was about six feet off the ground) and jump off onto the gymnasium floor." You should have seen her face. I can still remember the expression of horror to this day. Then I said, "Honey, I'm not going to pray for you to be healed. I'm just going to tell you what to do to get healed." I knew that action and a step of obedience was required of her. It had nothing to do with the prayer or the level of anointing. Again I said, "Get up on the platform. You are going to jump off and land on the floor." She looked at me and grabbed my arm exclaiming, "No, please!" Then she hung onto me like a child grabbing her father before he goes to work, trying to persuade him not to go. I start prying her arms off and said, "Get up there right now. Ushers help me. Get her up on that platform." I had to be firm. "That's right, get up there." Eventually she began walking up the stairs: Everyone in the service was watching, and I begin thinking, "There is going to be a major law suit if she jumps off that platform and she is not healed." She kind of inched her way to the edge and I shouted, "Go! Jump!" She groaned, "Ahhh!" and her face contorted with pain as she jumped. When she hit the ground, she stood and said, "Huh? Wow! Wow! Wow!" She was completely healed! Pain free!

That miracle demonstrates the power of acts of faith. We spend too much time begging God to do what He told us to do! We are trying to get God to cast out the devils He told us to cast them out. We are trying to get God to heal the sick that He told us to heal. He said, ***"Whatever city you enter… heal the sick there" (Lk. 10:8-9).***

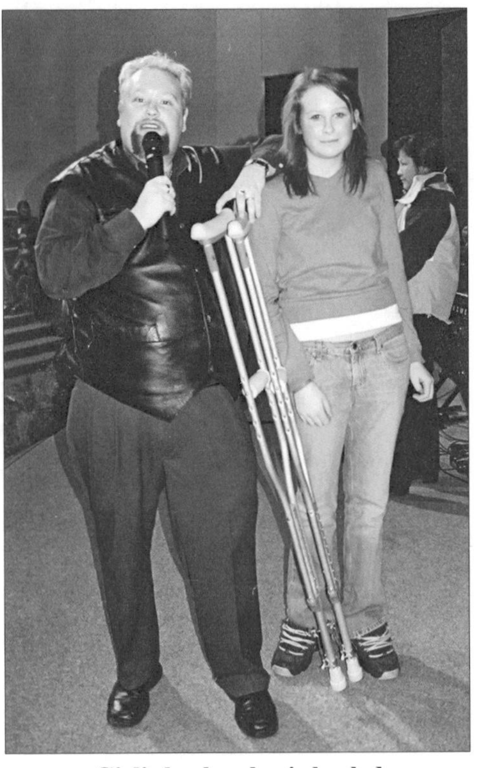

Girl's broken leg is healed

There are times when we need to be like Peter and speak what I call "the authoritative command of healing." We need to act on the commission we already have! ***"Silver and gold I do not have,"*** he said, ***"but what I do have I give you: In the name of Jesus Christ of Nazareth, rise up and walk" (Acts 3:6).*** Now that might sound a little arrogant. However, it's really just a man who knows who he is and what he has in Christ. Even though he offered the crippled man what he had, Peter knew that the healing power he had was a free gift of God's grace.

In the same way, God, in His grace and by His Holy Spirit, has given you the healing word, the healing gift, the healing power and the healing commission. At times, we don't see more healing in the church today because we are praying for God to do what God has called us to do. Sometimes those prayers just won't work until we speak the authoritative command of healing—that's where we tell someone's body what to do in Jesus' name.

Here are some authoritative commands: "Stretch out your hand!" or "I command you, spinal cord, to straighten out in the name of Jesus!" I'm not going to pray, "God, I ask that You would heal the spine." I actually tell the spine, the blind eye or the crippled leg what to do by the authority Jesus has given to me. "Begin to stretch out your leg. That's right—now leg, begin to move, begin to vibrate and begin to feel again. Come on nerve endings, begin to come alive." I actually begin to prophesy to body parts.

Like Peter, it's important that we know we've got something to give. That's just the start. Do you really know you have the healing power of God inside you to give? It's OK for you to act like you know that you have it, because you know that it came from Him and His grace. We're often just too timid. We act in false humility because we don't want to sound too proud or arrogant. However, humility is walking in faith in God's Word, as if we believe in His greatness and in the gifts He's given us. There is no time for false humility. People are dying! God needs reckless people of faith!

Radical Obedience for Healing

Think of all the people of radical faith throughout church history and the unusual acts that God has called them to take. Think of Elijah challenging the prophets of Baal to a trial by fire before the Lord revealed himself as the true God who is Lord of fire and power. Think about Jesus spitting on the blind man's eyes (Mk. 8:23); or yelling at the money changers and driving them out of the temple with a whip (John 2:14-16); or basically calling the pastor's and theologians of the day whitewashed, stinking graves (Matt. 23:27).

Then, in the 20th century, there was Smith Wigglesworth, the radical apostle of faith who would sometimes punch people in the stomach when he prayed for them… and they would be healed! Sometimes God needs a man or woman like that or an aggressive Jack Coe, healing minister, who takes authority over infirmity and commands the crippled person, "Come on! Get up!" God wants radical obedience. Just like Elijah, Jesus or these healing evangelists, God may ask us as Christians to take extreme steps of faith which may be offensive to people. However, if we are obeying God's word to us, we will see miracles. Radical acts of faith can sometimes look arrogant but God will always honor them—He will reveal himself as a miracle-working God.

Once I was in a meeting praying for cripples all night, yet no one was being healed. "What's going on God?" I asked. "I know that You can heal cripples. I've seen You do it in the past." Then the Lord spoke something that challenged my thinking. "Listen Todd, faith is more than believing." You see, I knew that God could heal based on what I've seen in the past. However, I had prayed for so many people without seeing any results that I was now just praying, hoping He would do it again, while really struggling to believe that He actually would. "Todd it's faith that gets the answer," said the Lord. "What do You mean 'its faith?'" I asked, "I'm praying the prayer! I'm praying it in faith!" Then God challenged me again. "No, I need some action like, 'Stretch forth your hand' or 'Take up your bed and walk.' Faith is action." So I asked

Him, "Well, what do You want me to do God?" His reply shocked me. "Grab that cripple's legs (in front of 50,000 people) and bang them up and down on the platform like a baseball bat—both legs." I said, "God, that seems so insensitive!" So I grabbed this cripple's legs and started banging them up and down like baseball bats. I obeyed; I acted in faith. Guess what happened? The crippled legs came alive and the person was healed!

In African crusades, sometimes the Holy Spirit tells me to say, "If you are crippled and need a miracle or a healing and you are listening to me over the radio, reach out and touch your radio right now." That's it—that simple. When they respond, they are healed. Their healing does not come because of the prayer. The power of God doesn't come on them first. When they act in obedience then they are healed. They come to the crusade the next night and share what happened. I am amazed at how easily it works. "God if I could just get people in America to move when I ask them."

Forgiveness and Healing

In God's eyes, forgiveness and healing are the same thing. Notice how the psalmist speaks of these two benefits from God in the same breath: ***"Bless the Lord, O my soul, and forget not all His benefits: who forgives all your iniquities, who heals all your diseases" (Ps. 103:3).*** The prophet Isaiah also prophesies about a day in the church when the inhabitants of the land would say, "I am not sick." Isaiah's prophecy came 800 years before the cross of Calvary and Jesus' redemptive, healing work. Look at his divinely inspired words: ***"And the inhabitant will not say, 'I am sick'; the people who dwell in it will be forgiven their iniquity" (Is. 33:24).*** I believe that Isaiah was talking about the day when Jesus went to the cross—from that day on every inhabitant in the land was able to say, "I am not sick." Jesus' sacrifice gave us this freedom from sickness and the ability to say, "I have been forgiven of my iniquity." Christians don't see forgiveness and healing (sin and sickness) as the same thing. We still see sickness and disease in the church today because we fail to look at sin and sickness through God's eyes.

Let's examine what the book of James says about this subject.

> ***"And the prayer of faith will save the sick, and the Lord will raise him up. And if he has committed sins, he will be forgiven. Confess your trespasses to one another, and pray for one another, that you may be healed" (Jas. 5:15-16).***

This is wild! Think about it—James is saying that the prayer of faith will save and raise up a sick person as well as grant him forgiveness of sins. Wait a minute! The guy gets healed of cancer and simultaneously, if he has sinned, the Lord will forgive him? Yes, that's what James is saying. This guy hasn't even asked for forgiveness of sin. But you see, because the Lord sees the forgiveness of sin and the healing of sickness as the same thing, the Lord will forgive you at the same time He heals you, even if you didn't ask the Lord to forgive you of your sin.

When you remove sickness and disease from the picture, sin is removed as well. There is no sickness or disease without sin. Romans 8:2 tells us that the Spirit of life in Christ Jesus sets us free from the law of sin and death. Sin became the door on earth for sickness and death. Sickness did not exist until sin came into the world. Sin is the door for disease. Sin is the door for poverty and lack. Sin is both spiritual and natural. The forgiveness of sin brings the healing and resurrection of people's dead spirits. Yes, the healing of sickness and disease is the healing and salvation of the physical part of your body. It's the same thing—this is the power of *Sozo*—salvation for the whole man.

It's vital that you have a deep heart revelation of these scriptural truths about God's desire for your complete wholeness—then you can begin to walk in faith to receive this inheritance. God wants you to be convinced that He desires to heal all, all the time. Faith will rise when you quit praying, "Lord if it be your will," and when you no longer need to figure out at the altar, if you pray for the sick, whether they will be healed. You will no longer pray a courtesy prayer while inside you're wondering if anything is really going to happen. Questions like: "Am I really called to this?" or "Should I really be doing this or should I leave it for Todd and Benny?" will no longer plague your mind.

When I first purposed in my heart that God was going to use me in the healing ministry, I went on a fast and spent weeks meditating on these truths. I did nothing else but meditate on these truths until I came to the place where I was absolutely convinced that there was no room for anything else in Scripture other than "all, all the time." It took time to really believe that. Eventually I also got the revelation that healing and forgiveness go together.

Throughout Scripture, even in the ministry of Jesus, God treats healing and the forgiveness of sin as if they were the same. A story in the gospel of Mark gives us a vivid example of this:

> ***"When Jesus saw their faith, He said to the paralytic, 'Son, your sins are forgiven you.' And some of the scribes were sitting there and reasoning in their hearts, 'Why does this Man speak blasphemies like this? Who can forgive sins but***

> ***God alone?' But immediately, when Jesus perceived in His spirit that they reasoned thus within themselves, He said to them, 'Why do you reason about these things in your hearts? Which is easier, to say to the paralytic, 'Your sins are forgiven you,' or to say, 'Arise, take up your bed and walk'? But that you may know that the Son of Man has power on earth to forgive sins--He said to the paralytic, 'I say to you, 'Arise, take up your bed, and go to your house'" (Mark 2:5-11).***

In this story four men carried the paralytic to Jesus but couldn't get past the crowd. So they uncovered the roof of the house where Jesus was. When they lowered the man down on a bed, Jesus "saw their faith" and said, "Son, your sins are forgiven you." Next, He healed the paralyzed man. The question is this: was it the sick man's faith combined with the other four or was it really the faith of the man's friends that Jesus recognized?

I can just imagine the guy yelling and screaming when they put him on the mat. When they carried him to the meeting and later when they lowered him through the roof. He was probably saying, "I don't want to go through the roof! Don't lower me through the roof!" But what could he do—he's totally paralyzed? His friends were probably saying: "We've got enough faith for you too. You are going in!" I can see the four guys telling the paralytic stories of all the people that had been healed in Jesus' ministry, trying to build his faith. When the men finally lowered their friend into the house in the middle of Jesus' sermon, the Lord said, "Son, your sins are forgiven you." Wait a minute. Perhaps the paralyzed man thought, "What does the forgiveness of my sin have to do with my need for healing?" The Scribes and Pharisees were astounded by these words because only God had the power to forgive sins. What they were really saying is: "You are not God. It's blasphemy for You to forgive sin."

However, unlike many Christians today, the Jewish people, Pharisees and Sadducees included, did not struggle with two aspects of God's redemptive nature. They believed that the Lord is both a God of forgiveness and a God of healing, according to Psalm 103:2-3: ***"Bless the LORD, O my soul, and forget not all His benefits: Who forgives all your iniquities, who heals all your diseases..."*** He forgives what? All our sins. Only God forgives sins. The religious leaders knew this and so they were thinking: "You don't have power on the earth to forgive sin because You are not God—this is blasphemy. Who are You to say, 'Son, your sins are forgiven You.'" On the other hand, the crippled guy is thinking, "What does the forgiveness of sin have to do with my healing?"

The other truth these people knew about God was, "He heals all my diseases." You see, they knew that God is Jehovah Rapha as demonstrated in Exodus 15 when the Israelites came up from Egypt and not one was sick, week or feeble. They believed at least these two absolutes about God: He forgives; He heals. You didn't have to preach divine healing to them. If you were to say, "God heals today", they would have said, "Duh! Of course He does! We know that! We understand the Passover and the freedom from sin, death and destruction that came through the sacrifice of the lamb. We celebrate that every year!" It's just in the church today that we don't have a full revelation of these truths!

Jesus eventually healed the paralyzed man after asking them, ***"Which is easier, to say to the paralytic, 'Your sins are forgiven you,' or to say, 'Arise, take up your bed and walk'?"*** With this statement and one act of healing, Jesus was proving, not only His power to heal, but His power to forgive, and consequently, He was demonstrating to the people that He was God. In this case, Christ's words and healing act were a strong rebuke to the religious leaders and a powerful testimony of His deity.

Touching God's Promise

I want to share three biblical stories with you of individuals who received divine healing because they touched God on covenant.

The Woman With an Issue of Blood

Scripture tells a powerful story about a woman with an issue of blood. Let's examine the passage to find some key reasons why she received her healing.

> ***"Now a certain woman had a flow of blood for twelve years, and had suffered many things from many physicians. She had spent all that she had and was no better, but rather grew worse. When she heard about Jesus, she came behind Him in the crowd and touched His garment. For she said, 'If only I may touch His clothes, I shall be made well.' Immediately the fountain of her blood was dried up, and she felt in her body that she was healed of the affliction. And Jesus, immediately knowing in Himself that power had gone out of Him, turned around in the crowd and said, 'Who touched My clothes?' But His disciples said to Him, 'You***

see the multitude thronging You, and You say, 'Who touched My clothes?'" (Mark 5:25-30).

What does the healing anointing feel like? The woman actually felt healing in her body. There was something so distinctive about the touch that she felt power and knew she was healed.

Jesus had hundreds, maybe thousands, of people pressing in at the same time. Everybody was pulling and grabbing—it was like being in the mosh pit of a rock concert where everyone is crammed in so tight that you can barely move. It's in this place that Jesus felt power flowing out of Him. Incredible! He actually turned around, with a huge crowd pressing in and asked who touched Him. His disciples are astounded at Jesus' question. "We are in a throng! Do You know how many people must have touched You in the last five minutes? What do You mean who touched You? It's impossible to know."

The woman, trembling with fear, came and fell before Him and told Him her story. Then He said to her, "Daughter, your faith has made you well. Go and be healed of your affliction." So it was the woman's faith that drew the Lord's healing power into her body.

But what kind of faith did the woman have? Was it faith in Jehovah Rapha? Was it her desperate faith for healing? Or was it something more? Besides the woman's desperation to press through the crowd and her confession that she would be healed if she touched Jesus' garment, I believe she was healed because of saving faith.

"Why saving faith Todd?" you may ask. First let's look at the context of this Scripture. Under Jewish law, only the high priest could enter the presence of God, the holy of holies. He would enter that place, only once a year, to offer a sacrifice to make atonement for the people's sins. The high priest wore a special garment that God had prescribed to Moses in Exodus. No other Jew would wear this garment. The hem was very significant. Attached to the high priest's garment, on the hem, were tassels, bells and pomegranates representing the law, the judgments and promises of God. God's people knew that Scripture spoke of the hem of God's garment and the authority it represented.

It was the hem of Jesus' garment; the hem of the Great High Priest, that the woman touched. She risked her life by being seen out in public with her physical condition—the legal penalty for an unclean woman with an issue of blood coming into the camp was death. She also risked being trampled to death by getting down on all fours in the midst of the pressing crowd to reach for the hem of His garment. Why didn't she just grab His shoulder? Why didn't she just push her hand through and grab the small of His back? Why didn't she just jump up and touch Jesus' head? Why did she go for the hem of His garment?

By reaching out in faith for Jesus' hem, I believe, she was acknowledging

Jesus as her great high priest who had atoned for her sins once and for all. She was acknowledging the authority of God's law and His promises. "I believe that You are God in the flesh," she was saying, "Behold the Lamb of God who takes away the sin of the world. I believe that You are the Messiah, the High Priest of Israel." By this one act, the woman was recognizing, with the eyes of faith, that Jesus was the high priest of her forgiveness, cleansing and healing. I believe it was THIS kind of saving faith that caused Jesus to turn around and tell the woman that her faith had made her well. It wasn't her desperation; it wasn't her pressing through or the faith of her verbal confession. Although, all those acts were important, I believe it was her act of faith and humility in reaching out to touch the hem of His garment that brought her healing.

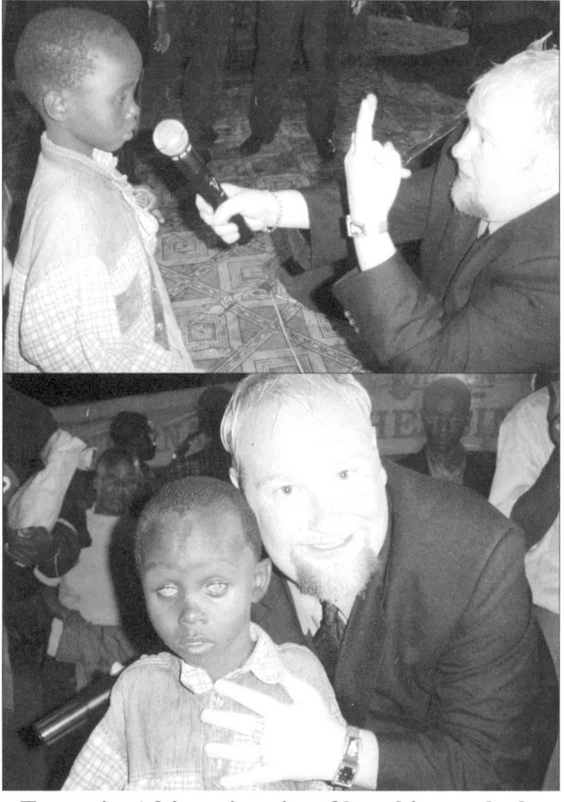

Tanzania, Africa—in spite of how his eyes look, blind boy now sees. It's a wonder!

Blind Bartimaeus

Now let's look at another story which illustrates the power of laying hold of covenant:

> ***"Now they came to Jericho. As He went out of Jericho with His disciples and a great multitude, blind Bartimaeus, the son of Timaeus, sat by the road begging. And when he heard that it was Jesus of Nazareth, he began to cry out and say, 'Jesus, Son of David, have mercy on me!' Then many warned him to be quiet; but he cried out all the more, 'Son of David, have mercy on me!' So Jesus stood still and commanded him to be called. Then they called the blind***

> ***man, saying to him, 'Be of good cheer. Rise, He is calling you.' And throwing aside his garment, he rose and came to Jesus. So Jesus answered and said to him, 'What do you want Me to do for you?' The blind man said to Him, 'Rabboni, that I may receive my sight.' Then Jesus said to him, 'Go your way; your faith has made you well.' And immediately he received his sight and followed Jesus on the road" (Mark 10:46-52).***

How was the faith of blind Bartimaeus released? Could it have been through his desperate cries for help even when people told him to be quiet? I believe there was another factor that gave him the right to be healed. (I call it the right to receive healing.)

Let's look at the story again. The blind man had heard about the healings that took place in Jesus' ministry and knew that He was passing by. It is important to note that the blind man called Jesus "Son of David." He didn't address Jesus as Jehovah Rapha (the God who heals). Instead, he used Jesus' messianic title. He used the name that spoke of Jesus as Savior, Messiah and Christ.

You see, what the rest of the people in Israel weren't willing to do was recognize that Jesus is the Son of David, because that title, Son of David, belonged to the coming Messiah. They didn't believe that the messiah had come yet.

Perhaps the blind man received even more than his healing. Remember that healing and forgiveness are one and the same. Could it be that by crying to the Messiah for mercy Bartimaeus also received forgiveness? He acknowledged Jesus as Messiah and Savior first and then asked for mercy—mercy from the Messiah, the One who saves. Although the blind man probably understood God as Jehovah Rapha, the healer, according to Exodus 15:26, he knew he needed something more than healing: "I need him to be merciful because of my sin. What good is the healing of my sickness without the forgiveness of my disease?"

I believe that this attitude was what released the blind man's healing. Now how do I know that he received salvation as well? Well, remember that blind Bartimaeus threw off his garment when he came to the Lord? Now why would he do that? In those days the Roman government actually issued a begging cloak which allowed certain people to legally ask for alms. That cloak let the people know that the wearers were really blind or disabled and that they weren't con-artists. That cloak gave beggars their identity—often when people saw it they would have mercy and give alms. So, for Bartimaeus, his garment was his identity--it's who he was. He would have been recognized in the city by his cloak. The first thing the blind man did when Jesus called him was throw off his cloak.

I believe he was saying, "I don't need this anymore—this represents the old man. The old things have passed away, all things have become new. I'm going to get rid of this thing because it's about yesterday. It's no longer who I am because Jesus has heard my cry. Bartimaeus knew that something more than a healing miracle was happening to him. When he threw off his garment, it was as if he was casting off the old man even before he received his eyesight. He knew that something had changed in his heart first.

A Gentile Woman's Faith

In conclusion, let's look at the story of the gentile woman with great faith as documented in the gospel of Mathew:

> ***"Then Jesus went out from there and departed to the region of Tyre and Sidon. And behold, a woman of Canaan came from that region and cried out to Him, saying, 'Have mercy on me, O Lord, Son of David! My daughter is severely demon-possessed.' But He answered her not a word. And His disciples came and urged Him, saying, 'Send her away, for she cries out after us.' But He answered and said, 'I was not sent except to the lost sheep of the house of Israel.' Then she came and worshiped Him, saying, 'Lord, help me!' But He answered and said, 'It is not good to take the children's bread and throw it to the little dogs.' And she said, 'Yes, Lord, yet even the little dogs eat the crumbs which fall from their masters' table.' Then Jesus answered and said to her, 'O woman, great is your faith! Let it be to you as you desire.' And her daughter was healed from that very hour" (Matt. 15:21–28).***

Jesus said that it wasn't right for Him to take the children's bread and give it to the gentiles, those outside God's covenant. In Scripture bread represents healing and deliverance. Bread also represents life, the Word and God's presence. In this particular Scripture, Jesus is speaking of the bread of deliverance—healing for the demon-possessed. Only God's covenant children of promise, the Israelites had a right to the bread of healing and deliverance. In the eyes of the Jews, the gentiles were unbelievers outside of relationship with God; they were outcasts who were as lowly as dogs, animals that needed to beg for scraps.

In a similar way, in the church today, we are begging for crumbs because we don't have a revelation of our covenant rights and the blessings Christ has provided for us. This same tragedy is illustrated in the parable of the prodigal son. The younger son comes home after living a sinful lifestyle for years. He's backslidden. When he arrives the father gives him a ring, a new robe and a huge feast. Dad kills the fattened calf and throws a big, joyful celebration—a type of renewal party. He's been out there in the world living a wasteful life, yet the father welcomes him with open arms. Despite this younger son's sinful past, he still had the right to the blessings of a covenant son.

However, I want to highlight the response of the older son. After watching how his younger brother was treated, he responded with angry words something like this: "All these years I've served you and what have you done for me? I've been in the ministry twenty years (or I've served faithfully in church) and not once have I turned my back, not once have I backslidden. Yet he gets to party; he gets the favor; he gets the best robe and the ring." You remember the story? It's the older brother syndrome—he didn't have a revelation of the father's love. When the father heard his older son's jealous words, he responds something like this: "Listen, all I have in my kingdom has been yours. You could have had a party any time you wanted. Didn't you know that you had access to everything every day? It was always there for the taking."

You see, that's just like it is in the church today. God's people are destroyed for lack of knowledge. We are begging for the crumbs of what is already ours or we are saying, "Lord, I'm not good enough." On the other hand, some are saying, "Lord, now I'm worthy because I haven't sinned for a week" or, "I recently fasted" or, "I went to the healing school." But the Lord is saying, "It's all there—the blessings are all free! You don't have to earn them. Everything in my kingdom is yours! Didn't you know?" You can just see the father in the Bible story totally astonished that the older son didn't even know he had access to everything. The son could have thrown parties every day if he wanted to, just because he was a son.

However, in the case of the Samaritan woman, even though she was not part of the covenant of blessing, she still believed that the Father had lots of blessings to go around. She wasn't offended at being called a dog. Her response was something like this: "Yes Lord, I have no rights. I am not in covenant. I have no relationship. It's not mine. I know that I don't meet the requirements—it belongs to the Jews. I have no claim on this thing. You are right. I am a sinner." Yet, she still had faith for her daughter's healing. She said, "I'll take the crumbs that fall from the Master's table." Then Jesus says, "Oh woman, great is your faith!"

What was so great about her faith? Did she show faith by showing desperation and persistence for her daughter's freedom even when others urged her to go away? Or was her great faith revealed some other way? I'll tell you what I believe was so great about her faith. Even when God's children of promise, who had a right to the bread of healing, wouldn't acknowledge who Jesus was, this gentile woman called Him the Son of David. While most Jews would not call Jesus the Christ, the Messiah, she did. She said, "Son of David have mercy on me!" Then, when Jesus pointed out that she was not part of the covenant of the Messiah, she said, "Yes Lord, I am a sinner outside of covenant relationship. I don't have the right to claim healing, but I will eat the crumbs that fall from the Master's table. You are the Master; you are the Lord." What kind of faith was that? Saving faith!

Blind Bartimaeus demonstrated the same kind of faith. Besides just crying out all the more, he acted in faith that old things had passed away: "This cloak is my identity. I don't need this anymore. I know I am not healed yet, but something has changed in my heart already because I have the attention of the Son of David. I need forgiveness of sins before I receive my healing." The woman with the issue of blood had the same kind of faith. Everyone else was pressing in and touching Jesus when this woman said, "I need to touch the hem of His garment." She knew enough to go for the hem, the area of the high priest's robe which symbolized the law and promises. You see, all three of these people of faith found something more than Jehovah Rapha; they found the Savior of their soul first. And the Savior quickly acknowledged their faith. In the moment that they came into faith in Christ, they received *Sozo*, complete salvation for their spirit, soul and body. For each of these three people, all the benefits of this multi-faceted salvation were received simultaneously.

Now here's the message, the bottom line. You may have been saved 20 years, yet you are still not healed. You need to get the revelation that this complete covenant salvation of body, soul and spirit is yours. When we minister to others, this is the full salvation blessing we need to offer to people before they come to know Christ. Then, at the moment of salvation, they can receive complete wholeness and healing. I preach this message in Africa and India—then, at the moment the lost ask Jesus to come into their heart, their blind eyes see, their deaf ears hear and their crippled bodies are restored.

Calvary's Covenant

Let's briefly examine two scriptures which clearly speak of the healing provision of the new covenant which Jesus paid for at Calvary. First, in the book of Isaiah, the prophet speaks of the healing provision that would come through Jesus.

"But He was wounded for our transgressions, He was bruised for our iniquities; the chastisement for our peace was upon Him, and by His stripes we are healed" (Is. 53:5).

Isaiah, speaking of the Christ, the Suffering Servant, speaks in the present tense saying, ***"By His stripes we are healed."*** Then, again, in the New Testament, Peter writes about the healing provision of Christ, this time in the past tense.

"...who Himself bore our sins in His own body on the tree, that we, having died to sins, might live for righteousness—by whose stripes you were healed" (1 Pet. 2:24).

Yes, many years ago, at Calvary, your sins were forgiven and your disease was healed. If you've already found the forgiveness of sins through Jesus Christ, then you can also believe for your disease to disappear in His name. The woman with the issue of blood got down and humbled herself before Jesus, the great High Priest. She honored the law and trusted that He would keep His promise. We can also place our trust in Jesus as priest, the One who came to forgive us and make us whole in every way.

I pray that each one of you reading this would receive a deep revelation of the Father's love and His passionate desire to give you the children's bread—salvation, healing, deliverance and all of Heaven's abundant provision. The Devil has lied to us all these years. Religion has lied to us all these years—it has tried to rob us of our blessings in Christ. So in faith today, let's take what is ours in Jesus' name. I also pray that the Lord would set us all free from the older brother syndrome, from the servant mentality. Let's begin to walk in the revelation that we are sons, not servants, children, not slaves. We are branches grafted into the vine, we need to relax and receive all the sap, strength and blessing, so we can produce fruit. As we abide in Christ, we will receive the abundant supply of heaven and be very fruitful. That's what soaking and waiting in His presence is all about—it's receiving the sap, the life of Christ. We just receive; it's God's job to make it happen.

So many people in the church today are trying to make it happen—they're desperately trying to get the blessings of God. Some of you will be healed by just lying two hours a day in His love and learning to receive; it won't come by working, fasting, confessing, repenting or getting everything clean and in order in your life. All you need to do is say, "Here I am, all messed up, lying in Your presence everyday for the next week, receiving Your sap, Your life."

Here is my challenge to you... be a branch! You don't have to do anything. Just lie there and receive sap from Jesus. People sometimes ask, "Have you ever felt guilty for receiving the Lord's presence?" My answer is "no" because I've realized that God loves for me to wait on Him and to receive His love and blessings.

I once had a three month season of 4 to12 hours a day of dedicated branch time. At first I actually started repenting because I wasn't "doing" anything during the actual prayer time. I felt as if I wasn't giving anything to the Lord. "I'm just being here, taking up space," I said. "That's what I want," the Lord would respond. "You mean I don't have to intercede? I don't have to spend time in praise, praying in tongues or reading the Word? I don't have to do anything but rest in Your presence and enjoy it?" To my surprise He said, "Go ahead, it's free. Just lie there—be a branch and receive My love."

As you've been reading, I believe the Lord has been releasing to you the grace to just receive His love and blessings, without work and without striving. Now continue to receive—let His covenant blessings flow in and through your life. Now pray with me:

> *"Father, thank You for Your covenant promises of forgiveness and healing through my great high priest, Jesus. Please continue speaking to me about Your promises. I know Your Word says that You always keep Your words for those who believe in them. Lord, help me to take action upon my belief in Your Word. I ask that You would build unshakable faith into my life and stir up a passionate desire to reach out and take hold of the miracles You have for me. Yes Lord, I expect Your miracles in my life. Father, help me to receive Your love and your promises for me. Also, give me the boldness to exercise my faith, standing in the gap for the healing of others. Today I choose to put feet to my faith and action to my belief in Your Word. Amen."*

Chapter Six

Thirty Reasons Why Miracles Happen

I will continue to build on the truths of divine healing in this chapter. God wants to establish faith in the power of the atonement in His people today so that we will see the manifestation of God's desire for all of His people to walk in divine health and to minister complete healing to others.

God's Word gives us many reasons why He has healed and will still heal today. I believe that through this teaching, you will be equipped further to release healing. You will also receive an impartation of faith and anointing to destroy the works of the Devil in people's bodies just like Jesus did.

Here are the 30 reasons why miracles happen:

1. God's Love

The number one reason miracles happen is the Father's heart of love for people. It was love that motivated Jesus' ministry: "***And when Jesus went out He saw a great multitude; and He was moved with compassion for them, and healed their sick" (Matt. 14:14).*** The word "compassion" in this verse speaks of pity, tender mercies and the feeling of affection deep down in the bowels. The tender mercies, or the pity of God, moved Him to heal people. Everything in the kingdom works by love. You can have faith, power and anointing, but they will be of no lasting value unless they are motivated by love. Scripture tells us that faith works by love (Gal. 5:6).

At times I've sensed that the manifestation of healing was hindered because I didn't have feelings of affection during prayer ministry—I was too removed from the situation when I prayed. Each person had become just another number, just another case of sickness and death. As callous as that may sound, when you're ministering to thousands around the world, it's easy to become hardened unless you trust the Lord to keep your heart tender and loving. For instance, in one crusade, we'll sometimes see 150 deaf mutes hear and speak for the first time. They're all deaf mutes. It's difficult in these situations to keep a compassionate heart engaged with the people and not to fall into a "just another deaf ear" mentality.

God wants us, like Jesus, to pray for every individual with compassion, with the revelation that he or she is dearly loved by a God who heals. We can't start thinking of people as just numbers, as "one of those 200 that got healed tonight." He wants us to feel their pain, to cry out for their healing and to rejoice with them when they are healed. I need affection and compassion, something that moves deep within my bowels for each one. When I am driven by love I see a greater manifestation of healing. When I am touched by people's infirmity then God's power increases.

Many people are just motivated by faith or truth. They say, "The Bible says it and I believe it. I'm a man of the Word and so that's it! I've got faith in God's power so I just have to lay hands on the sick and they'll recover. That's the Word and that's all I need." Yes, that kind of reckless faith is good, but if we don't have mercy fueling our faith and grace oiling our ministry, then God's healing power will not flow freely through us. Faith works through love.

All of God's covenants with man, including our healing covenant, have been fueled by love. In Genesis, God's covenant of blessing with Abraham was motivated by the love of His love. That is the main theological reason that God heals.

The Father's loving desire, expressed through the Abrahamic covenant thousands of years ago, now blesses us as 21st century believers with salvation, deliverance, prosperity and healing. Today, under the New Covenant, we can receive the blessing of Abraham because we have been redeemed from the curse of the law (Gal. 3:13-14). The curse of the law (Deut. 28), which includes sin, sickness, disease and poverty, no longer has power over us as God's children. Through Christ, we have received the blessing of Abraham. Later in the book we'll examine, in detail, all the blessings of Abraham. And don't forget, no matter what we're discussing, the fingerprint of God's love is on every reason we will study.

2. God Keeps His Covenants!

As mentioned in the chapter called Touching God on Covenant, we see how extremely powerful and totally sure God's covenant is because God is a God of His word. The Bible tells us that His promises are even surer than His name, than His very nature as God. Therefore, if He promises something, He does it—it's as simple as that! God's promise of healing, ***"…by whose stripes you were healed" (1 Peter 2:24)***, is a sure thing we can stand on. You can refer back to chapter five to remind yourself about God's nature as a covenant keeper.

3. God Wills It

Miracles also happen just because God wills it. That's a pretty good reason—the willingness of Jesus. He wants to heal. We don't have to jump through all the healing hoops and beg. God wills it. I mean, who doesn't know that He can heal? He's all powerful—of course He can. Christians today don't even struggle too much with the question of whether God is willing to heal. The question we grapple with is this: "Is God willing to heal **me**?" Most of us know that God can heal and wants to heal others, but we must come to the revelation, like the leper in the gospel of Matthew, that God really wants to heal us. The leprous man says, ***"Lord, if You are willing, You can make me clean" (Matt. 8:2).*** How did Jesus respond? The Bible tells us that He reached out and touched the man saying, "I am willing. Be cleansed."

We already talked about the centurion, whose servant was dreadfully tormented in another city. Even though this Roman centurion was a gentile outside of God's covenant, he had confidence in Jesus' ability and desire to heal his servant. Immediately after the centurion described his servant's condition, Jesus said, ***"I'll come and heal him" (Matt. 8:7).*** The centurion hadn't even asked Jesus to heal; he was still stating his case. How would you like that? You are about to make your request when the answer comes.

It's like that story of the disciples who are praying for God to release Peter from prison. Someone knocks at the door, Rhoda answers—it's Peter! The answer was so immediate they didn't even believe Rhoda's report. That's a picture of many Christians' prayer lives—if God ever did bring the answer while they were still asking, they might not believe it either.

Thousands are saved, healed and delivered at our crusades in Africa

Now back to the centurion. This gentile didn't have the scriptures or revelation the Jews had. Yet, when he came to Jesus he had total confidence in the answer the Lord would give. The centurion had barely finished telling his story, when the Lord said, "I want to heal him" and they were on their way to his house. Suddenly the centurion stopped the Lord and said something like, "Wait a minute. Lord, I'm not worthy for You to come under my roof." Next, the man spoke those powerful words of faith, "But only speak a word, and my servant will be healed."

Notice how eager Jesus was to heal the man's servant even before he asked. Jesus is just as willing to heal us—let's get that revelation of His goodness and His desire to heal. He is saying to each of us, "My son, my daughter—I am willing. Be made whole."

4. Mass Evangelism

The fourth reason why you can expect miracles and healing in your ministry is for the sake of mass evangelism. Some Christians may say, "Todd, why do you make such a big deal of divine healing? It's just one part of the gospel. You make it sound like healing is the whole gospel and there's nothing else." I emphasize healing so much because it is the number one tool for mass evangelism and lost souls are the passion of God's heart.

Others state, "Christianity has matured since the time of the first century church. We are not as dark and sinful today. They needed to see miracles back then because they didn't know about Jesus' power and deity and that He is a God who conquers the grave. They needed to know that! But we all know that today!"

That argument just doesn't make sense to me. We have a lot of powerless religion today—the Bible calls it a "form of godliness" that denies the power (2 Tim. 3:5). But we don't have as much demonstration of the Spirit as we need. The world is crying out, "Don't tell me God is real. Show me!"

Look at the impact of Jesus' miracles: ***"Then a great multitude followed Him, because they saw His signs which He performed on those who were diseased" (Jn. 6:2).*** That's it! God's power still draws people to Jesus today. I've gone to Africa and there were only 500 people at one of our first crusades. I'd say, "Oh God, 500 people! I wanted to reach a lot more." A few miracles happen and the next night we'd have 5,000!

Think about it. How did Jesus reach the multitudes all over the nation of Israel with the good news? Scripture tells us that He healed all kinds of sickness and disease and ***"… <u>then</u> His fame went throughout all Syria" (Matt. 4:24).*** When the people heard about Jesus' healing ministry: ***"…they***

brought to Him all sick people who were afflicted with various diseases and torments, and those who were demon-possessed, epileptics, and paralytics; and He healed them" (Matt. 4:24). Look at the result of these powerful healings: ***"Great multitudes followed Him!"*** That's it! There it is. Great multitudes followed Him. Why? He healed them! That's the way to reach unbelievers and to get their attention!

If there was no other reason for healing and miracles today except for mass evangelism, that's enough. That is why we need a greater anointing for healings and miracles. Forget all the theological stuff. If God healed today, not because of love, not because of His covenant or because of the atonement—if He only healed to reach the lost, that is all we should need.

Think of the story, in Acts 4, of the crippled man at the Gate Beautiful who gets healed. The Pharisees take counsel among themselves to decide what to do about Peter and John who had healed the man. The Pharisees were bewildered: ***"What shall we do to these men for indeed a notable miracle has been done through them, and it is evident to all who dwell in Jerusalem?. Everybody in the city knows, and we can not deny it" (Acts 4:16).*** Even these Jewish leaders recognized the powerful influence that the miraculous could have.

We saw this same impact of God's power in India. People ran to the altars every night to come to Jesus as they saw the healing miracles. Almost 11,000 Hindus and Muslims made commitments to Christ during that crusade. Even when we left, people kept getting healed. Some people would wake up healed a week later. I'm not talking about headaches, I'm talking about blind and crippled people who would just wake up healed.

In response to the power of the *Sozo* word of God, two men, completely blind from birth, who didn't even get prayer, were totally healed during the preaching. Days later they walked into a village where they were known as "the two blind men." People were amazed at their testimony of God's healing power. They saw a divine opportunity and said, "Let's plant a church." They planted a church and had 200 members the next day! Since then the church has grown by hundreds. Isn't that amazing! That's the evangelistic power of healing and miracles.

5. Demonstration of Deity

The healing power of God provides convincing proof of God's deity--it proves that He is God. Even Moses understood this truth. Remember when God basically told Moses in Exodus 33–34: "I'm not going with you. You take the people into the Promised Land. I'll send My angel with you, but I'm not going." Then Moses said, ***"If Your Presence does not go with us, do not bring us up from here. For how then will it be known that Your people and I have found grace in Your sight, except You go with us?" (Ex. 33: 15-16).***

Moses is saying that they are not going if God doesn't go with them because if God's glory doesn't go with them, they lose their distinction as God's people. Without God's presence, God's people are no different than the people of any other religion. What makes Christianity different? It's miracles! You take away the miracle-working power of God and Christianity is just another religion. What makes God, *God* other than the demonstration of His deity?

When I went to Africa for the first time, I needed a miracle more than ever before. The organizers told me when we got there: "Oh Todd, because we have advertised that miracles happen in your meetings, if they don't happen this week, they might kill you." I am serious! They laughed about it. I said, "Wait a minute. You're joking, right?" They said, "Well, we won't kill you. But some of the people might because they are tired of big ministries coming in with their big money and putting up their 'big miracle' ads and using the word "miracle," "prophetic" and "blessing" to get crowds as if it's magic. If it's not genuine they will stone you because you are a false prophet."

They were not talking about the Christians turning violent, but the Hindus and the Muslims who travel five days through the bush to bring their sick kids to a crusade advertising, "Bring your sick kids—they will be healed." These people are hungry. All they've heard is 'Healing, Miracles, Crusade and Evangelist.' They don't know that it may not be for them, especially since they heard "Miracles will happen!" The organizers said, "They've actually chased guys out of the city because nothing happened." I was stunned: "Wow! I need some miracles!" But God was faithful to pour out His power with healings and miracles that first crusade.

Another time we were in Africa, the radical Muslims threatened violence at a Jesus parade. (Please realize that many peace-loving Muslims and Hindus come to our meetings. God loves them all. These threats came from the radicals. Even Christianity has its violent radicals or corrupt televangelists that give us a bad name). People of every religion need a touch of Jesus' love. Many Muslims we meet, like so many Christians today, are just Muslim in name only. They're all searching for truth, love and a God who's real. So we were dealing with religious fanatics like you have in every religion. This happened to be a Muslim-dominated city—they threatened violence and bombings if we went ahead with the planned Jesus parade. Instead of the parade, we decided to take a small team of 50 people into the market place.

"All right," I said, "I want to demonstrate God in a public place. Let's go into the Muslim market and have a spontaneous meeting. We'll bring in the sound system and I'll give my testimony and an altar call. We'll take the crusade to them since they are not coming to the crusade." The pastors were horrified. "It's like a hornet's nest there—we don't want to go." But my team was still eager to go.

So, 500 Muslims gathered in this big fish market to hear us. A lot of them stood with arms crossed, looking skeptical, suspicious and angry. I gave my testimony and an altar call and 176 people got saved. It was great. However, I still felt a wall of resistance—skepticism and unbelief. By the look on their faces, it was as if they were thinking: "We also have testimonies in our religion of people that found God and converted to Islam." You can find stories in every religion of "revelations" of God. So, most of them were still not convinced. I certainly wasn't winning them over with my testimony and I wasn't winning them over by hammering out Scripture. Even though some of them were moved to salvation, for most of them, the theology just wasn't going over!

So I cried out to God and heard Him say to me, "Issue a challenge." That's when I said, "If the first three people that come up here are not healed, then everything I said is a lie, the crusade is a lie, God is a liar, and we will all turn our backs on God and go home."

Now the rest of the team was saying under their breath: "I didn't say that!" I forgot to tell the team that I was operating in the gift of faith and they weren't. God gave me a supernatural boldness which they didn't get at the time. This was the first time they had come on a ministry trip to Africa and they were shocked when they heard me say, "I want you to go get your children—blind, deaf, crippled, whatever—I guarantee healing for the first three." Nobody in the crowd moved. I had to give the challenge two or three times.

God gave me a word of knowledge that one of my team leaders was thinking, "God, anybody except for someone without legs! Anybody but . . ." I quickly turned around, looked at him and said, "Don't you believe God can grow legs?!" I mean, talk about the Bible! Jesus knew their thoughts.

The first three people that responded were completely healed. One person was blind, another was deaf and the last person had some sickness that I don't remember now—all three were healed.

We left our team to continue praying for the sick and the crowds just grew. In five days, we ended up reaching nearly a quarter of a million people in that crusade. The crowds just exploded, in part, because of the demonstration of God's power in the market place. I heard God, received the gift of faith and issued the challenge. God was faithful to His word to me and responded by demonstrating His power and deity. To convince these skeptical Muslims, we had to demonstrate that the kingdom of God is not in word only—we had to demonstrate the power of God!

In Malawi, after a Muslim was healed of total blindness, I asked him: "Now will you become a Christian?" He quickly responded "yes." God's miraculous power was the only thing that would win him over.

I often challenge people by saying that if God proves the Bible is true by healing you, then you and your whole family needs to convert and become Christians. Jesus does prove His deity through the miraculous. Earlier in the book we examined the story in Mark of the paralytic whom Jesus pronounced forgiven of his sins. Then, when the Pharisees protested Jesus' words, saying, "He was blaspheming by presuming to forgive sins," Jesus responded by saying:

> ***"Which is easier, to say to the paralytic, 'Your sins are forgiven you' or to say, 'Arise, take up your bed and walk'? But that you may know that the Son of Man has power on earth to forgive sins'—He said to the paralytic, 'I say to you, arise, take up your bed, and go to your house" (Mark 2:9-12).***

The religious leaders were really stating that Jesus wasn't God. However, Jesus promptly turned around and did something that only God can do—He healed the man, proving that He truly was God. With those words and one miraculous act, He confirmed that both healing and forgiveness of sin was the same thing. But what He was really saying was, "Let me demonstrate My deity."

Jesus began His ministry by turning water into wine. The Bible actually says of this act: "***This beginning of signs Jesus did in Cana of Galilee, and manifested His glory; and His disciples believed in Him" (Jn. 2:11).*** This miracle was a manifestation of His glory as God in the flesh. This was the first miracle to demonstrate His deity—it was necessary so that His disciples would be thoroughly convinced that He was God. Later in John's gospel Jesus says to His disciples: ***"Believe that I am in the Father and the Father is in me, or else believe me for the sake of the works themselves" (Jn. 14:11).***

6. To Fulfill the Prophetic Word

The sixth reason miracles happen today is to fulfill God's prophetic word. Isaiah gave us a prophetic promise of healing, hundreds of years before Christ. In Isaiah 53 he spoke of Christ's suffering for our pain, sin and sorrow before declaring: "***By His stripes we are healed" (vs. 5).*** By His stripes, <u>WE ARE</u>… WE ARE HEALED.

Those many centuries ago, God prophesied healing in the atonement. Isaiah prophesied that Christ would suffer for our pain, sorrow and sickness just as He would suffer for our sin. Healing is for ALL, in the same way as the forgiveness of sin is for ALL. It's not just for some! ALL! No one is excluded from salvation or healing.

Our earlier chapter about *sozo* affirms this truth. There is nothing greater than the power and testimony of the cross of Jesus. If people want to use the story of Paul and the guy he left at home sick, their argument still disappears in the light of the *sozo* power of the cross. Any verse or suggestion that seems to refute the healing power of God today holds absolutely no weight to the cross's provision in salvation, healing and deliverance. The cross is enough for me to have faith in the fact that healing is for today. I don't need anything else but the cross!

The gospel of Matthew even confirms that Jesus' ministry fulfilled Isaiah's prophecy:

> ***"When evening had come, they brought to Him many who were demon-possessed. And He cast out the spirits with a word, and healed all who were sick, that it might be fulfilled which was spoken by Isaiah the prophet, saying: "He Himself took our infirmities and bore our sicknesses" (Matt. 8:16-17).***

So the verse is clear—Jesus healed all in order to fulfill Isaiah's prophecy that He would eventually pay the price for our healing. Jesus didn't just come die for our sin, but for our sicknesses too. Jesus, through His healing ministry, established forever the prophetic promise of healing for those who put their faith in Him. That doesn't mean everyone will be healed, just as it doesn't mean that everyone will be saved. These are gifts to be received by faith. In another chapter, to balance out this teaching, we will discuss some reasons why people aren't healed.

7. Faith

For some people, faith is the only reason people are healed. Some healing ministers will actually go as far as to tell you, "Come back tomorrow when you have more faith." They don't have room for anything. If healing doesn't happen, it's your fault. That is an unbalanced healing theology. As you're seeing, there are many reasons people get healed today—I list 30. Some people have revelation of just one. However, today, as in Jesus' day, faith is still one vital element in healing ministry.

a. The Prayer of faith

The epistle of James describes the power of faith: "***Is anyone among you sick? Let him call for the elders of the church, and let them pray over him, anointing him with oil in the name of the Lord. And the prayer of faith will save the sick, and the Lord will raise him up" (James 5:14-15).*** Notice the certainty in this verse—the prayer of faith **will** save (or heal) the sick! No question about it. In this case, though, it's the faith of the person praying that is important, not necessarily the faith of the sick person. So, as we pray for others in faith, they will be healed.

b. Believe before you receive

According to Scripture, asking in faith can assure that our prayers are answered: ***"Therefore, I say to you, whatever things you ask when you pray, believe that you receive them and you will have them" (Mark 11:24).*** This verse tells us that faith-filled prayer involves believing you already have something when you pray. So, when we pray for healing, we are to believe in it before we see the healing manifested in the natural realm.

Faith involves seeing in the spirit. We see and receive our healing in the spiritual realm first—that's where all our blessings start out. Once we've received our answer in our spirit, once we know that we know that we've got it, it's only a matter of time before we see the healing come to pass. Think of the10 lepers who set out to show themselves to the priests, even though they were not yet healed. "***And so it was that as they went, they were cleansed" (Lu. 17:14).***

That's how we are to live a life of faith—we don't believe that we will one day receive our healing; we believe that we have it now before we actually see it in our body. What a powerful principle. That's why it's so important to develop the eyes of our heart—to see by faith, things that don't exist yet on earth. We are to" ***walk by faith, not by sight" (2 Cor. 5:7).***

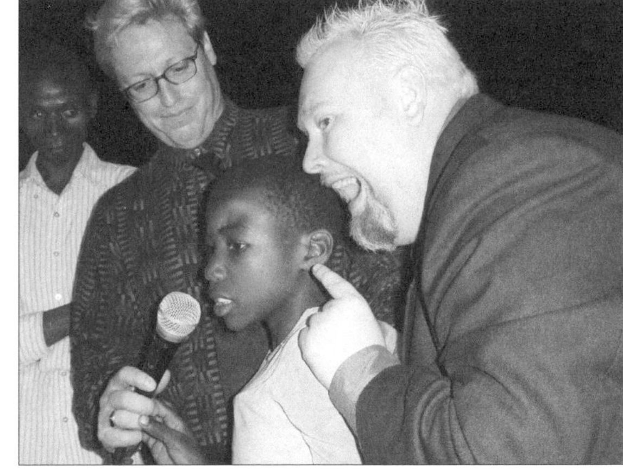

Deaf boy healed

c. Faith of the sick person

On many different occasions Jesus told people that their faith had healed them. When the woman with the issue of blood reached out to touch the hem of Jesus' garment, He said to her, ***"Be of good cheer, daughter; your faith has made you well" (Matt. 9:22).***

When two blind men shouted out for Jesus to have mercy on them, He asked them: "Do you believe that I am able to do this?" Then He said, ***"According to your faith, let it be to you" (Matt. 9:29).***

Clearly, in Scripture there is a place where the responsibility for receiving healing is on **us**. (At the same time, let's remember that it is the Lord that causes faith to grow as we allow Him to speak healing revelation into our hearts.) Jesus sometimes rebuked people for their unbelief or for their "little faith." Throughout the gospels Jesus also made statements like: "As you have believed. Whatever you ask for in prayer, believing, you shall receive them. Your faith has made you well. Do you believe that I am able to do this?"

We need to recognize that lack of faith is not the only reason healing doesn't happen—we'll talk about those other reasons later. However, receiving healing often has everything to do with your faith. Scripture is clear that the prayer of faith will save the sick—no maybe or probably!

d. Another person's faith

Although the individual's faith is very important, God often heals because of someone else's faith. Sometimes people are too weak or beaten down and they need others to exercise faith on their behalf.

Scripture shows us that the nobleman's dying son was healed because of his father's faith.

> ***"When he heard that Jesus had come out of Judea into Galilee, he went to Him and implored Him to come down and heal his son, for he was at the point of death.... The nobleman said to Him, 'Sir, come down before my child dies!' Jesus said to him, 'Go your way; your son lives.' So the man believed the word that Jesus spoke to him, and he went his way" (Jn. 4:47-50).***

Faith in Jesus and His desire and ability to heal is a vital ingredient for miracles.

8. Healing Anointing

The healing anointing is one important reason that healing and miracles happen. Think about the time when Jesus was surrounded by a crowd of people and the woman with the issue of blood was healed. One person was healed; hundreds weren't healed. On another occasion, Jesus was ministering and ***"the power of the Lord was present to heal them" (Lk. 5:17).*** That's when everybody was healed.

Now think about it—on one occasion, one woman was healed and hundreds weren't; another time hundreds were healed. Why was that? The power of the Lord was present and a healing atmosphere had settled in that place.

It's not always about the level of your faith; often it's about the level of God in the room. When the power of His manifest presence comes, sickness and disease is driven out. It doesn't have anything to do with people's ability to believe God for their healing—it has everything to do with how much God's presence is manifest on the person ministering healing. When a strong anointing of God's presence is on someone, when he/she lays hands on you, whether you believe or not, whether you are in sin or not, that sickness comes under the authority of the Presence. Sickness must bow to the manifest glory of the virtue of Jesus upon the minister or to the atmosphere of God in a city.

Often in our meetings, the manifestation of God's presence in the building becomes so strong that people are healed in their seats. Miracles happen just because God is near, because there is a powerful divine atmosphere in the air. Scripture tells us that people sick on beds waited in line for even Peter's shadow to touch them (Acts 5:15). Peter carried so much of God into the street that miracles happened.

One of the Old Testament prophets describes how this anointing will be seen in the last days: ***"His glory covered the heavens, and the earth was full of His praise. His brightness was like the light; He had rays flashing from His hand, and there His power was hidden. Before Him went pestilence, and fever followed at His feet" (Hab. 3:3-5).***

We know that at the presence of Jesus, pestilence was driven out and that fever came under the authority of His presence. I believe that God's power flashed as rays from Jesus' hands. In the ministry of John G. Lake, the 20th century healing apostle, this same phenomenon occurred. Lake spoke about the lightings of God that flashed from him to release healing and miracles.

I believe this type of anointing is being released to the church today. The prophet Malachi also promised this great day of God's healing power saying, ***"But to you who fear my name, the Son of Righteousness shall arise with healing in His wings" (Mal. 4:2).*** Yes, the Son of Righteousness is rising, or, as Habakkuk describes it—*"His brightness was like the light."* This is a dawning of a new day; the Morning Star is rising today with healing power. Malachi tells us the time-frame for this day of power: *"I will send you Elijah the prophet before the great and dreadful day of the Lord" (Mal. 4: 5).* When the forerunner anointing of Elijah comes before the great and dreadful day of the Lord (the second coming), the spirit and power of Elijah will come on the church to prepare the bride of Christ for its bridegroom.

The Bible is clear, I believe, that the Son of Righteousness will arise with healing in His wings when the forerunner anointing of the last days is released. That healing anointing will flash from the hands of God's people. Healing will come in "His wings" or His garment (Hebrew meaning) as His children *"abide under the shadow of the Almighty" (Ps. 91:1).*

Realize that the "wings" healing anointing is different than the one-on-one healing anointing. When the "wings" healing anointing shows up, the anointing covers and comes upon the entire service. This anointing rests on a meeting just like a mother hen who takes the chicks under her wings as she settles down onto the nest. God will sit on whole cities! They will be enveloped in the healing anointing under His wings and all the sick will be healed!

It's important to understand that miracles come through the healing anointing and manifest presence of God. The presence of Jesus drives away sickness. As is mentioned in Luke 6:19, in the Lord's ministry the *"power went out from Him and healed them all."*

9. To Prove the Ministry

The release of healing power is also an important way of proving or validating the ministry of God's people. How will people know that we truly serve a living, powerful God, unless they see the demonstration of power in our lives?

Look at what Peter said to the crowd at Pentecost; ***"Men of Israel, hear these words: Jesus of Nazareth, a man attested (proven) by God to you by miracles, wonders and signs which God did through Him in your midst..." (Acts 2:22).*** What proved the ministry of Jesus? Miracles, signs and wonders—we need this anointing in the church today to impact kings, presidents, leaders and nations.

Christianity in North America is just another religion without God's power. When we begin to walk in the miraculous, people will begin to respond to us like the woman did when Elijah raised her dead boy: ***"Now by this I know that you are a man of God, and that the word of the Lord in your mouth is the truth" (1Ki. 17:24).*** The woman was saying that by this miracle she knew that Elijah was a true prophet.

As the apostle Paul said, the kingdom of God is not in word only but in power. We need God's power to prove our ministry is genuine. We need genuine apostolic ministry—ministry marked by miracles, signs and wonders. ***"Truly the signs of an apostle were accomplished among you with all perseverance, in signs and wonders and mighty deeds" (2 Cor. 12:12).***

10. To Know Him

Here's a wonderful reason for God's power: every miracle is an invitation to know Him! Jesus rebuked the people in John 6:26 because they didn't recognize the true purpose of the signs: ***"Most assuredly I say to you, you seek me not because you saw the signs, but because you ate of the loaves and were filled."*** There is nothing wrong with signs as long as we understand the reason for them.

According to Jesus, signs should prompt you to seek Him. The sign is a whole lot more than the "Wow." He didn't rebuke them for seeking signs but for seeking physical blessings like bread, instead of the Bread of Heaven, Himself. He was saying, "The signs were an invitation to know Me. I revealed myself, My love and My goodness by healing you."

I meet people who receive a special impartation of the love of God along with their healing. They often say things like: "God loved me so much that He called out the details of my condition by a word of knowledge and cared enough about me that He healed my tumor. I feel a whole lot closer to Him."

My brother, my sister, you can be sure that you've had a touch of the divine when you have a massive cancer and a finger comes out of heaven, touches you and the cancer is gone. It leaves you with a greater desire to know this awesome God. Jesus ultimately wants us to seek Him, not for the loaves or the benefits, but to know Him personally. He wants relationship with us.

In John 6, the Lord spoke of Himself as the Bread of Life and called people to eat His flesh and drink His blood. This was His call for us to come into intimate relationship with Him. It's His desire that when He heals us that we will want to know Him, the source of healing, not just want more of His blessing.

11. He is Still the Same Today

We can also expect miracles today because Jesus is risen and alive today. He is ***the same yesterday, today and forever" (Heb. 13:8).*** He needs to act the same as He did 2,000 years ago. He still does miracles and wonders today because He is alive and He is the same. That's why miracles happen!

Miracles couldn't have passed away with the apostles because then He wouldn't be the same today. He is the "***Father of lights, with whom there is no variation or shadow of turning" (Jas. 1:17).*** God's methods may change, but His nature never does. He is the God who heals you (Ex. 15:26). If He doesn't heal the sick today then He has changed—but God cannot deny His own nature.

Jesus makes this powerful statement in the last book of the Bible: "***I am He who lives, and was dead, and behold, I am alive forevermore. Amen. And I have the keys of Hades and of Death" (Rev. 1:18).*** You see, God heals today to demonstrate His resurrection power and sovereign dominion over the influence of hell and death.

Woman rejoices—Jesus dissolved a large tumor!

12. Healing Commission

Miracles happen today because Jesus has commissioned us to work the miraculous in His name—He heals us and works in power through us because of this commission.

Look at Jesus' words to us: ***"Most assuredly, I say to you, he who believes in me, the works that I do he will do also; and greater works than these he will do, because I go to my Father" (Jn. 14:12).*** Miracles happen today because He said that whoever believes in Him will do the works that He did. That's why miracles happen today!

The Lord also gave another healing commission in Mark 16:15-18 when He said, ***"Go into all the world and preach the gospel… these signs will follow those who believe: In my name they will cast out demons; they will speak with other tongues… they will lay hands on the sick, and they will recover."*** That's why miracles happen today—it's the healing commission.

Realize, however, that signs and wonders do not automatically follow you because you are a Christian. No it's our belief in the signs and wonders ministry that releases the miraculous. It's ***"according to your faith, let it be to you" (Matt. 9:29).*** What's important is our belief in the ministry of Jesus to work miracles through people today. If you have no faith grid that God can use you in healing, God will use everyone else but you. You will only have faith for God to work through somebody else that has a healing gift.

If you actually believe healing passed away 2,000 years ago and you hang around people who believe the same way, there will be no healing. Even though everybody is a believer in Jesus there will be no healing because they don't believe in healing. You just won't see the miraculous in your life. That is why in some streams of the body of Christ we see miracles and in some streams we don't. In the same way, we have some groups that speak in tongues and some that don't. It's not that they can't, it's that they don't. But they can—these signs are for everyone who believes!

God wants to equip us; He wants to give us these powerful tools to spread the gospel. We are not special or elite Christians because we walk in supernatural power. We have just chosen to believe and to receive His power to fulfill the commission. We have realized that we are weak in ourselves and need all the help we can get. Most Christians don't yet know all the supernatural treasures of heaven that are available to them. However, we can begin to walk into the miraculous based on Jesus' commission.

13. Repentance

Repentance! With every miracle comes a responsibility to change. Healings can actually bring a judgment against entire cities. I believe God does miracles in some cities in North America as a sign to them that they don't know God—that they are Godless. Look at this:

> ***"Woe to you Chorazin! Woe to you Bethsaida. For if the mighty works which were done in you had been done in Tyre and Sidon, they would have repented long ago in sackcloth and ashes. But I say to you, it will be more tolerable for Tyre and Sidon in the day of judgment than for you. And you Capernaum, who are exalted to heaven, will be brought down to Hades; for if the mighty works which were done in you had been done in Sodom, it would have remained until this day." (Matt. 11:21-24).***

God does miracles in cities, and in the lives of believers, in the hope that they will repent of their sin and unbelief. Supernatural signs demonstrate how real and awesome our God is—they call us back to the Father so our hearts are totally after Him.

14. So That We Might Believe

God does signs and wonders today so that we will believe in His power to do the impossible. Jesus healed Lazarus so that people would "believe" that He was from God (John 11:42).

The apostle John confirmed this purpose of the miraculous: "***And truly Jesus did many other signs in the presence of His disciples, which are not written in this book; but these are written that you may believe that Jesus is the Christ, the Son of God, and that believing you may have life in His name" (Jn. 20:30).*** John was saying that Jesus performed signs to make people believe.

15. Goodness

Miracles happen because of God's goodness. Jesus said, ***"If you then, being evil, know how to give good gifts to your children, how much more will your Father who is in heaven give good things to those who ask Him?" (Matt 7:11).*** Our Heavenly Father is a very good God—the scriptures and nature testify of this over and over. He wants to lavish good gifts on us because "***every good gift and every perfect gift is from above" (Jas. 1:17).***

He gave His only Son to die for us and then He gave us the Holy Spirit to teach, comfort and empower us. He also wants to continually pour heavenly blessings on us who will receive them by faith. God is so good that He even wants to do "***exceedingly abundantly above all that we ask or think" (Eph. 3:20).***

16. God is Sovereign

This is a simple reason but it's "good enough for me." Clearly, the Bible shows us that God sometimes acts in sovereign ways and doesn't necessarily explain everything to us: ***"Do not be hasty to go from His presence, do not take your stand for an evil thing for He does whatever He pleases" (Ec. 8: 3).*** Healings why? Miracles why? Because He is sovereign and does whatever He pleases!

I remember when God was changing people's silver fillings to gold in Canada—we called them signs and wonders. They were signs that caused the unbeliever to wonder if Jesus really was alive. God had already started this gold dental work in Toronto just weeks before but we hadn't yet heard about it.

I was doing some meetings in Mission, BC, with Patricia King. What was planned for a couple of nights ended up going for three weeks—night after night. I remember those early days of ministry; I was green. I had only been in the ministry a few months and God was already blessing us with, not just healing, but with signs and wonders. God was healing, but in the form of dental miracles—some people received full gold crowns… supernaturally. People would open their mouths and have no gold. Then, as the meeting progressed, or as people received prayer, they would open their mouths again and have five gold crowns—it looked like a full bar of gold. When they went back to the dentist to have it checked out, they would have thousands of dollars worth of dental work in their mouths. We heard testimonies like this over and over again.

Also, as further signs of His presence, God sent gold dust and flakes and even emerald stones. There was such a manifestation of God's glory that the glory mist would fill the building, People often ask, "Why would God give people gold teeth or send other strange manifestations?" Why not? There is no great theological reason—it's just that God is sovereign. He does whatever He pleases!

A prophet friend of mine once said to the Lord: "God I am going to be doing a prophetic school and I want to share with the people how you speak and how to hear your voice. So I am going to put together a nice little lesson on "How God Speaks." So Lord, tell me how You speak." God's response came as quite a shock. The Lord actually came and yelled at him: "Tell the people that I speak any way that I want to!"

God is sovereign and He does whatever He pleases. Yes, God does give us principles as well as reasons for the things He does—but not always. If He wants to do something, He just does it; He doesn't have to explain it to us. He is God and we are not.

17. Charitable Giving

You will see more miracles in your ministry if you act on this point. The question is—can our offerings, our giving, truly open heaven so we can receive miracles? What does money have to do with miracles? Let's see what the Bible says about this:

> ***"At Joppa there was a certain disciple named Tabitha, which is translated Dorcas. This woman was full of good works and charitable deeds which she did. But it happened in those days that she became sick and died. When they had washed her, they laid her in an upper room" (Acts 9:36-37).***

Well, you probably know the story—Peter raised her from the dead. However, notice that right before the miracle happens, the Bible emphasizes the fact that the woman was ***full of charitable deeds and good works.*** So God brings Peter along to raise her from the dead because she was a woman of charitable deeds and good works.

In the next chapter of Acts, God brings salvation to the entire house of Cornelius because of his giving.

> ***"There was a certain man in Caesarea called Cornelius, a centurion of what was called the Italian Regiment, a devout man and one who feared God with all his household, who gave alms generously to the people…" (Acts 10:1-2).***

Alms are not the tithe. They are resources given to the poor above and beyond your tithe. They are actually a love offerings—special gifts to the poor or for children—for the sake of mercy.

In the case of Cornelius, it was both his giving and his praying that opened up heaven. That is an important key. Prayer and giving must go hand in hand. You can pray forever and never give or you can always give and never pray. However, you won't get an open heaven until you combine the two.

If people only knew the powerful breakthroughs that can happen as a result of giving, everyone in the church would want to tithe and give offerings. Look at what happened to Cornelius:

> ***"At about the ninth hour of the day he saw clearly in a vision an angel of God coming in and saying to him, 'Cornelius!' And when he observed him, he was afraid, and said, 'What is it, Lord?' So He said to him, 'Your prayers and your alms***

have come up for a memorial before God'" (Acts 10:3-4).

Wow! Think about it—he prays and gives to the poor, so God sends a vision of an angel. In the end revival comes to him and his family.

Scripture speaks so much about miracles that happen because of our giving. God actually promises divine healing and health for giving to the poor. God has ordained a greater healing anointing for giving to the poor. "***Blessed is he who considers the poor; the Lord will deliver him in time of trouble. The Lord will preserve him and keep him alive and he will be blessed on the earth" (Ps. 41:1-2).***

Everyone's understanding of "poor" is different. To some an income of $500 a week is poor, to others its $1,000. The word poor actually means "helpless and powerless." Most of the poor live in third world countries where, even if there is money in the system, the average person can't get it—they're victims of corrupt, ungodly government or social systems. Some countries run on a caste system which locks people into a particular social stratum their entire lives.

In the lower castes, they have no access to education; they are helpless and powerless to change their condition. In North America, at least we have social security, welfare, food banks and food stamps. These benefits don't exist in many countries so for many people, there is no alternative but to live on the street. Our situation is totally different from countries like India with its caste system or like Africa with war, child soldiers, famine and millions dying of starvation.

As we give to these helpless, powerless poor, the Lord promises to deliver us, to preserve us and to bless us. Scripture also promises, in Psalm 41:2-3 that He will give us victory over our enemies and strengthen us on our sickbed. These verses declare not just healing, but divine health. God will preserve you and keep you alive. He'll strengthen you on your bed of illness. Why would the Lord do all this? Because you consider the poor. That's why God does miracles today—charitable giving.

18. It's the Gospel

Miracles happen because of the good news. We need to preach the gospel! As the apostle Paul said, ***"I am not ashamed of the gospel because it is the power of God to salvation for everyone who believes" (Rom. 1:16).*** The gospel is the power of God for everyone who believes. You can't get someone saved without power. In the preaching of the message is found the power of God to salvation.

We would see more miracles in the church today if we knew how to preach the full gospel. Do you know what the full gospel is? In the book of Romans Paul talks about his ministry among unbelievers. He goes on to talk about the ministry of Jesus given to him: ***"... in mighty signs and wonders, by the power of the Spirit of God, so that from Jerusalem and round about to Illyricum I have fully preached the gospel of Christ" (Rom. 15:19).*** Do you know what Paul just said? He clearly says that he has not fully preached the gospel if he does not do it with miracles, signs and wonders in the power of the Holy Ghost! Wow! Signs and wonders are a powerful confirmation of the truth of the gospel. "***So then, after the Lord had spoken to them, He was received up into heaven, and sat down at the right hand of God. And they went out and preached everywhere, the Lord working with them and confirming the word through the accompanying signs" (Mark 16:19).*** What did they do? They preached everywhere. What did they preach? It was the full gospel message of salvation with power—signs which included deliverance, healing and miracles. Healing signs specifically accompany the message of the gospel of Christ.

19. Friendship With God

The nineteenth reason God heals today—friendship with God. Jesus said to His disciples:

> ***"No longer do I call you servants, for a servant does not know what his master is doing; but I have called you friends, for all things that I heard from my Father I have made known to you. You did not choose me, but I chose you and appointed you that you should go and bear fruit, and that your fruit should remain, that whatever you ask the Father in my name He may give you" (Jn. 15:15-16).***

When you become a friend of God, the first thing that you get is the inside scoop on what He is doing. Why? Because you are friends. Whatever you ask the Father He will give you. God hears the prayers of His friends. There is a wonderful connection between intimate friendship with God and working miracles today. As we abide in the vine, we ask whatever we wish and it happens. He is saying, "I am going to answer your prayer and you are going to bear much fruit."

20. The Glory of God

Miracles also happen in order to bring glory to - the God of Israel (Matt. 15:31). Jesus actually healed the maimed—this involved a creative miracle which restored arms, legs or other missing body parts. He also healed the mute, lame and blind. For what reason? So people would give glory to the God of Israel.

There are times in the church today when the Lord does miracles so we will praise Him because He has done a great work. When He does a miracle, we are again made aware that God is good and all-powerful and that He has visited us. When He gives us signs, He is saying, "I am going to heal someone just so that the people of this city will glorify the God of Israel. I am going to open someone's blind eyes so people will say, 'Praise the Lord!'"

You see, God wants to bless us by healing us and by revealing His powerful goodness. He knows that faith grows in us and we get breakthroughs in our lives when we see His faithfulness and give glory to Him. Scripture even tells us that Abraham grew strong in faith by giving glory to God (Rom. 4:20).

Let's look at another Bible story in which a miracle happened specifically to give God glory. In the gospel of John, after Jesus heals a blind man, the people ask, ***"Rabbi, who sinned, this man or his parents, that he was born blind?" (Jn. 9:1).*** To some, every sickness means that you are in sin. I don't believe that. Jesus answered them in verse three saying, ***"Neither this man nor his parents sinned."*** So why was he blind?

I meet people all the time trying to understand: "I didn't even have a chance to sin so the Devil could afflict me. I was just born this way." As Christians, we often think things like, "Why is that person crippled? He didn't do anything; he's a great person." I want you to realize that sometimes there is no reason why, other than the reason Jesus gives in verse three: ***"…that the works of God should be revealed in him."*** That's it. For God's glory!

I remember a story written about John G. Lake in a remote mountain region of Africa. He was in prayer on the mountain when he heard a child crying who had lost his mother. He looked to first make sure nobody was around then he quickly ran up and healed the boy before anybody could see.

Is that what we do in the church today? Come on! Often our intention is to first make sure everybody is watching. Then after God performs the miracle we yell, "Hey guys, look what God did through me!" Yes, at times we definitely need to testify of God's wonderful works, especially for the purpose of mass evangelism. However, the question is—what is our motive for telling our "God stories?" Is it to bring glory to God or to us?

I have actually been in meetings where God didn't heal anybody and

Blind man healed in Latvia

then He told me it was my fault. "Why God?" I asked. The Lord said, "I am not going to heal that person because if I do, there will be too much glory in it for you." He wasn't even saying that I would take the glory, but that too much glory would come to me. My tendency would be to think of what that great miracle could do for the meetings, how it could propel me to the next level, how it could raise the faith in the meetings or how it could triple the size of the crowd the next night. And sometimes God will use miracles for those reasons. However, sometimes God just says, "I am not going to heal that person right now, or in this way, because I won't share My glory." Then He'll just perform the healing sovereignly so He gets all the glory.

You need to make sure that your motive are right when you are involved in the miracle and healing ministry. Many believers are not seeing a great healing anointing because their motives are impure. Maybe some people are wishing, "God, just give me that one miracle out on the street then the whole city will know that I have a healing gift. Then I'll get hundreds of invitations."

Yes, God may use miracles to bring favor on our life and ministry. But if our motive for ministering healing is to get people's attention, then we are stealing God's glory. We need to be passionate that God gets all the glory. Yes, God does miracles so people will glorify Him and be drawn closer to Him when they see Him as the God of great power and goodness. Miracles are for the glory of God.

21. Curse of The Law

God also heals today because, according to ***Galatians 3:13, "Christ has redeemed us from the curse of the law."*** God will heal you today because Christ redeems from the curse of the law. Let's look at the entire passage:

> ***"Christ has redeemed us from the curse of the law, having become a curse for us (for it is written, 'Cursed is everyone who hangs on a tree'), that the blessing of Abraham might come upon the Gentiles in Christ Jesus…" (Gal. 3:13-14).***

God wants us to receive the blessing of Abraham. God wants to free us from all the diseases described under the curse of the law in Deuteronomy 28. That description includes just about every sickness that you can find in the world today as well as blindness, tumors, boils, skin conditions, madness, confusion, mental illness, chronic conditions and miscarriages. Although certain diseases today may have different names, they still fit under the criteria of "***every sickness and every plague, which is not written in this Book of the Law..." (Deut. 28:61).***

The bottom line is that to be redeemed from this curse of the law and to fulfill His covenant with us (which was paid with Jesus' blood), God has to heal you from every sickness and disease. Christ paid the price for our complete freedom from the curse of physical sickness.

22. Desperation

Here's another important reason miracles happen today—desperation! We've already gone over the gospel stories illustrating this point. Remember Blind Bartimaeus (Mark 10: 46-48) who, when He cried out, was told to be quiet? Yet he cried out all the more.

Think again about the desperation of the woman with the issue of blood who pushed through the crowds to touch the hem of Jesus' garment. (Mark 5:25-34). This woman could have been put to death for venturing into a populated area with an "unclean condition." She was desperate enough to risk her life!

Matthew gives us further illustrations of healing in response to desperation. You have the story of the Canaanite woman. Even though the disciples tried to get rid of her, and Jesus seemed unmoved by her request, she kept crying out for Jesus to have mercy and heal her daughter. She persisted (Matt. 15:27) saying, ***"Yes, Lord, yet even the little dogs eat the crumbs which***

fall from their masters' table." Jesus responded to her desperation and healed her daughter.

God still does miracles just because people cry out in desperation despite others who try to discourage them. They press through the crowd, through the obstacles and beyond the fear of what others think.

One of the greatest hindrances to healing in the church today is the fear of what someone will think if I pursue healing or respond to an altar call. We don't want to get up in front of all those people.

We need to press through the fear of man and continue to cry out even when they tell us to be quiet. We need to cry out all the more. When others say, "It's not time," "It's God's will that you are sick," or "It's God's thorn for you," we need to say, "No way!" Even when we've gotten prayer a hundred times and nothing has happened and the Devil says, "Give up!" we need to say, "NO!" and cry out all the more! There is something powerful about our desperation which releases miracles in the church today.

23. To Destroy the Devil's Work

Here is my favorite reason why God does miracles today. If God did miracles for no other reason than this one, it would be enough. He does miracles to destroy the Devil's work! Think about that truth for a minute. Here's what the Bible says: "***...God anointed Jesus of Nazareth with the Holy Spirit and with power, who went about doing good and healing all who were oppressed by the Devil, for God was with Him" (Acts 10:38).*** So Jesus went about doing good and healing! So say this with me, "Healing is good."

This Scripture also tells us that Jesus healed ALL. Say "All!" Think about that—All! All! All! All! Who? All who were oppressed of the Devil. So Jesus healed everyone oppressed by the Devil. Do we agree that everything that Jesus did was for the purpose of destroying the work of the Devil? Now think about the good works He did. He healed people of every kind of sickness and disease.

So disease is a work of the Devil! You may be thinking, "Wait a minute, Todd. Are you saying that I have a demon because I have migraines? I believe that there are some examples in the Scripture which show that demons cause sickness—but surely not every sickness can be demonic."

Well, let me explain it this way—He healed every sickness and every disease among the people (Matt. 9:35). Do you believe that? He also rebuked Peter's mother-in-law's fever! Just a fever! Why? He was rebuking a demonic source behind the fever. Remember, Jesus came to destroy the works of the Devil: "***For this purpose the Son of God was manifested, that He might***

destroy the works of the Devil" (1 Jn. 3:8). In God's eyes, fever is a work of the Devil. This does not mean that every person who is sick actually has a demon. However, in God's eyes any sickness and any disease is an oppression, a work of the Devil. That is how God sees it. It doesn't matter if people are blind, deaf, crippled or epileptic or whether they have fever, skin conditions, boils or prostate problems--God sees each physical affliction as a work of the Devil. Let me emphasize again--sickness doesn't mean you are demon-possessed.

Listen, just because George Bush doesn't live in my back yard doesn't mean that I'm not affected by what he does in government. Every decision he makes, whether good or bad, affects the whole nation of America, and often, other nations too.

Have you ever felt like you were an innocent victim of the decisions of big corporations or government and there was nothing you could do? When government decides to take the nation to war, some people agree while others disagree. Yet, everyone's life is affected. When our government raises the taxes, that's it! My family ends up paying the hike whether we like it or not.

In the same way, we live on someone else's turf—we live in a world in which, according to Scripture, Satan is the god or ruler. He is the Prince of the Air; we live in his system. You can put up all the no trespassing signs that you want to, but listen, the Devil will test to see whether you are an enforcer. God has passed a new law, the new covenant, which gives us, as children of God, spiritual rights and authority over the enemy's system. But remember, even when governments pass laws, people still break them—I sure did before I was saved. You could put up all the "No Trespassing" signs you wanted, but I was going to break in until you reinforced your rights.

The kingdom of God operates in a similar way. The Devil wants to know if you are going to respond to his attacks and if you are going to resist him. Are you just going to roll over and take everything he throws at you like you've done all those other times? You may talk big, but he's watching—he knows your track record of victory or defeat. After you've been rebuking devils all night at that meeting, he knows if you're going to go home and melt down when he begins to attack your most vulnerable areas. He remembers if you've reacted in fear in the past and said things like, "I'll just stay on the pew and leave the Devil alone if he'll leave me alone. If I don't go after him, he won't go after my family. I don't want to get too much into that spiritual warfare stuff because then I'm going to catch all that backlash."

As Christians, we often react that way. Even after we've ministered deliverance to someone all night, we get all worried that the demon on the person is going to get on us. I meet people all the time who are afraid of the Devil and his attacks. We need to learn to walk in our authority as kings and priests in Christ Jesus. We need to resist the Devil until he flees from us (James 4:7).

Hopefully by now you realize that the enemy is actually at work to afflict and destroy people's bodies. You also need to realize that we can resist sickness because Scripture tells us that every sickness and disease is an oppression of the Devil. We need to rise up in God's righteous anger to destroy the enemy's works—just like Jesus did!

24. The Name Of God

As we've discussed in a previous chapter, one of God's redemptive names is Jehovah Rapha—***"the Lord who heals you" (Ex. 15:26).*** That Hebrew word also means "physician" or "doctor." This word refers more to physical healing than inner healing, relational healing or national healing. He is Jehovah the Great Physician—by definition, He heals and makes healthy. His wisdom and power over disease is far greater than that of an earthly doctor. Let's put our faith in Jehovah Rapha, our healer.

25. Communion

It is vital that we understand the power of communion in healing and miracles according to ***1 Corinthians 11:29-30, "For he who eats and drinks in an unworthy manner eats and drinks judgment to himself, not discerning the Lord's body. For this reason many are weak and sick among you, and many sleep."*** I'll tell you why many in the church are sick and die prematurely today.

First, because many Christians don't have a revelation of the intimacy and communion God has called us to as the body of Christ. We don't discern His body properly—we often avoid (or don't pursue) close relationship with any believer who is not part of our stream.

We aren't discerning of the fact that Baptists, Catholics, Pentecostals and believers in every other denominational stream are just as important to Christ's body as we are. We become so inwardly focused—it becomes just about us and we don't discern the unity that God wants among all of his people. Every denomination, every independent church, every faith movement, the Lord wants us to actively recognize each part of His body and to embrace them. When we don't discern the Lord's body, divisions and factions arise within and between denominations and streams.

Second, the greatest reason that many people in the church are sick today—because they don't discern the healing power, in Christ's body, found in the atoning sacrifice. When we participate in communion, we don't see the healing that is found through His broken, beaten body. We understand the forgiveness of sin, but we don't understand the *Sozo*, the salvation, healing and deliverance at the moment of salvation for the body, soul and spirit. We don't understand that in the same way that He suffered for sin, He also suffered for sickness. In the same way that He wants everyone to be forgiven of their sin—and they can be—He also wants everyone to be healed. When we don't discern that Jesus' body was broken for our spiritual wholeness as well as our physical wholeness, like those in the Corinthian church, many become weak and sick or even die.

However, consider the healing power that would be released in us if we did discern the Lord's body rightly. If partaking of communion with poor discernment can cause sickness and death, think about the power for life and healing when we do take communion in a worthy manner with full revelation of Christ's body. If we really understood the power of communion, we would see great life where there is now death and we would see healing flow like a river through the church.

26. Gifts Of The Spirit

God has given His children, the gifts of the Spirit so we can walk in the same power Jesus did. As the apostle Paul says about these gifts: "***To another (is given) faith by the same spirit, to another gifts of healing by the same spirit, to another working of miracles" (1 Cor. 12: 9-10).*** Why do healings happen today? That verse is clear—He heals through and because of the gifts of the Spirit.

27. The Name of Jesus

Why did God heal the lame man at the Gate Beautiful? The answer is found in the Apostle Peter's words: ***"Silver and gold I do not have, but what I do have I give you: In the name of Jesus Christ of Nazareth, rise up and walk" (Acts 3:6).***

Clearly, healing happens because of the name of Jesus Christ. Later in this chapter, Peter confirms the power of Jesus' name saying: ***"And His name, through faith in His name, has made this man strong" (Acts 3:16).*** The name "Jesus" comes from the Hebrew root, Yeshua, meaning "Jehovah saved" (again pointing to *sozo*), while the name "Christ" means "the Messiah" or "anointed one" (such as a priest or king). As the Christ, Jesus was anointed with the Holy Spirit to release healing power. Healing is in Jesus' name and He is still the same today; He has not changed His name. That wonderful name is the only reason we need for healing and miracles today.

28. Filled With The Spirit

Being filled with the Spirit has always been a powerful key to the manifestation of healing power and anointing in my life and ministry. Still today, I need to get juiced regularly so I am always full of the virtue, the power and the strength of God. Just let me soak in the reality of Romans 8:11 for 5 minutes on my bed with the lights off and my eyes closed… then I'm in power!

Let's look at that verse: "***But if the Spirit of Him who raised Jesus from the dead dwells in you, He who raised Christ from the dead will also give life to your mortal bodies through His Spirit who dwells in you" (Rom. 8:11).*** Divine healing actually comes through His Spirit who dwells in you and brings life to your physical bodies. The healing anointing is in you. And the healing anointing in you comes through the Spirit that dwells in you, not the Holy Ghost from outside of you.

"I need Todd to lay hands on me. Let healing fall on me!" I hear that a lot. To these people healing seems to always be an outward thing. All the while God is trying to get their attention. He's saying, "You have the same Spirit!"

Now think about that for a few minutes—the same Spirit that empowered the ministry of Jesus to heal all those who were oppressed of the Devil lives in you. The same Spirit that came on Jesus in power and raised Him from the dead lives in you. The same Spirit that was involved in the creation of the entire universe lives in you.

Don't let this revelation pass you by. That is what is going to bring healing to your mortal body and life to your soul. It's the healing power within you. Be healed right now. Just close your eyes and let it out into your soul and into your body. People can get healed just meditating on this one truth about the Spirit within them. Christ in you is rising up! Speak it out: "The same Spirit that raised Jesus from the dead, lives in me, right now—in me! I am the temple of the Holy Ghost."

Look at that mountain, that obstacle or struggle in your life, your whole perspective on it is changing isn't it? A minute ago it was much bigger than you and now you are bigger than it.

Five minutes on my bed with that verse and I'm in power, I'm ready to go another hour. When His Spirit begins to be released in my life and my body by faith, life and healing begin to course through my veins. Yes, miracles happen today because the power of the Holy Spirit, the Spirit who created the universe and who raised Jesus from the dead lives in us!

29. I Am Saved

Another reason that miracles happen today is—one we discussed in an earlier chapter—we are saved! Remember, in God's eyes salvation, or *sozo*, doesn't just mean spiritual salvation and freedom from sin. Remember what Scripture says about Jesus' healing ministry? "***And as many as touched Him were made well" (Mark 6:56).*** That word "well" is actually *Sozo* or salvation—so everyone who touched Jesus was ***saved*** of their sickness. When we come to Jesus for salvation, we get the whole package—salvation, healing and deliverance. (See a few other *sozo* scriptures: Luke 7:50; Rom. 10:9.)

30. The Kingdom

The thirtieth reason why I can expect to be healed and see miracles in this life is the kingdom. Jesus said, ***"But if I cast out demons by the Spirit of God, surely the kingdom of God has come upon you" (Matt. 12:28).*** My favorite revelation about healing in the kingdom is Mathew 6:10. His disciples asked Jesus to teach them how to pray and Jesus said, ***"Your kingdom come. Your will be done on earth as it is in heaven."*** What is the kingdom of God? It is—"as it is in heaven!"

God's kingdom comes when heaven and earth synchronize, when heaven touches earth. His kingdom comes when heaven shows up in your world and your life lines up with God's world. That means no sorrow, no pain, no sickness or disease in your life. Those things don't exist in heaven. When the kingdom comes, everything that exists in heaven invades earth now.

Today on earth it is not as it is in heaven. However, it can be—that's why Jesus taught the disciples to pray for God's kingdom to come. He wants earth to become "as it is in heaven" now—not some day when we die and go to heaven. The enemy will do anything to oppose this wonderful divine plan. So when you pray, welcome the kingdom. Pray for the kingdom to come. Invite the atmosphere of heaven into your life, into your church and into your city. God does miracles and healings in the church today because they are a sign and a manifestation of His kingdom. When people see miracles manifest on the earth, they know that the kingdom of God has come upon them.

Chapter Seven

THE WORD OF KNOWLEDGE

In one of the first years of my ministry, I received a word of knowledge by a "supernatural visitation." I was in Oregon praying in the pastor's office when a woman "visited" me in the spirit. I was in a dream-like state, but I was awake. The woman grabbed me and shook me violently and shouted several times, "The headlines read, 'Boy Comes out of a Coma!'" She disappeared and I snapped out of it (I was never sleeping and I was still sitting up in a posture of prayer).

I called out to God for wisdom. I realized that He had given me a word of knowledge, but I didn't know what to do with it. "God, what do you want me to do with the word of knowledge?" I prayed. "The woman is in the hospital with the boy in the coma and she will send a man to your meeting tonight to ask you to specifically pray for the boy," said the Lord. "I want you to call him out before he can ask you to pray for him." I went into the meeting and said, "There is a man here and you've come on behalf of a woman who is in the hospital. She is with a boy who is in a coma and you've come specifically to ask me to pray for him." The man stood up for prayer and I simply declared, "The headlines read, 'Boy Comes out of a Coma!'" That's it. That's all there was to it.

Later I was ministering in another meeting in Oregon and some church elders said, "Listen Todd! Exactly as you said it, an article just appeared in the paper with headlines that read, 'Boy Comes out of a Coma!'" Not all words of knowledge are that exciting—some come as just a "knowing" about something and others as just a quick flash of a thought. But however words come, this supernatural knowledge from God often triggers the supernatural and releases God's power into situations.

In this chapter, I want to show you how to receive those words of knowledge that will bring heaven to earth and activate miracles. In the pages that follow, I will help you understand what the word of knowledge is and how it works with other gifts. I'll give New and Old Testament examples of this gift, list eight ways to receive a word and equip you to know the process of delivering a word of knowledge.

A Revelatory Gift

First, it is important to understand that your use of revelatory gifts must not be to impress people but to bless people. Knowledge is one of three revelatory gifts described in 1 Corinthians 12 at the top of this page. (The other six gifts of the Holy Spirit, not discussed here, are known as the power gifts). Scripture speaks very clearly about these different gifts and their purpose: "***But the manifestation of the Spirit is given to each one for the profit of all: for to one is given the word of wisdom, through the Spirit, to another the word of knowledge through the same Spirit, … to another discerning of spirits…" (1 Cor. 12:7, 8, 10).***

Word of Knowledge Defined

The word of knowledge is a supernatural insight or understanding of circumstances, situations and problems. It is a divine piece, but only a piece, of information about the past or present. It can be a knowing or a physical impression manifesting in your body. Most often the word of knowledge brings revelation about the past and present but not the future. Information about the future usually falls into the category of prophecy.

John Wimber defines the word of knowledge as follows:

> *"This is the supernatural revelation of fact about a person or situation, which is not learned through the efforts of the natural mind, but is a fragment of knowledge freely given by God, disclosing the truth which the Spirit wishes to be made*

known concerning a particular person or situation" (John Wimber, Vineyard Fellowships, U.S.A.).

Let me give you one more definition of the word of knowledge: "It is the supernatural ability to receive information and truth directly from God without natural means." In even simpler terms it is to know something without knowing how you know.

This is how the word of knowledge comes most often to me: as a definite conviction, impression, or knowing. I know that I know that I know… yet I don't know how I know. I become aware, for example, that a 24-year-old man in the audience was just healed of asthma. I can't explain how I know that; I didn't hear a voice and I didn't have a vision. The knowledge is just there like a thought that popped in as divine information.

Many people think they've heard God's voice but they're not sure it was God. In these cases, quite often it *was* God's voice. What they're really saying is "I think I know something but I don't know how I know it. I can't explain how I know it." They probably want to write it off because they feel they should be able to explain it. But, quite often, when it is God, you can't explain it! God often gives me a divine thought quite suddenly. I'll be lying on my bed going, "Jesus. Jesus. Jesus." Then, out of the blue, I'm thinking about cancer patients. That's a pretty good indication that God wants to do something with cancer patients in the meeting that night. Then I'll be thinking "Jesus. Jesus. Jesus" And suddenly my mind will think "gall bladder" and I'll know that God wants to heal someone's gall bladder.

Quite often I receive a word of knowledge by looking over a crowd. When I see someone's face, sometimes right away, with that face, may come a thought of a sickness.

Todd Bentley delivering a message

Then I'll say, "Stand up please" or ask, "Do you have this condition?" They'll say "yes," faith will rise in them because God has spoken and then healing will be released.

The Operation of the Word of Knowledge

An important aspect of any kind of prophetic or revelatory gift is specified in 1 Corinthians 13:9: ***"For we know in part and we prophesy in part."*** One individual never gets the full picture. That is why we need to work cooperatively with other members of the body of Christ. We only get a divine piece of information.

On one occasion I might know a man's first name and maybe his age and the city he is from, and another time I might know a woman's last name and where she is sitting in the room and what color skirt she is wearing. Then the next time I might know someone's address and the first name of his brother. I'm only given a divine piece because we only know in part.

Boy, who was a deaf mute, hears and speaks

It's OK not to have the full picture. What works best is to get a group of people together to get words of knowledge. All of them get a piece and then everyone shares and you put the puzzle together and get the ultimate word.

Quite often I'll tell our interns and disciples to each give me five words for the service that night. Or I'll call them to the platform and say, "You guys are going to prophesy over five people that I pick out." They don't even get to pick their own people, which makes it more difficult. They never know what to expect. When they write the words down for me, quite often they will have received the same words. When I look at the paper, I often get a divine knowing about which one is accurate and which details fit together so we get a more complete picture. We prophecy in part and we know in part.

Also, its really great for you and your spouse, independent of each other, to hear God about the same issues. Shonnah and I may pray separately before a meeting and then we compare notes. She'll tell me a word of knowledge that I didn't get, I'll just know that it is God and so I'll add it to my list.

The Word of Knowledge and the Word of Wisdom

The word of knowledge and the word of wisdom often work together. This is because when God gives a word of knowledge to us, it is important for us to know what to do with it. The word of wisdom helps us apply the word of knowledge properly. Wisdom is rightly applying knowledge.

With a word of knowledge there are three parts: revelation, interpretation and delivery. We want to make sure that we are accurate on all three of these. If you receive an accurate word, but miss the interpretation or your delivery makes the person feel condemned, you've dropped the ball. It's not enough to get the word of knowledge—that is only the first step.

It is not advisable to interpret supernatural knowledge with the natural mind. Wisdom allows us to comprehend what God is saying and then guides us in passing it to the person in an appropriate way they can receive. The way we relate to the person when we deliver the word is important and so is the tone of voice, especially to someone who is in anguish or pain.

The Word of Knowledge and the Word of Faith

Quite often the word of knowledge will release you into the faith that you need to see that miracle take place. I've come to the place of such confidence that when I believe I have accurately heard God, and if my word of knowledge comes with a name, an age, a condition, the name of their mother and the name of their son, I know that its a word from God and I know that their miracle will happen. The more detailed the word of knowledge, the more confidence that comes and the more faith imparted. If the word of knowledge is less specific, then there is less of a chance it will happen.

So that's why the word of knowledge and the gift of faith often partner together in releasing healing and miracles into people's lives.

The Word of Knowledge and Healing

Through the word of knowledge we have the operation of ***"the gifts of healing by the same Spirit…" (I Cor. 12:9)***—this is how it is most commonly manifest in the church today. Gifts of healing come out of the word of knowledge because the word of knowledge becomes the vehicle which releases the healing anointing to fulfill the word. The operation of the healing gift in a meeting can stir up a powerful anointing that releases creative miracles. Often a specific powerful word of knowledge will raise faith levels and lift the meeting to a higher and more powerful realm of instant miracles.

The Word of Knowledge and the Gift of Prophecy

The word of knowledge also works together with the gift of prophecy. I often come into the service, then look around the room and say, "God, who do you want me to prophesy over?" The Holy Spirit highlights somebody and my gaze keeps being drawn back to the same one. That's who needs the prophetic word.

Yes, a word of knowledge can direct me to someone who needs a word of prophecy. Although, the word of knowledge involves the past and present and the gift of prophecy usually involves the future, the two gifts can easily operate together and complement each other.

Do you see how all the gifts of the Spirit tend to work together... especially the word of wisdom and the word of knowledge; the gift of faith and the working of healing and miracles. If you operate in one, you tend to operate in four or five.

New Testament Examples of the Word of Knowledge

When we think about the word of knowledge we usually connect it with healing, but there are many other purposes for the word of knowledge in Scripture.

Jesus in Action

In these two verses Jesus instructed His disciples in specific detail. ***"Go into the village opposite you, where as you enter you will find a colt tied, which no one else has ever sat. Loose it and bring it here. And if anyone asks you, 'Why are you loosing it?' thus you shall say to him, 'Because the Lord has need of it'" (Luke 19:30-31).*** This is an example of Jesus in action using the word of knowledge. Pretty specific isn't it?

God still gives very specific words to His people today—we are now Jesus' hands and feet. I've gone into churches where I've known nothing about the churches and the five or ten people that I pick out that morning will all be networked together as key people in a movement. Everyone in the church will see and recognize the network of the ten and they will know that I don't know the network. At other times I'll pull people out from back to front, the side and the middle, and they will tell me that I pulled out all the deacons and elders without knowing. It has happened where a pastor will say, you have called out five people without knowing that they were all my leaders. At that point I have the attention of the entire church and now they will listen to the message I'm about to bring next.

A Soul-Winning Tool

Jesus operated in the word of knowledge with the Samaritan woman at the well. ***"You are right when you say you have no husband. The fact is, you have had five husbands, and the man you have now is not your husband." (John 4:17,18)*** As a result of that word of knowledge, the woman went into the city and said, ***"Come and see a man who told me everything I ever did."(v. 29)*** Then the whole city came out to hear the word and get healed. There was a great revival in the city because of one word of knowledge to one woman.

The word of knowledge is a great soul-winning tool. The key to reaching whole cities isn't just preaching to 5,000 but it's finding the one Samaritan woman, the one that you can give a word of knowledge or a prophecy to. If you can touch that one, they may just be the key to the whole city.

For years I avoided words of knowledge in Africa. "How could it work with 50, 000 people" I thought? If I give a word of knowledge that somebody has a bump in their back and I feel like the spine is bent a little bit, a thousand people will come to the altar. It works a little better in a meeting of 1,000."

One day the Lord said, "Why don't you go for it?" So I said, "OK, I will." God said, "There are four women here with problems in their wombs and reproductive systems." I said, "Oh great, God, them and 10,000 others! Every woman in Africa has problems with her reproductive system, wants to have a child or has some kind of tumor. It's common." But there was more to the word. "No. I want you to pray for four women who are pregnant, " He said. "Oh great, God. There could be 500 pregnant women here," I responded. "No. No. No. These are four women that have been to the witch doctor and had a curse placed on their reproductive system because they looked to the witch doctor, not Me, as the source of their child," explained the Lord. "These women have been pregnant for *years!*" Then I told the crowd what God had said and five women responded that had been pregnant between two to five years, each with a baby still alive in her womb! "It's impossible!" you may be saying. Think of these woman's situations as a miracle on the dark side. Satan has power too.

Another time in the Congo in Africa, I called out a word of knowledge about a woman in the crusade who just had the doctor tell her to leave the hospital and drive down to the meeting because he could do nothing for her. When I called out the word, she had just arrived. "Good, you are the woman that God wants to heal," I said. I prayed for this woman who had been pregnant too long and immediately she began to go into labor. Now that was a word of knowledge!

Because God healed her and others like her, the crowds grew to 60,000 during that crusade in Congo. People came to see the word of knowledge in action. They had never seen anything like that. The crowd's reaction was, "Wow! The witch doctors can't do this." The crowds just grew. The word of knowledge is a great tool for witnessing!

Revelation of Sin

The word of knowledge can reveal sin and corruption in the church. That comes in handy occasionally. In the book of Acts Peter received a word of knowledge that Ananias and Saphira were holding back part of the land and they were lying to the Holy Spirit (Acts 5:1-5).

Let me emphasize though, that this type of ministry is reserved for people who hold the office of prophets, not just those who flow in a revelatory gifting. When you give a word it should edify and encourage. If you receive a word that doesn't edify or encourage, the Lord probably gave it to you so you could pray for that person.

Divine Direction

Maybe you need some divine direction or knowledge in your life. It can come by the word of knowledge as it did in Acts 9:10-11:

> ***"Now there was a certain disciple at Damascus named Ananias; and to him the Lord said in a vision, 'Ananias.' And he said, 'Here I am, Lord.' So the Lord said to him, 'Arise and go to the street called Straight, and inquire at the house of Judas for one called Saul of Tarsus, for behold, he is praying. And in a vision he has seen a man named***

Ananias coming in and putting his hand on him, so that he might receive his sight.'"

That is the kind of specific word of knowledge that we need in the church today. ***"Arise and go the street called Straight…"*** That is divine direction. God told Ananias which street, which house, who lived in the house and He even told him what Paul was doing in the house. The Lord also told Ananias that Saul was expecting him because God had given him a vision.

So what was the result? Salvation for the Gentiles, the spread of the gospel throughout the world and ultimately, our salvation today! This great harvest came as a direct result of a word of knowledge!

Warning of Danger

In this Scripture, Paul was warned by a word of knowledge of a coming danger. This was not prophecy; it was a word of knowledge. Acts 22:17 says "***Now it happened, when I returned to Jerusalem and was praying in the temple, that I was in a trance and saw Him saying to me, 'Make haste and get out of Jerusalem quickly, for they will not receive your testimony concerning Me.'"*** It was a word of knowledge that came while he was in a trance. (I'll cover trances in more detail a little later in this chapter.)

Provision

The word of knowledge brings provision. Jesus gave a word of knowledge to Peter, that he would find the gold to pay his taxes in the fish's mouth (Matt. 17:27). How would you like to receive a word of knowledge like that to bring the provision of God and free you from a difficult financial situation?

It was a word of knowledge. God knew where the fish was, what lake Peter had to go to. He knew what fish was to be caught and that there would be a gold coin in its mouth to pay the taxes. It was a word of knowledge; it wasn't a prophecy. A prophecy would have spoken about Peter, in the future, finding a fish that was going to pay his taxes! But this divine message came as a word of knowledge about a fish that was already there with money in its mouth.

Isn't that a whole lot easier than praying for money? Just ask, "Where God?" And He'll say, "There will be 10 fish, but you take the first fish." Sometimes our provision is right under our nose and we just need knowledge to get it.

Its one thing to pray about something but it's another to be in position to receive what you prayed for. Some of you have been praying for the same thing and the Lord wants to give you the word of knowledge to get what He has already provided for you. So sometimes it requires a word of knowledge—what, where, when, why and who—because God already has that $50, 000 provision. We need to be asking questions like, "What phone call? What meeting? What offering do I need to receive and how do I receive it?"

Childrens' choir at one of our crusades in India

Rather than praying for your son to get saved, you should be asking God how to get your son saved. What about parents asking for words of knowledge about what their kids are doing so when they come home the parents can tell them everything that they did that night? I know a woman that did that with all her kids and the fear of God came on them! All her kids are serving the Lord and loving Him today.

Elisha used the word of knowledge to figure out how he was going to get the ax head. "I borrowed that ax! I need to give it back to my neighbor and the ax head fell off in the water." So the Lord gave him a word of knowledge about throwing a stick in the water and making the ax head float. Wow!

Old Testament Examples of the Word of Knowledge

Warning for a King

The kings of Syria and Israel were at war and the word of knowledge came to Elisha about the enemy king's battle plans. The word of knowledge was given to a prophet to warn the King of the enemy's plan (2 Kings 6:8-10).

Couldn't we use that in the Pentagon today? Wouldn't the U.S. Army Chiefs have liked a word of knowledge about where Saddam Hussein was? Or how about a word of knowledge about Osama planning and plotting his terrorist attacks? That type of specific information is going to be revealed to the church. The government and the world will take notice and realize that the church today has a spiritual gift from heaven that can give warning of what the enemy is planning to do. This gift is a whole lot better than the secret service--

God's eyes look to and fro throughout the whole earth. There is nothing hidden from before His sight. We need to begin to put our faith out there.

Boat-Building Instructions

Noah received a word of knowledge--divine knowledge that the rains and floods were coming and understanding of what to do about it (Genesis 9: 24). Nobody had ever seen rain before, much less a flood. Noah had knowledge of the measurements and what kind of wood to use--everything he needed to build the ark and to save anyone who believed his word of knowledge.

The Unveiling of a Lie

In this Scripture Elisha had a word of knowledge about Gehazi, his servant, lying to Naaman the Syrian and hiding a talent of silver and two changes of clothes. But do you know how he received the word of knowledge? He actually traveled in the spirit to where Gehazi was and watched it happen!

When Elisha confronted him, "Where did you go Gehazi?" Gehazi lied again, "Your servant did not go anywhere." Then Elisha said to him ***"Did not my heart ..."*** (and the word for heart is actually "spirit") ***go with you when the man turned back from the chariot to meet you? Is it time to receive money, and to receive clothing, olive groves, vineyards, sheep, oxen, male and female servants? (II Kings 5:20-26)."***

God sent me five different times in the spirit to see what one of my interns was doing and then I went and confronted him. Sometimes I know the thoughts of my staff. I can call them up and I know when there is some difficult situation that needs to be dealt with. It might take me a week or two to catch up with a problem situation, but it's hard to hide anything from me.

Knowledge of a successor

Elijah had a word of knowledge that Elisha would be his successor. He was told to anoint Elisha the son of Shaphat as the next prophet and Jehu the son of Nimshi as the next King (1 Kings 19:15-16). God knows the right people to get His work done because He knows everyone's heart. We tend to look at the outer appearance, but God truly knows each person's deepest motivations. As we wait on the Lord he will show us who He has appointed as leaders, elders, deacons or for other places in our ministries (or even our businesses).

Lost Property Found

The Old Testament gives us an example of the prophet receiving divine knowledge of where to find the king's lost property: ***"But as for your donkeys that were lost three days ago, do not be anxious about them, for they have been found" (I Sam. 9:20).*** Samuel knew that Saul's donkeys were lost. He knew that the donkeys were lost three days before and he knew that the donkeys had already been found.

On a more personal note about lost things--my wife gets words of knowledge about lost keys. She says, "Let's just stop and ask God where they are. God will do it." Then the Lord will say, "They're under the table in the living room," and my wife will walk right into the living room, look under the table and there they are. Consulting the Lord when you've lost something will sure take a lot of stress off you!

Sixteen Words of Knowledge

I want to look more closely at the passage about Samuel and Saul. Oh, I love this! We see more words of knowledge in 1 Samuel 9 and 10 than any other passage in the entire Bible—you can find at least 16 examples in these few verses.

The first word of knowledge is in 1 Samuel 9:16: ***"Tomorrow about this time, I will send you a man from the land of Benjamin."*** God is speaking to Samuel. God knew who Saul was and what tribe he would come from.

The second word of knowledge is that Samuel knew, by divine knowledge, that Saul would be the next King of Israel:. ***"...and you shall anoint him commander over My people Israel..." (verse 16).***

In the same verse God told Samuel that Saul would save His people from the hand of the Philistines. That's number three. ***"...that he may save My people from the hand of the Philistines...because their cry has come to Me."***

Verse 17 has the fourth example of the word of knowledge: ***"When Samuel saw Saul, the Lord said to him, "There he is, the man of whom I spoke to you."*** God specifically points Saul out to Samuel.

The fifth, sixth and seventh examples of the word of knowledge are in verse 20 which we looked at above: ***"But as for your donkeys that were lost three days ago, do not be anxious about them, for they have been found."***

The eighth example of the word of knowledge is in 1 Samuel 9:23. How about this for a word of knowledge? Samuel said to the cook, ***"Bring the portion of food which I gave you and I said for you to set it apart yesterday."***

By a word of knowledge, Samuel, in preparation for Saul's visit had already told the cook what to prepare and to save a portion for the next day. When Saul arrived Samuel just told the cook to bring in Saul's portion. Can you imagine? Saul just showed up and the prophet already had his meal on the table!

The ninth example of the word of knowledge is found in 1 Samuel 10: 3. ***"Then you shall go on forward from there and come to the terebinth tree of Tabor."*** This is direction given by the word of knowledge.

He said, ***"There three men going up to God at Bethel will meet you, one carrying three young goats, another carrying three loaves of bread, and another carrying a skin of wine."*** Here are the tenth, eleventh and twelfth examples: Three men, will greet you, carrying goats, bread and wine.

Then you have the fourteenth word of knowledge in verse 5. ***"After that you shall come to the hill of God."***

Example fifteen, still in verse 5, God told Samuel to tell Saul that he would meet a group of prophets. Not only would he meet a group of prophets but they would be carrying specific instruments. ***"And it will happen, when you have come there to the city, that you will meet a group of prophets coming down from the high place with a stringed instrument, a tambourine, a flute, and a harp before them; and they will be prophesying."***

The sixteenth example is in verse 6: ***"Then the spirit of the Lord will come upon you and you will prophesy and turn into another man."***

We have seen sixteen different examples of the word of knowledge in just a few verses from 1 Samuel 9:16 to 1 Samuel 10:6.

Growing in the Word of Knowledge

In Psalms 106:15 God declares ***"He sent a wasting disease or a leanness into their soul."*** Why did He treat the children of Israel in this way? The reason is given in verse 13: ***"They did not wait for His counsel."*** When I saw this I said, "Oh, there is something important about waiting quietly in His presence, about listening prayer and waiting for His counsel. So I began to take time to see what the Father was doing before I got to the service. I said, "God, you showed Smith Wigglesworth pictures of people's faces before he even got to a service. He knew what they looked like and what they were wearing so that when he got to the meeting he would recognize the people from his vision and he would call them up and they would be healed."

I thought, "Wouldn't that be a whole lot better than just going to the meeting and praying for the sick and trying to see who God wants to heal? Can I actually come to the meeting having seen the faces of the people that God wants to heal? I'd love it if I looked at the crowd and saw a man's face or a woman's face and I knew that it was the person that God wanted me to pray for."

So I began to sow into the ministry of waiting. And every day for a couple of months in a healing revival in Oregon, I spent one to three hours a day waiting in His presence to receive knowledge. I'd have a pen and paper and I'd say, "OK Father, show me what You are going to do tonight?" And I would wait.

That's when I received that powerful vision and supernatural knowledge about that boy in the hospital in a coma. That was one of the first times that I ever had any other kind of visitation along with the word of knowledge. Usually, as I was waiting before the Lord, I would have a knowing (I knew that I knew somehow) that cancer was going to be healed and I'd write that down. And then I'd have a knowing that back conditions were going to be healed—I didn't even know how I knew. At first I wasn't even having visions of a back being healed. I wasn't seeing faces. I just had the "I know that I know that I know" that backs would be healed, so I'd write that down.

If you're used to soaking prayer, all you need to do is adjust your focus a little to hear from God. Instead of soaking to receive more of the Lord's presence, you soak for the purpose of hearing God. Personally, I use the same soaking model of receiving to hear from God in preparation for a meeting. If I'm soaking, I'll just keep a journal beside me. It's really quite easy to hear from the Lord; it just takes practice and commitment everyday. That's it.

After a while I wasn't satisfied with a general word of knowledge. I learned that when I received a fragment of knowledge I could push for details. So I'm thinking "Jesus, Jesus, Jesus," and my mind thinks, "gall bladder." I can stop there and say, "God is going to heal someone's gall bladder," but that doesn't create much faith. In a meeting of 500 people I could just get up and say, "God is going to heal gall bladders, arthritis, tumors, hernias and headaches" and there is a pretty good chance that people would respond.

So I learned to push for details. I'd say, "God, is it a male or a female?" and right away my mind would think, "female," and I would go with the strongest sense. Then I would ask, "How old is she?" Even if the Lord didn't answer with a specific number, sometimes the Lord will give me an impression of the person's general age range. I'll have a flash of a woman the age of my mother-in-law or a flash of a child skipping rope." Then I'll have a ball park figure. Those extra details bring a little more credibility to my word of knowledge. By this point I know the person is a woman, I know that she has a gall bladder problem and I know that she is over 40-years-old.

Then I will take the leap and say, "I sense that the Lord showed me that there was a healing for a gall bladder and I am going to pray for anyone with this condition, but one specific case I felt was a female between the age of 40 and 42." Then three people may stand up with gall bladder problems, but only one of them would be a female about 40 years old. I would be thinking, "Wow, it worked!"

Note that I didn't say, "There is a woman here, a 40-year-old, with gall bladder problems." I made it clear that I would pray for anyone with gall bladder problems and then was more specific. In that way I left myself some room for error when I became more specific and said that I felt like there might be somebody here "around this age."

This is how I grew in the word of knowledge. I actually practiced this everyday for months in that healing revival. And it's "according to your faith…." If your faith is for names then you can get names. I taught almost all the guys on our team to get names and they came up to my level right away. If I set the standard: "Let's just expect to see it by vision, and push for details," all of a sudden the level of receiving gets higher.

I set the standard on what kinds of word of knowledge I go for. If I am in a prophetic conference I say, "I am going to go for prophetic words." If I am in a healing conference, "I am going for conditions." It all depends on what you ask for. I'll wait on the Lord and sometimes the Lord will tell me, "It's name's night" and other times I just decide that it's name's night. "Lord, will you give me ten names?" I'll ask. I actually set goals. You might want to start by asking the Lord for one or two names. ***"According to your faith let it be to you" (Matt. 9:29).***

I've been doing this for many years now so I usually go for 15 names. After I started getting 15 names I began asking for the names of people's mothers, so I pushed the envelope a little further. Then I would stretch my faith further and say, "Lord, tell me the name of her sister." Then I pushed for last names and addresses. It depends on how many details you want with each word of knowledge! You can press for it according to your faith level.

Let's say you get five details with one condition, so you discern gall bladder and five other things. One could be her age, address, her city, how many children she has and the name of her daughter. So now you might pick and choose which details you offer and you might take it slow. That way if you miss on one, at least you were accurate on two or three of the points and you didn't miss it on the whole word of knowledge.

I teach people to start by giving the condition, and then saying, "I sense that you might have a couple of children," because five people will stand up with the same condition and you want to narrow it down. So then you give the second detail. "We have five gall bladder problems but I know there is one person here that the Lord wants to heal right now. I'll pray for the other four in a minute. Let's get the specific woman." But they are all women with children so all five are still standing. So now you call out one detail at a time until one woman is left standing. Now you know you have the right lady.

Maybe you also had her mother's name but there is no need for you to give that because you already narrowed it down to the right one. And if you missed it on number three you can back track to detail number one and two and keep yourself covered. Don't just throw out all your pearls by saying "You are 56, your name is Mary, your mother is Jane, you have two sons and no daughters." What if you are right on every detail except that she has no sons and two daughters? If you had taken it a little slower you still would have built everyone's faith, but now that you just threw it all out there and no one responded—you just flat lined.

Worshipping the Lord during a crusade

I would have started with, "There is a bladder condition." If only one person stood up there would be no need for me to offer the other details. But if I wanted to, when she came up I could say, "Does this make sense?" Rather than, "This is the word of the Lord!" I could say "I sensed this, and sensed that." And the more she nodds her head the more the faith level rises in the meeting and the more I protect myself. If I give all the information and I am wrong in one of the five, I could still blow the faith level in the room.

Preparing To Receive Words

Divine Knowledge Only

Because the word of knowledge is supernatural, knowledge from our natural mind and senses can actually hinder us receiving insights from God. It's very difficult to receive a word of knowledge when you know too much about the person because the word of knowledge is divine knowledge that comes *without* prior knowing. I try to stay as detached as I can from knowing anything about where you came from, why you are at the meeting and what your needs are. Sometimes I'll say, "Don't tell me anything about yourself." Everyone wants to communicate with me about what they need or what is going on but that can actually be a hindrance for getting a specific word of knowledge about their lives.

Desire

The Bible says in1 Corinthians 14:1 that we are to earnestly desire spiritual gifts. God doesn't want you to desire something that He doesn't want you to have. Paul the apostle in Romans 1:11 wanted us to have the word of knowledge. ***"For I long to see you that I may impart on to you some spiritual gift to the end that you might be established."***

Every ministry has authority from the Lord to impart what they have as a spiritual gift to the believers they minister to. When I lay hands on you in the anointing service I am fulfilling Romans 1:11.

How Words of Knowledge Come

Thoughts or Impressions

A word of knowledge can come as a thought or an impression on the mind—it comes as a confident certainty, a knowing. Thoughts and impressions seem to be the most common way that people receive words of knowledge, especially when they are starting out. There comes a divine knowing—it's something that just pops into your thoughts and you know it.

A Body Impression

Quite often when people get words of knowledge, they get them in the realm of "I feel it." They get impressions in their body. You can actually feel the word of knowledge in the form of pain in your physical body. So, if God releases the anointing of the word of knowledge, many people might get pain that they didn't have before—that is also a word of knowledge.

Let's look at one other definition. A word of knowledge means "to know" but it also means "to feel." There is a realm of the word of knowledge that isn't just "I know that I know that I know." There is a realm of the word of knowledge that allows us to feel. My wife gets words of knowledge like this. She will come to the meeting and say, "Oh my chest! I have stabbing pains in my heart." When I ask what's wrong, she replies, "It's a word of knowledge." When she delivers that word of knowledge she is released from that pain.

The next day she may come into the meeting and say, "My back! My back! Ow!" And this time I'll say, "Oh, that's a word of knowledge." Or her neck will get stiff and she exclaims, "My neck, I can't move my neck." That's my clue that someone in the meeting has a neck problem. My wife often gets words of knowledge this way--by feeling. The word "to know" includes that aspect of feeling. As for me, though, I could probably count the number of times on one hand that I have felt a word of knowledge.

Trances

A trance is a dream-like state in which you never really go to sleep. A trance is not so much how you get revelation; it's a state that you go into where revelation happens. A trance is simply a state that you go into to receive a vision. If you look at Acts 10:10 Peter first goes into a trance and then he has a vision.

Having a trance is like going to the dentist for Novocain. It's God numbing your senses so that He can take you into the spirit realm. A trance is like going into a dream without being asleep. So if you aren't in bed sleeping and God wants to give you a dream, He gives you a trance instead. It's as if the Lord anesthetizes your body while you are awake so He can take you into a dream-like state.

In Acts 10:10-20 Peter has a trance and heaven opens. When Peter wonders within himself what this vision meant, the men who have been sent by Cornelius arrive at the gate of the house where Peter is staying. They call and ask whether Simon, whose surname is Peter, is lodging there. Peter has just seen heaven open and he is wondering what it means. He receives a word of knowledge as the Spirit says to him, ***"While Peter thought about the vision, the Spirit said to him, "Behold, three men are seeking you. Arise, go down and go with them, doubting nothing for I have sent them" (Acts 10:19-20).*** Peter has been in a trance and had a vision. Before these men even knock on the door, by a word of knowledge, Peter learns that they are there.

A Vision

This Scripture shows how a word of knowledge came for Paul as a vision while he was in a trance. Remember the trance is the state you're in and then you can receive revelation. Notice that Paul says that he "saw." He writes: ***"Now it happened, when I returned to Jerusalem and was praying in the temple, that I was in a trance and saw Him saying to me, 'Make haste and get out of Jerusalem quickly, for they will not receive your testimony concerning Me'" (Acts 22:17-18).***

Through Dreams

A word of knowledge came for Paul in a dream. Paul was shown where to go to preach the gospel. A man came to him in a dream and said, "Come to Macedonia." Paul had divine direction about where to go next (Acts 10: 9-10).

I actually receive whole downloads for services through dreams. I dream about who I should call out. I dream who is testifying on the microphone and when I wake up I write down all the testimonies that were given or all the people I called out.

Sometimes if I know that I have to minister the next morning and I may not have time to wake up and pray before the morning session I'll ask for dreams of tomorrow's healings before I go to bed. People ask, "Todd! How is it that you roll out of bed at 9:30 a.m. and you are in the pulpit by 10:00 a.m. and you still give all those detailed words of knowledge? It's so early in the morning; you haven't even had coffee yet. How did you flow like that?" I dream.

The Still Small Voice

God also gives words through His still small voice. We know how the still small voice of God in 1Kings 19 came to Elijah, but there is also a great story about receiving the word of knowledge in 1 Samuel 9:15-16. It says ***"And God spoke into Samuel's ear."***

I have been getting this quite often in the last few months. The Lord actually whispers to me in my ear and I hear Him. He says something like, "I am healing a woman with cancer; she is 19 and sitting on your left." Or, "I am healing somebody over here right now with a hip problem." I actually hear the Lord speaking into my ear, whispering what He is doing right at the moment that He is doing it.

The Word of God

"But the Helper, the Holy Spirit, whom the Father will send in My name, He will teach you all things, and bring to your remembrance all things that I said to you" (Jn. 14:26-27). In this Scripture Jesus talks about the Holy Spirit bringing to remembrance all the things that He has said to us.

This happens to me quite often. God will remind me of a certain healing that took place in the Bible and I'll just be thinking about that miracle and I'll know there is somebody in the meeting that is going to receive that same miracle. God can also remind you of a situation that applies to your meeting, it doesn't just have to be healing.

Another way the Holy Spirit will speak to me is by flashing me back to another meeting to a certain word of knowledge I gave then. The Lord gives me this flashback to tell me to deliver the same word. Often the Lord will bring me back to words of knowledge that I've given in past meetings to indicate that He wants to heal the same condition in the meeting that day.

I've been in at least two other meetings where the Lord reminded me of that December 5, 2000 word about the boy coming out of the coma. I went to a flashback and relived that word of knowledge—it was God's way of indicating that I was to give that same word of knowledge again.

Angels

In Acts 10:30 Cornelius says, ***"Four days ago I was fasting until this hour; and at the ninth hour I prayed in my house and behold, a man stood before me in bright clothing, and said, 'Cornelius, your prayer has been heard, and your alms are remembered in the sight of God.'"*** Sometimes the angel comes with a word of knowledge.

In my meetings, at times, an angel actually visits me. He is an angel called Healing Revival and he is like the angel that stirred the waters of

Bethesda in John 5. Angels in the Bible are actually ministering spirits. They obey God's Word but they are also messengers. When the angel visits me on the night of a service, in five minutes I could know 20 names. I'll have an increased knowing of accurate divine pieces of information. I'm given details like first, last and middle names and names of siblings. The presence of the angel comes and I can write down "Bob, and his Dad's name is Bill. Melanie Sue and her daughter's name is Wanda." This only happens when the angel comes. However, when the angel visits me, the frequency and accuracy of the word of knowledge just goes off the charts.

Naturally Supernatural

I expect many readers will be wondering about the details of such supernatural testimonies. I know it might be hard to accept and understand such experiences. I want to say, though, that this way of life has become so normal to me that I forget how abnormal it is to many others. If it seems sometimes that when I share I am a little bit flippant, it is because supernatural revelation has become so common to me, by God's grace, that I forget how uncommon it is for the rest of the church.

I'm sure I actually lose people when I talk about an angel here and a trance there and a vision everywhere. So if it seems like that, I am sorry. Even though these spiritual experiences my still be somewhat rare in the church today, I am convinced that they should be normal for all Christians. We are called to be naturally supernatural.

Giving A Word Of Knowledge

Questions to ask first:

When you receive a word of knowledge you should ask yourself four questions—these questions will help you understand the purpose of the word:

- Is this word for prayer only?
- Should I share this knowledge with the local church leaders first?
- Is this public or private information?
- Will this word bring edification to the individual and the church?

Now let me mention some checks and balances. I get words of knowledge about adultery, homosexuality, people's sexual sins and what is going on in their life at the time. I see all kinds of gross things. But I need to ask if it is for private or public information because a word of knowledge, just like prophecy, has to be for comfort, edification and exhortation. The word of knowledge is just like all the other gifts—it has to be for the profit of all. When giving out words in public meetings you *must* give them in such a way that the individual, and the meeting as a whole, is edified and encouraged. So if what you are sharing isn't going to profit everyone, then maybe it's not to be public information. If you have any doubts about the knowledge received or what you should do with it, check with your pastor, elder, church leader or whoever is giving oversight to the ministry.

Qualify Your Requests

People have said to me, "Todd, I have been able to diagnose sicknesses, but I don't seem to be able to do more than that. How do I deal with the correct diagnosis of a sickness but not having the ability or power to see the healing through?" I explain that I started asking God to show me only the ones that were going to be healed.

I instructed one of my disciples to make just that little adjustment in her prayer time. Now she asks God to only show her the ones that He is going to heal that night. After that prayer she no longer called out words of knowledge that were accurate but lacking the power to bring the healing to pass.

The Lord wants to release a new, or greater, ability to receive and activate powerful words of knowledge through our lives. Now, as I agree with you, pray this prayer to receive fresh impartation of revelatory knowledge:

> *"Father I ask for the word of knowledge. I ask You to come, Holy Spirit, and release the gift of the word of knowledge. Father I pray for the spirit of prophecy, for the spirit of wisdom and revelation in the knowledge of Him. Let there come an increase of wisdom. I cry out and ask for wisdom. I cry out and ask for knowledge. God I pray for the anointing of divine knowledge."*

> *"Lord, I give my thoughts; I give my mind; I give the realm of my imagination--I give them all to You. I ask You, Holy Spirit, for the mind of Christ. Let Your power come upon my mind. I am seeking the deep things; now please give me one God-thought, in Jesus' name."*

Chapter Eight

HIDDEN PRAYER AND HEALING

In this chapter, we'll focus on the main purposes of prayer. Prayer prepares and empowers us to do God's will; it brings strength for trials and revelation of God's purpose. These are very important, however, prayer's most important functions are that it hides us in Christ and keeps us dead to our old nature.

Prayer Prepares

Strength for Trials

In Mathew 26:35-39 Peter said to Jesus:

"'Even if I have to die with You, I will not deny You!' And so said all the disciples. Then Jesus came with them to a place called Gethsemane, and said, 'Sit here and watch with Me.' And He took with Him Peter and the two sons of Zebedee, and He began to be sorrowful and deeply distressed. Then He said to them, 'My soul is exceedingly sorrowful even to

> ***death. Stay here and watch with Me.' He went a little farther and fell on His face, and praying said, 'O My Father, if it is possible, let this cup pass from Me; nevertheless; not as I will.'"***

Jesus actually said, "Watch and pray." It was a call for the disciples to pray, not to just sit. The disciples all fell asleep instead of praying and because of the lack of prayer they all fell away. You see, if you don't prepare in prayer you will never have strength for trials. I believe that it was this prayer time in the garden that sustained Jesus through Calvary's cross. At the end of this prayer time the angels came and ministered to Him. I believe it was a divine impartation of strength.

Peter's heart was good, but like us, his flesh was weak. We are overcome by the weakness of our flesh when we don't pray. How many times have you found that you just don't do what you really want to do and you seem to be overcome by the lust of your flesh?

When I go more than a few days without the kind of intimacy that I need in His presence, I get overcome by the nature and the ways of the old man. I feel like saying, "God, I come out of the grave so quickly! Man, I start stinking after one day!" My spirit is willing, I still want to love and serve God, but it is amazing how quickly the flesh can become weak. It is because I didn't watch and pray with Him.

Revelation of Purpose

The revelation of purpose comes through prayer. Take a look at Jesus' words here:

> ***"Jesus departed and went into a deserted place. And the crowd sought Him and came to Him, and tried to keep Him from leaving them; but He said to them, 'I must preach the kingdom of God to the other cities also, because for this purpose I have been sent'" (Luke 4:42-43).***

Note the urgency when He says, "I must preach the kingdom of God to other cities also." How did He know that? God's purpose came to Him in prayer. The crowd said, "No, let's stay here in the healing revival; let's extend the meeting." But there was a sense of urgency to go on because He knew His purpose and assignment.

We see the same thing in ***Acts 10:9-10:***

"The next day, as they went on their journey and drew near the city, Peter went up onto the housetop to pray, about the sixth hour. Then he became very hungry and wanted to eat; but while they made ready, he fell into a trance… (Next the scriptures describe Peter's vision with the sheet coming down holding unclean animals.) While Peter thought about the vision, the Spirit said to Him, 'Behold, three men are seeking you. Arise therefore and go down and go with them, doubting nothing; for I have sent them.'"

You see prayer gives the vision. Peter was in prayer in the sixth hour on the roof-top. It prepared him to receive the vision that would radically change his deeply held religious beliefs. Prayer also opened up revival for Cornelius and his whole house to get saved and for the Holy Spirit to fall on the gentiles. It all came out of Peter's sixth hour prayers.

If you don't pray you will lose the sense of God's purpose and direction. If you don't have the purpose of God, you will end up trying to be somebody He doesn't want you to do something you shouldn't do. You don't need to emulate anyone else that God is using; you need to be who God has called you to be. The only place that you are going to get the revelation of God's purpose for your life is through prayer. Pray to receive the power to do what God has called you to do.

One of Jesus' most important goals in prayer was to see what the Father was doing. ***"Then Jesus answered and said unto them, 'Most assuredly, I say to you, The Son can do nothing of Himself, but what He sees the Father do; for whatever He does, the Son also does in like manner'" (John 5:19).*** It was in prayer all night on the mountain that Jesus received visions of what the Father wanted to do the next day and then Jesus went out and fulfilled those mandates.

Prayer Empowers

Jesus said in Luke 24:49, ***"But tarry in the city of Jerusalem until you are endued with power from on high."*** We see the fulfillment of the disciple's empowerment in Acts 2:1-3. The 120 are gathered together in the upper room. The power of God fell after ten days in prayer and supplication. They were all in one accord (one purpose) and in one place. Then we know that in Acts 2, on the day of Pentecost, they were filled with the Spirit and tongues as of fire rested upon each one of them. "***(They) began to speak with other tongues, as the Sprit gave them utterance" (Acts 2:4).***

I suggest that we have powerless Christianity today because we don't wait and tarry in consistent, ongoing prayer until God comes upon us. We give up too quickly. We pray a little here and we pray a little there, but we don't really have desperation. Ten days, day and night, in prayer with fasting until the power falls, that's how the old revivals were birthed. That is how the old revivalists set themselves on fire, they just decided, "I'm going to wait until it happens. I am going to pray day and night because I am desperate for His presence."

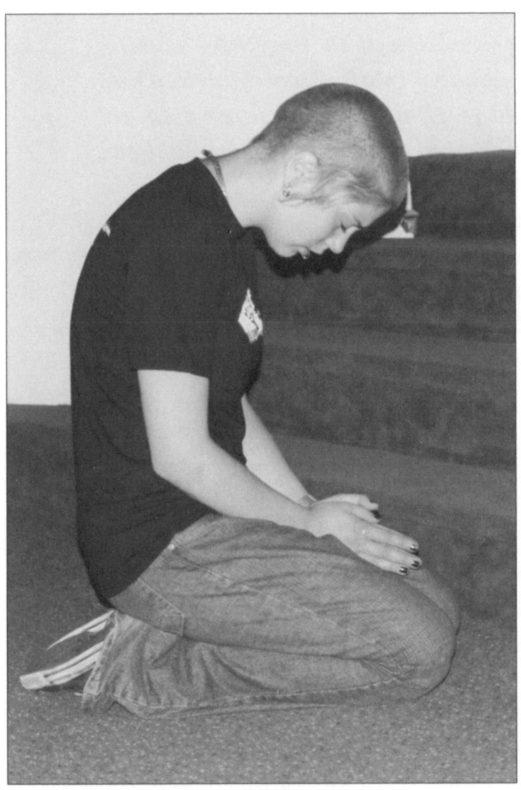

Waiting on the Lord at a Joel's Army Youth Conference

So even after God opened heaven and gave revival, (healings, salvations, deliverances, miracles and the birth of the early church) the disciples continued in Acts 2, 3, 4, doing what they did in the upper room. To sustain the level of what God gave them and to take them to the next level they continued on in prayer. If you read Acts 4:31, they are still together in daily prayer. Their attitude was, "Don't give up now."

When you read the book of Acts you might think that Chapter 3 happened the day after Chapter 2. The time between Acts 2:13 and Acts 2: 14 might actually have been months. So time went by and here they were still crying out. When they had prayed in Acts 4:31, the place where they had assembled together was shaken and they were all filled with the Holy Ghost *again*, and they spoke the Word with boldness.

Look what happens in Acts 4:33, which is years into the revival: "***And with great power the apostles gave witness to the resurrection of the Lord Jesus. And great grace was upon them all.***" They went from power to great power and from grace to great grace when they prayed. If you would like to have great power and great grace then pray!

Prayer Hides

This is the most important part of what I want to share about prayer. Prayer is not only about being empowered and anointed to do better. There is place in prayer that works together with healing. I discovered that just about every example of Jesus alone in prayer was either right after He did miracles or right before He did miracles.

I asked, "Jesus was that because You needed to prepare for tomorrow's healing service? Did You need to see what the Father was doing and get words of knowledge? Were You empty and needing to be filled?" The Holy Spirit spoke that Jesus withdrew because that was His way of being able to handle the fame and the growth. He had to withdraw into a place that was secret and quiet. Do you know what the word "withdrew" means? It means to give place. See, Jesus gave place to prayer. If Jesus needed to do this, we will be crushed by the demand of the crowds if we don't give the glory back to Him and run and hide in His presence.

It is vital for us to stay in hiddenness and prayer to help us remain humble in the midst of what God is going to do. The Devil is going to come and offer you the kingdom, the world, a reputation and a great big ministry. The only thing that is going to keep you in the midst of all that power and great healings is to go right back to the place of hiddenness where it all started and to worship Him and give Him honor and praise.

Jesus' Ministry Model

"Then a great multitude followed Him, because they saw His signs which He performed on those who were diseased" (John 6:2). Let's face it. Miracles and signs draw big crowds. But a later verse shows us Jesus' response to the crowds: ***"Therefore when Jesus perceived that they were about to come and take Him by force to make Him King, He departed again to the mountain by Himself alone" (John 6:15).***

Right after all these miracles took place the crowd began to grow and Jesus' first response was, "I must go back into a place of hiddeness and get alone with God." There really is something about being hidden away in that place where we can't be touched by the glory and fame that comes with the healing ministry.

So Jesus just didn't withdraw to prepare and Jesus didn't withdraw just to be empowered, Jesus withdrew to hide from the crowds. Sometimes the devil can't take you out with gold or girls so he just makes you busy. He just throws a little bit more fame at you or a little more success so that you are too busy trying to keep up with the momentum and you have no time to pray and seek His face. He knows that one day it will crush you.

Some of us wonder, "God why isn't there a greater anointing on my life for healing?" It's because our impure and immature motives can cause us to stumble and fall. Sometimes when God is moving in healing, our motives are for our benefit. If we still have worldly values, we might think, "What could this do for my ministry? If God would only use me to pray for one blind man and a powerful minister saw it, he might want me to travel with him. I'd have my big break."

Here's a good example to strive for: Remember when Jesus healed a leper and told him not to tell anyone about it? "***And He charged him to tell no one…. However, the report went around concerning Him all the more; and great multitudes came together to hear, and to be healed by Him of their infirmities. So He Himself often withdrew into the wilderness and prayed" (Luke 5:14-16).***

Not us. "Please. Let everybody know." But there was something about Jesus that caused Him to say, "Shhhhh, let's keep it quiet." There was something about Him that was untouched by the need for the big name, the big success. His response was, "We just healed all these people and now more people are coming so I am going to withdraw." He often withdrew into the wilderness and prayed. If it was necessary for Jesus, how much more so for you and me?

Look at Luke 9:10. "***Jesus took them and went aside privately into a deserted city…."*** The disciples have been casting out demons and healing the sick and they came back with mighty revival reports. Jesus knew that hiddenness was going to protect them when the crowds came. He said, "Let's go away to a deserted place for a while and pray. Because if you don't stay hidden in prayer, the crowds will crush you later." If God is going to use you mightily in miracles you need to have your life hidden with Christ in God. You have to hide from pride.

Heavenly Visitation

I remember in the early days of my ministry I would say, "I am going to prophesy over everyone who shows up tomorrow." I prepared in prayer before the service. When I was done at 4:00 a.m. all I wanted to do was go to bed! But when I came home I said, "I am going to pray like I did before I went to the service because I want to love God after, just like I loved Him before. I want to be hidden away."

I was lying in bed and I began to worship and call His name, "Oh

Jesus, wonderful Jesus! You are beautiful and I love you." I became aware of the Lord's presence. Just then the door opened. "Errrreeeee!" My heart just about jumped out of my chest. I looked and nobody was there but I heard the door go, "click!" Have you ever felt the Presence, but nobody was there? I was freaking out. Suddenly, colors came at me out of the darkness like a living rainbow, shimmering emerald, purple and yellow. I thought, *God, it's the coat of many colors!* Honestly, that was my first thought! It came toward the bed like a shimmering pillar of light with color and life.

It was Jesus. He sat down on the edge of my bed! The sheets moved; the mattress pressed down as if someone just sat down. Then He took His hand and cupped it over my face and I could smell vanilla, cinnamon, frankincense and myrrh. It was the fragrances of the Lord. Jesus said, "I am so pleased that you spent time with Me before the service and especially that you hid away with Me after the service."

I remember one snowy day my wife said to me, "Todd, everyone is going out to the snow hill." They were going to go tobogganing and then have hot chocolate.

I was thinking, "Hallelujah, what a great thing to do on a Sunday; there is three feet of snow. All right! I'm ready to go and hit that hill."

Just as I was about to walk to the door, the Holy Spirit said, "Stay with Me."

"But God, hot chocolate at the restaurant, I mean... You are going to be here in two hours when I get back. You are busy running the universe. Surely there are billions of other people that you can be with right now. I mean, God?"

"Well, Todd, you can go if you want to." So I made the sacrifice and I stayed.

My wife had been barren because of chemotherapy she had when she was an adolescent. We were struggling, unsuccessfully, to have a child the first year of marriage. My wife went to a service that evening and a prophet called out a word of knowledge and prayed for her. She felt fire go through her lower body. Seven days later she conceived. The Holy Spirit said it was because I had stayed alone with Him.

Remember Phillip (Acts 8:26-38) who was in a revival? There were miracles and the crowds were coming. God said, "I want you to go to one, the Ethiopian eunuch." There is something about God, bigger isn't always better.

Here's another example. John G. Lake, who had one of the biggest healing ministries, was out in the woods or the mountains alone in prayer. He saw a young crippled boy—for some reason the boy was alone and was screaming, "Mommy! Mommy"! John G. Lake made sure that nobody was there and then he snuck up to where the child was, laid hands on the boy, got him healed and ran away before anyone could see. What a good example of hiddenness in prayer.

After great miracle services the people want to make Jesus King, but He said no. "***Therefore when Jesus perceived that they were about to come and take Him by force to make Him king, He departed again to the mountain by Himself alone" (John 6:15).***

Throughout the Gospels Jesus hides Himself and prays because He knows if He hides by Himself after every great miracle, He'll be right in His heart and pure and free from the spirit of pride that wants to attack in the midst of great things.

Prayer Brings Death

We are going to talk about how prayer brings death and keeps us humble. Remember how Jesus went in the desert to be tempted? I want you to notice something in Luke 4:1 it says, ***"Jesus filled with the Spirit returned from the Jordan and was led by the Spirit into the wilderness, being tempted for forty days by the devil."***

Do you know that being *filled* with the Spirit is not the *power* of the Spirit? They are two different things. Jesus (already filled with the Spirit in Luke 4:1) is driven into the wilderness and then He comes out in Luke 4: 14 (in the power of the Spirit). "***Then Jesus returned in the power of the Spirit to Galilee..."*** Filled with the Spirit and the power of the Spirit are two different things. It was praying and dying to Himself that made the difference. Something happened during Jesus' forty days in the wilderness, as Jesus walked through that season of dying to self, that caused the power of the Holy Spirit to be released in His life.

Dying to Earthly Things

Colossians 3:1-4 gives us key to this glorious death to self:

> ***"If then you were raised with Christ, seek those things which are above, where Christ is, sitting at the right hand of God. Set your mind on things above, not on the things of the earth. For you died and your life is hidden with Christ in God."***

See the connection with "you died" and "your life is hidden with

Christ in God"? When you are no longer dead, your life is no longer hidden. If you want your life to be hidden with Christ in God, the key is for you to die. You might be asking, "How long do I need to die before I am really dead"? Paul the apostle said, ***"I die daily" (I Cor. 15:31).*** The key is to die to self daily. So I want to share some keys about dying to self and dying to sin.

Dying Daily

Romans 6 talks about the need to die to sin even after you are saved. Some people think it's done at the cross. "Why do anything that He has already done? I'm dead. What is all this talk about 'I must die? I must decrease, lay down my life, take up my cross'? I am dead in Christ, I am a new creation, and I am born again!" There is truth to that, but Paul teaching here in Romans 6: 3-12 makes it clear:

> ***"Or do you not know that as many of us as were baptized into Christ Jesus were baptized into His death? (He's speaking of the moment of salvation.) Therefore we were buried with Him through baptism into death, that just as Christ was raised from the dead by the glory of the Father. Even so we also should walk in the newness of life. For if we have been united together in the likeness of His death, certainly we also shall be in the likeness of His resurrection, knowing this, that our old man was crucified with Him, that the body of sin might be done away with, that we should no longer be slaves of sin. For he who has died has been freed from sin. Now if we died with Christ, we believe that we shall also live with Him, knowing that Christ, having been raised from the dead, dies no more. Death no longer has dominion over Him…Likewise you also, reckon yourselves to be dead indeed to sin, but alive to God in Christ Jesus our Lord. Therefore do not let sin reign in your mortal body…"***

As this Scripture teaches us, when we have died to our flesh or carnal nature, we will walk in the light and will not fall into persistent sin. Christians who live in habitual sin are really not dead to self. The minute that we sin we step out from under the umbrella of being hidden with Christ. We are no longer dead and we become open to the enemy's attack. We then need to confess our sin and fully submit carnal nature to the Lordship of Jesus once again.

Romans 6:13 confirms this message, "***And do not present your members as instruments of unrighteousness to sin, but present yourselves to God as being alive from the dead..."*** What happens if you let sin reign in your mortal body? Then you obey its lust. So now you become a slave to sin and death and you are no longer dead even though you are baptized into Jesus' death. When you let sin reign in your mortal body you are no longer counting yourself as dead and when you are not dead your life is not hidden in Christ any longer!

What is the next key to staying dead? ***"For you died and your life is hidden with Christ in God (Colossians 3:3)."*** You are only dead when you set your mind on the things of heaven, not when you set your mind on the things of earth. When you set your mind on the things of the earth you let sin reign in your mortal body and you come alive again. So the key to death is to set your mind on things above—that really can only take place in prayer.

Humility—Key to Death and Life

Humility is one of the keys. Do you know what humility is? Biblical humility is not someone who talks quietly, (thank goodness or I'd be immediately eliminated!) Biblical humility literally means obedience, total dependence on Him. You can think you are humble in character, but if you do not do what the Lord tells you every time the Lord tells you to do it, that is pride. To be totally dependent upon Him means that it's no longer I who live, but Christ who lives within me. So I do the when, what, where, and how as the Lord commands. When I don't it becomes my own way, disobedience, it becomes self. Humility is complete and total dependence on the Spirit, not when you feel like it, but when He says move. Paul talks about it in John 3:30: "***He must increase, but I must decrease.***" Humility is of the heart.

The only thing that is going to sustain us in the midst of the healing anointing that God wants to give is to be able to keep that place of death and humility in our hearts so that we can handle the success and crowds that come with the healing anointing.

Jesus understood the importance of staying dead to the pull of the world and hidden in the Father. It is just as important for believers today to understand hiddenness and prayer and to remain humble in the midst of what God is doing. The Devil is going to offer us the world, a kingdom, reputation and a great big ministry. Our hearts must be right in the midst of great power or we'll be crushed. If you want to stay hidden, you've got to stay dead. If you're going to stay dead, you have to stay conscious of the revelation God gives us in Romans 6. As we remain in that place of death to self, our reputation no longer matters. Now our only concern is bringing glory and fame to our Father. In that glorious place of death to self, we can experience the joy, peace, power and abundant life that God wants us to have.

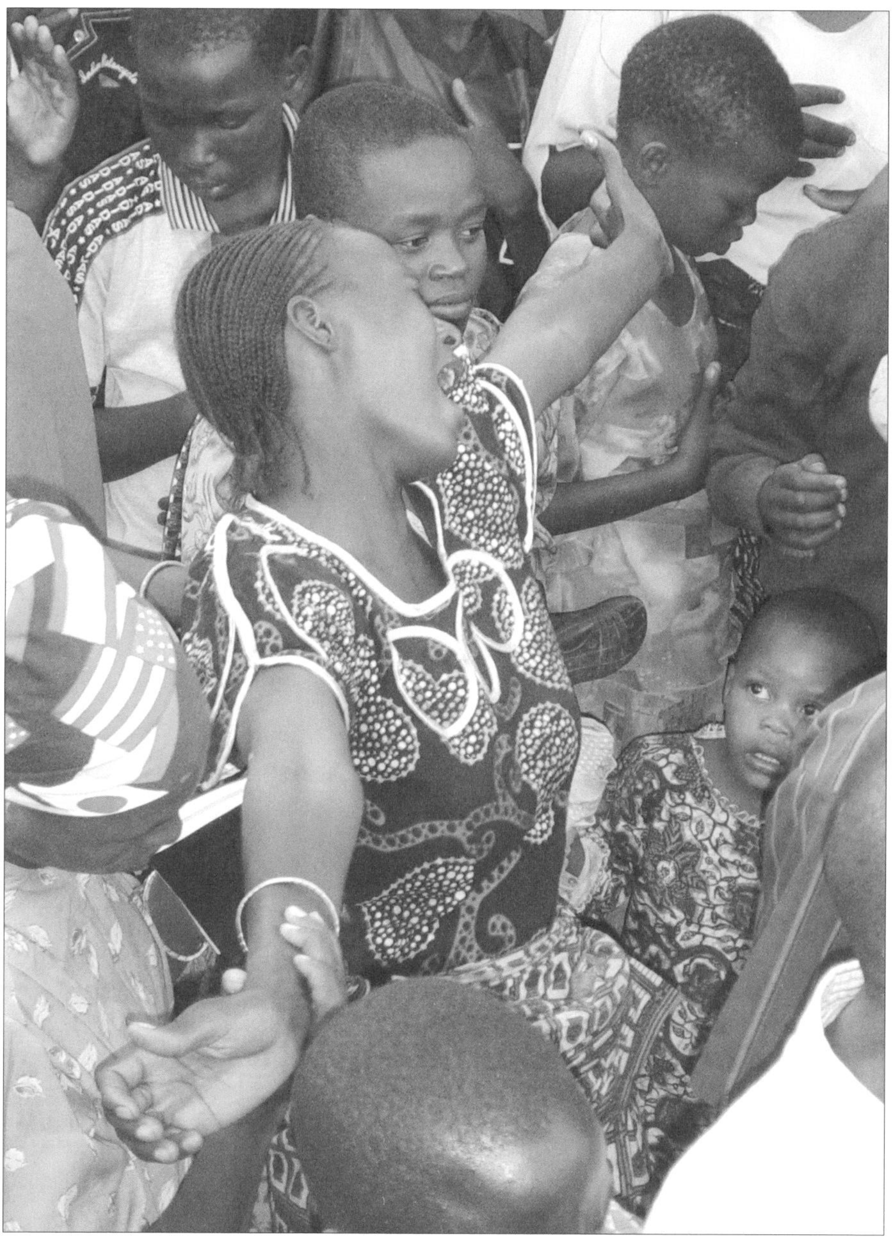

Woman crying out to God during a crusade in Africa

Chapter Nine

CREATIVE MIRACLES

We were conducting a crusade in Ginga, Uganda a few years ago. The Lord had been moving in great power in our services. Then He performed one of the most profound acts of power we had ever seen up till that day. He released not just one creative miracle but a series of creative miracles that almost blew all of our circuits. The second evening of the crusade, the Lord had me tell the crowd: "Take your hand and place it on the part of your body that needs healing." I then prayed a general prayer for healing over the entire crowd. There were so many thousands in attendance that it was impossible for me to lay hands on each one. "Holy Spirit come and heal sick bodies right where they are," I cried to the Lord. I also rebuked and took authority over spirits of infirmity and devils of cancer. Then I asked people to press their way up to the platform if they knew that God had just touched their body and given them a miracle. My staff began to interview the people who came forward.

That evening four powerful creative miracles took place. First a woman testified that she had breast cancer several years earlier and had been to all the voodoo magic practitioners and witch-doctors in the community for a cure. When all the attempts of these occult healers had failed, a medical doctor was forced to surgically remove her right breast. The woman was weeping and screaming as she told her story. Right where she stood in the crowd, God had grown her a brand new breast! The whole thing! Right there! We knew that this woman had grown a breast because several of the pastors' wives had physically examined her. And to everyone else her new breast was clearly visible. She was grabbing it with excitement as she told her amazing story. That was the first of a series of creative miracles.

Then another woman came running to the platform—cancer had been visibly eating the skin around her bosom, leaving raw flesh, blood and scabs around her breast area. Others described her former horrible condition. But God had given her new skin like that of a baby. She kept saying, "My breasts are like baby's breasts." She was so excited about what God had done that she flashed 20,000 people about four or five times as she displayed her miracle! (In African culture, it is not uncommon for woman to walk around with her breasts uncovered or to display her breasts as she feeds her baby.)

Right after that second miracle, a man testified to a miracle in his genital area. A large tumor had damaged his sexual organs, preventing him from having intimate relations with his wife for 15 years! His wife was divorcing him. He began to shout with excitement at the miracle God had performed. First, the Lord had dissolved the tumor. Then, because of damage the tumor had caused, the Lord had actually had to recreate parts to restore this man to normal.

The final miracle story came from a woman who told us that something creative had taken place in her female parts. So we asked her how she knew. Some kind of illness had caused a closing of the entrance to her womb but the Lord had opened it.

After watching this string of creative miracles, we sensed God was saying, "These miracles are a prophetic message to Uganda that I am restoring to the church the breast that nurtures as well as the fathering productivity to the church. I am opening the womb that gives birth to spiritual offspring." Out of thousands of people at that meeting, God first chose to release creative miracles to those four people—all in a row. How wild is that for some opening miracles at a meeting? Think about it—four different people, not knowing each other, show up at the platform, all reporting creative miracles involving sexual organs. That's just amazing! After that string of miracles, 34,000 got saved and the crowds grew to 60,000 people plus.

Because of all those creative miracles, the witch-doctors began to wonder what kind of power the "white soothsayer" possessed that he "could cause body parts to grow back." So the next night the witch-doctors, and all those who had been unsuccessfully treated by the witch-doctors, showed up at the crusade. They were saying, "If this white man's God can heal people that the witch-doctor couldn't treat, maybe He could heal us too." That night the Commander of the Army of the Lord directed us to deal with witchcraft; we counted over 1,800 on the ground violently manifesting devils. Numerous people went through deliverance and many people testified to healing of total paralysis, broken necks and total blindness—tremendous miracles took place!

Although some people think that God only does miracles overseas, over the years we've seen God perform many creative miracles in North American too. At an international healing conference in Minneapolis, Minnesota in October 2001, a young woman, Andie Meyer, testified to an incredible instant healing of her blind eye. Seven years earlier her eye had been severely damaged when her brother shot it out with a BB gun. The doctor had to reconstruct her eye using silicon and part of a cadaver. I was one of several guest speakers and the miracle took place over several days as she sat in the healing atmosphere. I can't think of one individual who specifically prayed for this creative miracle. In fact, because this woman was in a wheel chair, I and many others were actually praying that God would raise her up from her wheelchair. Then, one meeting, she passed through a "fire tunnel" (a sheep dip). When she came out the other side, God had recreated her eyeball. Only God can get the glory—so many people laid hands on her. When she went to visit the doctor, he was so confounded by the fact that she had a creative miracle in her eye that he called in five other doctors to examine her. They were all totally amazed after concluding that a woman who had her eye reconstructed with a cadaver and silicon could now see with perfect 20/20 vision.

I believe God wants to raise our faith to the level where creative miracles like these are normal events in our lives and ministries. He wants us to have a revelation of God as Creator so we can have faith to believe for, and to bring about, creative miracles. When we see the creative nature of the Holy Spirit and His creative power in us, we will realize how easy creative miracles are. The gospel is salvation, healing and deliverance to the body, soul and spirit. I believe a time is coming when our thinking will be so transformed that when someone says, "I was in a meeting last night and people's blind eyes were being opened," we won't be very surprised.

Right now when we talk about third heaven experiences, creative miracles or signs and wonders, people may say they believe, but they really wonder if those things still happen today. Supernatural experiences are not as common to us as they should be. We need our spirits to grow to the point where we simply believe in the creative power of God for today.

In this chapter, you will come to understand the differences between healings, miracles, signs and wonders and you will grow in faith to see their operation in your life. I believe that by the end of this chapter you won't just believe in healing—you are going to wonder why creative miracles don't happen more often. You will believe that creative miracles are easy for the Holy Ghost, as easy as speaking God's Word. You will have faith to believe that limbs can grow back and to even believe for a re-creative miracle in your body. I believe that the Lord is going to deposit faith in you for miracles, signs and wonders as you receive a revelation of Elohiym (the supreme creator God) and His creative power in us—this revelation will cause you to say, "Creative miracles are happening! It's the Holy Ghost's nature! He is a creator. How could miracles or healings not happen, Todd, it's the gospel? The gospel is salvation, healing and deliverance – body, soul and spirit."

Yes, I truly believe that we are going to reach a place where the supernatural will be common place. As we walk in God's supernatural realm we begin to grow in kingdom levels in our spirit.

I have definitely grown in levels of healing in my ministry. I remember

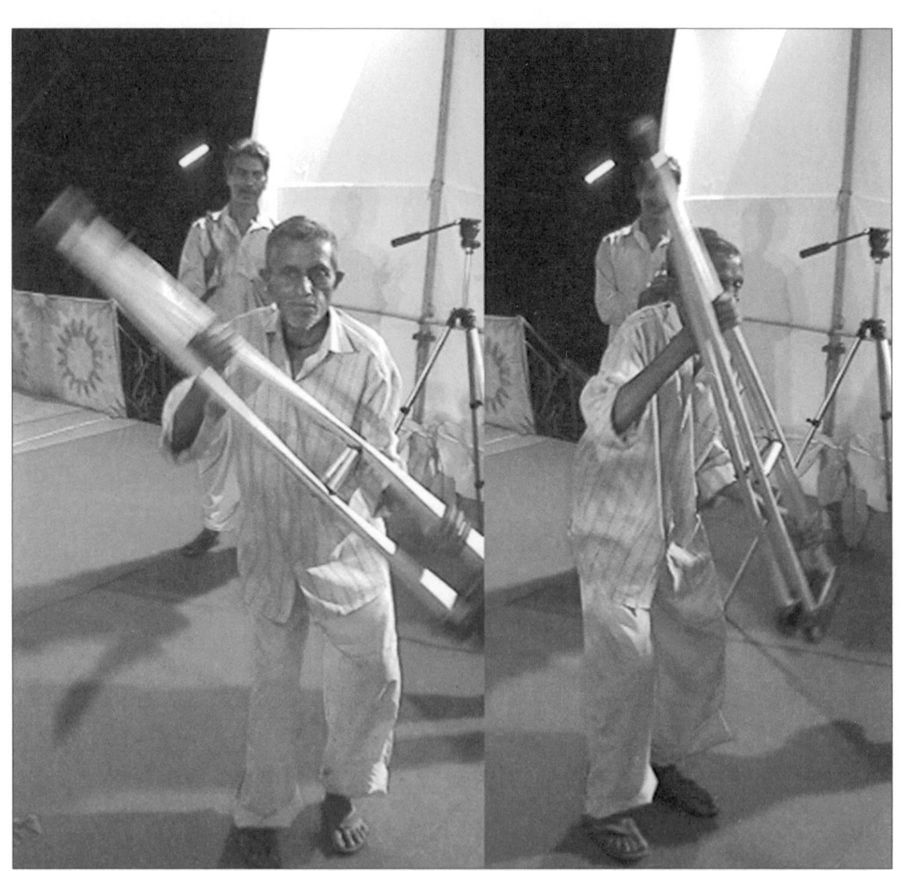

At a crusade in India, a lame man is healed and starts dancing on the platform, waving his crutches in the air.

when a headache or back pain was intimidating. Today we see people coming out of wheelchairs or being healed of incurable diseases. I am growing in my spirit to a kingdom place of authority in the area of creative miracles.

As I've mentioned in another chapter, there is a difference between healings, miracles, signs and wonders. Healings are usually a process; they are progressive. You will lay hands on the sick and they will recover. He didn't say they would recover instantly. Instant healings are actually called miracles. These divine phenomena take place when God's supernatural laws override man's natural laws and defy the laws of medical science. Both miracles and healings can be considered signs which point to Jesus and wonders that cause people to wonder about God's great power.

However, signs and wonders also operate at another level, as described in ***Acts 2:19: "I will show wonders in heaven above and signs in the earth beneath."*** When the sun stood still at Joshua's command, it was a sign and a wonder. When Jesus took authority over the waves and the wind, that was a sign and a wonder. When the Virgin Mary gave birth to Jesus, the son of God, that was a sign and a wonder. When Jesus walked on the water, that was a sign and that was a wonder.

I believe that signs and wonders are miracles that contradict the laws of physics and override the natural earthly order. Like Elijah, believers walking in a signs and wonders authority can call for a drought or they can call for the rain. They can turn water into blood and command a tornado to stop. Yes, these are the signs and wonders God is going to release through His anointed people who are walking in a powerful dimension of His authority on earth.

Get ready to receive a new revelation of this divine supernatural realm, especially in the area of miracles. I believe God will release the miraculous on your life as you receive revelation of Elohiym, the God of creation. You will begin to get a picture of God's creative power in you and become excited about the next opportunity you have to believe for a creative miracle.

Creative Miracles in the Beginning

From the beginning of the Bible, we see God revealed as a miracle-working creator. In Genesis 1, we see that God created the heavens and the earth.

> ***"In the beginning God created the heavens and the earth. The earth was without form, and void; and darkness was on the face of the deep. And the Spirit of God was hovering over***

the face of the waters. Then God said, 'Let there be light'; and there was light" (Gen. 1:1-3).

This is Elohiym's creative power at work. We see the creative Word; we see the atmosphere and the moving of the Holy Spirit. Whenever we see creation, we always see the Spirit of God at work. When God formed man He breathed His Spirit, His Life, the essence of who He was into that lifeless lump of clay. Then Adam became a living being. The Holy Spirit was and is always a vital partner in God's amazing creative works. Here is the first revelation for you: it is as easy to operate in creative power as it is to be in the presence of the Holy Spirit.

Holy Spirit Creativity

The Bible declares in Psalm 104:30 that ***"You send forth Your Spirit, they are created; and You renew the face of the earth."*** At the Father's word, the Holy Spirit was sent out to create. It was the Holy Spirit who completed the final miraculous works of creating heaven and earth and of creating Adam and Eve. Each of us is also a miracle, a creation of the Spirit of God.

Let's look at how the Holy Spirit was involved in every aspect of Jesus' life on earth. He was involved in the Jesus' creation—His power came on Mary and overshadowed her. Only then did she conceive and give birth to the Son of God. Also, the ministry of Jesus—the creative miracles and healing ministry—did not happen without the Holy Ghost. Scripture tells us that ***"... God anointed Jesus of Nazareth with the Holy Spirit and with power, who went about doing good and healing all who were oppressed by the devil, for God was with Him" (Acts 10:38).*** (Let me re-emphasize this important point--healings destroy the oppression of the Devil.)

The Holy Spirit continued to rest on and strengthen Him until His death and Jesus' created body died when the Holy Ghost left. The Bible tells us that while Jesus was on the cross God forsook Him (Matt. 27:46), or the Spirit of God left Him. Then Jesus said "It is finished" (John 19:30), He "gave up the ghost" and died. When the spirit of God left, creation died. It's the same for us, the Bible also tells us that when God takes away the Spirit, or when He takes away the breath, man returns to the dust (Ps. 104:29).

But the Holy Spirit didn't leave Jesus in the tomb. Scripture speaks of ***"the Spirit of Him who raised Jesus from the dead" (Rom. 8:11a).*** Jesus wasn't just raised from the dead, a creative miracle of regeneration and resurrection was released into His body by the power of the Holy Spirit. It was a creative miracle because his organs were damaged and His flesh was shredded from the beatings He endured. After three days He was decomposing. This event wasn't just a resurrection; it involved a series of creative miracles. The power of the Spirit restored torn flesh and released life back into dead organs. It was the same power of the Holy Ghost involved in the creation of the heavens and the earth.

I want you to have a revelation today of the creator God, performer of creative miracles. Realize that miracles are as easy as the presence and atmosphere of the Holy Ghost. Jesus released the era of the manifestation of the Holy Ghost, the era of salvation and the era of miracles. He said, ***"But if I cast out demons by the Spirit of God, surely the kingdom of God has come upon you" (Matt. 12:28).*** Jesus also called people to repent and believe in the gospel, for the kingdom of heaven was at hand. The kingdom era of deliverance had come upon them. Freedom, healing, deliverance from sin, sickness and disease had come upon them; kingdom power also came to God's people because the Holy Ghost had come upon them.

Miracles Living Inside of Us

Creative miracles and healings only happen when the Spirit of God hovers, when He begins to work. The Bible says that the same Spirit that raised Jesus from the dead lives in you and me. That means creation lives in us; creative power lives in you. When we walk into the presence and the atmosphere of the Holy Ghost, we begin to operate in the realm of creative miracles.

When God spoke the words, "Let there be light," the Holy Spirit performed the word and there was light. Creative miracles are as easy as believing the Word of God and speaking it into the atmosphere of the presence of the Holy Ghost. Creative miracles must happen because the creator of heaven and earth lives inside of us. The same Spirit that recreated and raised Jesus from the dead lives inside of you. The same Holy Ghost that was involved in the creation of heaven and earth lives inside of you and He is released by what you speak with your mouth in His presence. Creative miracles are that easy! I want you to see that creative miracles are as easy as having a revelation of the power of God in creation.

As you read these pages, I believe the Lord wants to make a road in the wilderness of your life; He wants to make a river in the desert of your broken dreams and He wants to open up the Red Sea of your circumstances. God can perform every kind of miracle, not just healing miracles—He can perform an instant miracle in your finances or in your marriage. He can activate an instant miracle in your ministry. He could even birth a ministry with the creative anointing to build, plant, root up and pull down. God has put creation inside of us—gifts of entrepreneurship, art, music, drama and dance. People's passion to create and express themselves through worship, art and flags is an aspect of divine creativity.

When you get a revelation of creative power in your spirit, you will go a long way in God's kingdom. God releases destiny dreams and visions in our spirits to inspire faith to believe for creative miracles. Creative miracles are released merely with a word like: "Let there be light." The Bible actually says that the God who called those things that are not as though they were (Rom. 4:17), has given us the same authority (as Jesus had on earth) to allow and disallow things by our words:

> ***"Assuredly, I say to you, whatever you bind on earth will be bound in heaven, and whatever you loose on earth will be loosed in heaven. "Again I say to you that if two of you agree on earth concerning anything that they ask, it will be done for them by My Father in heaven." (Matt. 18:18-19).***

We need to pull on that anointing to speak the miraculous into reality. We need to lay hold of things that already exist in the spirit realm. God has given us creative supernatural power to do even greater works, greater miracles than Jesus did (John 5:20). Whenever creation takes place, you are watching the presence of the Holy Ghost acting in response to the speaking of God's Word. We can all release those powerful miracle-working words when we get a revelation that the same supernatural Spirit that raised Jesus from the dead lives in us.

Creative Miracles in Nature

Jesus had such a revelation of the power of the creative spoken word that He could even control the weather:

> ***"On the same day, when evening had come, He said to them, 'Let us cross over to the other side.' And a great windstorm arose, and the waves beat into the boat, so that it was already filling. But He was in the stern, asleep on a pillow. And they awoke Him and said to Him, 'Teacher, do You not care that we are perishing?' Then He arose and rebuked the wind, and said to the sea, 'Peace, be still!' And the wind ceased***

and there was a great calm. But He said to them, 'Why are you so fearful? How is it that you have no faith?' And they feared exceedingly, and said to one another, 'Who can this be, that even the wind and the sea obey Him?'" (Mark 4:35-41)

Jesus must have been thinking: "Of course the winds and the seas obey Me. I am Elohiym; I am creator God! Not only do the winds and the waves obey me, but the laws of natural science, the heavens, the earth and the universe are all subject to Me, your body obeys me and heaven and earth obey me. Every angel and demon obeys me because I am Creator. I am Elohiym. Didn't you know that nothing was created unless it was created through the Word of God? You shouldn't be surprised that creation is subject to Me. I am Elohiym!"

Just a few chapters later in the gospel of Mark, Jesus again demonstrates His authority over nature when He walked out to the disciples' boat on the water in the midst of a storm. When he got in the boat the storm immediately stopped. ***"Then He went up into the boat to them, and the wind ceased. And they were greatly amazed in themselves beyond measure, and marveled. For they had not understood about the loaves, because their heart was hardened" (Mark 6:52).***

Notice that the disciples still didn't have a revelation of Elohiym, the creator. He had already commanded the wind and waves to be still and had walked on water. Jesus had also just fed the five thousand by multiplying a few loaves and fish. Over twelve baskets of fragments were left over. Yet, they still didn't realize that Jesus was the creator God.

In Matthew 16:5-12 Jesus warns the disciples to beware of the doctrine of the Sadducees and Pharisees. He referred to it as "the leaven of the Pharisees." The disciples actually thought He was rebuking them for not bringing any bread. Then Jesus looked at them and said something like this:

"Don't you understand yet? Haven't you had a revelation of how easy it is for me to create and release miracles, healings, signs and wonders, and especially bread? I am Elohiym. Yes, I walk on water! Of course I do—creation is subject to me. Of course the winds and the waves obey me – creation is subject to me. Of course I can speak to the man with the withered hand and say, "Stretch out your hand" and his hand becomes as whole as anyone else's. I am Elohiym! I am the Creator of heaven and earth! All of creation is subject to me. Of course I created 5,000 loaves

and 5,000 fish from just a few. I am Elohiym! I am creator of heaven and earth. All of creation is subject to me."

The disciples just didn't have a revelation of how easy it was for Jesus to create. They didn't truly realize that it was God who dwelt among them. When you receive Jesus as God; when you see Him as the powerful Creator of heaven and earth and when you have a revelation of Him releasing creative miracles by speaking Holy Spirit inspired words, you will also be eager, like Peter, to get out of the boat and walk on the water.

Peter began to recognize that Jesus could command the wind and the waves to be still, that He was the God of creation. He believed that Jesus, as Elohiym, God, had authority over the water and that He could command it to be subject to him as well. Peter's revelation of Jesus gave him the faith and boldness to step out onto the water and walk.

A Resurrection Miracle

Let's examine another Bible example of a creative miracle—the story of Lazarus' resurrection. Lazarus had already been dead four days—his flesh was decomposing; his body stunk. Yet, Jesus' words carry such creative power that when He commanded "Lazarus, come forth!" His words immediately triggered a creative miracle.

Do you know why He called Lazarus by name? Because if He said "Hey dead, come forth!" everyone in the grave yard would have come out. His words carried great power! I mean, there was an anointing there! When you have a revelation of the God of creation, that He is the resurrection and the life, you'll know that creative miracles are as easy as believing that He is Creator God. Then His creative miracle power will be released merely through speaking God's Word.

All of creation is subject to God—He made it. What is it to God to grow another arm? He formed your original arms. What's it to God to grow some teeth in your mouth? I mean, really, what's it to God to give you a new thyroid gland? He gave you the first so why can't He recreate it? Hey, even if you need a new heart, it's really no sweat for God to give you one. When you have this kingdom revelation of God's creative power, you can boldly say to the sick, "I don't care if you don't have a leg or an ear drum—just come on up here! God will create one for you!"

We make the ministry of healing and miracles so hard. Let's get the revelation of Elohiym's power of. I'm ready for creative miracles. I'm ready for people with no limbs to receive limbs. When we go to Africa, I'm now looking for the lepers, for the dead and for those needing creative miracles. Yes, take me to the cancer clinics; take me to where they have locked the lunatics away—I tell you, that is where you are going to see miracles.

Supernatural Signs that Follow

The Bible tells us that healings and supernatural signs are part of the believer's inheritance:

> ***"And these signs will follow those who believe: In My name they will cast out demons; they will speak with new tongues; they will take up serpents; and if they drink anything deadly, it will by no means hurt them; they will lay hands on the sick, and they will recover" (Mark 16:18).***

Mass deliverance from demonic oppression

Yes, we as believers can cast out demons and see instant miracles. Or we can speak with new tongues as a sign to the world of a powerful God at work. God wants to pour out His Spirit on His children in these days and manifest miraculous wonders in and through them. In the book of Acts, speaking of the outpouring of the Spirit and the gift of tongues, Peter quotes the prophet Joel:

> ***"And it shall come to pass in the last days, says God, That I will pour out of My Spirit on all flesh; Your sons and your daughters shall prophesy, Your young men shall see visions, Your old men shall dream dreams. And on My menservants and on My maidservants I will pour out My Spirit in those days; And they shall prophesy. I will show wonders in heaven above And signs in the earth beneath: Blood and fire and vapor of smoke. The sun shall be turned into darkness,***

And the moon into blood, Before the coming of the great and awesome day of the LORD" (Acts 2:17-20).

Not only will the Lord give His children the gift of tongues or prophecy, He will also manifest wonders in the heavens and signs on the earth! Yes, God, through His people operating in their authority, can even change the natural elements and cycles of the earth. Read what the Lord did through Joshua:

"So the sun stood still, and the moon stopped, till the people had revenge upon their enemies. Is this not written in the Book of Jasher? So the sun stood still in the midst of heaven, and did not hasten to go down for about a whole day" (Jos. 10:13).

Isn't that an amazing sign and wonder? God actually used Joshua to stop time! The sun and the moon actually stopped!

Today God still gives supernatural heavenly signs to His people. In many of our overseas crusades the Lord has given us signs such as rainbows over the platform, glory clouds and heavenly portholes. One of the most dramatic manifestations happened in Uganda on the last night of one of our crusades. The previous night a huge windstorm destroyed our platform and we had to quickly rebuild it. By the final night we needed some encouragement. Well, God really saved the best for last. During the worship service, a huge mushroom-shaped, shining, glory cloud appeared over the platform for all to see. Above the cloud was a rainbow-colored porthole opening up into heaven. In the rainbow colors of this divine sign appeared the shape of a lion's head. We knew that God was giving us a prophetic sign of a spiritual open heaven over the crusade that night. Well, God was true to the sign He gave us—that night we saw a huge explosion of His power, far greater than the four nights before. This open heaven resulted in hundreds saved, thousands filled with the Holy Spirit and numerous powerful miracles.

The Revelation of Christ in You

The Bible tells us that the same Spirit that raised Jesus from the dead lives in us (Rom. 8:11). We have God's creative power working in us. The apostle John emphasized the creative power of the Word working in the beginning, during the creation of the universe.

"In the beginning was the Word, and the Word was with

> ***God, and the Word was God. He was in the beginning with God. 3 All things were made through Him, and without Him nothing was made that was made" (John 1:1-3).***

Can you see the power of the Word? Jesus, the Word, was in the beginning with God. All things were made through Him. Creation was released through what? The Word of God. The Scripture is clear—"without Him nothing was made that was made." God and His Word are one. Creation is linked to His Word. The apostle John again tells us the source of all created life: ***"In Him was life, and the life was the light of men" (Jn. 1:4).***

However, as John points out, the world was only the beginning of God's creative work. With Jesus' life and death, the Father prepared the way for the creation of new spirits, of new creations in Christ (2 Cor. 5:17) and of spiritual sons and daughters.

> ***"He was in the world, and the world was made through Him, and the world did not know Him. He came to His own, and His own did not receive Him. But as many as received Him, to them He gave the right to become children of God, to those who believe in His name: who were born, not of blood, nor of the will of the flesh, nor of the will of man, but of God" (John 1:10-13).***

Today God is still performing creative miracles, both inside His people and in the world through His people who have a revelation of His greatness and power.

The Moses & Elijah Anointings

A powerful authority for creative miracles is coming to the church—it will come in the form of two anointings that will revolutionize the church. The book of Revelation describes these two witnesses (representing two anointings):

> ***"These have power to shut heaven, so that no rain falls in the days of their prophecy; and they have power over waters to turn them to blood, and to strike the earth with all plagues, as often as they desire" (Rev. 11:6).***

Who are these two people? Well, in this passage they are strikingly similar to Moses (Ex. 7-11) and Elijah (1 Kin. 17:1; Mal. 4:5). These two witnesses will prophesy with incredible power. During the days of their prophecy, they will stop the rain (like Elijah as described in James 5:17) and they will strike the earth with plagues (like Moses in Ex. 7-11).

I believe the Lord is saying, in this passage that He is going to put this same anointing for creative miracles on His people who are rulers and judges with divine connections. Like the two witnesses, God's anointed people will release healings and miracles or even signs and wonders in the heavens and earth, "as often as they desire." This is the anointing God is about to release on the earth.

I don't believe Revelation 11 is talking about two witnesses (one Moses and one Elijah) but rather, an anointing like that which rested on these two prophets. I don't believe that Scripture is talking about two big, mega, end-times ministries twenty times bigger than Billy Graham and Benny Hinn's ministries together. No, it isn't about one big ministry with the anointing of Elijah and one with the anointing of Moses that are doing such dramatic works for God that the rest of God's people can just relax and leave the world harvest to them. No, that interpretation would go against the biblical model of training and equipping the saints for the work of the ministry. God wants everyone to be doing the work of the ministry.

In the New Testament it started with the 12 disciples, then it was the 70, the 120, the 3,000 and eventually the ones that the Lord added to the church daily. Yes God gives apostles, prophets, teachers, pastors and evangelists to train and equip the saints for the ministry.

I believe that these witnesses represent the spirit of Moses and the spirit of Elijah that will come on the church—this view seems more consistent with God's discipling model. This anointing on the church will mean that some will walk more in a Moses-type anointing and others more in an Elijah-type anointing.

Why do I believe that it is the church? Revelations was originally introduced as a book of signs and symbols. And we know that the two witnesses, according to Rev. 11:4, are the ***"two olive trees and the two menorot (lamp-stands), standing before the Lord."*** God often speaks through numbers and signs and symbols, so we need to be careful not to interpret this so literally.

Do you know what the lamp-stands are? Revelation 1 speaks of lamp-stands as representing churches. Guess what? There were more than seven churches in Asia at the time. Does that mean that only seven of the churches were really "saved churches"? These letters were for the churches of Asia at that time, churches that were birthed under Paul's apostolic ministry. I believe the letters represented messages to seven *types* of churches at the time and messages for everyone in the church age today. There are still churches like the one in Ephesus or Sardis. So, I believe it is clear that the lamp-stands in Revelation 11 speak of the churches or the people of God. It's you and it's me!

God is going to release the anointing of the spirit of Elijah and the anointing of the spirit of Moses on you and me. He is going to release such a creative anointing for healing, signs and wonders; He will trust us with such power that we can release miracles as often as we desire.

According to this Scripture, God will give power to the witnesses; they will prophesy and signs and wonders will take place. These things will take place, not at God's command, but at the command of the witnesses. Just like Elijah spoke and drought, rain or fire was released, so too, God's people will speak and release supernatural signs. God was waiting for Elijah's word--that is why Elijah went up on Mt. Carmel and birthed what God had already said. God is including your word in His plan.

God also chose for Moses' word to be vital to His plan in Egypt: "Moses, I have made you a god unto Pharaoh." The Lord told Him that he would have to speak and act as an ambassador of the Almighty.

Jesus gave the same commissioning and authority to His disciples. He briefed His disciples something like this:

> ***"Yes, I am leaving, but you are going to do greater works than I did. Why? Because I am giving my ministry on earth to you. You need to continue to release salvation, healing and deliverance. Preach the gospel in the nations of the earth and then the end will come. I've done my part—it's finished. The Holy Ghost who was with me now lives in you. Now I am waiting for you, as a ruler and a judge with divine connections to take all I have given you—the power, the victory, the atonement—and release it to the world as often as you like. I am going to release an anointing on you that is going to be creative. Life and death are in the power of the tongue—you are going to have to watch what you say" (Matt. 16:19; Mark 11:23; Mark 16:17,18).***

Elijah and Elisha both knew the power of the tongue. The Bible speaks of various supernatural events that took place ***"according to the word of the LORD which Elijah had spoken" (1 Ki. 17:16; 2 Ki. 1:17; 10:10).*** You see it again and again throughout Scripture: "According to the word of Elijah. According to the word of Moses." He is saying the same to us: "According to Bill's words. According to the word of Angela. According to Mike's words."

It's no different than God honoring the word of His anointed servants in Scripture.

According to the New Testament scriptures listed above, God has said that He will not work except at your word. Your word is involved in this. God is saying,

> *"I put a creative anointing, a creative power, in you. I've done what I've done and now I want you to do the rest. Creation is going to be released and healing is going to be released as you believe in Me and believe that I've given you My power. As you begin to open up your mouth and speak, creative miracles will be released—they are as easy as believing that the presence of the Holy Ghost is here. You've had a revelation of the God of creation, of Elohiym—I am the one to whom all creation is subject. Of course creative miracles are happening—signs and wonders should be normal in the church. Of course people are being healed. How could people not be healed when My word is spoken? It's not that I don't want to touch the sick—It's just that My people have been destroyed for a lack of knowledge."*

Creative Multiplication

Now let's examine an incredible passage of Scripture where we again see Jesus' creative, supernatural power at work. In John 6 huge crowds followed Jesus to the other side of the Sea of Galilee because they had seen His signs. They saw the creative miracles and healings which He performed on those who were diseased. When Jesus saw the great multitude of over 5,000 men, not including the women and children, He knew they were tired and hungry. Many of them still needed Him to minister to their soul and body—they needed their diseases healed. So He looked at Phillip and asked, "Hey Phil, where are we going to buy bread so all these people can eat?" This was a test for Phillip. Jesus was really asking:

> *"Have you had a revelation of creation and of the Creator, Phillip? Have you had a revelation of My miraculous power to heal and create? You have been with Me, but have you really seen the signs that I performed among those who were diseased? You were with Me when I commanded that man with a withered hand to stretch out his arm. You were with Me when*

> *the wind and the seas obeyed Me. You were with Me when I walked on the water to show that all of creation is subject to Me. I even told you that you can also walk on the water if you would believe. You saw all the signs, wonders and miracles—the blind eyes, the deaf ears, the mute spirit and the devils I cast out. Have you yet got a revelation of My creative power?"*

Jesus wanted to know if Phillip believed that he, Phillip, could do creative miracles. Jesus already knew He could take 5 loaves and a few fish, multiply them and feed 5,000 people. Yet he wanted to know whether Phillip and His other followers believed that creative miracles are easy. He was asking, "Have you seen my Elohiym power yet? Have you had a revelation that I am God and that all of creation is subject to Me? Do you realize yet that it is easy for Me to make something out of nothing today?"

But look at Phillip's answer: ***"Two hundred denarii worth of bread is not sufficient for them, that every one of them may have a little" (Jn. 6:7).*** Even after seeing all of Jesus' creative power, Phillip was saying, "We don't have enough money to feed all these people!"

Then Simon Peter's brother says to Him, ***"There is a lad here who has five barley loaves and two small fish, but what are they among so many" (Jn. 6:9)?*** See, they still didn't get it. So Jesus said to them, ***"Make the people sit down" (6:10).*** Look what happened that day:

> ***"… Now there was much grass in the place. So the men sat down, in number about five thousand. 11 And Jesus took the loaves, and when He had given thanks He distributed them to the disciples, and the disciples to those sitting down; and likewise of the fish, as much as they wanted. 12 So when they were filled, He said to His disciples, 'Gather up the fragments that remain, so that nothing is lost.' 13 Therefore they gathered them up, and filled twelve baskets with the fragments of the five barley loaves which were left over by those who had eaten" (Jn. 6:10-13).***

We can read about this same creative miracle in the gospel of Matthew. However, here the writer records that Jesus actually said to his disciples, "you give them something to eat!" What He was actually saying was,

> *"You have the God of creation with you. You have a revelation of My creative power with you. You have watched my miracles long enough; now I want you to do a creative miracle! This*

is a test! What are we going to do about all these people? I want you to give them something to eat and I want you to participate in a creative miracle."

I'll tell you something: when Jesus took the loaves and the fish and He broke and He blessed them He didn't create 5,000 loaves and put them in a big pile. Do you know how much space that would have taken? Jesus multiplied the food as it was being distributed.

You can't understand creative miracles. They don't make sense to the mind. I can imagine the disciples thinking: "Ok Jesus! You just blessed the five fish and the loaves, *but we still only have five fish and five loaves*. Ok, You just broke them in pieces and we all have a piece in our hands, *but we still don't see any creative miracle*."

In our case, when we are believing for a creative miracle, like the disciples were, it's hard not to think, "This guy is still missing an arm. He is still missing a kidney; he still doesn't have a thyroid. The creative miracle still hasn't happened. I don't see anything yet."

To see a creative miracle, we must believe that we have it before we see it:

"For assuredly, I say to you, whoever says to this mountain, 'Be removed and be cast into the sea,' and does not doubt in his heart, but believes that those things he says will be done, he will have whatever he says" (Mark 11:23).

When Jesus told the disciples to give away the bread and fish, maybe they were thinking, "I don't understand how these creative miracles work. What do you mean give it away? I don't have anything to give away. I've still only got half a fish and half a loaf and there are still 5,000 people!" But, to their credit, the disciples just obeyed Jesus. As they gave away what they had received, even before they could see or figure out the miracle, the food was multiplied.

Man's deaf ears open in Wales

Even though the disciples couldn't see the 5,000 loaves and fishes before they started to distribute them, I think they started to believe that the God of creation, the Miracle-Worker was among them. Even though, in the natural, it still looked absolutely foolish because the miracle had not manifested, as they gave away the food, the miracle they believed they had came into being.

God wants us to believe we have the miracle even though we can't see the miracle; God wants us to believe that we have the ability to minister the creative miracle even when it seems impossible. The disciples did their part by believing, so God did His part by creating through them.

Jesus must have had a talk with His disciples later. Maybe they were eating leftovers after the crowd had dispersed:

> *"Come on guys! How could you not believe in creative miracles? Creative miracles are as easy as believing creative power is here because the Holy Ghost is here and because I am here. Do you understand this now?"*

In the same way, we can also be involved in creative miracles. Say, for instance, a man comes to the altar and says, "I am missing a kidney." You need to look at that man and say something like this to yourself:

> *"I am involved in this. God has put that creative power in me. God is in me; the same Spirit that raised Jesus from the dead is in me—the Miracle Worker is here through the presence and power of the Holy Spirit. I am able to release this miracle with my mouth even though I don't see it. I must believe I already have this creative miracle in the spirit realm. I've got it even though I can't see it; with God's power, I can make something out of nothing!"*

Elijah and the Hungry Widow

Let me share two more examples of creative miracles. Perhaps you recall the story in which Elijah meets a widow who only has a little jar of oil and a little flour. Elijah tells her that God is going to perform a creative miracle:

> ***"And Elijah said to her, 'Do not fear; go and do as you have said, but make me a small cake from it first, and bring it to me; and afterward make some for yourself and your son. For thus says the LORD God of Israel: 'The bin of flour***

> ***shall not be used up, nor shall the jar of oil run dry, until the day the LORD sends rain on the earth.' So she went away and did according to the word of Elijah; and she and he and her household ate for many days. The bin of flour was not used up, nor did the jar of oil run dry, according to the word of the LORD which He spoke by Elijah" (1 Kg. 17:13-17).***

Amazing! Before the miracle even happened, Elijah told the woman that God would take the little oil and flour and would feed him, the woman and her son for three years—the supplies would not run dry. "We are going to eat like kings at a feast," he was saying.

In the natural she sure didn't understand the prophet's instructions to give him the last of her food. It must have seemed absolutely foolish. "You want me to give you the last of what I have (which is barely enough to feed me and my son) to feed you first? And once it's gone more is going to appear?" It sounded like a con job. "You are telling me that if I do as you say, God will cause our tiny food supply to last for three years?" You see, God wanted to include her in the creative miracle. She saved her life and her son's life by following Elijah's instructions.

God also wants to include us in creative miracles. The first step to being involved in such supernatural acts is believing that God will do them through us. We've each got our little jar of oil and a little bit of flour. OK, perhaps you are believing for restoration of a missing arm, limb, organ, tooth or some other body part. Then God wants you to start participating in your miracle through prayer and faith. As you give in prayer God will release your miracle.

Remember, the miracle didn't happen in the widow's case until she became involved and followed Elijah's instructions. Like the widow, you only need the word of the Lord to release a creative miracle. As you believe the word of the Lord and pray it out or act on it, you *will* see your miracle.

You have now read the word of God about the creative power that lives in you. Begin to get it deep into your heart and then watch what happens!

Elisha and the Bankrupt Widow

Now let's look at 2 Kings 4:1-8. Elisha also meets a widow—this time the woman is in debt and the creditors are coming. Her desperate situation looked something like this: "They are taking back my house; they are taking back my car. They are taking my kids away. I am in debt and I have absolutely nothing. I need a spiritual breakthrough!"

So Elisha basically says, "I am not doing a creative miracle unless you are willing to be involved. What do you have in the house? Gather your empty vessels. Go get some from your neighbors, get as many as you can." So she gathered a great many empty vessels and brought them home. She still didn't have the manifestation, but she obviously believed that she was going to get it.

Then Elisah told her to pour the little jar of oil into the big vessels until they were full. In the natural that goes against everything we know. Pour the oil and it doesn't run out. Give away one fish and there is another one. Come on, this is impossible! Yes, it is—naturally speaking. You'll never understand it; so just leave it alone. God wants you to believe that you can minister creative miracles, even though you can't understand them. Even though you can't understand it; you can't see it, just believe that you have it and you can do it. It's that easy."

Well, the widow believed. So she said, "yes" and began to pour the oil and the miracle was there. The level in the little jar never changed until the big ones got full. You'll never understand it. Don't make miracles so complicated. It is as easy as believing in the God of creation and that the Creative Power, the Holy Spirit, lives in you. The same spirit that raised Jesus from the dead lives in you.

God is asking, "What do you have in your house?" He wants you to launch out in faith and get involved in miracles. The Holy Ghost lives inside you and is waiting for you to speak the word and release miracles. How can creative miracles not happen?

Keys to Faith for Creative Miracles

Scripture gives us some keys to unlocking creative miracles in our lives and ministries. Here are a few of them:

Revelation of the Power of Elohiym

The first key to having faith for creative miracles is having a revelation of Elohiym. When Scripture opens with "In the beginning God created…." it uses the plural Hebrew word Elohiym which actually means "the Gods." So, as the curtain opens on the history of the world, we see the Trinity—the Father, Son and Holy Spirit—on stage, fully involved in creation. Yes, together the Father, Son and Holy Ghost created the heavens and the earth.

Later in Genesis, God speaks as a plural being again saying, "Let **Us** make man in **Our** image," (Gen. 1:26) and "…let **Us** go down and there and confuse their language" (Gen. 11:7). You can't get away from the "Us."

Well, who do you think the "Us" is? If you have a hard time with the Trinity, those scriptures will throw your theology out the window. We need a revelation of this supreme God, the Trinity that created everything.

The Creative Power of gods

The second key to having faith for creative miracles, as I've already mentioned, is having a revelation of creative power in us. King David says,

> ***"I said, 'You are gods, and all of you are children of the Most High. But you shall die like men, and fall like one of the princes.' Arise, O God, judge the earth; for You shall inherit all nations" (Ps. 82:6-8).***

The psalmist actually speaks of the people as gods (or mighty ones) because they are children of the heavenly Father. In John 10, Jesus refers to this passage during a debate with the Pharisees, who were offended when Jesus spoke of Himself as the Son of God. He basically said, "You have a hard time with Me calling Myself the Son of God, even when David has called you gods"?

Notice, in your Bible, that this passage speaks of god with a little "g." He is addressing children of the Most High as gods—that's us, you and me. Here, David is actually using the word Elohiym, but this time it's singular usage, not plural. He is really saying to us, "You are rulers with divine connections. You can rule as God, be god-like and function in all the authority that God has for you because you have divine connections with the Most High, Creator of heaven and earth."

This passage isn't suggesting that you are actually God. You don't have the free will to do absolutely anything you want; you do not have the abilities of God to be omniscient (present everywhere) or omnipotent (all powerful). You are not God in essence, however, you are given all authority on earth (like Jesus) to extend His kingdom on earth. You are also given the same glorious inheritance as Jesus. The Father's words to the prodigal son's older brother also apply to us. ***"Son, you are always with me, and all that I have is yours" (Lk. 15:31).***

Think about it: the Father has made you a joint-heir with Jesus with the same power, authority and provision. He has made you to sit as an equal (in function) with Jesus, in heavenly places far above all power, dominion, and principalities (Eph. 2:6). God has made the angels a little lower than you—He has given you a place above the angels of heaven. The Father has made you sit in that place where He rules and reigns as the King of Kings and Lord of Lords. He has not made you like Him in essence or in attributes, but He has made you a god (spiritual, mighty ruler) on earth with the ability to create and exercise power over sin, sickness, disease and death.

In the same passage David refers to God's people (us) as gods, he also gives a warning. He tells us that in spite of this great privilege, we will still return to dust. Even though the creator has made us gods able to walk in victory, authority and power, as administrators and ambassadors of His kingdom, we are still going to die like men. We still need to remember that God is the Most High and that we are children of the Most High God. Because He is the Most High God, He has made us gods – little "g," rulers who can tap into God's kingdom resources and power because of the victory He won at Calvary. He has put creative ability in us to build, to root up, to pull down and to plant. We can use that creative ability for good or for evil; we can release creative power for healing and creative miracles by speaking God's Word.

In the book of Exodus, again using the Hebrew word Elohiym, the Lord says to Moses: ***"I have made you as God to Pharaoh..." (Ex. 7:1).*** Again that word God is Elohiym. He was saying to Moses that He had made him a judge, a ruler with divine connections. In His commission as God to Pharaoh, Moses was going to release creative miracles and signs and wonders. He would release plagues and later He would command water to come from the rock. Moses would also stretch his hand over the Red Sea and part the waters. God was saying to Moses that He would not do anything unless He did it with His servant.

The Power of the Spoken Word

As gods, just like Moses, we can also perform creative miracles as we exercise our authority and speak commands as ambassadors of the Almighty. I'll say it again: miracles are as easy as releasing the atmosphere of the Spirit of God and speaking words of creation. Miracles are as easy as, ***"he sent forth his word, and healed them, and delivered them from destruction" (Ps. 107:20).***

There is power in God's Word. The Bible says that the word that goes out of God's mouth will not return to Him without doing its job (Is. 55:11). It will prosper and do what God sent it to accomplish. There is a creative power in the Word, especially when it is spoken out of a revelation from God, an understanding of our authority in Christ's kingdom as creative beings, combined with the power and authority of the Holy Spirit. We need a deep revelation that the nature of God lives inside of us, that we are rulers and judges with divine connections.

Creative miracles are released by what you say. We know that the Bible says life and death are in the power of the tongue (Pr. 18:21). Watch what you say with your mouth. You are going to eat the fruit of the words you speak—Scripture tells us that life and healing, blessing and cursing are in the tongue. You reap what you sow. Be careful of letting your tongue release criticism, judgments or gossip. However, my main emphasis in this teaching is the creative power of the tongue in the context of commanding creative healing, miracles, signs and wonders. God has put creation in you and that creation is released out of you as you begin to speak out the Word like God who ***"...calls those things which do not exist as though they did..." (Rom. 4:17).*** Those signs and wonders are released as you hear God and speak the creative words He directs you to speak.

We need a revelation of the power of God's word like the centurion who came to Jesus seeking a miracle for his servant. The centurion began telling Jesus about how his servant was lying at home paralyzed and dreadfully tormented. When Jesus offered to go to the man's house to heal his servant, the centurion said, ***"Lord, I am not worthy that You should come under my roof. But only speak a word, and my servant will be healed"*** **(Matt. 8:8).** Because the centurion, as a man who understood authority, knew the power of spoken commands, he had a revelation of the force of the creative spoken word. Like this Centurion, we need the revelation that the creative power of Elohiym can be released when we speak something with our mouth.

The same creative Holy Spirit that raised Jesus from the dead lives in us (Rom. 8:11). That creative power in us is released when we have faith in the God of creation and the power of God's word through us when we command a body to regenerate or a limb to grow back. As we receive that revelation of the power of the Holy Spirit inside of us, we will be able to boldly say, "Stretch out your withered arm in Jesus name," or "Begin to move your paralyzed leg." Miracles will happen! When we speak God's word with divine authority, creative miracles must happen!

Pioneering the Ministry of the Supernatural

Few are willing to believe such a message. Among those who do believe, few are willing to take the onslaught, attack, opposition and reproach that come with having a ministry of miracles and healing. The persecution is enormous. I have been ripped apart on radio programs and debates. People accuse me of having a deceptive spirit, of hypnotizing people and of operating in the spirit of Beelzebub. Christ's supernatural ministry cuts across the grain of what most people are doing—the world comes against it and the media comes against it and much of the church comes against it.

The big healing evangelists of the 40s and 50s, as well as the televangelists of the 80s, brought a reproach on the miracle and healing ministry. That reproach is still in effect today. Some of these early evangelists fell into sin or error. In many people's minds, the failings of these evangelist's, these Generals of the Faith, have stained or disqualified this supernatural ministry. These mental strongholds are hindering what God wants to do today.

Even pastors that believe in the ministry of miracles don't want to touch this stuff because there is so much controversy that comes with it. The miracle ministry challenges what most people believe and what most ministries are doing.

But somebody just has to break through! Somebody has got to be willing to pioneer healing and miracles again to see the power of God restored to the church. We have got to get the fullness of God's kingdom back into the body of Christ! We've got to have faith, not only for healings and miracles, but we have to have faith for creative healings and miracles again! They are really so easy when we come to know creator God.

We must not be afraid of failure. We cannot be afraid of praying for someone and having them die. Not all the sick are going to be healed when you pray for them. There will be angry people and those who will persecute the ministry. But God is not going to do it without us.

We have to realize, it's not that God has stopped doing miracles—we have! It's still business as usual in heaven! Just as it was 2,000 years ago, so it is today—business as usual. But you only see the miraculous in the lives of a few because few are willing to take the persecution and opposition that comes when you really begin to step out with this supernatural ministry.

When Jesus broke the five loaves and two fish, He told the disciples to give it to the people—they did and five thousand were fed. When Elisha told the widow to pour out her oil, she did, and a great number of large vessels were filled. When Jesus told the people to roll away the tombstone, they did, and Lazarus walked out of his grave, alive, at Jesus' command. Before performing each creative miracle, God first wanted people to do something with what they had. In the same way, we are to just give God all we have and He will do the rest.

With so much opposition to the miraculous, why did God launch me into this ministry? People often wonder why God pulled me out of the pit of drugs and alcohol ten years ago. Why did He take me out of the saw mill when I was nobody, and say, "Todd I want to send you all over the world with the gospel and with saving, healing, delivering power"? Well, when the Lord said that to me, I didn't spend much time wondering why. I just said,

> *"God, I am willing. Here I am—send me. I can hardly wait Lord! Even if I face opposition, persecution, or reproach; even if I have to fight in a spiritual war, praise God—that is for me! I am not going to be destroyed for a lack of knowledge. I am going to believe the Word of God. And whatever comes my way in reproach, because I choose to believe God's Word, I know God will move in miracles!"*

It's time for us, as God's people, to press for the anointing. We've got to be bold; we've got to stand out. We have to roll back the reproach and not be afraid of failure. We need courage even if we lay hands on 500 sick people and nobody is healed or when we lay hands on someone and that person still dies. Even when everyone comes to us and says, "You prayed for him. Where is this miracle power that you talk about? That person died. Where was the miracle?" No matter what, we need to press through to victory.

And you know what? This worst-case scenario will not happen to you! You will see people healed if you step out in faith—God will honor your action. Get a revelation of the creative power that is in you. Believe that Jesus wants to release miracles in and through your life today.

We will never understand miracles and healings while we are still in our human bodies. So we might as well forget trying to figure them out. When we give what we have, there is still more. We shouldn't make it too complicated. Creation does not happen without the Holy Spirit. And, remember, the same Spirit that raised Christ from the dead lives in you and me. It is as simple as that.

Chapter Ten

FAITH TO RAISE THE DEAD

Our God is not only a healer but He is also in the resurrection business. When Jesus said He must be about His Father's business, I believe He was talking about the resurrection business. That's an amazing business to be in—in our world the market for resurrection is huge. Death is everywhere. Millions of people are dying in their sins; they're crying because of dreams and hopes that have died; they're mourning the death of loved ones and they're suffering from physical sicknesses leading to death.

The Bible tells us that Jesus came that we would have life and have it more abundantly (John 10:10). Jesus also tells us in Scripture that He is the resurrection and the life and that whoever believes in Him will live even though he is dead (John 11:25). Wow! Think about it—Jesus is the author of life; He is resurrection in bodily form. The Bible also tells us that, as born-again believers, the same Spirit that raised Jesus from the dead lives in us—resurrection lives inside of us (Rom. 8:11).

Like many in our world, you too may need a tangible touch of Jesus' resurrection life. As you read this chapter, I pray that God's resurrection life and power would quicken your finances, your marriage and the areas of death in your soul and body. I'm asking God to resurrect bankrupt businesses, ministry's that have collapsed and churches that have closed their doors. I believe that new life will arise wherever the spirit of death has destroyed the vision, purpose and destiny of God; where hope deferred has made the heart grow sick. May the Spirit of resurrection release joy instead of heaviness and depression, as well as vision where confusion and despair have reigned. I pray that the divine nuclear force of God's life would release resurrection in you and illumine the principles in these pages. Then, may He give you the authority and weapons which will enable you to war and contend for resurrection miracles in other's lives... even those whose ***body's*** have died!

I remember being part of a conference in which we prayed for a nurse who worked at a local hospital—we prayed for an impartation for faith and an anointing to raise the dead. Working around sickness everyday, seeing people dying of various diseases and feeling powerless to do anything had made her desperate to see God's healing power in operation. She so wanted to see the miracles that she had read about in the Bible that she requested an impartation of God's healing power and resurrection life from me and several of the speakers.

Within days this woman had returned to the hospital and discovered that a baby in her ward had died. She was preparing the baby for the morgue when she remembered the impartation she had received. So she commanded life and the child came alive! She testified that she had received that impartation of power for resurrection life at the conference.

My wife and I once had to lay hold of that resurrection life—we had an encounter with the spirit of death that really shook us, yet taught us our authority in Christ. Years ago my oldest child, Lauralee, had an accident when she was several months old. An entire pepper shaker had accidentally spilled in her face. She began to choke; she stopped breathing and went blue in the face. We panicked. After several minutes my wife scooped up Lauralee's limp body and ran outside. She held her up to God and said, "God if you want us to have this child, then cause her to start to breathe." Instantly Lauralee started crying and breathing again. Although she hadn't been pronounced clinically dead, minutes had gone by without a breath. It was as if the spirit of death tried to take my child. That was the first experience where I began to learn about our authority over death.

Raising Dead Bodies

Warning: raising the dead is not like healing the sick! People say to me: "Todd if we want to raise the dead, or practice raising the dead, why can't we just go to the morgue and pray for corpses?" Remember, God has promised the healing of every sickness and disease and we can be confident that healing is in the atonement. Also, Jesus has commissioned us to "heal the sick, cleanse the lepers (and) raise the dead," according to Matthew 10:8. However, raising those who have died physically takes place at the command of Jesus. Yes, although we can claim Jesus' promises of spiritual resurrection, we must hear His word for those whose bodies have died. When you hear testimonies of those that have raised the dead, remember that Jesus said, ***"I only do those things I see the Father doing" (Jn. 5:19).*** So you can't just, at will, go to the graveyard or interrupt a funeral procession and pray for the dead.

Recently, in Malawi, a young child was run over by a 10-ton truck on our crusade grounds. Everybody on our team said, "Todd, let's go raise him from the dead. Let's go down to the morgue and pray for the child!" I said, "Well, I don't know that the parents want us to pray for the child." People on the team just kept pushing to go raise the child. I thought, "You've got to be sensitive to the family. You can't just barge into the hospital, ask the police for the body and pray for the child to be raised from the dead." Insensitivity could cause an offense, especially if the parents haven't asked us to pray for their child. So, eventually, we decided not to go pray for the child.

It's a whole different situation if people invite us to pray for a dead relative, or if they bring the dead body to a crusade. Even if we pray for the body in my "raise the dead" tent (which we set up in my crusades in Africa) we have more authority in the spirit. In these cases, if we do pray for a dead body and it is not raised, what did we lose? The relatives were the ones that initiated, acting on their faith, saying, "Todd, I want you to pray for my child. I understand if it happens it happens, if it doesn't, it doesn't. So I brought my child to you." This situation is very different from one in which I go trying to pry open an opportunity to raise a dead person and offend everyone along the way.

In the Morgue

I was in Africa and was talking about raising the dead. One of the pastors had a nephew who had died of Malaria a few days earlier. He made arrangements for us to come to the morgue and pray. My mission's director, John, and I went into the morgue where we met the mortician and looked around. Morgues in Africa are not neat and clean like they are in North America. I saw three or four bodies laying around in various stages of autopsy. I just wasn't prepared to go into that kind of situation and raise the dead. The mortician pulled out a box and opened it up—the boy was lying there with two or three bodies beside his. One of the people had been in a car accident and blood was everywhere. "Great. Praise God," I said. Yet, everything looked impossible around me. "Let's raise the dead," I said, "Let's go for it." I kind of climbed on top of the body and shouted, "Life! Life! Life! Life!" trying to raise the boy from the dead. Then, holding the boy's dead toe I said, "Life! I command you to come alive. I command your spirit to come back into your body. I take authority over the spirit of death. I rebuke the spirit of death in the name of Jesus. I command your spirit to come back into your body."

A Dispute in Heaven

Suddenly, I was in the second heaven where I saw a battle involving the spirit of death, who had a legal right to claim to this unsaved boy's soul. But, because I was a child of God taking authority and commanding the child's spirit to come back, a dispute arose. The scene was similar to the scene in heaven when the Devil came before God to accuse Job and get permission to afflict him. In the spirit realm, a legal battle raged.

On the one side I, as a child of God, was commanding something to take place. The Father was listening to my prayer and the Devil was contesting my claim. It was as if Satan was saying, "No way is Todd going to raise him from the dead—this child died as a non-believer. He is not a Christian; his soul is legally mine because he died without Christ. If Todd raises him from

Some beautiful African children we met during an outreach

the dead he'll get saved and I'll lose him from my kingdom—you can't have him."

As this dispute continued, I stood in the gap, trying to take dominion over the spirits of death that were hindering the boy's spirit from returning to his body. I knew if his spirit returned, he would be raised from the dead and I could lead him to Christ. The Devil opposed and resisted me in the second heaven.

I continued to appeal to heaven illegally, without God having spoken to me that it was His will to raise the boy. As I continued I was attacked by the spirit of death— it came out of the boy's body and climbed up my arm. I felt it grab hold of me and it took two hours to get it off.

That was the first time I was attacked by a demon like that. But I quickly learned some things about raising the dead— the keys are listening for instructions from God and then acting on our authority in Christ. You don't just go out to the morgue or the grave and pray for the dead unless family members have invited you or you've heard God's direction to go.

These situations are different than if God shows me in a vision, before I get to Africa, that I will raise the dead. You can believe if somebody dies while I'm there under those circumstances, I'm going to go for it because then I have the authority to release resurrection life.

Today, in various parts of the world, more and more ministries are beginning to have experiences with God's resurrection power (like Heidi Baker's and Reinhard Bonnke's ministry). I believe that as we continue to go out and do Christ's works in the nations, both you and I will have many opportunities to raise the dead at God's command.

Raising Those Without Purpose and Hope

As New Testament believers, we are also called to raise another kind of dead— those who are still breathing but who lack purpose and hope. Scripture speaks of these types of people saying, ***"Where there is no vision the people perish" (Prov. 29:18 KJV).*** They become lazy and complacent. So, at times when people have lost purpose and hope, we need to release Jesus' resurrection life.

Maybe a place in your heart has died; deferred hope has made your heart sick. Perhaps you've experienced years of discouragement and disappointment in your marriage; the romance has died or you've experienced serious relational struggles, separation or divorce. Maybe your business is bankrupt—it's dead and you've lost all your money. Maybe your ministry had died and you've closed all the doors to your church. Death. Perhaps the doctors have diagnosed a terminal condition and you are as good as dead, or you're so depressed that your emotions are dead. Maybe it's a son and daughter who is dead in sin and you want to see them spiritually raised and made alive in Christ. Like many Christians, you've probably suffered from the death of visions in your life—God wants to resurrect those dreams. He wants to resurrect every area of death and to breathe life to your prophetic promises and words. Its time to hope again!

Seeing Life Through Jesus' Eyes

If we begin to see situations through Jesus' eyes, we will begin to walk in the resurrection life that He has for us. Jesus views situations a whole lot differently than we do. Let's look again at the story of Jesus' friend Lazarus.

Lazarus lived in Bethany with his sisters Mary and Martha. It was this Mary that anointed Jesus with fragrant oil. In John 11:3 the sisters sent Jesus a message: ***"Lord, behold, he who you love is sick."*** However, the passage says, ***"Jesus knew that this sickness wouldn't end in death, but that it would bring glory to God" (v. 4).*** Lazarus was sick on his deathbed without even one day to live. He just had hours—it was either "Jesus come now or Lazarus will die!" In spite of the desperate situation, Jesus stayed where He was for two more days.

Have you ever been in a situation where just when you thought it couldn't get any worse, it seemed like God disappeared? It seemed like God was late. God delayed when you thought it couldn't get any darker and then it got darker. But remember, God is never late; it just seems like He's late. To Mary and Martha God seemed very late.

Not Dead, Just Sleeping

You may have also been in a desperate life situation like Lazarus' sisters. You needed God to act before disaster struck and it seemed like He failed you. Usually, however, our desperation comes from not understanding God's workings or His timing. To us God seems to be late; He waited too long. What is it about God that causes Him never to come through early? God is a five 'till midnight God.

Jesus eventually decides to go to Bethany: ***"'Our friend Lazarus sleeps, but I go that I might wake him up.' Then His disciples said, 'Lord, if He sleeps he will get well.' However, even when Jesus spoke of His death, they thought He was speaking about sleeping" (Jn. 11:11-13).***

Now was Jesus lying? He said, "Our friend Lazarus sleeps." But Lazarus was dead, not sleeping. Just as with Lazarus, you may have heard the final death rattle in an area of your life or ministry and you're saying, "It's dead. It's over. I can't. It's impossible. Look at the doctor's diagnosis; look at the mountain of hindrance. It's impossible." Yet, all the while Jesus is saying, "It's sleeping."

You see, when we see things through Jesus' eyes we will also begin to see life when everything in the natural speaks of death. Jesus sees it a whole lot differently than you do. You say Lazarus is dead. Jesus says He is sleeping. Later in the story Jesus actually tells them plainly that Lazarus is dead. Then He says something shocking in verse 15: ***"I am glad for your sakes that I was not there, that you might believe."*** I can imagine Mary, Martha and the disciples by now are angry, confused and disappointed—they had told Jesus the need and He hadn't come through. They didn't understand the reasons God waits. What is it about the eleventh hour? What is it about the last minute? They can't figure out why Jesus didn't come when He got their urgent news; they didn't realize that He wanted to teach them something.

God sees impossible circumstances as opportunity—to Him ***Impossibility = Opportunity.*** Without impossible circumstances in our lives, we have no opportunity to really believe in an awesome God of the impossible. The next time you face a mountain of impossibility you can say, ***"Who are you, oh mountain…" (Zech. 4:7)?*** So how does Jesus handle this "impossible" circumstance? When He arrives in Bethany, Lazarus had already been in the tomb for four days.

> ***"Many of the Jews were comforting Martha and Mary in their mourning. As soon as she heard that Jesus had entered the city, Martha went to meet Him. She said, 'Lord if you had been here, my brother would not have died, but even now I know that whatever you ask of God, God will give you'" (Jn. 11:19-22).***

A Test of Faith

Martha sounds like a woman of faith—what a great confession! My brother is dead, but "even now I know." It's like saying, "The doctors diagnosed me with cancer but even now I know I can be healed." But the Lord is about to test her faith. When we make a decision to stand and believe God, He will test us to see if we really believe what we say we believe. I can imagine Jesus thinking, "OK, let's see if you really believe that your brother will rise again."

Like Martha, there are all kinds of Christians who are programmed to carefully speak only the "right things." Sometimes there is not even room for joking in their lives. Yes, we need to be careful with our confession. I believe in good confession and prophetic decrees. I believe in calling those things that aren't as though they were. However, we may speak the promises of God and quote the Scripture saying, "By His stripes I am healed" but the true test of what we believe is when we are confronted by an impossible situation.

Here in Bethany Martha is talking like many Christians do. "Even now I know that whatever you ask of God will happen." It sounds really good. "I don't have the money but even now I know God is Jehovah Jireh brother; everything is good in my life!" They talk like this but see very little manifest in their lives. Or, if God provides, they're actually shocked.

In our story, Jesus turns around and says something like, "OK, do you really believe that your brother will rise again?" Suddenly her faith withers and we see that her words weren't really words of faith at all. Her faith was actually just hope because she responded saying that she knows he will rise again one day out there in the future. Hope is always tomorrow.

Many Christians, when put to the test, talk the same way: "I know I will be healed Todd—one day I will be healed. You are right, God does heal all. When you die and get to heaven that is a healing." Like Martha, God's people also put God's promises way out in the future. When Jesus tests Martha's faith, her attitude is: "OK, I know that my brother will rise again because the word of God is true—what God said is true." But her idea of how and when God would fulfill His word did not line up.

Now take a look at Jesus' response***: "I am the resurrection and the life. He who believes in Me, though he may die, he shall live. And whoever lives and believes in Me shall never die. Do you believe this" (v. 25-26)?*** She responds by saying***, "Yes, Lord, I believe that you are the Christ, the Son of God, who is to come into the world" (v. 27).***

Further in the passage we read that famous verse 35, ***"Jesus wept."*** Did Jesus weep out of compassion? Or could it be that Jesus wept because of their unbelief or because they were so angry that He had not come earlier? Perhaps Jesus wept because, although their confession was, "Even now I know that whatever you ask of God, God will give you," yet they later failed the test of their faith. It was just empty words.

As modern-day believers, we also need to realize that when we take a stand for something, God will test us. When the testing begins, we really find out what we are made of. It is easy to believe in healing until *you* are the one who is sick. It's easy to look at others who and say, "Just believe God," until you go to the doctor and he says that you have cancer. Then it's a whole different ball game.

When Jesus wept they said, ***"See how he loved him" (v. 35).*** I think they misread Jesus. I don't believe He wept because of His love for Lazarus—Jesus knew that he was going to rise again. From Jesus' perspective, there was no need to weep for Lazarus. In fact, earlier Jesus was actually rejoicing, saying things like: "I am glad for your sakes that he's dead. I am glad that I wasn't here. Hallelujah! I want you to learn to believe. I want to teach you something here."

When the Lord tells them to take away the stone, Martha responds, ***"Lord, by this time there is a stench, for he has been dead four days."*** Then Jesus reminds her saying, ***"Did I not say to you that if you would believe you would see the glory of God?" (v. 39).*** In that instant Martha must have remembered her great confession of faith earlier—she began to understand that she didn't really believe what she thought she believed.

Eleventh-hour Provision

Just like Martha, often when I've thought I was strong in faith, God brings some huge obstacle into my life such as a great financial need. In this test, as I'm beginning to doubt God or work out how I can save myself if God doesn't rescue me, He reminds me of the many times He's come through for me by looking after my rent or paying a bill. As I remember God's last-minute, eleventh-hour provision in the past, I cry out again, "God help!" And God comes through again, right at the last minute. Then I repent that I didn't believe God and ask Him to forgive me: "I'll never doubt again. I'm sorry that I got so worried and that I was trying to figure out how I would get out of it just in case you didn't come through."

We all tend to do this. We convince ourselves that we are really trusting God, yet we give God a deadline saying: "I'll trust you until then. But if you don't answer by then, I can't wait any longer. So I will have to call Bill or Susie to help." We work it through in our head and then God comes through in the end. We discover that for us God also just stayed where He was two more days until it seemed like it was too late. When He comes through later, we find out how perfect His timing was. Looking back we say, "Oh God, I should have trusted You all the way through. Now I see why You delayed."

Over and over again, in similar situations, we tend to fall into doubt. Then we pray, "God! Help! Forgive me for my unbelief!" God wants us to understand why He often allows already dark circumstances to get darker—it's so that you might believe; so that you can be stronger next time. God wants to teach you something about raising the dead. Jesus wanted Mary and Martha to learn that it didn't take any more faith for Him to raise Lazarus from the dead than it would have taken two days earlier to heal him. In Jesus' eyes, Lazarus was only sleeping. You see, what we call dead or what we think is impossible in our lives is only sleeping. Jesus wants to come and wake those things up.

Only Possibilities

When God looks at naturally impossible situations in our lives, He sees only possibilities. With God all things are possible (Matt. 19:26)! God makes dead ends into highways. Do you believe that? He makes every mountain low, every valley high, every crooked place straight (Isa. 40:3-4). That's just who God is. He says, ***"Who are you, oh great mountain? ...you shall become a plain!" (Zech. 4:7)*** When we start thinking like God does, we realize that we can lay hold of the answer to our impossible situation by faith. When we walk in faith, we lay hold of the spiritual substance in the heavenly realm and bring our promise, our answer to prayer, into our natural realm.

God is Never Early and Never Late

On our time schedule, we may consider God to be constantly late. However, from His eternal, heavenly perspective, God is always on time, never early and never late. Mark 5 illustrates this perfect, heavenly punctuality:

> ***"Now when Jesus had crossed over again by boat to the other side, a great multitude gathered to Him; and He was by the sea. And behold, one of the rulers of the synagogue came, Jairus by name. And when he saw him, he fell at His feet and begged him earnestly, saying, "My little daughter lies at the point of death" (Mrk. 5:21-23).***

The man's daughter, just like Lazarus, is not quite dead but just about there. Now look at the confession, the confidence, the boldness. ***"Come lay your hands on her and she will live" (v. 23).***

He is saying, "I believe God in the midst of this impossible situation—my daughter lies at the point of death but I know that I know! I am in faith!" Then, suddenly, in verse 35, ***"while he was still speaking"*** terrible news came—the girl had died.

As believers today, we may have had similar experiences. Just when we're starting to believe for a breakthrough, things get worse—perhaps the phone rings and the voice on the line says, "It's not just cancer – its melanoma cancer. He has three months to live."

In Jairus' case, the messenger not only brought the bad news, but encouraged him to give up believing: ***"Why trouble the teacher any further" (v. 35)?*** You can just hear Jairus: "Yeah, you're right. Why trouble the teacher any further?" And you can just hear the Devil bombarding Jairus with the same negative thoughts, "Why trouble the teacher any further?"

Faith-Shaking Events

Have you ever had a similar experience? You were absolutely convinced that God was going to heal that dear woman in the church—the prophets prophesied about Tina's healing and others in the congregation have had prophetic promises about her ministry a year or two from now. Now the question is: "If God has this great destiny for Tina, then how can she be dying of cancer?" We conclude that this must mean that she is going to be healed. We pray for her, she feels the fire of God and the symptoms of cancer start to leave—it seems like we are getting the victory. The congregation is meeting every Friday night; they are holding prayer vigils to war and press in for Tina's healing.

Two girls, who were both deaf, are totally healed during mass prayer at a crusade in India

"We got the prophetic word; we got God's healing promises. We had the healing school with Todd Bentley and everyone's faith is off the charts. Our faith has been fueled to pray for Tina. It looks like we are winning and the Devil has the short end of the stick." Then you get the phone call—Tina has died. Pop! In an instant, your faith balloon has burst. I've seen this story repeated again and again around the world in various ways. People's faith is on the up and then the phone rings to say that their son died in a car accident. Or, they're on a roll—people are getting healed and things are going on in the ministry when some faith-shaking event takes place.

Recently our Fresh Fire team was in the midst of a crusade in Malawi. God was doing creative miracles—a new eyeball had grown where no eye was; a baby's enlarged head was instantly restored to normal; huge tumors had fallen off people's bodies and 10,000 people had been saved. On the crusade grounds one afternoon, a ten-ton truck backed over a child and crushed him to death. The child dies on the crusade grounds right in the midst of a revival. Everyone knows that it was on our crusade grounds that the nine-year-old boy was killed. Yet, we're the ones proclaiming the goodness and healing power of God with testimonies of healing every night. And now we're supposed to get up on the platform that next night and say, "Celebrate, Jesus, celebrate!"

When the Darkness gets Darker

In Jairus' case, I wonder how long it had taken him to muster up enough faith to come to Jesus. He had been hearing the testimonies of what Jesus was doing all over the city and hope had come alive in his heart. He said, "You know what guys? My daughter is lying at the point of death. But if Jesus can heal all those others, He can do it for my little girl." So he left his house to find Jesus and, with all the faith within him says, "Come lay your hands on her – she will live." What confidence! "I am going to believe God. He is going to provide." And just then, while he is still speaking, the message comes: "Your daughter is dead." Unbelief hits like a freight train. Here is Jairus at the crossroads of faith "You're right. Why trouble the teacher any further?"

As soon as Jesus heard the negative confession and saw Jairus begin to falter, He began to steady his wavering faith. I can imagine Jesus grabbing Jairus's by the shoulders and looking him in the eyes, "Steady, Jairus. Only believe. Only believe! It doesn't take any more faith for Me to raise her from the dead than to heal her illness. It doesn't take any more power for me to heal a blind eye than it does to heal a headache. It doesn't take any more faith for me to heal a crippled man than it does for me to heal arthritis. It doesn't take any more power for me to call Lazarus out of the tomb than to rebuke Peter's mother-in-law's fever. Jairus, nothing has changed. Only believe!"

Only Believe!

Jesus makes it sound so simple. How many times have you been in a place in your life where the last thing you wanted to hear was "Well, brother, just believe God"? Perhaps Jairus is thinking, "Who wants to hear, 'only believe'? My daughter is dead! And Jesus you're telling me to 'just believe!'" Yet Jesus was saying, "Jairus, just have the faith that you had a moment ago when you believed I could heal her. Even though she is dead, nothing has really changed except for the circumstance. To you it's impossible, but I see it as an opportunity. Only believe."

Jesus is trying to teach Jairus to see through the eyes of faith. In the same way, Jesus wants us to see impossible situations like He does. When we see the obstacles His way, we can begin praising and thanking Him even before the miracle happens. Even though the girl had died, I believe, as in the story of Lazarus, Jesus is excited. He is in faith and is thanking the Father for this opportunity to glorify Him. If we're looking through Jesus' lenses of faith, we will also see the breakthrough before it manifests and we will be inspired to worship Him. Just like Abraham, the father of faith, we will be ***"strengthened in faith, (by) giving glory to God" (Rom. 4:20).*** Then, as our faith grows, we continue to thank and worship Him in advance—and the heavens begin to open over our situation.

Nothing but Faith, Hope and Love

You see, when everything else fails, three things still remain—faith, hope and love (1 Cor. 13:13). When I stepped into the healing ministry I had to make the decision to exclude everything from my vocabulary but faith, hope, and love. I realized that the only way that I could overcome the disappointment when people weren't healed was by embracing Hebrews 11:39. It is a powerful Scripture: ***"Many died not yet receiving the promise."***

So how long are you going to believe God for healing? Are you dead yet? How many times do I need to get prayer at the altar? Are you dead yet? Think about the man with the infirmity in John 5—he had suffered for 38 years when Jesus showed up. Can you believe that? Jesus doesn't apologize for being late or not healing him sooner. Perhaps the man looked back over his life and said, "Hmmmmm, let's see—how many thousands of times did I go down to the altar and get prayer from all the healing guys? After all those years of waiting, the man received his miracle.

However, Scripture also tells us that many died not receiving the promise. I came to realize something in the healing ministry a long time ago—

there will be disappointments and some people will even die. You may be thinking, "There it is—a bad confession again Todd. Some people won't get healed—how can you say that? That is why they don't get healed."

Come on, let's get serious! Because none of us has perfected faith yet, if you decide to risk launching into the healing ministry, you are going to pray for people and some are going to die. Sometimes, you are going to pray for people and they are not going to be healed. People will be disappointed and you will experience failure. You might pray for a hundred and nobody gets healed. Yet, faith must persevere. If you pray for a thousand and nobody is healed, then you must pray for another thousand. Because there are three things that abide—faith, hope and love. You don't have any other choice—there is no option that involves giving up. The Bible tells us some died not receiving the promise.

Remember that all these people in Hebrews 11 are called the *heroes* of the faith! God didn't chastise them for clinging to their faith until their last dying breath. He is proud of them for keeping the faith! ***"But now they desire a better, that is, a heavenly country. Therefore God is not ashamed to be called their God, for He has prepared a city for them.... And all these, having obtained a good testimony through faith, did not receive the promise" (Heb. 11:16-17, 39).***

He says that they obtained a "good testimony." That's awesome, how would you like to hear God pronounce that over you?

Let's take our cue from Jesus. When John the Baptist, great friend of Jesus, the Bridegroom, was beheaded, what did Jesus do? The next day he went out and did miracles.

I've learned the lesson of persistent faith in the school of hard knocks. A few years ago I was at a great healing revival in Albany, Oregon; people were coming from around the word to receive healing. In the midst of that whole thing people were getting saved and mighty miracles were happening everywhere—it was awesome! Then, suddenly, I got news that my Mom had died of a stroke at age 46. All the while, people were being healed of the effects of stroke in our meetings. So, what did I do? I got on an airplane and flew to the next crusade. The funeral would be in five days. I finished the crusade, came home, buried my mom and went out again. What else could I do? She was with Jesus... it was over!

That's when I said, "Well Devil, now you are going to have to give me a hundred stroke victims!" I could have gotten disappointed, angry, confused and given up, never to pray for the sick again. That would have been to deny my call and God's word. My choice was—either give up or add more fuel to my fire for healing ministry. I grieved on the inside, but this setback just made me stronger.

So many Christians have given up their call, ministry, promises or even their faith because of a devastating failure or disappointment. Many have fallen along the way. But this is war. This is war! We are on the front lines and people die. But there is faith, hope and love. See, there is no other choice for Todd Bentley but faith, hope and love. There is no disappointment or anything else. Either believe God, or give up. Get in or get out—that's it! Recognizing this harsh reality helped me go on.

Victorious Faith Like Abraham's

We're in a life and death struggle against demonic forces trying to destroy our faith. However, we can overcome the enemy by standing firm in our faith. Scripture emphasizes this truth: ***"...this is the victory that has overcome the world—our faith" (1 Jn. 5:4).***

If we want to learn about faith we need to look at the life of Abraham, the father of faith. Why do they call Abraham the father of faith? What gave Abraham faith—what sustained him? Well, according to Romans 4:17, Abraham's kind of faith ***"...calls those things that do not exist as though they did."***

Abraham's faith declarations, according to the book of Hebrews, released a powerful force of life: ***"These all died in faith, not having received the promises, but having seen them afar off, were assured of them, embraced them and confessed that they were strangers and pilgrims of this earth" (Heb. 11:13).*** These believers saw the promises in the spirit from afar; they saw them coming out of the heavens. And that supernatural vision is what sustained Abraham when God tested his faith.

God told Abraham to take his only son and offer him up as a sacrifice. "Kill him." Everything within Abraham must have screamed, "That has got to be the devil. My son is all I have in the natural to fulfill God's promise to me. How can that be God? What am I going to say to the police—'The Devil made me do it?' What am I going to tell the neighbors when they ask me why Isaac isn't playing in the backyard with all the kids anymore? How am I going to tell this to my wife after it took so long for her to believe God's promise of a son in the first place? Now God is asking me to kill the only means of fulfilling God's promise to make me a father of many nations?"

I'm sure Abraham was working all the scenarios through in his head: "Well, maybe I'll get up there and the Second Coming will happen. Maybe He's just looking for me to step out in obedience." I bet Abraham didn't sleep the night before. But Abraham had one belief that he clung to, something that sustained his faith

> ***"...in the presence of him who he believed--God who gives life to the dead and calls those things which do not exist as though they did; who, contrary to hope, in hope believed, so that he became the father of many nations, according to what was spoken, 'So shall your descendants be'" (Rom. 14:17-18).***

I'm sure this was one of the scenarios he imagined: "OK, I get up on the mountain, put my son on the altar and I kill him with the knife. God will raise him from the dead and I have him back again. That's it. Hallelujah."

Your Miracle Begins in Your Spirit

Eventually Abraham comes to terms with God's command. You see, some things, you will never do in the natural until you've worked it through in your spirit first. Now he had confidence that even if he killed his son on the altar God would give new life and raise him from the dead. There is something powerful about seeing what is about to happen before it does. That is why, when God first promised Abraham he would be a father of nations, He took Abraham outside, and showed him a natural illustration of his inheritance. God said to him:

> *"You see the stars; how innumerable they are? Now think about the sands of the sea shore, how innumerable they are. Get a vision in your eye gate. You become what you behold. You produce after what you see. I want you to get the vision. I want you to get it in your imagination. I want you to see it. Look at the stars. Those are your descendants right there. Look at the sand of the sea shore, that's how great the multitude of your descendents will be. You see that Abraham?"*

After God's object lesson, Abraham was able to visualize his destiny. Seeing is so much more powerful than just hearing. Reading a story is great but watching a book come to life on the movie screen is more impacting. We are visual people.

You need to see your miracle in your spirit before it will manifest. You need to see it as finished. Abraham thought, "I already see Isaac killed, dead, and raised again. ***"God gives life to the dead and calls those things which do not exist as though they did."*** So, if I bring him up there and kill him, God will resurrect him." Like Abraham, we must see our resurrection promises

Mass prayer for healing in Mexico

in our spirit first. We must catch a vision and revelation of what Jesus has already done. We must see ourselves healed.

When Jesus raised Lazarus from the dead, He did not have to lay hands on the dead body. There was authority in the Word of God He spoke. Now think about those things that are dead in your life? Maybe your faith is dead. Maybe your relationship with God, your marriage, your children, your body, your church or even your ministry is dead. See the situation and command resurrection power to be released. Let your hope rise again and your faith be resurrected. Contend for miracles as your vision is restored. See the power of His life come. He is the Resurrection and Life!

Warring and Contending for Miracles

I am going to show you what real resurrection faith is. You see, in the church today, we need to have an understanding of what real faith is and know that it is OK to ask God for the same thing more than once. Remember, when the disciples asked Jesus to teach them how to pray? He told them the parable of the persistent widow who kept on coming to make her request (Luke 18:1-8) and the parable about the friend that just kept asking for food, even though it was midnight (Luke 11:5-10). Some people in the kingdom think that if they ever ask God for the same thing more than once that they aren't going to get it because they didn't believe God the first time they asked.

Perhaps they think, "I should only get prayer once and then I should believe that when Todd prayed for me I was healed. Wouldn't that be unbelief if I went to the altar again? How long do I believe God?" Well, I believe Scripture shows us that if you don't get healed tonight you're to come back tomorrow. If you don't get healed tomorrow, come back the next day. If the healing hasn't manifested yet, come back again the next day. According to Matthew 7:7, you are to ***"keep on asking and it will be given you; keep on seeking and you will find; keep on knocking and the door will be opened to you" (Amp.).***

We are to be like the persistent widow and continue to weary the Lord with our petitions. "God, don't forget You said that You would heal me. Don't forget You said You would heal me. Don't forget You said that You would heal me!" Then get prayer ministry at every opportunity. Asking God for something more than once doesn't mean that you don't believe God or that your faith is weak. In fact, the Bible teaches that those walking in real faith war and contend for miracles according to Hebrews 11:6: ***"But without faith it is impossible to please Him, for He who comes to Him must believe that He is and that He is a rewarder of those who diligently seek Him."*** Yes, God wants us to be diligent, to continue to ask, seek and knock until the answer comes. God rewards those who diligently seek Him!

The Power of Persistent Prayer

I believe that often we don't see the miracles we want because we only pray once. The ministry success of John G. Lake, pioneer of one of the greatest healing/miracle ministries in the last 100 years, can largely be attributed to persistent prayer. He would sometimes pray for three days without any food or drink and, at times, even without sleep or rest—just to see one person healed. When I heard about this tenacity I said, "Oh God… five minutes and I am done!" I mean, I might pray three hours at the altar, but any longer than five minutes for one person and I'm thinking, "Bring me the next one. If he isn't healed by now, he isn't getting it." I'm just being honest.

But, if you go to the Toronto Airport Vineyard, you'll find prayer teams that will pray with you for four hours: "More Lord, more Lord, more Lord!" Whereas, when I minister, I'd rather just lay out a whole bench of people with one single nuclear prayer. "Bam! Oh, you want it again? Bam!" That's it. Then I move on to the next people. You see, I am not really programmed for those long prayers. However, Scripture emphasizes the spiritual force of desperate, pray-till-something-happens tenacity. We all need a greater revelation of the power of persistent prayer.

The story, in 2 Kings 4, of Elisha and the Shunammite woman, illustrates this principle. Let me paraphrase: this Shunammite had been so good to Elisha—giving him a place to stay and food whenever he came into town—that Elisha decides he wants to do something for her. When Elisha asks his servant Gehazi what he can do, Gehazi answers: "Well, actually, the woman has no child, and her husband is old." In the natural it is impossible. Who knows how many years the couple had already tried to have children and how long since they had given up?

Resurrecting Dreams

What about you? How many years have you had a dream in your heart or how long have you believed God for the fulfillment of a prophetic word? Perhaps you've come to a place of disillusionment and you just don't want to hear another prophetic word. Or you may have met people who talk like this: "Don't tell me things that are too good to be true because I've heard all the prophetic words. I've waited so long and I haven't seen their fulfillment—I don't know if I can handle another disappointment, another broken relationship, another possible financial or ministry breakthrough that doesn't happen or another…." Most of us can recall the times we've been repeatedly let down by someone and we start to say things like "Don't tell me that again. You broke my trust. After the tenth broken promise I stopped believing you." Often, after repeated disappointments, we just give up.

I believe that's how the Shunammite woman felt. However, she was about to get a sure word from God. In the Old Testament, when the prophet spoke, it was as if it was God Himself. In those days, you went to the seer prophet when you wanted to hear God's word. In 2 Kings 4:16 the prophet Elisha speaks a divinely authoritative word which would dramatically change the woman's world. ***"About this time next year you shall embrace a son."*** However, out of her deep discouragement, she answered, ***"No, my Lord. Man of God, do not lie to your maidservant."***

How many times have you been in a meeting where you've heard the truth about God's desire to heal all and about His promised gift of healing? Yet you've been disappointed—you've stood on that promise for a long time but still haven't seen healing manifest. Eventually you've begun to think, "I don't even want to hear another person tell me it's God's will to heal everyone all the time because I am so disappointed that I'm not healed. I've been let down so many times before."

You see, that was the Shunammite woman's state, ***"No my Lord… do not lie to your maidservant."*** She was saying, "Don't tell me things that are too good to be true. I've been disappointed. I've tried for so long and my hopes have been dashed." Despite her protests, the word of the Lord comes to pass and she conceives. At God's word, something happened to this woman; something happened to her faith. God did what He said He would do. He did it! Hallelujah! The answer! Doesn't that do something for your faith?

Passing Tests of Faith

When God answers your prayer, doesn't that make it easier for you to believe Him in that area next time? Even though she had seen a powerful miracle, the Shunammite woman's faith would be tested again. Later in the story, her boy is with his father out in the harvest field, when he begins to experience head pain and dies. What a devastating and confusing situation for the woman.

Perhaps you've been in a similar situation. God gives you a wonderful gift; you really believe that was *the* ministry He gave you, or you know that this person is the one who will become your spouse. You believe He gave you that business idea or told you to move to that city. It's wonderful when we get these sure words from the Lord. However, the question is, how long do we stand in unwavering faith when we get these words?

So often people come into our churches and say things like: "God told me that I was supposed to come to this church and give this much money. He told me I'm going to be your right hand man and I'm going to do 'this and that.'" Next thing you know, they're gone again. Everyone else is left wondering whatever happened to their "word from God." Perhaps you've even had Christian brothers and sisters around you who change their mind like the wind. From day to day you don't know if you can really believe what they say they've heard from God. So your response becomes, "Oh yeah, that's great. God bless you in that new vision." It's the hundredth one this week. Unlike such wavering "unbelievable" Christians, God is trustworthy and wants us to learn to cling to His words with all our might. ***"God is not a man, that He should lie, Nor a son of man, that He should repent. Has He said, and will He not do? Or has He spoken, and will He not make it good" (Nu. 23:19)?***

Pursuing the Promises

The Lord wanted the Shunammite to learn this lesson too:

> ***"When he (the husband) had taken him and brought him to his mother, he sat on her knees till noon, and then died. And she went up and laid him on the bed of the man of God, shut the door upon him, and went out. Then she called to her husband, and said, 'Please send me one of the young men and one of the donkeys, that I may run to the man of God and come back.' So he said, 'Why are you going to him today? It is neither the New Moon nor the Sabbath'" (II Ki. 4:20-23).***

Talk about desperation, focus and looking to Jesus. Her attitude says,

"I am going to run to the man of God, right back to the source of my prophetic word. Forget the waves and the wind trying to discourage me. Get me a donkey; I am going to the Word."

As she takes these bold steps of faith, in verse 23 discouragement comes knocking on her door just like it does for us when we decide to press in for a promise, a healing or to take a stand for Jesus. ***"So he said, 'Why are you going to him today?'"*** Just when we really purpose in our heart to get on fire, verse 23 comes like a bucket of cold water. Right after you leave the healing school, verse 23 will want to visit your house. Everyone is trying to persuade you to abandon your convictions: "Come on, we don't want to be that committed to Christ. We don't want to be a Jesus-freak, fanatic. You don't really have to serve God that hard. Let's just make it to heaven and have fun."

Or, perhaps your verse 23 sounded like this: "What makes you think that God wants to heal you? He didn't heal me. And if God was going to heal anyone He would've healed me because. I've been trying to get healed for ten years." When these discouraging words come at you, just say to others, "I am going to the healing school to get an impartation. I am going to get healed and I am going to get involved in the ministry of Jesus and God is going to use me to heal the sick." Stand firm on the truth.

The Shunammite's verse 23 came in the form of her husband's words, which went something like this: "Why are you going to him today? It's not God's time. It is neither the new moon nor the Sabbath!" But look at her response: "It is well (which, in the Hebrew, means 'it *will be* well')." What a powerful confession of faith in a very dark situation. Then she got on her donkey and told her servant to drive fast and not to slow down. Talk about desperation. From a distance Elisha saw her coming and said to Gehazi, ***"Look, the Shunammite woman! Please run now to meet her, and say to her, 'Is it well with you? Is it well with your husband? Is it well with your child?'" (vs. 25-26).***

She answers in faith: "It is well." When Elisha notices the woman's distress, he says that the Lord has hidden things from him or "I have no supernatural revelation and understanding about what is going on in her life." Yet the Lord, through the prophet, asked the woman a question to test her faith. With her words, ***"It is well"*** she passed the first test just as Martha had passed her first test by saying, ***"...even now I know that whatever you ask of God He will give it."*** Will the Shunammite woman's faith pass the next test, unlike Martha's? Is she just speaking words or are they backed up with true faith? You see, until the word of the Lord comes to pass, it is going to test you. God hears your confession.

No More Tiptoeing Around Heaven

God has also tested me in the healing ministry. He said, "Todd, let's see if you will really pray for another thousand if no one in the first thousand is healed." I've had to press through many times when the blind didn't see and the deaf didn't hear. But I had the word of the Lord that the miracles would happen—so I went the distance. Many people start to pray for the sick, but when they don't see healings right away, they give up. We need to get a revelation that God truly **is** a rewarder of those who diligently seek Him (Heb.11:6).

You see, it's easy in the healing school to go, "Ra, ra, ra. Yes, yes, yes. I'm going to believe God." But what are you doing six weeks later? What do you do when you pray for a thousand and see no results? Most pastors won't even go to the hospital to pray for the sick—just in case they prayed and God didn't heal. They'll go and pray that God will comfort them but usually they're just not really convinced that God does want to heal.

In the church today, we approach the healing ministry timidly, leaving the back door open so we can save face in case nothing happens. Well, that's not faith! Faith means taking radical risks; launching out into the deep. We are so cautious because we have a, "Lord-if-it-be-Your-will" attitude. We aren't really convinced that it's God's will to heal everyone. We haven't yet gotten a revelation of God's heart for healing. We approach healing like we're tiptoeing around heaven; we're afraid to come into His presence boldly to bring our requests.

Let's look at how the Shunammite woman's story ends. Elisha tells his servant to take his staff, run ahead, go up to the room and lay the staff on the child. However, in verse 31, Gehazi returns reporting that ***"the child has not awakened."*** Now Elisha arrives at the house—the child is dead in the bed. Elisha goes in, shuts the door, prays again and continues to pray.

Worshipping the Lord during a conference

How many times do you need to get prayer? Are you dead yet? Then keep praying as long as you have breath. Keep on asking; keep on seeking. In Elisha's case he needed to pray three times. He first prayed then he went and lay on the child—at this the child's flesh became warm. Then Elisha and Gehazi began to pace up and down. Who knows what they were doing as they walked back and forth in the house. Elisha probably did a little intercession before he went back and laid hands on the boy again. He got himself juiced up with power. Then, when he was ready, he returned to the bedroom. Again he laid on the child as he prayed and the child came to life.

Keep On Praying

Do we persist like this until healing manifests? Many have this experience: "OK, Todd, I am feeling a little heat now. I am feeling a little electricity. I'm feeling a little movement. Now the pain is just a little less." Then they go home and say they weren't healed.

However, in Elisha's case, even after the manifestation started to happen, he prayed again. This time, as he stretched himself out on the child, the child sneezed seven times and opened his eyes. God is a rewarder of those who diligently seek Him. If we are going to have faith for raising the dead and for creative miracles, we need to say, "I am going to war and I'm going to contend. I am not going to give up because many died not yet receiving the promise." How long am I going to believe God? Am I dead yet?" You need to see impossible circumstances as opportunities. You need to understand that, from Jesus' perspective, what you call dead He says is just sleeping. And if it's just sleeping, God can wake it up.

Praying Like Elisha

Now, let's begin to pray like Elisha did; let's begin to resurrect areas of death now. If you have something dead in your life right now, let's begin to pray and contend until resurrection comes. Hebrews 11:35 says that by faith women received their dead back to life again. If you have sons and daughters dead in their sins, you can also receive them back to life again by faith.

It's time to war, contend and lay hold of this thing in the spirit realm. Like that Shunammite woman, I want you to say, "I'm not going to slacken the pace. I am going to lay hold of the promise of what God said. I'm going to pray and I'm going to receive my dead back to life right now."

Now, just like Elisha the prophet in 2 Kings 4, I want you to see yourself in the spirit realm climbing up onto whatever is dead right now. Come on. Climb up on top of that thing. Lay hold of it! Whether it's your business, your marriage or one of your kids who's not serving God, see them lying there right now and bring the situation before the Lord. Begin to prophesy life to it. Life! Begin to speak to those bones. Life! Prophesy to the wind: "Oh wind! Oh breath of heaven! Oh wind of the Holy Spirit, blow over every dead area of my life! Come! I speak life and rebuke the spirit of death. New life, come forth in the name of Jesus."

Co-workers With God

In His Word, God calls us His co-workers (1 Cor. 3:9). Therefore, just as He is in the resurrection business, so are we. It's time for us to join our God in prophesying life. Call forth those things that are not! Come on saints, prophecy! Rebuke the spirit of death. Ask God for resurrection life, resurrection power—pray, pray, pray.

> *"God I ask for sons and daughters made alive in Christ Jesus! I call them by name. "Melanie, Mitch, Bob... come forth! Come out of the darkness! Come out of your prison! Be made alive in Christ Jesus."*

Now agree with me as I pray for you:

> *"God I ask for life for dead sons and daughters. I ask for life! God I speak life to sick bodies. I rebuke death, tumors, cancers and terminal illness. God, I ask for healing in the name of Jesus! Sovereign Holy Spirit come! God I ask for the healing of hope, the healing of vision, the resurrection of purpose. Lord we release these things now in the name of Jesus. We stretch our bodies right now over those things in faith and we see them resurrecting."*

Can you see the resurrection in your spirit? Can you see the healing and restoration coming to pass? Begin to see areas of death coming to life, promises being resurrected, dreams being fulfilled and people coming out of dark prisons into glorious new life.

Chapter Eleven

DUNAMIS POWER

Before He ascended into heaven, Jesus' gave His disciples some final instructions. He told them to wait in Jerusalem until they were ***"endued with power from on high" (Luke 24:49).*** The disciples waited for ten days until the Holy Spirit came upon them, supernaturally gave them new languages and empowered them. God's Spirit had come to fill their lives with dunamis, explosive power, so they would be able to take the gospel to the world.

When I got saved I knew that I also needed this same power. I needed the Holy Spirit to empower me to fulfill my destiny. I vividly remember my first Holy Spirit power encounter. I was in my home praying, "Lord I want to know what it is like to have Your power come on my flesh." I had prayed that way many times.

As I laid on my bed crying out to God, it wasn't God's presence that came but His power—it felt as if a 500-pound weight was pressing me into the mattress. I couldn't even raise my head off the bed, let alone any other part of my body. I felt electricity come in through my legs, course through my body into my head and then explode. Then the power flowed from my head down to my legs and exploded in my toes. This Holy Spirit current went back and forth through my body like waves of generated electricity. I shook and vibrated uncontrollably.

In the midst of this encounter, one of my friends came into the room and asked what was happening to me.

> "I can't get off the bed and I can't stop shaking. It's the power of God," I said.
> "This is the devil."
> "No, it's the Lord!" I replied.
> "Well, how come you can't get up?" he asked.
> "I don't know, but I've got electricity coursing through my body; it's like a heavy weight. I can't even lift a finger. I know I am in the power of God."

My friend actually got scared because he didn't understand my power encounter. In recent years, in some of my meetings, I've seen others have similar experiences. I've even watched as four or five guys struggled to pick up a 120 pound woman—it was as if she weighed 500 pounds.

In my encounter, the Spirit came to fill me with His power. But that wasn't enough to endue me with power for the next ten years. I would need to continue to have encounters to keep myself full of God's power so I could take Christ's healing touch to the world. I make it my goal to have as many encounters in the power as I can. I want those experiences daily if possible, not just one every few years. It's those fresh touches, those power encounters that keep me full of the anointing.

When I pray, I don't just ask for the anointing, I pray myself into an experience, until God's power comes. Sometimes I do this by speaking in

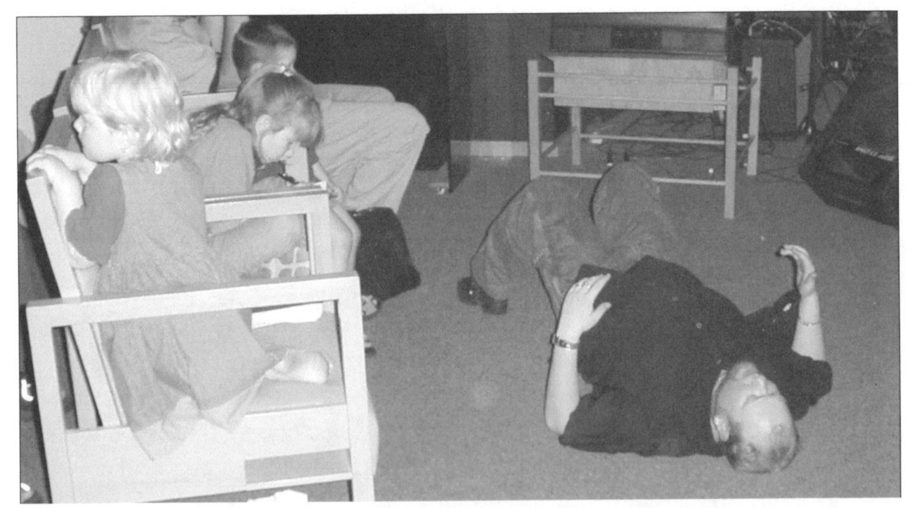

Todd being touched by the Holy Spirit, with his three children sitting to the left

tongues until I feel my faith rise and my spirit strengthened. At other times I charge myself up by just waiting on the Lord saying, "Here I am Lord. Holy Spirit, come. I love Your presence. I want Your power to come on my flesh. I want to go into the meeting tonight and know Your anointing is on me." I talk to God about His power and the anointing and tell Him why I want it. I also decree God's power over my life, that when the anointing comes it is going to break yokes and remove bondages. I specifically ask the Lord that I would sense the anointing and that it would come upon my body.

Like the disciples, I wait until I am endued with power. At times I will wait, soaking in the Spirit and fasting eight hours a day for three days. During that time there will be sweet fellowship with the Holy Ghost. I tell Him how wonderful He is and how wonderful the anointing is. "I thank you for the anointing Holy Spirit; I really want the anointing to come upon me. I love the way the anointing feels Holy Ghost." Through communion with the Holy Ghost, making decrees about the power in my life and praying in tongues, my spiritual battery will be totally recharged with God's dunamis power.

Dunamis is a Greek word meaning miraculous power—the word literally means "the dynamo, dynamite, explosive power of God; a miracle itself; ability, abundance, might, worker of miracles, power, violence, strength and wonderful." It's what everyone wants but few are willing to pay the price for in faithfulness and seeking after God. Scripture tells us that we are only endued with power when the Holy Ghost comes, when we have an encounter with Him. We need to have ongoing encounters, ongoing baptisms of the Holy Spirit to continue to operate in dunamis. One encounter or baptism of the Spirit isn't going to get the job done. He comes in power as we wait on Him. What kind of power? Miraculous power.

So let me ask you this question. Why would the healing and miracle ministry not be for every believer? Isn't the Holy Spirit's enduement for every believer? Yes it is! Therefore, every believer is called to miracle ministry because the promise of the Holy Spirit is for all. I believe that the promise of the Spirit is a promise for every believer to have a healing anointing like Benny Hinn. Every believer can have an anointing like I have. That doesn't mean you are going to fill stadiums. The Lord may not give you the same sphere of influence but you can have the same anointing for healing as I can because Scripture tells us that when the Holy Spirit has come you shall receive dunamis power.

Now why would God come upon you with miraculous power if you weren't going to use that miraculous power to preach the gospel, heal the sick, cleanse the leper, raise the dead and cast out devils? Forget about receiving the healing anointing if you're not going to use it. Why would you need it? The anointing is for action; it's for being a witness in Jerusalem, Judea and Samaria and to the ends of the earth. So if you are planning on praying for the sick and reaching out to the lost then you need the anointing.

Four Kinds of Power

The original scriptures use various Greek words in place of our English word for power. One of those words is *dunamis*, which we've already discussed. I want to examine three other words for power (or strength) which I believe work together. As we learn to activate each one, we will be able to more readily activate the full force of *dunamis*. Here are the four official definitions from the Strong's Exhaustive Concordance of the Bible, in the order that I believe they function:

1. **exousia,** *ex-oo-see'-ah;* from exesti - exesti 1832 (in the sense of ability); privilege, i.e. (subjectively) force, capacity, competency, freedom, or (objectively) mastery (concretely, magistrate, superhuman, potentate, token of control), delegated influence:--authority, jurisdiction, liberty, power, right, strength. (# 1849)[1]

As you can see, *exousia* speaks of delegated authority, the kind of authority Jesus gave to His disciples when He commissioned them with ***"power (exousia) over unclean spirits, to cast them out, and to heal all kinds of sickness and all kinds of disease" (Matt. 10:1).*** In this verse, Jesus uses a variation of the word *exousia*. Later in this same book Jesus speaks of this *exousia* authority that the Father had given him, saying, ***"… All authority has been given to Me in heaven and on earth"*** just before He sends them out again with authority: ***"Go therefore and make disciples of all the nations, baptizing them…."***

2. **ischus,** *is-khoos';* from a derivative of is (force; compare eschon, a form of 2192); forcefulness (literally or figuratively): --ability, might(-ily), power, strength. (# 2479)[2]

Ischus power (or strength) comes through prayer that energizes. Sometimes your *dunamis* battery needs to be energized through prayer. I believe it's the same kind of persistent prayer of faith Elijah prayed in James 5:17-18 that called down rain on the drought-stricken land. The Apostle Paul uses a version of the word *ischus* when, in the book of Ephesians, he describes Christ's work in every believer as ***"…the exceeding greatness of His power toward us***

who believe, according to the working of His mighty power" (Eph. 1:19).

3. **dunamis,** *doo'-nam-is;* from dunamai - dunamai 1410; force (literally or figuratively); specially, miraculous power (usually by implication, a miracle itself):--ability, abundance, meaning, might(-ily, -y, -y deed), (worker of) miracle(-s), power, strength, violence, mighty (wonderful) work. (# 1411)[3]

As mentioned earlier, *dunamis* is the expolosive power of God for working miracles. It's the might of God working through His people, enabling them to do mighty works. Using a variation of the word *dunamis*, Jesus tells His followers that they will be ***"endued with power from on high" (Luke 24:49).*** Many of those who saw Jesus minister ***"...were astonished, saying, 'Where did this Man get these things? And what wisdom is this which is given to Him, that such mighty (dunamis) works are performed by His hands!'" (Mark. 6:2).***

4. **kratos,** *krat'-os;* perhaps a primary word; vigor ("great") (literally or figuratively):--dominion, might(-ily), power, strength. (2904)[4]

Kratos power is defined as manifest dominion or strength. In the days of the early church, Scripture tells us that ***"...the word of the Lord grew mightily (kratos) and prevailed" (Acts 19:20).*** The word of the Lord began to have dominion in the earth. In the book of Revelation Scripture also speaks of Jesus' final *kratos* dominion:

> ***"And every creature which is in heaven and on the earth and under the earth and such as are in the sea, and all that are in them, I heard saying: 'Blessing and honor and glory and power (kratos) Be to Him who sits on the throne, And to the Lamb, forever and ever'" (Rev. 5:13)!***

I believe these four different kinds of power work together to equip believers to do the work of the kingdom. When we understand the delegated *exousia* authority Jesus has given us as His ambassadors, we can begin to walk into His kingdom of power. His kingdom is not in word only but in power! Then we can begin to charge our battery though persistent, Elijah-style energizing prayer so we can receive *ischus* power, the exceeding greatness of His power toward us. Next, we can begin to walk in dynamite, miracle-working power or *dunamis* to release healings and miracles. After we've received and walked in *dunamis* power, we can begin to establish Christ's rule on earth and so *kratos*, manifest dominion, begins to operate through us. *Kratos* is in operation when there is a manifestation of God's dominion in a region or nation through His empowered people on earth.

Authority versus Dunamis

Now I want to focus on two of those words—exousia and dunamis—and explain how they can operate in our lives. Not every Christian that walks in divine miracles and healing necessarily operates in dunamis power. Supernatural ministry can also operate through authority. Even without dunamis empowerment, all believers can first learn to stand on their authority in Christ, which is their right in the Word to cast out demons and heal the sick. Let's briefly examine the difference between these biblical terms, so we as believers can learn to walk in both His authority (the faith principle) and dunamis power (the anointing).

Did you know that before the disciples received dunamis they received another type of power? In Mathew 10:1 Jesus commissioned the twelve: ***"And when He had called His twelve disciples to Him, He gave them power over unclean spirits, to cast them out, and to heal all kinds of sickness and all kinds of disease."*** In this instance, although the Scripture uses the word "power," the actual Greek word is "exousia," which means delegated authority. But it's not the same power as in Acts 1:8: ***"But you shall receive power when the Holy Spirit has come upon you…."*** In this Scripture the Greek word for power is dunamis, which speaks of fire, heat and tangible electrical power. Yet, what the disciples first received in Matthew 10 and Luke 10, before dunamis was released in Acts 1:8, was the authority to heal.

Jesus gave the disciples authority to preach the gospel, heal the sick and cast out demons (Luke 9:1). You see, in authority there isn't fire, lightning bolts, angels, words of knowledge, vision, and electricity coursing through your body. It's just, "Do it because I said you could do it. You are who I said you are; you can do what I said you can do." Authority is in the Word regardless of what you feel and regardless of what you see. Based on your authority in Christ's commission to you as a believer (Mark 16:15-18), whether you feel like you have a healing anointing or not, start praying for the sick.

Faith healing and healing by anointing are two different things. I birthed a healing ministry by authority which, I believe, is the same as healing by faith. Faith healing is authority, healing with anointing is dunamis. Some of you want the dunamis anointing to heal but first you need to be faithful with the Word and authority and operate in faith.

You need to pray for a thousand and if nobody is healed pray for another thousand. Do this because the Bible has promised that there is an anointing on you for healing whether you are aware of it or not. It doesn't matter whether a prophet has called you out and said you have a healing ministry. The Bible says these signs follow them that believe, so all you need to do is believe and keep on believing.

The 12 and the 70 Commissioned with Authority

Before the Lord will trust us with dunamis, we need to prove ourselves faithful with authority. The same delegated authority (exousia) to heal that Jesus gave His 12 disciples in Mathew 10:1, he also gave in Luke 10. Here He sends the 70 out with the authority to preach the gospel and to heal. Even though they didn't feel the power, they were just supposed to go and do the works of Jesus based on delegated authority. They probably went out wondering whether anything would happen: "Me cast out demons? Me heal every sickness? Me heal every disease?" But when they came back they said, ***"Lord, even the demons are subject to us in Your name" (Luke 10:17)!***

I can imagine the Lord saying, "Of course it worked! I told you if you would lay hands on the sick they would recover. I said, 'He who believes in Me will do the works that I do and even greater works.' Of course it worked. These signs will follow those who believe!"

In verse 19 Jesus gives them more authority; this time it's to ***"... trample on serpents and scorpions, and over all the power of the enemy, and nothing shall by any means hurt you."*** What does it mean that He gave them authority"? He already gave them authority in Mathew 10:1. I believe He was saying that they had been faithful with the measure given them so He was going to give them another level of authority. Do you know that there are levels in the kingdom of God?

Think about the parable of the master who gave talents to his servants—to one he gave five, another two and to another he gave one (Matt. 25:15). When the Lord came back, the first two servants had doubled their investment. He rewarded them with more authority and more responsibility. However, the third servant said, "Lord, I didn't do anything with what You gave me; I just buried it in the ground. But I still have what You gave me." When He heard this report the master took away what He had given the servant and gave it to another who had been faithful to use the talents given him.

This story highlights a principle of the kingdom—if you want more (and if you want dunamis) you must be faithful and step out in the authority that God has given you, regardless of what you feel and see. Many of us in the church today don't want to move unless there is an anointing. But God is saying, "Faith first!" Authority before power. He has already given us authority. We have power (exousia authority) over unclean spirits, over sickness and over all kinds of disease.

Dunamis Power

As we are faithful with what God gives us, and we continue walking in our exousia authority, and seeking the Lord for His power, we can receive downloads of dunamis.

But what exactly is dunamis power? What happens when the Holy Spirit comes upon you? You receive what? POWER. What kind of power? Miraculous power! DUNAMIS—dynamo, explosive, miraculous power to release miracles in abundance. It's anointing; it's the tangible power to heal. Dunamis is experience oriented; it changes you, empowers you and releases miracles; it also brings boldness. What does dunamis power look like? It looks like Peter's shadow in Acts 5. That's what you can expect when you get the healing anointing.

Here is what I want to emphasize: What was the fruit of the outpouring of the Holy Spirit's power in Acts 2? The church saw daily salvations, miracles, devils cast out, and the dead raised—all the same tremendous miracles that took place in Jesus' ministry. When did it happen? When the Holy Ghost came. Why? Because when the Holy Ghost came upon them they got something. What did they get? Dunamis. The Greek word for power (dunamis) in Acts 1:8 also means "the mighty strength" and "to make the impossible possible."

Dunamis power means the power of the Lord is present to heal. Jesus said in Acts 1:8 that when the Holy Spirit would come upon the disciples in the upper room they would receive dunamis power (dynamite, explosive power that makes the impossible possible, and releases miracles in abundance). In Scripture the word virtue is sometimes used in place of power: ***"For I perceived power (virtue) going out from Me" (Luke 8:46).*** So virtue suggests strength in the area of healing. When the woman touched the Lord's garment, dunamis virtue flowed into her and she was totally healed.

The word dunamis doesn't just mean miracles, but mighty miracles in abundance. The Father used dunamis power when He raised Jesus from the dead. Dunamis is the power to raise the dead.

Dunamis in experience is very demonstrative. When dunamis anointing comes upon your life you know you are anointed because you can feel the fire and the electricity of the Holy Ghost coursing through your body.

It's like, "Somebody come and get it, the anointing is on my hand. Who wants it?" It becomes very easy to minister because you *feel* anointed. How many times have you felt like you had nothing to give? You said, "I don't feel like I have a healing anointing. I don't feel any kind of fire or heat." It's very easy to minister when you are shaking under the power of God, or when you feel something like lightning bolts coming out of your hand.

Praying for a girl's healing during a crusade

What does dunamis power look like? I will show you in ***Habakkuk 3: 4: "His brightness was like the light; He had rays flashing from His hand, and there His power was hidden. Before Him went pestilence, and fever followed at His feet."*** There is a description of dunamis power. At the presence of Jesus the pestilence left! The fever bowed beneath His feet. The power in this verse flashed from His hand like bright light, the lightnings of God.

The Keys to Dunamis

The first key to dunamis is being faithful with authority. The second key is experiencing God now, not in the distant past. I meet men and woman who remember a time when the power was flowing. Maybe it was three months, a week or a year ago. "It's like God's power waned on my life. What happened, Todd? "

You see, the power only comes when the Holy Spirit has come upon you. There has to be a hunger and desperation in the church today to have continuous experiences in His presence.

Once we get dunamis we need to be like Paul who says in ***Ephesians 5:18 "Be filled with the Spirit…."*** That verse is in the present tense, suggesting a constant encounter with power. We need to have the Holy Spirit fall on us tonight and tomorrow. We need to be like Charles Finney, who said, "God, I am going to go out in the woods and I'm going to pray until You meet with me." People asked him, "Well how do you know when God is going to meet you?" Finney replied, "I don't know but I will tell you when it happens.

I am just going to pray until God comes down."

Like Finney, people need to get hungry and say, "If God doesn't come down, I'm going up." Jesus said to ***"tarry in the city of Jerusalem until you are endued with power from on high" (Luke 24:49).*** Many of us stop waiting just before the power is about to come. But remember, the key is to wait UNTIL. Tarry UNTIL you have been endued with power from on high. How do we move from positional truth to experiential truth? We have to get desperate and say, "I am going to pray until something happens." How do I know when something happens? How do I know when I've received power? Because it's dynamo, dynamite! How do I know that I have been endued with power from on high? Because I can't stop shaking and I can't get up off the floor. The electricity of God is coursing through my body. See, then I know that I've got the power of God.

Charles Finney went out in the woods and he prayed until he was baptized with the fire of God. The disciples waited ten days in the upper room. We can't even wait an hour. We need to set apart time until we have an experience. We need to pray until something happens. I will be satisfied that I have power when I have a visitation and when I begin to see the manifestation of healing and miracles. Until then, let's just be humble enough to admit that we are empty. We don't see a manifestation of His power, so that tells me we are empty. We are not having enough experiences when the Holy Ghost comes upon us in power.

Small Beginnings with Authority

You know how I started my ministry? It started with authority (exousia). All I had in the beginning was the authority of God's Word which commissioned me to lay hands on the sick and see them recover. All I had was everything the Bible promised about divine healing. I had a revelation that it was just as much God's will to heal the sick as to forgive sins. I believed I was who God said I was and I could do what God said I could do even though I didn't have any kind of dunamis experience. So I stepped out feeling nothing until I saw the manifestation of God's power. I started with authority.

People think, "Well, Todd just ended up in the place where He is today in the ministry." I am young and God has put great favor on my life and ministry. But, what people don't know is that as a brand new Christian, even in the first few months, I went to the skateboard park or to the mall every day and preached the gospel. Sometimes I'd win 20 or 30 souls in an afternoon.

There was another season when I spent almost every day in the park evangelizing and doing open air preaching. I had a coffee house ministry in the basement of my small church for people on the streets. Then I'd take everyone out on Saturday nights to evangelize those that didn't come to the coffee shop. That was my life for years. I gave my testimony at Full Gospel Business Men's luncheons. You know, I would prepare four hours in prayer before I would speak ten minutes. I so wanted God to move in power.

One time I went to a Christian school to share. Most of the kids weren't even saved. I had spent hours praying, "Holy Spirit I love you; fill me. Holy Spirit come with me to the school. As I walk into the school, walk in with me." When I started speaking about the reality of the Holy Spirit, He showed up and all the students got drunk with laughter. Revival broke out in the school. I came home from that meeting and I worshipped the Holy Spirit in my living room saying, "Thank you Holy Spirit that You came to the school with me. You are beautiful. When I walk I sense You walking with me. Holy Spirit I love that."

God wants you to operate in authority. Do you know why the body of Christ doesn't move in miracles, signs and wonders? It's waiting for dunamis. But Dunamis won't come until you are faithful with authority.

I meet people all over the world that talk about the healing anointing they have, and the call of God to heal the sick. I say, "What are you waiting for? Why aren't you in the hospitals? How come you're not exercising and contending and birthing and maturing and nurturing what God's given you?" They respond, "Well, the power hasn't come. I'm waiting for something to… I don't know… supernaturally possess me and bring me onto the platform."

We can be too experience-oriented. Yes, the power experience will eventually come. The anointing will come. But when there is nothing else, there is authority. God always rewards authority. He always blesses as we are faithful to invest, multiply, contend and pray. We need to keep pressing in even if it seems like nothing is happening.

It's like King David; he didn't become King until 15 years after he was anointed. First he was faithful in the wilderness with a bunch of misfits, then he became the King over Judah and finally God said, "You're faithful. Now it's time for you to be King over Israel." The wilderness is inhabited by misfits; it's dry and there is little fruit, but you must continue to pray, even when you don't see results.

I started to apply those principles in my ministry. I got ruthless; I started to war against the kingdom of Satan. I got aggressive. I said, "My God, it doesn't matter what I think, it doesn't matter what I feel and it doesn't matter what I see. This is what You said." It all started with authority and faith in God's Word. But as I was faithful with authority, one day God said, "Now I'm going to release power. When power comes, you'll never be the same again."

People make too many excuses, "The pastor won't give me an

opportunity. No one will let me on the prayer team." You're looking at everyone else to make it happen for you. If God has called others to help make it happen for you then they will help. If He didn't, make your own platform. The world is my parish.

Some are waiting for God to speak to them about having authority. He already gave it to you 2,000 years ago. It's in the Word. Others are waiting for God to manifest dunamis and God is saying, "You won't even use the authority I gave you."

Explosive Power

Acts 1:8, "But you shall receive power when the Holy Spirit has come upon you…" What kind of power? Dynamo, dynamite, explosive power. What's the power going to do? It's the same power the Father used to raise the dead. It's the power to bring forth miracles in abundance. What kind of power is it? It's healing power.

Acts 5:15 describes this anointing. They laid the sick out in the streets so that Peter's shadow might fall on them. In the Greek the word shadow means to overshadow. It's the same word used when the Holy Spirit came upon Mary and caused her to conceive Jesus. The Spirit overshadowed her and power from on high came upon her (Luke 1:35). It speaks of the covering, hovering, canopy of the manifest anointing that can come upon your life. It surrounds you like a sphere and when anybody gets within six feet of your presence they are healed because of how much of God you carry. It's greater than the corporate or personal anointing that ministers to people one by one.

When Scripture speaks of Jesus, the Son of Righteousness, arising with healing in His wings (Mal. 4:2), it is painting a picture of a whole congregation coming underneath His wings just like a mother hen protecting her chicks from harm. It will be as if God is sitting on entire congregations and healing everybody. Now that is dunamis power!

Much of the church is still operating in the authority years. We are sowing in faith regardless of what we see. Many of us are stepping out with the principals of healing and seeing a limited measure of success. We are saying, "We are going to be faithful with authority because God said that He gave us the right and permission. We are stepping out with the Word and we are seeking to release healing even if we aren't experiencing this great dunamis power yet. But, in Malachi 4:5, the Lord prophesies of a glorious day: ***"I will send you Elijah the prophet before the coming of the great and dreadful day of the Lord (the second coming)."***

That's when the Son of Righteousness will begin to arise with healing in His wings. It will be an end-time healing revival that ushers in the Second Coming of Jesus! It's beginning now! When it will come in full power, no-one will be able to stop it until Jesus comes again! It will not just last for ten years! It will carry us into the next millennium!

For You and Your Children

Look what Peter said in Acts 2:39, ***"For the promise is to you and to your children, and all who are afar off, as many as the Lord our God will call."*** So, you are included in that verse. What was the promise? Not the baptism of the Holy Ghost and speaking in tongues. Yes, that happens too, but that is not what that verse is talking about. That verse is saying, ***"Wait in Jerusalem until you are endued with power from on high"* (Luke 24:49).** Then, ***"'...you shall be baptized with the Holy Spirit not many days from now'" (Acts 1:5).*** And when that happens, ***"...you shall receive power when the Holy Spirit has come upon you..." (Acts 1:8).***

The Holy Ghost is going to come upon you and you are going to get miraculous power just like Peter in Acts 2. He got up and preached to the thousands that gathered at Pentecost after they witnessed the explosion of God by the Holy Ghost. And then he said, "Hey, this is for all of you here. This same power that we just received to preach the gospel, heal the sick, cleanse the leper, raise the dead, cast out devils like Mathew 10:1 promised – this is for you guys. Oh, and if you have kids they can have it too. Oh, and *anybody* that gets saved from this day forward has the same anointing available to them as we apostles do." Peter is saying that what they received wasn't just speaking in tongues. What they received was dunamis, dynamite power, to make the impossible possible and bring forth miracles in abundance and raise the dead. That's what they received.

Who is going to get the healing anointing, the healing power? It's for you and your children and it's for anyone from this day forward that is called into the kingdom; they are going to receive what Peter received. It's a believer's ministry. God wants to give it to you. He really wants you to have it.

The Primary Call for All Believers

Even though dunamis is available to us, many people in the church don't really want to take advantage of it. In our ministry, our least popular tape is "Power Evangelism." It's as if the church sees the word evangelism and says, "I don't want to be friends with the unsaved." Even though they'd like the impartation of healing anointing, they aren't really willing to step out of their comfort zone to reach the lost.

Jesus said that the Holy Spirit would come upon them and they would receive power to be His witnesses to the ends of the earth (Acts 1:8). The more we witness, the greater manifestation of God's power we will receive.

Power Evangelism shouldn't be the least popular tape series we sell. Mathew 10:7 is the primary call to all believers. ***"As you go, preach, saying, 'The kingdom of heaven is at hand.'"*** You see, it's *power to be My witness*. How does dunamis work? As you go. As we go what are we going to do? We are going to preach. We are going to say the kingdom of heaven is at hand and to prove it we are going to ***"heal the sick, cleanse the lepers, raise the dead and cast out demons" (Matt. 10:8).***

Now when we read Mathew 10:8 we tend to break it up into ministry categories and categories of difficulty. This is how we read it: "Some of you preach the gospel, (pastors and teachers), some of you heal the sick, (evangelists and apostles and some with prophetic gifts). Some of you really anointed apostolic types cleanse lepers and raise the dead. You deliverance ministries you are the guys who cast out demons."

Yes, there is a difference between gifts of healings (plural, more than one healing gift) and gifts of miracles, (plural, more than one miracle gift). Everyone has one of these ministry categories where they are more gifted than the other categories. That's ok. But don't automatically believe the rest of the gifts are not for you also. Pastors and teachers believe that miracles, signs and wonders are for everybody else. Most pastors wouldn't even go after a healing wave. They wait until they bring in the evangelist or the apostles. We have to get people believing this is for them.

Dunamis power is for us all! What are we going to do with the power and authority He gave us? We are going to preach the gospel, we're going to heal the sick, cleanse the leper, raise the dead and cast out demons.

The next thing we do is break this Scripture into categories of difficulty and we say, "It's easier to preach the gospel than it is to heal the sick. When you get really anointed and fast and pray and have faith, then you graduate to the level of cleansing lepers. That takes way more anointing and faith than it does to preach and heal the 'regular' sick. Then when you are really apostolic and really really super- anointed, then the ultimate, which takes the most faith and power, you raise the dead."

But this list is not from easiest to hardest because the last thing listed is casting out demons. I would say preach the gospel, cast out demons, heal the sick, cleanse the lepers and the ultimate, raise the dead. But that's not what He said either. He said it in one breath. He said if you can preach the gospel you can heal the sick. If you can heal the sick, you can cleanse the leper. If you can cleanse the leper you can raise the dead. If you can raise the dead you can cast out a demon! Why? It's the same thing. It isn't any harder to preach the gospel than it is to heal the sick. It doesn't take any more faith.

When I look at the church today, I see the kingdom in word, but where is the power? If you leave everyone else to do the healing wave there will be no healing that will ever happen through you. If you want to heal the sick, you need to go to where the sick are. If you want to win souls and preach the gospel, you need to go where the lost are. How can I cleanse the lepers in America?

In India I rented a bus and had lepers brought to the crusade. They are outcasts living in isolation from the rest of the population. They are not allowed to touch any other non-leprous human being. Most of these children have never felt the human touch or affection of any human being outside their own colony. When people want to feed the lepers they just throw scraps over the fence into the little area where they live.

At the crusade the lepers sit in their own special area away from the rest of the people. I said to my whole ministry team, "Jump off the platform. Let's go to where the lepers are. Lay your hands on them and make sure you get your hands on the afflicted areas."

Some children we met in India

When we touched them, they wept. All they wanted to do was hug us. They didn't even care if they got healed. They were overwhelmed just because somebody cared enough to show them God's love. They said, "Oh, that these people would come and give us human affection. We have never felt the touch of a non-leprous human being." They were weeping and the children were weeping. It was no longer about whether they got healed but that there was enough love in our hearts that we weren't afraid of their disease.

People want to raise the dead today. How can you raise the dead if you don't pray for the dead? I had to make opportunities for the dead to come to me. So I started a little faith project, my "How to Raise the Dead Tent." I have it there in all my African crusades and I announce on TV, radio and on my crusade posters that if anyone dies bring them to the crusade and I will pray for them. See, I am doing it in faith. Sowing into it and praying for the dead. How many dead have you prayed for? I believe God for the full gospel!

Pray with me:

"*Father, I thank You that You have commissioned me to walk in authority and to take Your healing and miracle power to needy people. I ask for Your forgiveness for waiting for some special experience and not being fully faithful to walk out the authority You have given me. Let me be so compelled by Jesus' love that I will have to do His works. Help me to walk by faith, birthing, nurturing and maturing Your commission of authority to me until I see the dunamis power of God released through my life. I choose to be faithful and I know You will keep Your word–as I go out in Your name to heal, cleanse, raise and deliver You will cause signs to follow me! Thank You Lord.*"

* [1, 2, 3, 4] Strong's Exhaustive Concordance of the Bible, James Strong, World Bible Publishers, (1986) Iowa Falls, Ia.

THE COMING HEALING REVIVAL

Let's talk about the incredible future that lies before us. We talked about the coming healing revival in my last book, *Journey Into The Miraculous*. However, I believe it is important, for those who haven't read my testimony book, for us to cover this topic again.

God is getting ready to do amazing things. Get ready for supernatural visitation and open heavens—the supernatural is about to become natural. There's coming a release of an apostolic anointing, which I call the "popcorn release" into ministry, where men and women are going to be thrust into worldwide ministry overnight. Tomorrow you're going to go to work and the next day your city is going to be in revival. Can a nation be born in a day? ***"Can a country be born in a day or a nation be brought forth in a moment?" (Is. 66:8).*** Yes they can!

Get ready. There are things that are about to happen in the church that eye has not seen and ear has not heard and you can be part of it. Even if I told you, you wouldn't believe it. ***"For the earth will be filled with the knowledge of the glory of the Lord, as the waters cover the sea" (Hab. 2:14).*** I want to share with you several aspects of the coming healing revival that I believe we are about to witness in our individual lives and in the church.

Aspects of the Coming Revival

Healing Revival

"And the inhabitant of the land shall not say I am sick" (Is. 33:24). I believe that this verse is speaking of a time in the church where there will be such a level of healing-anointing that no sickness or disease will touch God's people, just like when Israel came up out of Egypt. ***"He also brought them out with silver and gold, and there was none feeble among His tribes" (Psalm 105:37).*** Not one feeble or weak? Think about that, more than three million people healed after 400 years in oppression and bondage!

Kathryn Kuhlman prophesied that there would be a day when the church would say, "I am not sick!" and in some meetings every single person would be healed. Many others have prophesied a great healing revival in the end times, including John G. Lake. There will be a renewed focus on the message of repentance. Sickness and disease started with sin. In the beginning the Garden of Eden was paradise without sickness, disease, poverty or death. That was always God's plan for us! When sin entered the world then came sickness, disease and death. ***"Therefore, just as through one man sin entered the world, and death through sin, and thus death spread to all men, because all sinned" (Rom. 5:12).***

But with the resurrection of Jesus came a new law. Romans 8:1-2 states, ***"There is therefore now no condemnation to those who are in Christ Jesus, who do not walk according to the flesh, but according to the Spirit. For the law of the Spirit of life in Christ Jesus has made me free from the law of sin and death."***

A new force is in motion today to empower us to live holy lives and be made righteousness. All the angels of Heaven are prepared to back up that law. ***"For the law of the Spirit of life in Christ Jesus has made me free from the law of sin and death" (Rom. 8:2).***

We are redeemed from the curse of the law. ***"Christ has redeemed us from the curse of the law, having become a curse for us (for it is written, 'Cursed is everyone who hangs on a tree') that the blessing of Abraham might come upon the Gentiles in Christ Jesus, that we might receive the promise of the Spirit through faith" (Gal. 3:13-14).***

Today God's will is 3 John 1:2, ***"Beloved, I pray that you may prosper in all things and be in health, just as your soul prospers."***

Most of the world's sickness and disease stems from turning away from God to other idols and false religions. Whole nations are under curses (Deuteronomy 28) because they have turned to other gods. When we examine the beliefs of countries in Africa, India and South America, many are rooted

A street in a poor area of the Congo, Africa

in witchcraft or idol worship. In India alone, they worship over three million gods. I have been in many nations and have seen innocent children affected by poverty, famine, hunger, war, and sickness. I have grieved as I've driven down some streets and seen a temple on every corner. The innocent suffer because of the unrighteousness of governments and leaders.

In order for us to see a greater wave of healing in the church today there needs to be a renewed focus on repentance and personal holiness because many times our own sins of bitterness, envy, jealousy unforgiveness, sexual sins, etc. are not only the roots but the hindrances to healings. In the coming healing outpouring, as people repent of their willful sin and make a fresh commitment to holiness, then when healing is preached we will see more miracles.

James 5:15-16 says, ***"And the prayer of faith will save the sick, and the Lord will raise him up. And if he has committed sins, he will be forgiven. Confess your trespasses to one another, and pray for one another, that you may be healed."***

The Lord has also showed me that as the church and as nations repent of corruption and worldly ways and turn back to God, He will bring a mighty healing revival. Hosea 6:1-2 implores: ***"Come, and let us return to the Lord; For He has torn, but He will heal us; He has stricken, but He will bind us up. After two days He will revive us; on the third day He will raise us up, that we may live in His sight."***

As repentance and the revival of righteousness sweeps through the church, so will more healings and miracles. Healing will take place supernaturally without the laying on of hands. In Jesus' ministry He healed every sickness and disease among the people. ***"When evening had come, they brought to Him many who were demon-possessed. And He cast out the spirits with a word, and healed all who were sick" (Matt. 8:16).***

Saints' Revival

Another thing we'll see in the future will be a saints' revival. God is going to do away with a clergy/layman mentality and raise up the saints—the body of Christ—to do the work of the ministry. I strongly believe in the local church and godly leaders, the fivefold ministry and apostolic relationships built on trust and friendship. But, it will not be just the pastors or evangelists, but the saints released by God who will begin to preach the gospel and heal the sick. It has always been God's plan that every believer gets involved in the ministry of Jesus. John 14:12 says, ***"He who believes in me, the works that I do he will do also; and greater works than these he will do, because I go to my Father."***

I believe that when the early church was birthed, many ordinary people moved in signs and wonders. ***"The Apostles called out seven men full of good reputation and the Holy Spirit. They laid their hands on them… The number of the disciples increased greatly" (Acts 6:1-7).*** We all know Stephen, full of faith and power, was doing signs and wonders, but who were the rest in verse five? We never hear of them again or their works of power. But, I believe they flowed in an anointing just like Stephen. God is going to use the church deacons, businessmen, cashiers, housewives and children to work His great power—"nobodies," as it were, a nameless faceless generation. People we don't know, just like those chosen by the apostles, will flow in this anointing.

Through the church God will show signs and wonders in the heavens and the earth. The church will have the same power as Jesus over the natural elements—the winds and the sea obeyed Him. We will move into a ministry of wonders, fulfilling Joel 2:30-31. We will speak to limbs like Jesus did in Luke 6:10, when He said, "Stretch forth your hand…." and the limbs will become whole.

The wonders we will perform will be like in the days of Elijah or Moses. We will walk in authority like Joshua who spoke and the sun stood still. I don't just see healings and miracles, but signs and wonders of great proportion, which will jolt people from their busy lifestyles—the world will stop and see the glory cloud literally come down upon the church just like it did with Moses. In some cities we will witness signs of the Lord's glory for days that will even capture the media's attention.

"These have power to shut heaven, so that no rain falls in the days of their prophecy; and they have power over waters to turn them to blood, and to strike the earth with all plagues, as often as they desire" (Rev. 11:6). This Scripture says, concerning the two witnesses, that they could do their signs as often as they desired. Now that's power! Pray it in. Let's believe God to confirm His Word and trust us with the last-days anointing we'll need for the last-days harvest. The God of Abraham, Isaac, Jacob and Moses will once again begin to show up in the church just like He visited His people in Old Testament times.

Children's Ministry

I have seen a great move of healings and miracles by the hands of children. I had a vision of an eight-year-old boy with a Bible in his hand preaching with fire and boldness to thousands. He preached the word of the Lord and the sick recovered in their seats. I see children being used to grow limbs working creative miracles by the spoken word and faith. Some children will become part of the prophetic Samuel generation as young as eleven or twelve years old.

Girl on the left was healed of her deafness; then she prayed for the girl on the right (who was also deaf) and she was also healed.

We know that the kingdom isn't in word only but in power. Children are going to move in the power of the kingdom, drive out spirits and heal the sick because the kingdom is theirs. Jesus said in Matthew 19:14: "Let the little children come to me do not forbid them, for of such is the kingdom of heaven."

Last Days Anointing of Power

I have seen a glimpse of the anointing that will be on the last days church. We think the book of Acts was glorious but the glory of the latter house will be greater than the former. We are going out with a bigger bang than we came in with.

The end time anointing is the Elijah anointing! The Elijah anointing turns the hearts of the nations to God like it did in I Kings 18, where Elijah called down fire on Mt. Carmel in a confrontation with the prophets of Baal. In these last days, it won't be Elijah as one man, but it will be the Spirit and anointing of Elijah working through the church that will get the job done. We'll do miracles and signs like Elijah did. Some thought John the Baptist was Elijah the man, but they were actually seeing the Elijah-anointing on his life.

In Matthew 17 on the Mount of Transfiguration, the Father sent Moses and Elijah as a prophetic fulfillment and to show that Jesus was who He said He was. I believe as we near the second coming of Christ, God will again confirm the church as His voice in the land. He will do this by bringing the spirit and power of Moses and Elijah upon His end-time army to release forerunners to prepare the way of the Lord and to prepare the nations for God.

"Behold, I will send you Elijah the prophet before the coming of the great and dreadful day of the Lord. And he will turn the hearts of the fathers to the children, and the hearts of the children to their fathers, lest I come and strike the earth with a curse" (Mal. 4:5-6).

Desperate for God

It will be a movement of the prophetic, power evangelism and healing that will turn nations to God—some in a day! I'll develop this is more detail in the next vision. That hour is at hand and you need to reach out for this. The supernatural needs to be natural. It shouldn't be rare in the body of Christ. I believe that those who are hungry to have an encounter with the Holy Spirit will be filled. It's not about who you are, or your righteousness, it's not about your ability, it's about your availability. It's about the time we live in and a mighty God who has chosen to work through weak human vessels. The Spirit and the anointing have the power and the wisdom. ***"Not by might, not by power, but by my Spirit says the Lord" (Zechariah 4:6).***

Houses of Prayer Facilitate the Great Harvest

Recently I was in Latvia, a small Baltic state in Eastern Europe, formerly under Soviet rule. While traveling to an evening crusade I was caught up in an interactive vision. I saw the great harvest field already white. The angels were working in this field.

Then Jesus came to me. I knew in my spirit He was the Lord of the Harvest but He came to me dressed as the Good Shepherd (John 10) and holding a staff. I wondered why the Lord of Psalm 23 was the Lord of the Harvest. Then I understood – this is not just about winning souls but also about discipling these same souls. Jesus doesn't want to just be Savior but He also wants to be the great overseer of their souls and He wants to lead them into the depth of Psalms 23. He desires to restore their souls and to lead them beside the still waters.

Immediately these scriptures came to my mind:

> ***"The earth is the Lord's, and all its fullness, the world and those who dwell therein" (Psalms 24:1).***
>
> ***"The kingdoms of this world have become the kingdoms of our Lord and of His Christ, and He shall reign forever and ever!" (Revelation 11:15).***
>
> ***"Behold, the nations are as a drop in a bucket, and are counted as the small dust on the scales; Look, He lifts up the isles as a very little thing" (Isaiah 40:15).***
>
> ***"Ask of Me, and I will give you the nations for your inheritance, and the ends of the earth for Your possession." (Psalm 2:8).***

This was a faith level where whole cities and nations can be saved in a day. The Lord said to me, "Todd, enter into My harvest power! It's the Harvest of Amos 9:13: ***"'Behold, the days are coming,' says the Lord, 'When the plowman shall overtake the reaper, and the treader of grapes him who***

sows seed; the mountains shall drip with sweet wine, and all the hills shall flow with it.'"

There is coming an acceleration of the laws of sowing and reaping. The seed will be planted and as soon as the seed is sown it will be reaped. There will be harvest until the days of sowing and sowing until the days of harvest—a holy overlapping of continual sowing and reaping. When this acceleration happens, men and women will cry out, "What must I do to be saved?"

As I continued to walk in the harvest I noticed a tent in the field and asked, "Lord, what is that tent doing in the harvest and why does it look so old and ragged? It's not as glorious and golden as these fields." The Lord responded, "Todd, this is the tabernacle of David and it looks that way because, for many, prayer is so uninviting. It is a matter of perspective and priority. To many prayer is tedious work but to others it is the glory. Most importantly the tabernacle releases the Amos 9:13 harvest."

In the book of Acts, Paul, Barnabas, Peter and their ministry teams are seeing tremendous harvest in cities. Churches are being planted and the Holy Ghost is falling on the Gentile believers as well as the Jews. In Acts 15 they meet for the Jerusalem council and give reports of the harvest and discuss whether Gentile believers need to be circumcised. In the midst of this James quotes Amos 9:11-12:

> ***"After this I will return And will rebuild the tabernacle of David, which has fallen down; I will rebuild its ruins, and I will set it up; so that the rest of mankind may seek the Lord, even all the Gentiles who are called by My name, says the Lord who does all these things" (Acts 15:16-17).***

I said, "God there it is again—the great harvest and the house of David."

Night and day prayer, 24 hours a day, seven days a week is already taking place in the church. These houses of prayer are essential to the releasing of an end-time signs and wonders movement, healing revival and the geographic healing centers.

The Healing Centers

I've already spoken about the many healing pools of Bethesda (as in John 5) that I've seen throughout North America and different countries. The grace of God will give us an outpouring of the rains of healing and miracles, until the power of God increases and we have a flood of miracle rain and many pools of healing. Once again great multitudes will come from all over the world to geographical healing centers just like God did in Spokane in the early 1900's with John Lake's ministry. This coming healing outpouring will be the forerunner to the great harvest.

Elijah Anointing

God has promised the spirit and power of Elijah in these last days. With the spirit and power of Elijah we also have a promised healing revival in Malachi 4:2: ***"But to you who fear My name The Son of Righteousness shall arise with healing in His wings; and you shall go out and grow fat like stall-fed calves."***

The great prayer movement is the key to the release of the great healing revival that comes in the day of the Elijah spirit. But, before God releases the power to the church spoken of in Revelation 11:3, ("And I will give power to my two witnesses, and they will prophesy one thousand two hundred and sixty days, clothed in sackcloth.") the Lord conducts an evaluation of the church in Revelation 11:1: ***"Then I was given a reed like a measuring rod. And the angel stood, saying, 'Rise and measure the temple of God, the altar, and those who worship there.'"*** The angel was to measure three things: the temple of God, the altar, and those who worship there. The temple can represent the believers lives or the church, local, citywide or national. When the levels of worship, prayer and intercession are right in the church, God will release His end-time power and the promise of the spirit of Elijah. Only when the bowls of Revelation 8:3-5 are full will God release His power:

> ***"Then another angel, having a golden censer, came and stood at the altar. He was given much incense, that he should offer it with the prayers of all the saints upon the golden altar which was before the throne. And the smoke of the incense, with the prayers of the saints, ascended before God from the angel's hand. Then the angel took the censer, filled it with fire from the altar, and threw it to the earth. And there were noises, thunderings, lightnings, and an earthquake."***

God is checking the levels of intercession, worship and prayer in the believer's life, in churches, in cities and in nations. And when the levels are right then He will give power to the two witnesses. The House of David model (24 hours, seven days a week, day and night prayer, worship, intercession and intimacy with Jesus) are key to releasing power to prophesy and witness with signs following to the last day generation.

Now here is the part of the vision that should encourage us, but also make us tremble. When I asked the Lord which cities would have these healing centers He replied, "Which cities want them? I am checking the levels of worship, intercession and prayer. Their hunger will be the deciding factor. Every city has equal opportunity."

If there was ever a time to press in and go for it, now is that time. I repeat the question I asked at the beginning of the book. If not now, when? If not you, who?

My life has been marked by the supernatural: my conversion; three-month visitation; move to Abbotsford; marriage; three months of soaking and God launching me into an international ministry with supernatural miracles, signs and wonders.

Maybe you are reading this and getting discouraged or feeling jealous. You're asking the Lord why things like this haven't happened to you. I want to say, I'm a sovereign vessel in a sovereign time. God will use and anoint anyone but He has a timetable and makes sovereign choices. God is God and we are not.

I encourage you who have been serving the Lord and waiting for the prophetic promises that haven't come true yet, to keep your eyes on Jesus and hold on to God's Word. Jesus loves you as much as he loves me. I am only where I am because of faithful laborers who have come before me. Some of you were praying for this move of God while I was getting high on drugs! I'm the first-fruit of your labor. God's quick work in my life is not because of my righteousness but because of the kairos time we are living in. I'm looking forward to seeing many other members of this Elijah generation who will go far beyond where I have ever gone.

Don't forget the parable of the laborers in the vineyard (Matt. 20:1-16) who worked for one hour and got paid the same as those who labored all day. No matter how long you have labored or how long you have been contending for your promises, the Lord wants to reward you with the same Elijah anointing he has for every believer in this last days army. It's not about how long you've been running or what track you run on; the reward goes to every person that finishes the race they started. Fight the good of faith!

Dare to Ask!

I wrote this book to help you understand what God is doing in our time and to encourage you to take steps of faith in areas where you may have been holding back. I want your heart to be inflamed with passion for Him and your vision to soar. I'm boasting in a big God. I'm excited about what He's done, but I'm more excited about what He's going to do. He wants the supernatural to be natural. In Daniel 11:32 the Lord says, ***"... the people who know their God shall be strong, and carry out great exploits."*** That refers to you too, not just me.

One of Todd's crusades in India

I encourage you to believe in a big God and dare to ask Him to fulfill big dreams. This has become a key verse for me: ***"Ask of Me, and I will give You the nations for Your inheritance, and the ends of the earth for Your possession" (Psalm 2:8).***

God will do amazing things with ordinary people who totally yield their lives to Him.

My Prayer for You

After receiving several e-mail requests asking for the transfer of the healing anointing through the internet, I felt God prompt me to also release that anointing through this book for those who would come into agreement with a prophetic proclamation calling for the release of God's miraculous power.

First, let's establish a biblical precedent for this. We know that Jesus didn't have a laptop and they weren't "on line" in Jerusalem. But consider the story of the centurion who said to Jesus, ***"Just say the word, and my servant will be healed" (Matt. 8:5-13, Luke 7:1-10).*** Jesus marveled at the centurion's faith, not because he believed Jesus could heal, but because he believed Jesus could heal even though He was far from the sick person physically. Jesus lavished praise on the centurion, saying he had more faith than anyone He had met in all of Israel! How would you like to have Jesus say that about you?

> ***"When Jesus heard it, He marveled, and said to those who followed, 'Assuredly, I say to you, I have not found such great faith, not even in Israel...' Then Jesus said to the***

centurion, 'Go your way; and as you have believed, so let it be done for you.' And his servant was healed that same hour" (Matt. 8:10,13).

There are other New Testament examples of people getting healed "from a distance." The use of prayer cloths is one example. ***"Now God worked unusual miracles by the hands of Paul, so that even handkerchiefs or aprons were brought from his body to the sick, and the diseases left them and the evil spirits went out of them" (Acts 19:11-12).*** It's funny that people think it's an awesome miracle when they read about Paul using prayer cloths, but when we try the same thing, or a variation of it today, the same people think it's weird or "New Age-y."

Praying for people to be healed over cell phones, during a conference, and they are healed

In my ministry I've seen the healing anointing transferred through prayer cloths and over cell phones. People are regularly healed, even of AIDS, when listening to my crusades over the radio. One of my favorite stories about this comes from Cal Pierce at the Spokane Healing rooms. He tells how a woman in Africa was healed when someone made a Xerox copy of a prayer cloth and faxed the copy of the cloth to Africa. What great faith! What great use of technology!

Can this transference really happen through a book? Well, if God can heal through cloths, over telephone lines and through radio waves, it's safe to assume He can also work through the printed page. In fact, He's done it before because people used to get healed when they would read John G. Lake's newsletters.

All these examples indicate what we really already know—God is not limited by time and space. If you believe that the anointing is transferable and you want to agree with me that a greater release of His healing virtue is going to come into your life, ministry and church, I want you to align yourself in simple faith with this prayer. Here's the prayer I've prayed for you:

> *"Father I ask You right now in the name of Jesus to begin to release Your transferable, tangible healing anointing for those asking for more of Your power on their life and ministry. I release healing virtue in Jesus' name! Let an explosion of miracles and healing come to them now. I pray that they would be forerunners; that they would lead the way into the coming healing revival. I pray that the spirit of Elijah would fall on them and that they would evangelize in the market place with signs and wonders confirming their message. Lord let them enter in to the night and day prayers of the tabernacle of David. Father, pour out Your power and grace, I ask, that those agreeing with this prayer will receive a fresh anointing now in Jesus' name."*

Now, I want you to pray out loud:

> *"Father, I want more of the anointing transferred into my life. I believe now for the healing power to fill me. Give me a greater release of miracles, signs and wonders from this day forward. Come now Holy Spirit – I receive. I exercise my faith and declare that, 'The same spirit that raised Jesus from the dead lives in me.' I will take this healing gift to the sick in Jesus' name."*

From this day forward, I want you to believe God, to preach the gospel and to heal the sick! Go lay hands on them and see them recover. Start where you live, one person at a time. Now if you need a healing miracle get ready! If you are believing God for a healing right now I want you to put your hand on the part of your body that needs to be healed. Or, if there is someone in your house that needs a healing, lay hands on them and pray this prayer of faith with me:

> *"Come Holy Spirit; heal me now in Jesus' name. Father I command this sickness to go; I command my infirmity to go. Satan loose me now in Jesus name. Touch me Jesus. I receive my healing!"* I stand in agreement with your prayer: *"Lord, I pray that you would let Your healing touch every infirmity of those reading this book, right now."*

Rise up in Jesus' name and do something you couldn't do before. Move your body; thank God now for healing you. He's got an unlimited storehouse and He loves you—continue asking for more. Here's one final prayer you can pray to begin to receive all the wisdom, power and anointing He has for you as you prepare for your part in the coming healing revival:

> *"Father, I want to cooperate with what You are doing in heaven, so I pray for the Spirit of wisdom, revelation, council and might. Please give me eyes to see and ears to hear so that I can understand eternal things. I earnestly desire spiritual gifts, especially that I would prophesy. Let it come right now Lord—let the Holy Spirit fall with that prophetic mantle. Holy Spirit come! I want a download of the Spirit of prophecy.*
>
> *"Lord give me the word of knowledge for my workplace and for my school. Let me go into the marketplace with Your anointing, authority and mantle. Let me hear Your word, wherever I am, whenever the lost and hurting need Your loving touch. Oh God, let your mantle fall on me for healing and for prophetic evangelism. Lord, thank you for the coming power, miracles, healings, signs and wonders. According to Your word Father, as I speak words of faith, I can see supernatural manifestations. Let the authority and spirit of Elijah come again—let it come into my life. Surprise me Lord, it's not by my might or power but it's through Your Spirit.*
>
> *"Let me produce 100-fold fruit that remains for your kingdom. Help me to do exceedingly, abundantly above all I can ask or think for Your glory. Lord, draw me into night and day intercession too. I want to help fill those golden bowls to hasten Your coming. Let me not grow weary; open my eyes to see the power and impact of my simple prayers on the lives of others. Thank you Father for answering this cry of my heart."*

Chapter Thirteen

HEALING CRUSADE REPORTS

After traveling in ministry within North America for just under two years, the Lord launched me into overseas crusade ministry through an open-eye vision. During a conversation with the Lord, He commissioned me to go to South Africa and then gave me a vision of the dates I would go—March 10-27, 2000. Shortly after that experience, when a local pastor and prophet from South Africa, Keith Abrahams, called with an invitation to his home land, the dates coincided exactly with those the Lord had given me.

This invitation came just after a season in which I was studying the Life of John G. Lake, the Canadian who planted over 600 churches in South Africa through miracle and healing ministry. He later moved to the United States, in the early 1900s, and started healing rooms in different cities of the nation. He is widely considered to be a healing apostle by many. When the Lord gave me a vision of the coming healing revival and called me to go to South Africa, He gave me a clear commission: "Go to South Africa on a prophetic Journey. I want you to go and get the anointing of John G. Lake." That word of the Lord was confirmed the night before I left on this journey. Patricia King called with a word that I was going to South Africa to get the anointing of John Lake and that when I got it I was going to bring a healing revival to North America.

It was in South Africa that I first began to preach at open-air crusades. The Lord powerfully confirmed the word with signs following—we saw many hundreds saved and healed out doors and on the streets. When I returned from this trip, the signs and wonders in my ministry began to increase. Within six months, our first visit to the Vineyard Christian Fellowship in Albany, Oregon would turn into a revival of healing that would attract international attention. This revival lasted for months, continuing even after I left to minister in other places. I believe the South Africa trip, and the anointing I received, helped launch Fresh Fire's international crusade ministry.

Since this prophetic journey, we have been traveling to the nations, doing crusade ministry with powerful healings and miracles in evidence. It's as if the Lord just dramatically turned up the anointing and favor. Today, the crusade arm of our ministry travels to various continents—Africa, Asia, North America, South America and Europe—almost once a month. Some of our recent crusades have drawn hundreds of thousands of people and have yielded incredible harvest and miracles. In 2003 the Lord allowed us to introduce over 140,000 people to Jesus for the first time—what a privilege to lead all those precious souls in the sinner's prayer and then pray to see their bodies made whole as well. In a recent crusade, as reported below, over 139,000 people made decisions for Christ, in just five days, in the atmosphere of His powerful presence with healings, miracles, signs and wonders demonstrated.

Below you can read about some of the powerful things the Lord did in two recent overseas crusades. These are examples of a typical crusade with its accompanying harvest and miracles. If you want to read more crusade reports you can go to our website www.freshfire.ca and click on Revival Reports. I encourage you to read these reports in faith, believing that you too will begin to receive some of that same anointing for healing revival that the Lord has deposited into my life.

Miracle Explosion in Tanzania
March 3 - 10, 2004

By Kevin Basconi

Wednesday, March 3, 2004 (Arusha, Tanzania). Todd Bentley and his team traveled over 18,000 miles to preach the gospel in Tanzania. After a grueling two-day journey from Melbourne, Australia the team arrived in Arusha, Tanzania excited about what God was going to do. The team arrived at the crusade grounds at 5:00 p.m. where a crowd of 15,000 was waiting. Todd didn't preach but told them that he was going to demonstrate the power of the

Preaching to the people of Arusha, Tanzania

Holy Ghost. He released three words of knowledge the Lord gave him during afternoon prayer. God was going to heal the deaf, a woman with a tumor on her right breast and a woman with a blind right eye.

Immediately a seven-year-old boy who was totally deaf received prayer and was able to hear and also began to speak! The crowd went wild, and celebrated Jesus' goodness. After they calmed down, six more deaf were healed and the crowd swelled to nearly 18,000. Several blind people received prayer and seven were totally healed. The most remarkable healings of blindness were those of three women, all blind in their right eyes for 20 years. This was the exact word of knowledge that Todd called out at the beginning of the crusade.

Woman testifies of how Jesus healed her by removing the tumor in her breast

There were four women who responded to the word of knowledge about tumors and lumps in the right breast. The crowd cheered and pressed closer to see the miracles and healings. All four women went behind the platform to check their breasts and all four returned and reported that the tumors were totally gone!

With the testimonies of the healings continuing, Todd released a healing wave of the anointing. Immediately dozens in the crowd began to manifest demons. As the ushers carried them, kicking and screaming to the altar, many were totally delivered and set free. One demonized eight-year-old girl was throwing five grown men around. Todd called for her to be brought to the platform. After several demons were cast out of her in Jesus' name she was totally free. Todd told the crowd that he had done what he promised and that God had confirmed the gospel. "I didn't even preach the Word and you have seen mighty miracles. The blind see, the deaf hear and devils are cast out. This Gospel I preach is real!" When Todd opened the altars for salvation, hundreds ran forward to give their lives to Christ.

Thursday, March 4, 2004. Todd released the healing anointing to the team this afternoon and they wasted no time taking the anointing to the people. One team traveled to a local school to pray for children. They saw six salvations and several healings. One deaf child had his hearing restored and the fire of God fell in the school. Another team ministered in a local hospital. Six patients left the hospital's waiting room healed without even seeing a doctor! A third team was released into the marketplace to preach to a group of 200. After a team member released a word of knowledge for deafness, five deaf ears opened. Many other healings took place, such as a girl with a withered hand who was totally restored. After a brief message 62 people came forward to receive Jesus. At a second open air meeting, 66 more got saved after two more deaf were healed in a Muslim village. In all, 133 were saved in the afternoon outreaches.

The crusade began that evening with about 25,000 on hand. Many had brought the sick after hearing reports from those who had witnessed miracles last night. Todd opened the meeting operating under the gift of faith. He told the crowd, under the Spirit's inspiration, that he had seen five healings in visions during his prayer time before the crusade and that he guaranteed these five miracles would happen. He called out the people by name and age. First, a woman who was paralyzed on her right side would be healed. Three women

People pray to receive Jesus as Savior in Arusha, Tanzania

who were paralyzed on their right sides came forward and the power of Jesus healed all three.

Boy who was a deaf mute is totally healed—he begins to both hear and speak

Then Todd called for a 16 to 18-year-old boy who was totally deaf, and who had been brought to the crusade by a friend who had faith for his healing. A 16-year-old deaf mute was led to the platform by a friend. The power hit him and he began to both hear and speak!

Next, Todd called out a woman who had been paralyzed by a serious bout of malaria. He also noted that this woman had been carried to the crusade by a friend. Immediately several people carried a paralyzed woman to the platform on a mat. She could not walk and her friends had, indeed, carried her to the meetings. The power of God coursed into her and she immediately began to move her legs. Before too long she was walking across the platform! The crowd went into a frenzy and shouted in amazement! A man who had a tumor in his stomach also responded to a word of knowledge and was immediately able to bend over with no pain—the tumor had disappeared.

Finally Todd called a teenage girl who had been paralyzed in her right leg from polio. When she walked to the platform Todd proclaimed to the crowd, which had now swelled to over 30,000, that he guaranteed her healing, and that she would walk normally. The Lord was faithful to honor that bold declaration.

That night Todd shared his testimony, telling the crowd how Jesus restores all things. He told them about how he and his father were delivered from years of drugs and addictions. Todd told them that Jesus had restored his family and freed his father from 30 years of drug addiction. Dave joined Todd on the platform and the crowd cheered with reckless abandonment! When he opened the altars for those who wanted to accept Jesus as Lord and Savior 1060 came forward! Todd continued to minister in healing and released the teams into the crowd to pray for the sick.

The Elijah Challenge in Tanzania

Friday March 5, 2004. During the day teams continued ministering in the hospitals, schools, and marketplaces. One young man on the team gave a startling testimony: "I heard Todd guarantee that Jesus would heal deaf ears last night. I was preaching in the street and something just came over me. I told the crowd that Jesus would heal the first deaf person who came forward even if they were Muslim! I prayed for a deaf girl and Jesus healed her right on the spot! Then 17 people gave their lives to Jesus!"

That evening several local witches just outside the crusade grounds chanted and cursed the meeting. Todd stepped onto the platform and confronted the powers of darkness and witchcraft. It was a challenge just like Elijah gave to the prophets of Baal on Mount Carmel. Todd called forth the angelic realm to help in the battle and told the crowd that when God's power came that devils would manifest. He taught the crowd of 38,000 that infirmity and sickness are caused by demonic oppression. He told them that because many people in Tanzania, even Christians, visited witch doctors; they constantly opened the door for the devil to attack their lives. This open door allowed Satan to hold the people in bondage to sin and to afflict them with sickness and death. Many had made blood covenants with the devil and demonic gods. These people had been cursed by witch doctors. He went on to explain that the ministry of Jesus was to cast out devils and that He would heal sickness by casting out demons. Todd asked those involved in witchcraft to repent—he even invited the witch doctors to come to the altar. "Let's see who is stronger—Jesus or the devil!" Thousands of hands went up through the grounds, acknowledging involvement in witchcraft and indicating a desire to repent.

Even before the prayer to renounce the power of witchcraft and the authority of the devil began, demons started manifesting. Soon the altar was full of writhing bodies, hundreds of people screaming and acting out violently. During deliverance, many people were healed and set free! The Fresh Fire team worked feverishly to gather testimonies. As the crowd swelled to 40,000, many people gave miracle testimonies. Many tumors and cysts had dissolved and a woman with epilepsy had been delivered.

Todd saw a woman violently thrashing and resisting six ushers. He asked her if she was a witch—she was. The team ministered to her for about

People manifesting demons and getting delivered during the crusade

thirty minutes. Finally, all the devils were cast out and she cried out, "I want Jesus!" After she was gloriously saved and delivered, she gave her testimony to the cheering crowd!

An incredible series of testimonies followed this deliverance. A young girl's leg grew several inches after she was delivered—she was set free from a life-long limp. One woman with a paralyzed right arm was totally healed and began to move it freely. As people gave their testimonies, the crowd cheered and worshipped Jesus with reckless abandon! One man testified that tumors, which had been in his nose for 19 years, were totally gone. A paralytic began to walk back and forth across the stage while the crowd applauded Jesus! Also, a woman testified, through tears of joy, that she could see clearly for the first time in years. A man who had terrorized the community for years, who was widely known as a madman who lived at the city dump, came forward to receive Jesus as His savior. One person who had been totally deaf for ten years was also set free and healed during the Elijah challenge. When Todd heard this testimony he called for other deaf people to come to the platform. Todd guaranteed the Muslims that Jesus would heal any deaf they brought to the crusade Saturday. He told the crowd that he loved the Muslims, but he was going to prove that Jesus was the one true God and not just a prophet.

Todd prayed for five who were totally deaf. Then, before the crowd of 40,000, including thousands of Muslims, all five were totally healed! The crowd again went into a frenzy until Todd asked them to listen. Todd gave an altar call and when the ushers dropped the ropes, hundreds ran to the altar. In all, 825 were saved. Through tears, Todd told the crowd, "This is the greatest miracle of all"!

Healing for All

Saturday, March 6, 2004. Through the power of the Holy Spirit, the Fresh Fire Mission's teams continue to shake the city of Arusha, Tanzania. We have heard reports of over 130 salvations in the streets, markets and hospitals today. The hospital team saw dozens saved and healed. As they ministered in the waiting room, several people who had come for malaria treatment, they never saw a doctor but went home healed. One team member prayed for a Muslim man's wife; she was totally healed and received Jesus as her

A crippled woman, who was lying on pillows because of severe pain, is totally healed—she testifies at the Arusha, Tanzania crusade.

savior. Next, a totally deaf woman was healed through prayer and a lump on a woman's breast instantly dissolved.

The city of Arusha has been stirred by the reports of the miracles, signs and wonders happening in their midst. About 35,000 people came tonight to witness the power of Jesus first hand. Todd told the crowd that he was going to give them the word of God today. He told them that healing was in the Word, and asked the crowd to pray in agreement for God's glory and the Holy Ghost to fill the grounds. Todd taught about the Bible's promise of healing and how to receive salvation, healing and deliverance. He outlined the differences between the Christian, Muslim, and Hindu religions. Todd told the crowd that only Jesus offered the free gift of eternal life and that all others were by works and not grace. Then he taught on the power of the cross, how the blood of Jesus paid for the remission of our sins, and that the Lord bought more than eternal life. When Jesus took the 39 lashes he bought the world healing from sickness and disease. Todd told the crowd that God wants us to prosper and to be in health as our soul prospers. When the altar was opened, 1,120 were born into the kingdom. Todd prayed for the new converts to receive the baptism of the Holy Ghost and fire. Hundreds at the altar were gloriously filled with the Spirit and began speaking in tongues. Suddenly the fire of God fell through the crusade grounds and hundreds more were baptized!

Woman has her sight restored

Todd released a healing wave and dozens were hit by the power of God. A light rain fell on the meeting and the crowd began to scatter for cover. The hundreds at the altar continued speaking in their new Holy Spirit language!

Todd called for the deaf to be brought to the platform. The previous night Todd had invited people to bring the deaf and they responded! The rain increased to a steady down fall, yet thousands remained hungry for a touch from the Lord. Others stayed to see the miracles. Soon 26 deaf were lined up on the platform. The ministry team prayed in the rain and 22 deaf ears were opened.

Todd called for those in wheel chairs to be put on the platform. The stage was a commotion of healings, miracles and testimonies. Three totally paralyzed people got up from their wheel chairs and walked. One small child who had been blind from birth received an unusual miracle. After prayer, although his eyes still appeared to be blind, he was able to see normally. Todd told the crowd that it was one of the most unusual miracles he had ever seen. After an hour of concentrated prayer from several team members a three-year-old child, paralyzed and deaf, was hearing and walking!

A Miraculous Harvest

God has truly prospered the crusade and the outreaches, confirming the Word with hundreds of miracles, signs and wonders in the city of Arusha, Tanzania. On the final night of the crusade, Todd preached a dynamic salvation message to 55,000 people. The crowd listened with great interest to the gospel. Thousands had come from outlying villages to see miracles for themselves. Todd encouraged the crowd telling them that Jesus always saves the best wine for last. He started by sharing a few testimonies of the previous night's miracles including a seven-year-old boy, an AIDS orphan, who was totally blind. He had been carried miles to the crusade by a woman who had the faith for his healing. The boy was indeed healed. Although his eyes still appeared to be blind he could see and count fingers! After this miracle testimony Todd said that he had faith for unusual creative miracles that night as had happened in past crusades… miracles like the woman who grew a brand new breast, or the man, Leonard from Malawi, who grew a new eyeball where he had an empty socket.

Todd told the hundreds of Muslims who had gathered at the rear of the crusade that one reason Jesus still did miracles today is to prove that He is real and that He is the one true God. The second reason that God releases miracles is that He is moved with compassion for the people. Todd told the crowd that the Holy Spirit had spoken to him and stirred up compassion in his heart to return to Tanzania! The crowd cheered wildly as Todd announced that Fresh Fire was planning two crusades in 2006 in Mwanza and Arusha, Tanzania.

Over 1,500 new converts came to the altar to pray the salvation prayer. Then Todd invited those who wanted the baptism of the Holy Ghost to also come forward! Tens of thousands came to the front, forming a sea of people! The power of God swept over entire areas filling thousands with the Holy Spirit! Dozens began to manifest demons. After a few minutes, Todd encouraged everyone on the grounds who could speak in the heavenly language to all pray at once. It was absolutely wonderful to hear thousands upon thousands praying in tongues! It sounded like an orchestra of prayer.

Dozens were instantly healed by a powerful anointing moving over the crowd. One woman testified that, as she was standing in the crowd, her deaf ear popped open. She told the thousands, which were pressing closer to the stage, that she had been deaf for over 30 years. She also testified that a tumor in her ear and on her leg had disappeared! In all, there were nine people who testified that tumors had been completely healed.

Eight people who were deaf in one or both ears were totally healed as Todd cast out the deaf and dumb spirit. The crowd cheered as each deaf mute uttered words for the first time! Todd invited the crowd to bring sick babies to the stage. Over 60 babies were lined up as he ministered with tenderness to each child.

The ministry team pushed their way into the masses to pray for the sick and reported dozens more miracles in the crowd. The city of Arusha, Tanzania has indeed been shaken by the power of Jesus. Todd Bentley and his entire team have preached the gospel with a demonstration of the power of God like the town has never witnessed before!

Tanzania Crusade Totals:

Here are the totals of confirmed salvations, miracles and healings from the five days of ministry in Tanzania:

Salvations 5297

Blind Eyes 51

Partial Blind 20

Deaf Ears 120

Deaf Mutes 22

Tumors 67

Paralyzed Limbs 26

Paralytics Healed 11

In addition to these healings, hundreds of other healings were reported by the teams who preached the gospel in the villages, marketplaces, schools and hospitals. Only God truly knows the number of those touched by His power and the lives that have been transformed. To God we give all the Glory!

After the final crusade, the Fresh Fire team embarked on a two-day safari into the Serengeti National Park. It is reported to be the best safari adventure in the world.

Great Harvest in India!
May 5 - 20, 2004

by Ken Greter

Look and see what the Lord has done in just the first three days!!

- *Over 120,000 in attendance in three nights*
- *300 pastors from the local village participating*
- *Between 58-60,000 make decisions for Christ*
- *Thousands receive Baptism in the Holy Spirit*
- *16 year old boy stricken with Polio and constant seizures walks*
- *Tumors on legs, backs and breasts disappear*
- *3 blind eyes open just in night*
- *Dozens of deaf and mute hear*

A team of 37, from US and Canada including a number of FFM staff, were spiritually armed and ready to fulfill Matt.10:7-8 in Podili, Andhra Pradesh, India. In spite of the sweltering heat (peaking 100° F at times) during the long journey we all had a strong sense of anticipation of a massive harvest to come in India. FFM was originally slated to hold a Jesus Festival in Ongole, a city of approximately 300,000 located in the state of Andhra Pradesh, South India, where crowds of up to 100,000 were expected nightly. However, due to the turbulence revolving around the elections that may well have forced the

The India crusade crowd—***many hungry for Jesus!***

crusade to be shut down, our India contacts felt it best to host two smaller crusades. One in Podili, about an hours drive from Ongole and one in Medara Metla, about 45 minutes in the other direction from Ongole. Very little Christian witness has ever penetrated these areas, as many as 90% of those who attended the evening crusades were Hindu, or Muslim.

A market in Andhra Pradesh, India

Pastors are Fed—Spiritually and Physically

Approximately 1,500 pastors and Christian leaders were registered to attend a three day conference but because elections interfered, a number were unable to be there. Those who did make the journey, some as far away as 200 kilometers, were treated to free accommodation and food, compliments of the FFM partners. Pastor after pastor came with tears in his eyes, showing their depth of appreciation for being served a first class meal (chicken, rice and lentils, a rare treat for a village pastor) and for the excellent teaching from Todd Bentley, B.B. Rail and Ken Greter. To be sure, these pastors will be going back with a special fire in their soul, excited about evangelizing in their villages, and fulfilling Matt. 10:7- 8.

Nearly 20,000 Receive Jesus The First Night

The people of India are steeped in the Hindu religion, worshipping as many 3 million gods—the monkey god, the cow god, the elephant god and a host of others—you name it they have it. Yet, their hearts seem to be longing for spiritual reality. According to Psalms, the people of the land become like the god they worship, in this case lifeless and robotic with no hope or peace.

The people came to the crusade from everywhere, and in all kinds of vehicles. Over 200 busses and or grain trucks containing 100 people per vehicle escorted these precious souls to the crusade grounds. Others came in rickshaws, some on motorcycles, other on foot, still others in wagons pulled by tractors. We even had some riding in carts pulled by oxen.

On the first night Todd welcomed everyone, no matter what religious background. He challenged the audience of approximately 20-30,000 people to follow after the one true God of the universe—His Name is Jesus Christ—and to abandon all the other false gods. Todd shared his testimony of how God saved and delivered him after living a life of drugs and alcohol addiction and prison time. "If God can do it for me He can do it for you," Todd boldly declared over the loud PA system. To further demonstrate that Jesus is alive, Todd brought a challenge to the people, "Bring me the deaf and dumb and I guarantee the Lord will heal at least five." The deaf came and received prayer and to God be the glory, they were healed. Hallelujah! Jesus reigns over India.

When the altar call was given, to everyone's surprise, most of the hands

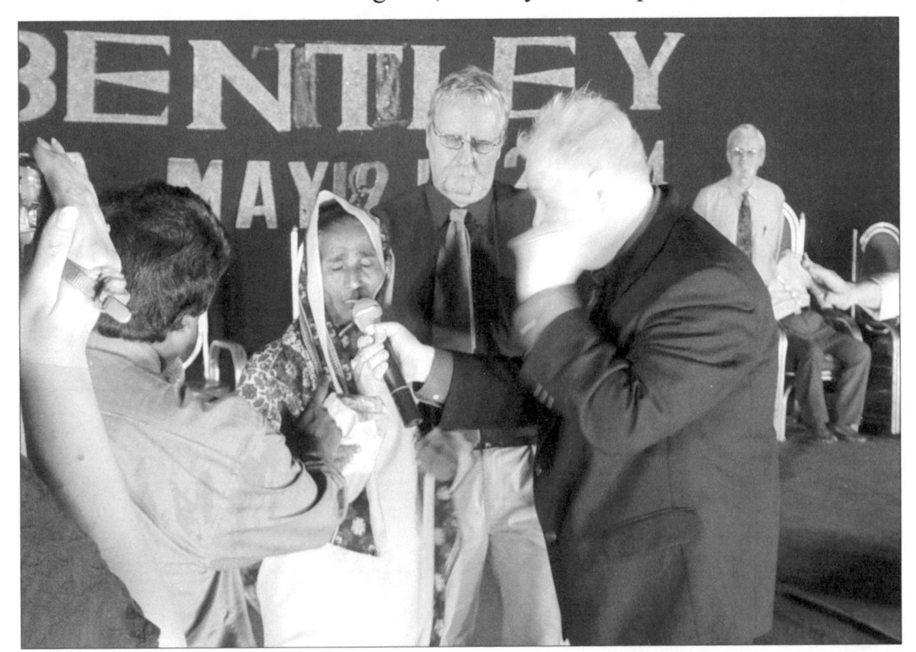

Woman who was deaf testifies of Jesus healing her

went up. Just to make sure that they truly understood the decision they were making Todd clarified, "Jesus Christ alone is to be worshipped and no other gods." The number didn't change. Never before had FFM recorded this many salvations in a single night.

Can you imagine more souls coming into the kingdom of God in 6 nights of crusade meetings than make up the entire population of Todd Bentley's home town—Abbotsford? With this colossal harvest, one immediately questions, "But what about the follow up?" Thanks to James Rebbavarapu and his tireless 30+ staff members, hundreds of participating pastors began an immediate follow-up program, assigned to each village represented. Between 170-180 transportation vehicles went into villages carrying as many as 100 people per vehicle. One pastor was assigned to each vehicle and was responsible to ensure that new converts who were riding in his vehicle received follow-up material and became nurtured in a church and/or home Bible study. What an effective strategy from the Lord!

Spirit of Leviathan Opposes Crusade

During the late evening of the second night of our second crusade a vicious cyclone surfaced out of nowhere causing major damage to the FFM crusade platform and the tent where the pastors meetings were held. The speed of the winds literally twisted the stage's steel frame. Equipment and other paraphernalia were strewn all over the grounds. It seemed to be an apparent victory for the enemy, as the tail of leviathan struck us, obviously unhappy with so many proclaiming the Lordship of Jesus Christ. To our amazement, Pastor James, with his proficient organizational skills, mobilized his energetic crew of 30+ spiritual troopers and just like a colony of hard-working ants, in no time at all, had the crusade venue and stage looking as good as new. What the enemy intended for evil, God truly turned around for good, as another 30,000 souls were committed to Christ on the final night of the crusade.

Near Riot Takes Place on Final Night

Night after night, Todd called out words of knowledge, promising Jesus is the same yesterday, today and forever. An unusual number of people were receiving instant miracles as Todd began to operate in the gift of faith. The blind were seeing, growths were disappearing, and the deaf were hearing. An AIDS victim claimed she was now healed after she felt the power of God shoot through her body like a lightning bolt. As we were nearing the end of the final night, a sense of desperation rose among the many thousands still hoping to receive prayer. The crowd became frenzied. Thirty officers failed to contain them, barricades gave way and the crowd began streaming to the platform begging for prayer. Ladies threw their babies to the platform, hoping Todd would touch them. What an amazing sight! People around the platform were packed in like sardines, and began pressing the FFM team, so much so that we had to escort them back onto the stage, lest they be crushed. Police officers guarded the stairs on either side of the platform to keep people off the stage. Before long even the metal welding was being torn away. After Todd released a mass prayer for healing, Pastor James encouraged the FFM staff to immediately leave the grounds. We reluctantly, and as inconspicuously as possible, headed to our vehicles and pulled away. Oh, the tearing in our hearts at the awareness that the need is so great, and the laborers so few. Lord Jesus, send forth laborers in your fields in India!

Response to Altar Call Surprises Everyone

Night after night, bus loads of curious Indians expressed their desire to forsake their 3 million gods and only follow Jesus. Did they truly understand as Todd gave the altar call? Eighty to ninety per cent of the crowd lifted their hands on any given night to follow Jesus. Over and over again Todd re-iterated the gravity of the decision—to follow Jesus was to abandon their old religion—only to find the same willing response among the spiritually hungry people of India. Never have we witnessed such a ripe harvest in any other country. ***"The harvest is plentiful…" (Matt. 9: 37-38).*** has definitely taken on a new meaning for us.

The Lord touches a young man's crippled hand

Medical Doctor Accompanies FFM to Authenticate Miracles

Doctor Rod Thompson, a medical doctor from the Pacific North West in the USA, was able to check and document the validity of many healing testimonies. If this procedure does not convince the skeptic, nothing will. Again and again, after examining the people the doctor verified Jesus Christ still heals today. Here is part of his report:

> *"Todd had called out a word of knowledge for a blind 13 or 14-year-old girl. A 13-year-old girl came for prayer. I examined her eyes with an ophthalmoscope and found a dense cataract in the left eye. She reported that she was totally blind in that eye. After Todd prayed for her, she reported partial sight. I re-examined the eye and to my amazement, the cataract looked like it had broken into several pieces. Medically, this does not make*

sense, but that is what I observed. I believe God was breaking up the cataract and restoring her sight.
I also examined a golf ball-sized goiter in a young lady's neck. Larry and B.B.Rail and I prayed for her. I re-examined the neck mass and it was smaller. We prayed a second time and it was smaller yet. We prayed a third time and it was virtually gone. In less than three minutes, a golf ball-sized thyroid tumor had dissolved. This can only be a miracle. Neither of these healings could be explained by medicine or science."

Special clinics were set up at the crusade site, where 10 FFM team members assisted Dr. Thompson with free medical care and supplies. FFM purchased approximately $18,000 US worth of medical equipment (for a substantial discount) in order to bless the poor in India. Nearly 60 people got prayer and medical treatment during the first outing. Scriptures throughout the Old and New Testament emphasize ministering to the poor in spirit, soul and body. Thank you FFM partners. Your contributions are truly making a difference among the people of India!

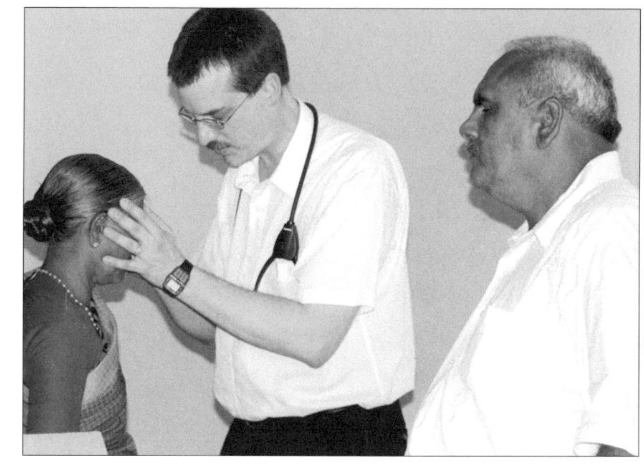

Dr. Rod Thompson ministering to an Indian woman in one of our medical clinics

Three Days and Nights in Coimbatore

Following on the heels of a 15 member team from Che Ahn's ministry in California, Todd ministered two evenings in Coimbatore to a nightly crowd of approximately 10-12,000. B.B. Rail, Ken Greter, Ray Makula and Todd shared at the pastors' and leaders' meetings. The final meeting concluded with a time of impartation, and literal Holy Ghost fire fell on the 300+ participants. We definitely experienced another "Upper Room Pentecost" in Coimbatore.

Poor Villages Receive Food Supplies

Pastor James selected 10 of the poorest villages in the area, (each village containing approximately 100 families per village) to receive free bags of rice and lentils, compliments once again of the FFM partners. These villages are members of the lowest caste system in India. The people are trapped within this demonic system believing they will never be able to break free from slavery and poverty because this is their eternal allotment in life. Thankfully, Jesus has come to set the captives free. No more slavery. Todd promised more humanitarianaid,including food supplies, to be given in 2005 to those remote villages.

Larry Rail, Todd and Dave Bentley praying over the food supplies to be distributed to the poor

The Final Record Harvest in India!

Over 139,200 decisions for Christ!

- *Nearly a quarter of a million attend the Jesus Festival held over 6 nights*
- *Over 170 deaf and/or mute miraculously healed*
- *Tens of thousands receive Baptism of the Holy Spirit*
- *Large golf-size lump on lady's throat instantly disappears*
- *Boy's twisted arm becomes straight*
- *Lady deaf for over 40 years receives hearing*
- *Numerous cancers and growths healed*
- *Dozens of blind receive sight*
- *Even a number of crippled walk*

The harvest is truly ripe, but the laborers are few, and India is most assuredly ready for the harvest. Come on, North American Evangelists, thrust in the sickle and reap a mighty end-time harvest in India while the doors remain open.

Reports from FFM Team Members

Martha Crenshaw – age 70; Eugene, Oregon

When I was 17 years old, I went out to the garden every day to pray. There was a wheat field on one side of the garden and the Lord gave me this

Scripture, "Lift up your eyes and look on the fields for they are white, ready to harvest." I looked at the stalks of grain, and they turned into black people who bowed their heads and accepted Jesus as their Savior. I knew it was God calling me to the mission field, but I made a wrong decision and got married instead. When I was 70 years old, I went to Todd Bentley's crusade to India, May 6-16th. It was amazing that on the first night, I saw the same vision I had seen when I was 17. As far as I could see there were black people, and Todd gave an altar call after he had prayed for 5 people. All 5 were healed and many were saved that night. I knew that God was calling me again to work in the end-time harvest. I just want to be one of the workers, I know that there will be opportunities as God leads, and I do not want to miss God's plan for me now.

Shannon and Dawn Reece; Colorado Springs, Colorado

We have seen so many miracles that it is impossible to count them or even remember them all. Virtually every one we are praying for is getting healed. Headaches, ear pain, back pain, chest pain, barrenness, kidney problems, stomach problems, and eye problems.

Deaf baby's ears are opened

- *4 blind eyes opened*
- *3 deaf ears opened*
- *One lady had severe back problems and couldn't bend over. She was totally healed and could touch her toes when we were done.*
- *One lady had a metal rod in her hand and her fingers had been frozen straight. After prayer she could move her fingers and make a fist.*

FFM's Future in India

With such huge interest from as many as 15 different cities in India desiring to host a FFM Jesus festival, Todd is establishing an international office in Hyderabad, a city of approximately 6 million, located in South India. Also, the ministry is launching our television program, *Journey in the Miraculous* in India. The viewing audience could reach as many as 1 billion people and will also include countries such as Afghanistan, South Asia, China and Iraq. Future crusades are already scheduled. Come and change the world with us as we see Matt. 10:7-8 fulfilled before our eyes.

Special thanks to all the team members who accompanied us on this trip to India including Keith Salmonson, who at the feisty "Caleb" age of 82, thoroughly enjoyed laying hands on the sick and casting out devils. Team, you were awesome. Also, Todd and Shonnah express heart-felt thanks to all the FFM partners who represent the back-bone of this ministry, with their monthly prayer and financial support. Your rewards will be great in heaven.

Chapter Fourteen

HEALING TESTIMONIES

A book about God's power to heal today would not be complete without personal testimonies of people who have experienced Christ's healing touch themselves, or who have seen Him work powerfully through them to heal others. Telling these testimonies brings glory to God and also delivers death blows to the demonic spirit of unbelief that hinders God's power today. As the Bible says, ***"And they overcame him by the blood of the Lamb and by the word of their testimony…" (Rev. 12:11).*** Over the years of taking the full message of Sozo (wholeness for spirit, soul and body) to the nations, our Fresh Fire Ministry team has seen thousands of powerful healings and miracles. Jesus has touched so many people, we could not possibly have enough healing books to record every healing and miracle. In some conferences or crusades, so many hundreds or even thousands of healings take place that, really, only heaven knows.

However, in this final chapter, we would like to encourage you with some healing stories—stories of people like you, who God has touched, or ordinary people that God has used to heal others. We have tried to choose a variety of stories; some testimonies which people may consider "smaller healings," to show that God cares about the small things, as well as other stories which could be considered "dramatic creative miracles," to demonstrate how incredibly powerful God is. However, in the light of the great majesty and power of Jehovah Rapha, really, every healing is "small" or "easy." After all, it was Him who created the human body in the first place. Surely He knows how to fix our bodies today!

So, as you read these testimonies, open your heart to God and let Him stir up new faith in your heart to receive His healing power for yourself and for the needy multitudes around you. I pray that God would also give you and your ministry personal stories like the testimonies that follow:

Blind Eye Sees

In January of 2002, I experienced a miracle that changed my life forever. We went to a small church in the inner city called Precious Fragments. Todd Bentley was teaching and praying for healings of people's diseases, illnesses and physical injuries. I watched in disbelief—I still did not believe that the Lord could use men to heal people.

Todd prophesied that there was someone in the audience that had their left eye injured and blinded from an accident. It seemed weird to me because I was blind in my left eye from an accident involving drugs! The accident happened approximately 15 years ago while I was riding in the back of a limousine—I was not a Christian at the time. I was opening a bottle of champagne and the cork blew up into my left eye, leaving me totally blind. I have had five (unsuccessful) corrective surgeries, the most recent in 1999.

(After) I got up and walked up to the stage, Todd came over and said, "Your injury was caused by a drug accident." I started feeling the Holy Spirit consume my body as he covered my eye with his hand and began to pray. He took his hand off my eye and asked me, "Can you see anything?" I put my hand on my right eye and started seeing things move in a circular motion in my left eye. Within moments, I started seeing color, although nothing very clearly. He continued to pray for me and about 15 minutes later the Lord had restored total vision in my eye! I fell to the ground in tears just thanking Jesus.

A few days after this incredible experience, the doctor (examined) my left eye thoroughly. He looked at my previous prescription glasses and said, "You must have had a great surgeon." My wife kept motioning to me to tell him what happened and I kept shaking my head, "no." She then told him, "He had the best surgeon there is" and proceeded to tell him about the prayer and healing that took place two days earlier. The doctor looked a little perplexed but then said "I believe you." We were able to share Christ with this man. He said he had heard of healings before but never knew anyone who had experienced one.

Before I went to the healing conference, my vision was 20/1000, which is considered legally blind. My vision after the conference was 20/20! The Lord can use men to perform His healing miracles and this just shows the awesome power and glory of Jesus Christ our Lord and Savior.

Scott Levine
Kansas City, Missouri

Todd ministering at the Abbotsford Revival Tent Meetings

Lump in Breast Disappeared at Abbotsford Tent Meeting

My name is Ursula Debrowska. Less than a year ago I discovered a lump in my right breast. I didn't go see a doctor for a diagnosis because I felt to trust God to heal me. I was sitting in the tent on August 11, 2004 at the Rivers of Revival Holy Ghost tent meetings in Abbotsford, BC when I felt a lot of heat come all over my body. I knew the heat meant God was healing the lump because before I went to the tent meeting God told me that I would be healed that night. As I was experiencing the healing power of God I checked the lump and it was getting smaller and smaller. Before the service was over the lump was completely gone! I went forward and testified in front of the whole meeting to give God the glory!

Ursula Debrowska,
Abbotsford, BC

Healed from Astigmatisms

I went to the Healing School in Fremont, California about nine months ago. During the conference which followed Todd had a word of knowledge that there was a healing anointing for astigmatisms. I turned to my aunt with a grin and told her it must be for me because just the day before I told her I wanted to have laser eye surgery and part of my diagnosis was astigmatism. I also had said "maybe God will heal it first." So when the word came forth I knew God was touching me.

I had intended to verify the healing when I got back to my home town but got very busy and actually forgot all about it. Last month I went for my yearly eye exam. I told my doctor that my contacts had been blurry for a couple months but nothing else was bothering me. Upon completing my exam, my doctor was amazed. He told me that the reason my contacts were blurry is because I no longer have astigmatism. Praise God. I shared with my doctor what had taken place and he actually asked if he could share that with other people.

Monica Caudillo
Hanford, CA

Healed from Chronic Fatigue and Lupus

I attended the conference at Sonrise Chapel in Everett, WA in March 2004. For a couple of years I have been quite sick with Chronic Fatigue Syndrome caused by Mono Virus. I've also had positive test results for Lupus as well. Many people have prayed for my healing over the years.

Saturday evening when Todd ministered he called out a word of knowledge: "There is a woman in the back row. An angel is touching you right now." Right before he said that I felt some sort of supernatural power touching me. I began to feel like I was inside the whirlwind, and my body was literally shaking up and down and side to side at the same time.

Then I heard Todd saying, "Jesus is here, wearing crimson robe, He is walking in the midst of us." As I was hearing it, my spirit ran after Him. I was so desperate for Him. I began to feel His presence. He whispered in my ears: "When I am in the midst of you, if you touch the hem of My garment with faith… anyone who touches me will be healed." This voice was so real and penetrating. I sobbed for a long time. As I was sharing (my testimony that night), I began to cry and then I began to laugh very hard for at least 30 minutes. Then, I was drunk in the spirit.

Two days later, I met with my doctor for the scheduled follow-up appointment. She said that I must have turned the corner and felt like I was about 90% normal. I said 100%. She drew some blood for the routine tests to confirm her belief. A week later I received the test results. IT SHOWED EVERYTHING IS NORMAL. My husband and I celebrated Lord's mercy and His Grace!

Stay-See Chon
Everett, WA

Set Free from Hepatitis C

During the autumn of 2003 I went to the doctor and was diagnosed with fibrosis of the liver caused by the Hepatitis C virus. My liver was not working as it should and I was feeling the physical effects of rapidly dying liver cells. I learned that there was no cure. My wife and I to have a rather somber Christian season that year.

In January, 2004 I did not feel well enough to continue work and had to stay at home and do a lot of resting. I had a mental image or dream of Jesus asking me what I had done with my life and I didn't have an answer! At this time I turned to God and told him to forgive me for wasting much of my life with selfish pursuits. For the first time ever I committed All of my life to Him – no hidden things or areas in my life anymore.

I learned of a Miracles, Signs and Wonders conference in Everett, Washington and decided to check out Todd Bentley. On the first day of the conference I told my wife, "Stop crying Catherine. God is going to heal me because He wants me to do something in Africa and that's why I know I'm going to be healed." I was somewhat surprised at what I had said to comfort my wife.

That evening another speaker, Mahesh Chavda, stopped his message and asked whoever had Hepatitis to come forward and be healed. As I was prayed for I felt a peace and joy and I knew I had been healed. That same afternoon a ministry team member prayed that I would be healed from some of the most unpleasant side effects of my treatment. That evening the common side effects (nausea and shaking) were gone.

That evening… Todd was praying for someone. He stopped, looked at me, and asked who had a liver problem. I raised my hand and he said that God was giving me a new liver; then went back to praying for the other person. I felt nothing at the time but 2 hours later my liver started tingling and I felt something like pin pricks in my liver for the next 2 days. It was about six weeks later after praying that I was finally tested to determine the amount of hepatitis virus in my body. The lab could find no evidence of the virus or a liver function problem!

My ALT test results went from 300 to 56 immediately after prayer. Two weeks later the ALT test results were 26. All of my tests after prayer indicate that they can find nothing wrong with me. I am amazed at what God has done for me.

Vincent Hewgill
Prince Rupert, BC

Miracle of Perfect Hearing

In early November 2001, I visited Lighthouse Church in Stony Plain where Todd Bentley was speaking at a weekend conference. Todd was praying over ears, in particular for freedom from deaf and dumb spirit. I took my daughter Jessica forward. She was 2 years old at the time and had significant hearing loss in her left ear.

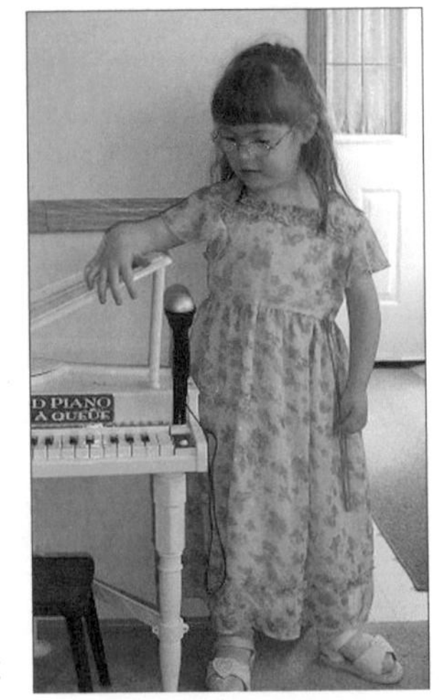

Jessica Lonergan

The same week following the healing services, she underwent an ABR (hearing) test under general anesthesia. Following the procedure, the Doctor came to me and said, "Mrs. Lonergan, we can't figure it out. All of the other testing we have done on Jessica prior to now has indicated a significant hearing loss in her left ear, with minor hearing loss in her right ear. We can't find anything wrong with either of her ears. Her hearing is perfectly normal and there are no issues to discuss!"

For a child with multiple disabilities, Jessica who is now five years old continues to amaze the professionals with her speech and language development. She loves to sing and knows the Lord's Prayer from memory. Praise the Lord for answered prayer!

Joy-Grace Lonergan
Stony Plain, AB

Healed from WWP Syndrome, TMJ Pain and an Issue of Blood

I first received healing at Rock Lake, Manitoba. Todd called for anyone with heart disease. I responded as I had a congenital heart condition called "Wolfe Parkinson White Syndrome" which was a defective SA node in my heart (this node is the pace maker of your heart that send the signals). Mine used to send an extra signal that caused my heart to go into arrhythmias—it could beat up to 160 beats a minute and cause me to faint.

I learned to control it with my mind and by pressing my jugular vein in my neck. Well, I don't have to do that anymore. When I was hooked up to a halter monitor for 24 hours they could not detect any arrhythmias. (The doctor) said, "Don't bother coming back to me about this unless you start having symptoms again." She recorded me as being "asymptomatic" (not displaying symptoms of the syndrome).

Also, at the Radical Kingdom Conference on October18, 2001 in Brandon, Manitoba Todd called me out by a word of knowledge about a lady with an issue of blood. I had a hormone imbalance that caused profuse continuous bleeding. I was prescribed "Medroxy Progesterone" to stop the bleeding.

I responded to the call and Todd laid hands on me. I fell very suddenly under the electrical power of God. The next morning the bleeding had stopped. I was bleeding heavily the night before I had just stopped the 14 days cycle of the progesterone. I gave the testimony the next night. Todd prayed and I fell again to the floor and Todd had another word of knowledge and said that it was a hormone imbalance. I had not told him the cause of it. Today, years later I still have no bleeding. I'm back in balance. Amen!

Saturday evening, October 20, 2001 Todd began the service with words of knowledge. He called for trauma due to a blow to the right side and TMJ pain on the right side. The doctors basically said I had to live with it. As he called this out the power of God was already on me. He prayed for me and my right arm shot up like a disco dancer. It was a little embarrassing. Then electricity went through me and I lost control of my body. I shook all over and got slammed down on the floor while the electricity still flowed through me. Then I began to feel a coolness along the right side of my jaw and into my right ear. It also felt like it as puffy and swollen. I went back to my seat and the power of God was still on me for the rest of the service. The next morning I woke up and was pain free!

Karol Quesnel
Brandon, MB

God's Gift of Miracle Arches!

While I was attending a FFM healing conference July, 2003 at Bethel Church in Redding, CA I received a healing of my flat feet. I was born with flat feet—they used to call me Fred Flintstone feet. Todd called anyone with flat feet to come quickly come to the front! I jumped up out of my seat and ran to the front. A young lady from Bethel's prayer team laid hands on me and started to pray. She was on fire, I was on fire, and my feet were on fire. During this prayer, I could literally feel my feet begin to curl up; however, when I went back to my seat, I did not see any difference but I knew I received a healing. My husband and I went back to our hotel and went to sleep.

When I woke up the next morning, I had arches. No lie! My flat Fred Flintstone feet were now pretty dancer's feet. I am on our church's dance troop. Though, it's been a year, I still look at my feet and smile because I always hated my flat feet. That's what a loving God we serve. He knew I hated my feet and He did something about it. It may seem small to someone else, but to me it is a great gift my Daddy gave me through Todd Bentley and the fervent prayers of a young lady at Bethel Church.

For 33 years I had to live with those flat feet and now I am free to walk, run, dance and anything else I want to, without pain. Well, now I have arches and they are real pretty!! Thanks a bunch!

Lisa R. Thomas
Gardnerville, NV

Deliverance from the Spirit of Death on the Womb

I was healed at a conference in Albany, Oregon at the Vineyard in January, 2002. Shortly after I married my husband, I had a miscarriage, then proceeded to get pregnant with my son, who is now five. After that, I got pregnant a year and a half later and carried a baby girl to full term, but she was stillborn a day after her due date. I got pregnant after that and miscarried again. So I felt that I needed prayer, and that I needed to have Todd pray for me.

Todd was praying for people after the service and he asked me what I needed prayer for. After I told him the details, he prayed against the Spirit of Death and prayed that the Spirit of Life would come. I fell under the power of the Spirit, which I had never done before. I was floating on a high for days!

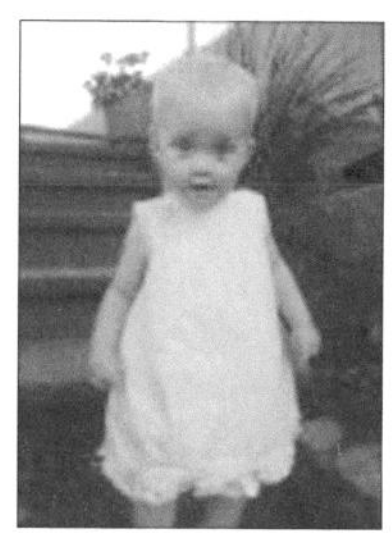

Allaire

Five months later I was pregnant again, and everything went perfectly. I now have another daughter, Allaire, who is 16 months old and an incredible joy to my husband and me! We praise the Lord for His wonderful mercy!

Suzanne Gilder
Albany, OR

Healed from NASH Disease

Before God miraculously touched my body, my symptoms were as follows: weakness, pressure from inside my abdominal cavity, searing pain, bruising pain and feeling lousy because of a back up of toxins and blood that was pooling around the liver area. I was swollen and had much heat radiating from that particular side and pain radiating down my underarm and shooting down my back.

When I ate the wrong kinds of foods (like high proteins and ice cream) my pain grew worse. I had been bedridden most of the time. I took many pain killers… when I could no longer stand the pain. I was depressed and tired of pain. I was also full of doubt and unbelief, and although trying to be joyful in the midst of these circumstances, I felt hopeless. After 2 years (of tests) the official diagnosis of my condition was: a liver disease called NASH a (Nonalcoholic Steatohepatitis).

(When I went for prayer at) the Vancouver Healing rooms Todd came over to me and said he saw a demonic presence that had attached itself to my liver area. He commanded it to loose. I felt a twisting and searing pain as if something was ripping and squeezing my liver. I felt it "let go" and I fell in a heap onto the floor. (Todd prayed for me the second night, again breaking the power of the enemy.) The Glory of the Lord's Presence upon me was thick and heavy and I knew Jesus was completing the work.

From the day Todd prayed for me, I knew I had been delivered from defeat, despair, depression, discouragement, hopelessness, doubt, unbelief and even my pain! I was back on the road to life, recovery and health. I had renewed energy again and even worked from 7:30 a.m. to 9:30 p.m. painting our new home the following week. In 5 days I had painted the whole house with supernatural energy!!

I was amazed and so was everyone else who saw me. My brother and sister in law could not believe it. Even as Mennonites they could not argue that surely God had completed a work. My mom couldn't believe it!! Even people at church were surprised!! Even though my husband was full of doubt and unbelief he was astounded and had to admit God must have done something. I even lifted a huge bag of dog food the very next day with no pain!! WOW! I was in awe of my BIG GOD! Before this, lifting a water pitcher sent pain shooting everywhere.

God is Faithful! He is the HEALER and Deliverer! Thank You Jesus!

Holly Wiens
Abbotsford, BC

Stage Three Aggressive Cancer Healed

In August, 2002, I was diagnosed with stage three, aggressive cancer. At the Todd Bentley Conference in Abbotsford in September I was prayed over by Todd, Mahesh Chavda and Kingsley Fletcher. When Mahesh prayed he told me I would live. He told me the glory of God was all over me. Mahesh instructed me not to wash my shirt, but to place it under my pillow. I did. I still refer to it as my "Glory Shirt"!

Because of heart, respiratory, obesity, and diabetic conditions, my doctors did not expect me to survive surgery. I am too medically fragile. The surgeon placed the liability on the cardiologist and the pulmonologist for my surgical survival. They delayed and ran voluminous tests hoping my death would release them from responsibility.

Sonogram results came in November that the uterine lining had shrunk, (not increased), from 19mil., in August, to 11mil. In January, 2002, it was 8mil (normal is <5mil). The doctor had no explanation. However, results of a second biopsy returned: stage 3, aggressive. The surgeon waited until January, 2003, to operate.

After the operation, the first question I asked was for the pathology report. The doctor said no one could explain it, or understand it. The doctors do not operate unless they are sure the cancer had invaded at least 50%. I was stage 3 in August. I should have been dead. The report revealed the cancer was <10%, closer to 5%, stage 1, passive, fully contained. No chemotherapy or radiation was recommended. God had reversed the cancer! If we had had additional delays, God would have gotten it all! But this way, we know for absolute sure, not on faith, that it was God, who healed me. All other tissues were pink and healthy! God healed the cancer!

Thank you for your ministry. God bless you, Mahesh, Todd and Kingsley.

Reanna Thatcher
Edmonds, WA

Delivered from Attention Deficit Disorder and Learning Disability

My name is Tim Andrews and I live in Southern California. I have struggled with school all my life. Through testing in the second grade it was determined that I had some learning disabilities along with Attention Deficit Disorder. It was hard to recall facts for tests and I always felt rushed. When I did not pass sixth grade my parents pulled me out of public school to home school me. During the school year 2001-2002 I was taken to one of Todd's meetings at Harvest Rock Church in Pasadena. Todd shared about some students he prayed for that were healed of ADD and then he prayed for all of us with learning problems. I couldn't tell if anything happened at that time; however, my parents put me in a charter school that was really hard compared to the regular public schools and I started to get C's and B's instead of F's. Todd visited our church in May of 2002 and I got more prayer for my learning problems. Last school year 2003-2004 my final report card was straight A's! Now I am 16 and I have been on two Fresh Fire ministry trips that really have changed my life. I decided I wanted to do home school again so that I could go to conferences and more ministry trips without being held back by school schedules.

Tim Andrews
Temecula, CA

Twist in the Bowel

I and my husband attended the Strategic Keys conference in Abbotsford in 2004. While we were there Todd gave a word of knowledge that a woman had a lump in her stomach on the left side and also had a twist in the bowel. I had been suffering for some time with discomfort on my left side from a lump and for a couple weeks had been having trouble with my bowels.

While in prayer one day the Holy Spirit had dropped into my spirit the words, "twisted" and "bowel". So when he gave the word of knowledge I knew it was me. I went forward for prayer and I was and am completely healed of both conditions. Praise the Lord. He is so good all the time!

I would like to add that after that conference I felt instant relief but I still battled the enemy for my complete healing. I put on Todd's Voice of Healing CD every day for at least 2 weeks and I literally felt the last of the pain and discomfort leave as I prayed and confessed the Word with Todd. I also prayed the prayer at the end of Todd's book every day and covered myself with the blood of Jesus. The best advice I could give someone other than what I've already written is....never give up! God loves you and wants to heal you!

Cheryl Burns
Edmonton, AB

Endometriosis Healed—Pregnancy Miracle

The doctors say I had Endometriosis since I was about 13 years old. I got married in September 1999 and just two months later the Endometriosis got so bad that I had to leave work at least one day early per month; this was brought on by monthly cycle. It also hindered the sexual intimacy of my marriage. In May of 2000 I had surgery for it but they couldn't remove it all because the doctors were afraid of rupturing my bladder. Needless to say it didn't help too much. Ever since I was a little girl it was my dream to be a mother; however, the doctors told me I probably wouldn't be able to have babies.

Todd Bentley came to Nanaimo late 2000 or early 2001 to Southside Christian Fellowship. One night he had a word of knowledge for a woman. He didn't know the name of what was being diagnosed by the doctors but he said, "There is a woman here tonight with an issue of blood . . . her uterus . . . doctors say you can't have babies." He kept giving more details that explained my condition without knowing the name. My husband and I were in the front row and we knew it was me that God was calling for healing that night! I slowly started walking to him, but saw a lady come up from the center row so I started walking back to my seat. But Todd looked directly in my eyes and pointed at me and said, "I knew it was you. Come here".

The next time I walked into Southside was September 2002, three weeks before my due date. Everyone in the church kept coming up to me saying, "Hey? You weren't supposed to have babies! Praise God!!" Makayla Joy was born on October 10, 2002 at 8:27 pm weighing nine lbs. 9oz. She is healthy and a joyous little girl. I do not have any pain or other symptoms since I got pregnant—I know that I have been healed of Endometriosis and know that it was by "His stripes that I am healed". Praise God!

Sarah Price
Nanaimo, BC

God Does Gold-Teeth Dentistry

My testimony is from about 5 years ago in March of 1999. I was at a healing service where Todd was ministering in Mission at a church there. That evening during the worship time I saw a gold rain coming down. Then when Todd started his healing time someone from my church in Maple Ridge saw (while I was talking) that I had gold teeth. God gave me three gold teeth! He was gracious and healed me from the inside out. Before this time I hated myself. I was fascinated with guns. I really wanted peace (like other people had from my church) but thought I would forever be depressed. I disliked my parents and family. After I received my gold teeth God gave me an inner peace and I started to like my self and my family. Before I was impossible to live with and now my husband has seen a change in me too and likes it. I still get mad, but I don't stay mad for long. I used to be skinny and now I am slim. There were many things I couldn't handle than I can handle now, like some jokes from family members and friends. It has made a huge impact on my life. I always needed confirmation of the love from my parents and I never really knew if God loved me. He gave me three gold teeth to show His love! I praise Him on a continuous basis for His love to me. I don't question His love anymore. He is an awesome God.

Sharon
Pitt Meadows, BC

Undiagnosable Shoulder Pain Healed

For several weeks, when standing straight, with my arms at my side, I would notice a slight pulling sensation in the muscles of my left arm. Then one day when I woke up I couldn't raise my left arm, like it was stuck somehow. It was also very painful, with very limited movement and constant throbbing. It became both difficult and very painful to do simple tasks like comb my hair or brush my teeth. I am also left-handed, which added to the difficulties. If I made a sudden jerking movement, like to catch my balance, it would shoot sharp pains through my body.

I went to my chiropractor and he worked on it for months. He took x-rays and nothing showed up. He was baffled by my shoulder's inability to move, and couldn't figure out what it was. He tried several different treatments and nothing budged the shoulder. I also went to my naturopathic doctor. He also couldn't figure out what was wrong with my shoulder either.

During this time, I was not able to sleep; the throbbing was constant. I would lie in bed at night moving in and out from prayer to a semi-delirious state of being. It felt like an endless torture and that there was no escape. However, also during this time, the Lord met me where I was. He communed with me. I felt very much like He told me that He would heal my shoulder. I just had to wait for His move on my life. Every chance I got, I went up for prayer for my shoulder. Hundreds of prayers went up on behalf of my mysterious affliction.

This whole thing went on for over a year. Both doctors gave up on my shoulder. They were baffled by it and were unable to help. My chiropractor told me that the best that could be done was to go to a medical doctor and have them do some sort of invasive surgery, which may or may not help. I didn't have medical insurance. I decided to wait on the promises of the Lord instead.

Last year, in October, Todd and his team were in Albany. I went down for the conference. The first night I was there, someone from the prayer team prayed for me. My whole arm started violently shaking and then got hot. God healed me! I could raise my arm over my head for the first time in over a year. As instantly as the affliction came upon me, I was healed. For months I had been unable to move or function and in seconds I was restored to complete health!

Kerrie Hubbard
Clackamas, OR

Healed of Fibromyalgia

A few years ago my teenage daughter Beth was diagnosed with Fibromyalgia by Dr Susan Ballinger of Pediatric Rheumatology, Riley's Children's Hospital in Indianapolis, IN. She had significant muscle and joint pain that was growing increasingly worse with time. She was so bad that if she bent over to tie her shoes, she couldn't get back up again. She cried frequently because of the pain. The doctor didn't hold out any hope of finding a "cure", and couldn't come up with any medications that offered any degree of relief for Beth. She prescribed specific stretching exercises she said were imperative for us to do with her on a daily basis but the pain Beth endured afterward left all of us crying. Beth missed numerous days of school and was forced to give up extracurricular activities. We began intensive intercession for her healing.

While studying Todd Bentley's teachings on the web-site I saw that he would be visiting a small Vineyard Church in Valparaiso, IN the following month. During a corporate prayer for healing, Beth related that she felt a tingling sensation begin on the top of her head, then spread downward until it covered her entire body. The tingling sensation continued for the duration of the service.

As the service ended and we began to leave, Beth said the sensation began to lift off of her, and with it went all the pain. She was healed and has been pain free ever since! Praise be to God! We didn't take her back to Riley's simply because of the long drive and time we would miss at work. We knew she was healed, and that's all that mattered to us at that point. My daughter, now 19, has not had the first symptom of Fibromyalgia since that night God healed her at Todd Bentley's meeting in Valparaiso, IN.

Cheryl Shull (mother of Beth)
Churubusco, IN

Pelvis Healed and Supernatural Weight Loss

Two years ago I experienced the healing power of God at my church, Trinity Worship Center in Texas. I had been experiencing daily discomfort and pain for two or three years in my right hip and thigh where it joins my pelvis, as well was pain shooting up my back. My chiropractor said I had a pinched sciatic nerve as well as an arthritic condition in some of my vertebrae. I went for chiropractic treatments for nine months but the pain persisted. I used up all my medical coverage that I received from a car accident and then stopped going for treatment.

At the church meeting Todd Bentley called out a word of knowledge about a lady in her 40's with pain in her right hip and leg and asked her to come forward because God wanted to heal her right now. I was really surprised because I had never prayed to ask God to do this for me. When I went forward I felt heat in the pelvic area where I had experienced the pain and I knew that I was healed.

I was especially touched with the realization that God was concerned about me even though my condition wasn't life threatening. This miracle showed me that the Lord cares about both little and big things. Nothing is too unimportant or hard for the Lord. It has been two years now and I am pain free!

At another service that weekend I brought my daughter Chelsea forward to receive prayer from Todd. I asked him to pray specifically for a miracle with her weight. She was 14 years old and weighed 165 lbs. Since she was 10 she started to eat compulsively and was pretty sedentary. She is very strong willed so I had to remove certain foods from the house because when nobody was watching she would go to the fridge and eat and keep eating.

Todd prayed for her and I didn't think about until two weeks later when Chelsea got on a scale to weigh her self. This was very unusual because Chelsea never wants to be weighed. I noticed she had gone from 165 to 135 lbs in two weeks! After another week she was down to 120 lbs! She hadn't been exercising more but had stopped eating incessantly. I took her to the doctor and testified to the doctors that it was a miracle.

Lynda Currie
McAllen, TX

Daughter Walks Without Cane

Thank you all at Fresh Fire! You are impacting thousands including me. My daughter was partially healed at Thornhill Vineyard (Toronto) in November of 2001. She was not even at the meeting where Todd was ministering. I had gone up for healing for myself (when) Todd touched my shoulder and started telling me about… stuff in my family. My daughter's condition came up and he prayed and also asked everyone in the meeting to pray. A few days later my daughter who is not even saved told me she does not need to have a cane any longer!!

Rima Anani
Toronto, Ont.

Healed of Menier's Syndrome

Praise God. My name is Salvatore Vincenti. I am the youth leader of New Hope Fellowship Church. I have been healed of deafness in my right ear which was caused by Menier's Syndrome, an inner ear disorder which causes vertigo and permanent loss of hearing. About a year and a half ago I was healed of vertigo when my Pastor's wife, Theresa, and others from the prayer ministry team prayed for me; I was able to bow down rapidly without any nausea. That was a miracle and I have not had an attack of vertigo since. However, I was not healed of the deafness that occurred from Menier's syndrome. I have continued to believe God for a full healing when I receive my hearing back. I was not able to hear any kind of faint noises that occurred at a home or at work.

Recently when Todd Bentley and his ministry team attended New Hope Fellowship Church in Brooklyn, on August 8th, 2004, my wife and a gentleman from the ministry team prayed for me with authority that I would be healed. I felt heat in my right ear and moments later we tested to see if I did receive my hearing back and I was able to hear my wife whisper very, very softly in my ear which I have not heard in the past three years. Also, my hearing in my left ear seemed stronger. In addition, when I was home, I asked my wife, "What's that noise?" and it was the mechanics of the wall oven, refrigerator, etc. in the kitchen. We laughed and she said the noise has always been there. I have also been able to hear from my right ear when I use my cell phone throughout the day. God is a faithful God and when man says it's impossible—God says all things are possible!

Salvatore Vincenti
Brooklyn, New York

Set Free from ADD

In 2003, before I received prayer from Todd, my school notes from the ground school fourth grade were all together about 3,2. I didn't like going to school. My teacher wrote in my school report card that I had problems concentrating and that I take more time to work on my school lessons. My concentration went up and down and because of this I made a lot of mistakes on the tests which could have been avoided. I was very silent and I didn't ask any questions. I hated to go to school because of all of this.

Dominic Vial

In 2004 I went to the main school fifth grade class. My school notes all together changed into 2,2 and I became the class-speaker and the second best in the class. Now I talk a lot during the school lesson, but not with the neighbor! I also ask a lot of questions. My concentration has risen up to very strong. Now when I read something on a subject I am able to hold this for a long time in my mind. I am also starting to argue with the teacher on the subject "RELIGION" when he says something about the Bible which is not right. Now I have summer holidays but I will be happy when the school starts again!

Dominic Vial
Düsseldorf, Germany

Dominic's Parent's Verify His Testimony:

We want to give you a testimony about our son Dominic. Todd, you prayed for him in the summer in Düsseldorf, Germany. You prayed for him because he had problems concentrating at school and bad notes from his teachers. Dominic told us that during the prayer he felt something leave him from his mind. Now he has super notes, it is easy for him to concentrate and easy for him to learn. PRAISE THE LORD! We bless you and the ministry and are thankful that you are more and more a blessing to the nations. In His great love,

Emanuel, Claudia
Düsseldorf, Germany

Testimonies from Missions to the Nations

Deaf Ears Opened in India

It was the first night of the first crusade in Ongole, India. I was just so excited to be in India and on the stage and seeing 20 thousand people in front of us. Todd spoke for an hour or so and then we as a team were all to go down the steps into this area designated to start praying for the masses of people. The masses of people were right there in front of us. I just asked my interpreter, "What is wrong with her?" (She signaled to me that the woman is deaf.)

"On the first time I ever pray for anyone in India I get a deaf person!" I thought. "What are you nuts?!" I said to myself and possibly aiming my question to God as well. But all of a sudden my arms went out—BAM—and my hands went over her ears. I prayed, "I command you deaf and dumb spirit to go in Jesus name! Ears be opened NOW!" It really surprised me to tell you the truth as I am usually not that bold.

Then I started snapping my fingers in front of her ears and she nodded her head sideways. And I said to my interpreter; "can she hear?"..."YES." I said, "she can?!" Inside I was saying, "WOW! Thank you JESUS!" I was shocked. The interpreter smiled. Talk about a faith booster, man! Then I had to collect myself and continue praying for many, many others.

See, God can work through us—even those of us who didn't have as much faith as we should have! I said before I left on this trip, "God use me as your vessel", and He did. I give Him all the Glory! I saw many miracles on that trip to India and the Lord … has given me boldness. I am so grateful. I love you Jesus!

Judith Martin
Kitchener, Ontario, Canada

Team Member Reports Healings in Africa

I was on the Mwanza, Tanzania team in 2002. On our first day, a little 7-9 year old boy in an orphanage for the mentally handicapped walked for the first time. He had been abandoned, and this church had provided an orphanage for children like him. He was wearing a diaper and had been carried around since birth. This child took his first staggering steps, while holding onto one of our team member's fingers and a finger of the director, just like a young toddler would first walk. Then he quickly began to walk around the room. While the team and the orphanage staff were praising Jesus for this healing, whooping and hollering, another boy grabbed his ears and began pulling at them and screaming loudly, as two men prayed for him. He was hearing for the first time!

Debby Spruill rejoicing in Africa

At the crusade, another woman on the

team and I prayed for a woman, who looked maybe 50-60 and was bent way over like an old woman. I felt two large curves (in her spine). She also struggled for breath because of this infirmity. She had had polio fifteen years earlier. This was not just a misalignment; the woman's head only came up to my waist.

We began to pray. I closed my eyes, put my hands on her waist and prayed. I can't say that I had a ton of faith. But I remembered the boys in the orphanage who were healed. Suddenly I felt her body jump. This woman turned completely around, standing just as straight and tall as I am (5' 9") and looked me straight in the eye. Our gazes locked, mine in shock! The woman's eyes (lit up) in total thankfulness to God. We praised Jesus for a minute. Then I took her to the stage, where she gave a testimony. The crowd rejoiced and more people surged forward for prayer because they knew this woman had been bent over for 15 years. Thank you, Jesus!

Debby Spruill
Kansas City, Missouri

Teen Prays for Miracles in Mexico

Going on this trip I desired two things from God. They were (1) to be used by him and (2) to be spiritually transformed. I was happy to receive both by making myself a willing and available vessel to do God's work, admitting also that it was very stretching. During the second night of the crusade in Cabo San Lucas I was praying for a lady who dealt with back pain or arthritis and the Holy Spirit led me to ask if she was living in unforgiveness. Her reply was, "Yes" and I proceeded to tell her that forgiving that person would not make what they did right. She was willing to forgive the person. Then I prayed for her healing and she said that the pain was 90 % gone and I told her that sometimes God heals us gradually. On the evening of the next day as we were praying for the sick again, that same lady came up to me with a big and beautiful smile on her

Stephanie Banai ministering to youth in Mexico

face. She said that the pain was now 100 % gone! She told me that she had gotten saved (I believe the night I prayed for her) and brought her son who she said was "almost" a Christian.

Stephanie Banai
Fifteen years old
Surrey, BC

Tuberculosis Ward Emptied in Malawi!!

June 22, 2003. Oh Hallelujah! I just got word from Malawi of an incredible report and had to tell you right away! Two weeks ago in Malawi, Iris Ministries partnered with Fresh Fire Ministries to hold open-air meetings in the city of Lilongwe, Malawi for 4 evenings. I was in charge of organizing outreaches to take place during the day in which the Gospel was preached and food was distributed in each of 7 locations. One of these locations was a "hospital" with very poor humanitarian and sanitary conditions. Many of the patients in this particular hospital had to sleep on the floor and we found many desperate people there. We distributed food to every patient and every member of the hospital staff. This brought much joy, and word of what we were doing spread throughout the city.

We also went through the entire hospital and prayed for every patient to be healed. Well, I've just received word that within 24 hours all the patients in the tuberculosis ward were healed and discharged from the TB ward!! All of them! There were over 65 patients in this ward, many of them on oxygen and in advanced stages of Tuberculosis! Not one patient remained in the hospital!

More and more reports are coming in from people in Lilongwe, Malawi about how they were healed. God is so amazing!

Linda Pallone
Iris Ministries, Malawi, Africa

Creative Miracles: Eye Ball Grows Back

Prior to traveling with Todd Bentley to Malawi, Africa in 2003, I had been in a season of prayer. The Lord told to me to expect Him to release creative miracles. I was expecting to see Jesus grow missing limbs and digits etc. The first person I met in Malawi was a man named Leonard. He was our bus driver. Several of the team noticed that Leonard was driving a little "erratically."

I tapped him on the shoulder (thinking I'd check whether he may be drunk) and when he turned to the left to speak to me I could see that he was missing his right eye ball. Immediately, Holy Spirit reminded me of the Lord's promise, and that I was to pray with boldness. I asked Leonard if we could pray that Jesus would grow his eye back. He agreed.

When we reached the hotel, I laid my hands on his eye and prayed (along with) a young woman named Shara. The anointing and power of God filled Leonard and an unpleasant white liquid began to weep from his eye socket. Leonard was getting drunk in the Spirit. When I removed my hand he was able to see light, and there appeared to be a little white "seed" of an eye in the socket. The "seed" was about the size of a BB.

The next day… Leonard wanted me to pray for him again. I laid hands on him in the name of Jesus and began to pray with boldness, commanding his new eye to grow. Several team members joined in the prayer. Again, when I removed my hand I could see Leonard's new eye was about the size of a pea. He told the team he could now see light, and shadows. After more prayer Leonard told us that he could see a fuzzy outline of my hand (like the blind man in Mark 8 who saw men walking "as trees").

The next day… I again laid hands on his "growing eye" for the third consecutive day. His new eye was now about the size of a small marble. He was beginning to see well with his new eye, and Leonard was laughing and praising God for his creative miracle. Todd invited Leonard to the platform that night and also prayed for his eye ball to grow (in front of a crowd of about 25,000). Todd then had Leonard cover his good eye, as we had done, and Leonard was able to see! He identified a hand, a Bible, a pair of glasses, and finally a small life saver candy!

The next day Leonard wanted more prayer! I checked his new eye and by now it was about the size of a small grape and the iris and pupil had formed. Leonard told me "I can see well, but I want more"! I laid hands upon him again and it appeared that his eye grew a little more and he told me he was seeing "better" out of his new eye.

About that time the camera man for the Malawi National TV station came by. I had met him earlier and told him about Leonard's unusual miracle. He asked Leonard and me to share the testimony with the country of Malawi. Now I found myself interviewing Leonard on the national television station! We were able to pray for Leonard for the next three days and each time the eye appeared to grow more.

The last time I saw Leonard's new eye it was nearly normal size and he was seeing "very well" according to his testimony.

(Leonard's creative miracle triggered many more healings in Africa.) During my time in Malawi I saw 62 totally blind eyes open in the name of Jesus!

During this time my team was at a second refugee camp. Two team members went to the translator at the sound system and announced: "Bring your blind to the white people under the tree and Jesus will open their blind eyes right now." I witnessed 42 blind eyes open in about 45 minutes. "With men this is impossible, but with God all things are possible." (Matt. 19:26)

Kevin Basconi and Leonard, who received a new eye from the Lord

Kevin Basconi
Kansas City, KA
King of Glory Ministries International

Child with Enlarged Head Healed

During a Fresh Fire Crusade in Malawi, Africa in June 2003, a mother brought her three-year-old hydrocephalic child to me for prayer. (The condition caused accumulation of fluid on the brain.) The child had a scull about twice the size of normal and his face was disfigured because of the enlarged size of his head. The mother asked if we would pray that God would heal her son. As me and several others around began to pray, I felt a "pop" under my hand. I immediately noticed that the head had become normal and the facial disfiguration was gone. When I asked the mother to check the child, she began to cry and told the interpreter that her son was healed. When the mother and child were brought up on the platform, everyone could see the extra flaps of skin at the back of the child's head where the enlarged scull had been. His face and head had been totally restored by the power of God!

Sammy Robinson
16 years old
Abbotsford, BC

YOUR COMMISSIONING INTO HEALING MINISTRY

My desire is to make the commission of Mark 16:17-18 no longer just words on a page, but an exciting everyday reality. ***"And these signs will follow those who believe: In My name they will cast out demons; they will speak with new tongues… they will lay hands on the sick, and they will recover."*** If you're a believer, then you're a candidate for this commissioning.

Now that you know and understand the commission and the promises examined in this book, it is your responsibility to pursue the reality of it. You must take an active role by stepping out, praying and laying hands on the sick. Just learning about healing is not enough—there is no substitute for experience. So start taking risks and doing the stuff! Pray for everyone you can find who needs healing, trust the Holy Spirit to help—He is a great teacher. Just do what Jesus did and follow the promptings of the Holy Spirit. Some of you may see healing manifest right away. Others may have to pray for 1,000 people before they see an actual healing or miracle. However, remember, if you persist, you will see God's power manifest.

My prayer is that you have already begun to receive healing and have started a wonderful journey of walking in divine health. I trust that this book has greatly built your faith and given you boldness to pray for the sick at home, at church, in your neighborhood, at work and wherever you are in the world. The lost need to know the healing power of our awesome God.

Remember, it's absolutely essential for you to begin warring and contending for God's power so you can be a channel of healing blessing to the world. In Matthew 7:7-8 Jesus tells us to keep asking, seeking, and knocking ***"for everyone who asks receives, and he who seeks finds, and to him who knocks it will be opened."*** (Volume II will also greatly help you in contending for healing anointing and authority.)

Once you begin to see the manifestation of healings and miracles, you will need to continue nurturing the anointing and gifts in your life. As you are faithful with little, God will bless you with much. Together, let's do it!

Allow the Holy Spirit to continue to mentor you in healing ministry so you will grow in passion and power to change the world with Christ's Healing Touch.

"Heal the sick, raise the dead, cleanse the lepers, cast out demons. Freely you received, freely give" (Matt. 10:8).

Heidi Baker of Iris Ministries and Todd Bentley rejoice after seeing many people in Malawi, Africa healed, set free and touched by the compassion of Christ.

THE HEALING TOUCH
BOOK COVER ARTWORK BY: ARTIST STEVE STANCZYK

NOW AVAILABLE AS POSTER OR CANVAS PRINT!

The Healing Touch is an image depicting Jesus healing a blind man with a dove above them, representing the Holy Spirit and the Anointing which 'destroys the yoke.'

There are also lightnings in the background representing God's dunamis power and faded scriptures across the image which are Acts 10:38 and Isaiah 61:1-3.

The image was commissioned by Todd Bentley for the cover of this book, "Christ's Healing Touch."

The artwork is the result of several different creative processes, including photography, drawing, and digital art.

AVAILABLE AS:

Art Poster: 15" x 23" inches
Art Canvas: Archival print on cotton canvas stretched onto a wood frame: 15" x 24" x 3/4" inches (looks exactly like an original canvas painting ready to hang)

TO ORDER, PLEASE CONTACT FRESH FIRE MINISTRIES:
Toll Free: 1.866.853.9041 or Online: www.freshfire.ca

For a larger, custom size canvas print, contact Steve directly at: steve@healingtouchart.com and visit: www.healingtouchart.com

The artist Steve Stanczyk lives in Abbotsford, BC Canada. His desire is to express God's heart and glory through the arts to minister to the church and to the lost. For more info about Steve, and to see more of his artwork, please visit: www.stevestanczyk.com

Other Resources By Todd Bentley

Journey Into The Miraculous

Todd Bentley's life story will do more than merely entertain you; it will inspire you to believe in a bigger God than you've ever known. You'll read how this supernatural God can take an ordinary man and do extraordinary works through him. Todd's life is truly a miracle! His story testifies to the Father's grace, love and transforming power; it demonstrates that God is truly looking for ordinary people with a "yes" in their spirit to do the "greater works than these" that Jesus prophesied. If you've ever felt disqualified or inadequate to do big things for God then this book will revolutionize your thinking.

The passion of Todd's life and ministry to the nations is to see others come into the reality of intimate relationship with Jesus and to experience the transferable, tangible anointing of the Holy Spirit. Today God is releasing His presence and power through Todd's life to the point where the blind see, the deaf hear and the lame walk, confirming that Jesus still heals every sickness and disease. This anointing is available to enable all believers to fulfill the great commission with miracles, signs and wonders following the message.

Journey Into The Miraculous will give you a greater passion for intimacy with God and convince you that Jesus' words are really true for you, yes; even you…and they're for today. "Preach the Gospel, heal the sick, cleanse the lepers, raise the dead, cast out demons... (Matt. 10:8)" What are you waiting for?

ENDORSEMENT:

"I love this book. Journey Into the Miraculous is a moving story about the extravagant grace of God. While Todd Bentley is a wonderful man with an unusual gift, this book is more than a story about his life. It's a prophetic declaration of God's intent for an entire generation. It invites those who are hungry and desperate for God to abandon themselves for the treasure of His presence. This book will ignite a holy passion for a holy God!"

***Bill Johnson**, Senior Pastor Bethel Church, Redding, California*
Author of "When Heaven Invades Earth"

Other Resources By Todd Bentley

Soaking In The Secret Place

Prayers for the manifest presence - Audio CD

Todd Bentley's brand new CD on Soaking and Intimacy is finally available after 4 years of Ministry. People have asked all over the world, Todd do you have a music CD we can use when we want to SOAK and wait on the Lord? If you have ever heard Todd's teaching on the Secret Place (Soaking), or as he puts it, pickling in the presence, then this new prayer CD will help you come into the Father's House and sit at the feet of Jesus.

Join Todd on a journey into the Presence of God using prayers from the bible and prayers that come from a deep passion and longing for Him. Prayers for the Manifest Presence is a meditative, contemplative CD with music, combining piano style music, and numerous sounds such as: rain, flute, trumpet, shofar, and more for a deep prayer experience. Instrumental version is also available.

The Voice Of Healing

Healing prayers set to original music - Audio CD

This CD takes prophetic declarations of the coming healing revival, healing prayers from the bible and sets them to original music. It is similar to the Praying the Bible series with Wesley and Stacey Campbell of Revival Now Ministries.

The Voice of Healing is a spontaneous project that will bring the transferable, tangible healing anointing and atmosphere to your home, hospital room or healing service. This is not just a healing prayer CD but a healing experience. This CD will bring you into a healing commission and release faith for the coming healing revival. Experience through healing prayers and music, the healing word that you may be delivered from your destruction. Produced by Revival Now Ministries with Wesley & Stacey Campbell.

Other Resources By Todd Bentley

ACTIVATING YOUR SPIRITUAL SENSES
On this new teaching message Todd will share with you nine keys to help anoint your eyes and ears so that the Holy Spirit will begin to visit you in extreme ways and not just the prophets. Todd will teach you to experience visions, trances, angelic visitations, third heaven experiences and throne zone encounters.

BONDAGE BREAKER - The Deliverance Series
Learn about and how to identify and expose the spirit of python and how to overcome it. Todd will also teach on breaking generational curses such as sickness, poverty, witchcraft and how they are passed down. Finally, Todd teaches on the power of the blood of Jesus and how to apply it to our daily lives.

COMMUNION
In this message Todd teaches on healing in Communion, how the emblems are more than represntations but rather spiritual impartation of the power of the blood and the presence of Christ. Learn how to have intimacy in the Lord's supper. -- NEWLY REVISED MESSAGE!

HEAVENLY COURTS AND DIVINE COUNCIL
Learn about the "moving" throne of Revelation 4 and 5 and its relevance to the triune God head. Todd will take you through scriptures which show how the throne room, heavenly courts, and divine council room are not just for the end times. These places are in session today so that we, as God's children, can go boldly before the throne to ask for the judgments that are rightfully due to us in the name of Jesus.

HOW TO RECEIVE THE ANOINTING
The first message is a teaching on how to drink the new wine. This is a soaking message. Todd shares on : "How do I receive the Holy Ghost?" "How do I overcome a hard to receive mentality and open up my spirit to experience the joys and blessings of renewal?" If you want more of God, but don't know how to get it, How To Receive The Anointing will make you sensitive to the presence of God.

Other Resources By Todd Bentley

OPEN HEAVENS VOL.I
On Open Heavens Vol.1 Bob Jones, Todd Bentley, Lou Engle, and Stacey Campbell, relate their stories, visions, experiences, and encounters with God and His angels. Listen as contemporary prophets and visionaries reveal what the Spirit is saying to us today. Open Heavens Vol.1 describes the calling of a prophet and relates visions of the end-time harvest. These supernatural stories will build your faith.

OPEN HEAVENS VOL.II
Prophets are a unique group of people. Ezekiel said, "I saw visions of God!" Whether they were seeing into heaven or predicting the future, prophets have always given guidance to the people of God. On this second CD of the "Open Heavens" series, Todd Bentley, Bob Jones, and Stacey Campbell, relate their stories, visions, experiences, and encounters with God and His angels.

THE SECRET PLACE
A powerful, prophetic revelation on the nine levels of intimacy and prayer. Todd was taken into a prophetic experience and brought into nine rooms in the Father's House. Todd will help you understand the different levels of communion with God, help you to develop a passion for his presence & help you make God the "Most High" of all that you are and lift you into a victorious, conquering spirit.

ENCOUNTERS OF THE KINGDOM KIND
This 6 message series, on how to encounter the realities of the kingdom realm, will truly transform your life. In this teaching, Todd goes into great detail on the throne room of Revelation chapter four and describes how to minister with the seven spirits of God. You will learn why seven lamps are burning before God's throne and why the sea of glass is like crystal. You will also discover why there are thunderings, lightenings and voices coming from the throne plus more.

OPEN HEAVENS
A powerful teaching series on the third heaven, prophetic experiences and being caught up into the spirit. Todd shares on how "Natural" it is to have "Supernatural" encounters. Through scripture, we see common people having extra ordinary, unusual visitations of the presence of God. What is an open heaven? How do you open the windows of heaven, when the heavens above are "brass" and the earth beneath is "iron?"

Other Resources By Todd Bentley

HEALINGS, MIRACLES, SIGNS AND WONDERS
Training & Equipping Healing School
This training school is great for pastors, evangelists, ministries, hungry saints and those who want to move in a greater dimension of healing. Go through the school with your youth groups, home groups, and churches. The school is also a great time of preparation for individuals who need healing and want to sit under powerful teaching. Practical examples of how to receive and maintain your healing, how to overcome hindrances to healing, building your faith and understanding of the function of miracles will also be taught.

The teachings you will recieve are: Seven Redemptive names of God, Freedom from Sickness and Disease, Faith for Creative Miracles, The Working of Faith, Healing, and Miracles, Four Levels of Healing, Hidden Prayer and Healing, Touching God on Covenant, SOZO - Salvation Deliverance and Healing, The Roots of Sickness, Dunamis Power, The Spirit of Python, The Deaf and Dumb Spirit, 30 Reasons why Miracles Happen, How to Maintain Your Healing, Faith to Raise the Dead, 30 Reasons why Miracles Don't Happen, The Word of Knowledge, Breaking Generational Curses.

This trianing school includes a single school manual. The workbook is designed to reinforce, and compile the lessons on each of the audio/video lessons focused on healings and miracles. Each lesson is set-up with a Key Bible Verse, Reinforcement Helpers, Life Application, and a Prayer. Additional manuals available.

THE SCHOOL OF
THE SUPERNATURAL REALMS OF HEAVEN
Training & Equipping Supernatural School

This exciting new school by Todd Bentley and Fresh Fire Ministries combines teaching on prophetic ministry with instruction on how to engage the revelatory realm of Heaven. This audio teaching series consists of 18 hours of teaching in which Todd shares and imparts everything he has learned and experienced in the area of prophecy and revelation. Todd shares many of his prophetic experiences and teaches how to activate spiritual senses.

In the School of The Supernatural Training series, you will learn how to: Birth and deliver a prophetic word, Use proper prophetic manners, Release breakthroughs with prophetic decrees, Understand the levels of the prophetic mantel, Experience the Open Heavens and angelic realm, Understand the seven Spirits of God, Stir up wisdom and revelation and Enter into intimacy with God in His secret place.

The training school comes with a 110-page student manual to help you follow the lessons and study many of the related scriptures. Saints, get ready to fly like an eagle into the supernatural realm! This teaching series will help launch you there. Additional manuals available.

FFM Partnership & Missions Trips

BECOME A PARTNER: Will you consider partnering financially together with FFM to take salvation and healing to the nations? Todd Bentley believes that when you become a partner with him in taking the gospel to the nations, the anointing, covering, blessing and fruit that God gives the ministry will also become yours.

As a Covenant Partner with this ministry, you receive one of the latest of Todd Bentley's messages, our monthly mail out and newsletters from crusades around the nation and abroad. You will also receive a new teaching in the mail every month. Another benefit of becoming a partner with us is our commitment to pray for you and your family. Also, as a partner, you can participate in any of our missions trips at a special partner discount and you can join us once a year for a trip solely for partners.

W: www.FreshFire.ca E: Partners@freshfire.ca T: 1.604.853.9041

GO ON A MISSIONS TRIP: Do you long to see the works of the Lord and greater works than these in our world today? Have you ever longed to see the paralytics walk, the deaf hear, the blind see, the lepers cleansed and the demonized set free? Do you want to feed the hungry, minister to the orphans and widows, preach and do the ministry of Jesus? If so, a Fresh Fire missions trip could be the trip for you. Come participate with Todd Bentley and the Fresh Fire Mission's Team on a life-changing missions trip.

W: www.FreshFire.ca E: Missions@freshfire.ca T: 1.604.853.9041

To Order Products: W: www.FreshFire.ca E: Orders@freshfire.ca
T: Toll Free: 1.866.853.9041 F: 1.604.853.5077